Alcohol in World History

From the origins of drinking to the use and abuse of alcohol in the present day, this global historical study draws on approaches and research from biology, anthropology, sociology, and psychology. Topics covered include:

- the impact of colonialism
- alcohol before the world economy
- industrialization and alcohol
- globalization, consumer society, and alcohol.

Gina Hames argues that the production, trade, consumption, and regulation of alcohol have shaped virtually every civilization in numerous ways. It has perpetuated the development of both domestic and international trade; helped create identity and define religion; provided a tool for oppression as well as a tool for cultural and political resistance; and has supplied governments with essential revenues as well as a means of control over minority groups.

Alcohol in World History is one of the first studies to pull together such a wide range of sources in order to compare the role of alcohol throughout time and across both Western and non-Western civilizations.

Gina Hames is an assistant professor at Pacific Lutheran University. Her research interests include alcohol and the creation of identity in early twentieth-century Bolivia and in the late twentieth- and early twenty-first-century United States.

Themes in World History
Series editor: Peter N. Stearns

The *Themes in World History* series offers focused treatment of a range of human experiences and institutions in the world history context. The purpose is to provide serious, if brief, discussions of important topics as additions to textbook coverage and document collections. The treatments will allow students to probe particular facets of the human story in greater depth than textbook coverage allows, and to gain a fuller sense of historians' analytical methods and debates in the process. Each topic is handled over time – allowing discussions of changes and continuities. Each topic is assessed in terms of a range of different societies and religions – allowing comparisons of relevant similarities and differences. Each book in the series helps readers deal with world history in action, evaluating global contexts as they work through some of the key components of human society and human life.

Alcohol in World History

Gina Hames

Routledge
Taylor & Francis Group

LONDON AND NEW YORK

First published 2012
by Routledge
2 Park Square, Milton Park, Abingdon, Oxon OX14 4RN

Simultaneously published in the USA and Canada
by Routledge
711 Third Avenue, New York, NY 10017

Routledge is an imprint of the Taylor & Francis Group, an informa business

British Library Cataloguing in Publication Data
A catalogue record for this book is available from the British Library

Library of Congress Cataloging in Publication Data
Hames, Gina.
  Alcohol in world history / Gina Hames.
    p. cm. – (Themes in world history)
  Includes bibliographical references.
  1. Drinking of alcoholic beverages–History. 2. Alcoholic beverages–Social
aspects–History. 3. Alcoholic beverage industry–Social aspects–History. I.
Title.
  HV5020.H36 2012
  394.1'309–dc23
            2011044427

ISBN: 978-0-415-31151-9 (hbk)
ISBN: 978-0-415-31152-6 (pbk)
ISBN: 978-0-203-46305-5 (ebk)

Typeset in Times New Roman
by Taylor & Francis Books

Contents

Acknowledgements

I especially thank Peter N. Stearns for his continued support. I also thank the editors at Routledge who have been very helpful to me throughout this project. Finally, I would like to thank my very talented student research assistants, Margaret Cox, Samm Thompson, Breanne Compton, Luke Dolge, and Ronan Rooney who assisted me during the beginning stages of the research.

Introduction

Alcohol has influenced virtually every civilization. Alcohol production, trade, consumption, and regulation have helped shape the cultural, social, political, and economic spheres in societies around the world. Consumption of alcohol began when humans discovered natural fermentation as hunter-gatherers. When people settled into agricultural societies, one of the first substances they produced was alcohol. Moreover, alcohol was one of the first commodities traded among groups. Alcohol has been central in the most important social and cultural ceremonies, especially rites of passage such as births, funerals, initiations, and marriages. It has also been a vital part of feasts, magic rites, worship, and hospitality.

Alcohol has provided people in many cultures with essential, daily nourishment, as well as safe fluids to drink where water remained contaminated. Alcohol has shaped traditional medicinal remedies in most cultures and has continued to be used in that way into the twenty-first-century. The meanings and uses of alcohol have affected gender roles, class stratification, social hierarchies, and ethnic identities. Governments have capitalized on the popularity of alcohol, regulating its production, sale, and consumption to gain power and money. And economies have flourished because of its trade. In fact, many have argued that alcohol has been the most significant form of material culture in the lives of the world's peoples.

Academic disciplines study alcohol

Each academic discipline has approached the study of alcohol differently. Chemists have been interested in the chemical processes of the fermentation of alcohol, meaning what happens at the molecular level. Economists have studied the market for alcohol. They have been interested in the factors that have led to the amount of alcohol purchased and the amount produced and sold. Anthropologists have concentrated on the meanings of alcohol in cultural and social rituals, and sociologists have focused on alcohol use in social activities. People's behavioral reactions to alcohol have been studied by social scientists, including sociologists, anthropologists, and psychologists. The regulation of alcohol has been studied by political scientists, who have focused on the individual and structural constraints surrounding alcohol. Finally, historians have been interested in the role of alcohol across civilizations, the change or continuity in that role over time, and the causes of those changes or continuities.

Several disciplines have focused on the abuse and disease aspects of alcohol. Sociologists and psychologists have studied the disease and treatment of alcoholism. Sociologists, psychologists, and social workers have studied alcohol abuse. Sociologists have analyzed how alcohol has been defined as a disease as well as the social indicators that have caused the disease, such as family background, gender, and class. They have also wanted to know the prevalence of the disease in society. Psychologists have questioned the etiology of the abuse of alcohol, in other words the neuro-chemical, behavioral, and genetic origins of the abuse of alcohol. Moreover, they have studied the prevention of abuse as well as treatment of abuse through behavioral, pharmacological, and social support means. In the hard sciences, chemists have analyzed the chemical process of alcohol metabolism in the body as well as the long-term chemical and physical effects of alcohol on certain organs of the body, like the brain, heart, kidneys, and liver. They have also asked questions about the biochemical basis of alcohol addiction. Biologists have also sought to pinpoint the physical effects of alcohol, especially the effects of abuse. They have tested insects, animals, and humans in order to find out how alcohol is metabolized.

This work uses both the natural and social sciences in a global context to understand more fully alcohol in world history. One way to begin to synthesize the links between the bio-chemical, socio-psychological, and cultural–historical approaches to alcohol studies is to compare alcohol production, trade, consumption, and regulation across cultures and through time. Human interactions during these processes highlight themes such as religious rituals, gender relations, class structures, ethnic identities, political structures, and economic systems, all of which help to understand world history.

What is alcohol?

The word alcohol originated in Arabic. A popular theory contends that it comes from the word al-kuhul. According to this theory, the meaning of al-kuhul was first used to describe distilled substances in general, and then narrowed to mean specifically ethanol. By 1672 this conjectured etymology began circulating in Britain, and now can be found in many dictionaries. There are three kinds of alcoholic beverages: wine, beer, and spirits. Wines are fermented from the sap of plants, honey, milk, and fruits or berries, especially grapes. Beers are fermented from grains such as wheat, corn, hops, and barley. Spirits are distilled from beer, wine, or other substances. The main ingredient that provides the effect of all these beverages is ethyl alcohol, or ethanol.

Alcoholic beverages contain more than ethyl alcohol, however. They contain secondary ingredients such as acids, aldehydes, ketones, phenols, tannins, vitamins, and minerals. Alcohol content varies by product. Commercially produced beer contains between 2 and 8 percent alcohol; wine contains between 8 and 14 percent alcohol; fortified wines, such as port, contain between 20 and 21 percent alcohol; and spirits such as vodka and gin contain between 40 and 50 percent alcohol. Traditionally made alcoholic beverages, such as corn beer, or *chicha*, in the Andes, fermented maguey juice, or *pulque*, in Mexico, palm wine and banana beer in parts of Africa, and *kumiss*, made from mare's milk in Mongolia, can contain anywhere from less than 1 percent alcohol up to 4 percent, depending upon the individual maker. Furthermore, there are nutritional differences between beer and wine. For example, in the nutritional comparison between one drink of wine, about 3 ½ ounces, and one drink of beer, about 12 ounces, beer wins with almost twice as much energy as wine. In fact, the food value of strong beers such as lager is similar to that of milk, but milk contains much more fat and cholesterol.

Outline of the book

The book is divided into seven chapters. Each chapter explores, in some combination, the production, trade, consumption, and regulation of alcohol across cultures and within cultures in a particular time period. First, the production and trade of alcohol are viewed through an economic as well as socio-cultural lens. Second, the consumption of alcohol, which includes nutritional, medicinal, social, and ritual uses of alcohol, are examined through a biological, anthropological, and sociological lens. Third, the regulation of alcohol is studied from political, sociological, and anthropological perspectives. Finally, all of these aspects of alcohol are analyzed historically. Historical questions include: Is there more change or continuity over time? Are there more differences or similarities across civilizations within the same time period? And what are the results of global contacts among civilizations over time?

Chapters 1, 2, and 3 examine alcohol in pre-modern world history, up to roughly 1450. The first chapter explains the origins of alcohol using archaeological evidence. It examines the kinds of alcohol, their contents, and their processes of production as well as alcohol's influence on the development of ancient Egypt, Mesopotamia (including Jewish society), China, India, and the Americas. Chapter 2 concentrates on the Classical period. It examines alcohol in the classical societies of Greece and Rome, China, and India, studying especially the uses of alcohol for nutrition and rituals, as well as how alcohol was used to signify social hierarchies. Chapter 3 moves on to the Post-Classical era in the Middle East, the isolated Aztec and Inca empires, medieval Eastern and Western Europe, and Japan, focusing on the spread of culture in the Middle East, the social and cultural meanings of production and use in the Americas, Eastern Europe, and Japan, and the modernization of trade in the West.

Chapters 4 through 7 explain the role of alcohol in societies from roughly 1450 up to the beginning of the twenty-first-century. Chapter 4 first analyzes the role of alcohol in the world economic system, using the perspective of the

West. It then explains the significance of alcohol in the Atlantic slave trade and the subsequent influence of alcohol in Africa. Next, it focuses on colonial contact in Latin America and North America, especially religious contact and its influence on drinking patterns. Last it analyzes the political agendas behind the regulation of alcohol by the colonial governments.

Chapter 5 discusses the uses and regulations of alcohol during industrialization, focusing on the Western countries of Britain, Ireland, France, and the United States, as well as the non-Western countries of Japan and Russia. It also compares the temperance movements across these societies. Chapter 6 examines the second great wave of colonialism in Africa, India, and Australia. It investigates how colonialism changed drinking patterns in all of these areas, as well as how the colonized used alcohol to maintain their traditions in the face of change. Chapter 7 covers the twentieth-century and the beginnings of the twenty-first-centuries, concentrating on the functions of alcohol in the process of cultural and economic globalization, especially the infiltration of Western culture into non-Western societies. The chapter uses Latin America, Africa, Saudi Arabia, India, China, Japan, Russia, France, and the United States to illustrate these trends.

The book pays particular attention to the following issues: (1) the significance of place and agriculture for the creation of alcohol; (2) the meanings of alcohol use in cultural construction; (3) the ritual significance of alcohol; (4) the beliefs about alcohol that reinforce patriarchy and, alternatively, those that empower women; (5) the role of alcohol in supporting existing social hierarchies or conversely upsetting the status quo; (6) alcohol culture as a means for Westernization or on the contrary as a tool to resist Westernization; (7) the uses of alcohol by governments; and (8) the significance of alcohol as a commodity.

1 The origins of alcohol

Between 8000 and 3500 BCE, sometimes called the Neolithic Age, or the new Stone Age, humans made one of the biggest shifts in human history; they moved from hunting and gathering to agricultural production. The development of stable, permanent agricultural societies occurred over a period of thousands of years. The rise of agriculture meant that larger groups of people could live within a prescribed area, because agriculture could support more people per parcel of land than could hunting and gathering. These concentrated groups invented better tools and began writing for the first time, which led to a higher degree of social complexity.

Many authors argue that in addition to tools and writing, the use of alcohol in emerging civilizations represented a higher level of social sophistication. For example, Alexander Joffe in his article "Alcohol and Social Complexity in Ancient Western Asia" posits that "the production, exchange, and consumption of alcoholic beverages form a significant element and regularity in the emergence of complex, hierarchically organized societies, along with the restructuring of labor and gender relations." For the major civilizations, then, one of the most important world events, the development of agriculture and the settling of societies, depended in part on the production, trade, consumption, and regulation of alcohol.

The very beginnings of human settlement show evidence of the domestication of grain and grape. Wild cereals and wild grapes grew in many areas. The existence of wild cereals facilitated the domestication of grains such as wheat and barley, which were used in the production of beer. Some historians argue that the production of beer even came before the production of bread. The argument asserts that the kind of wheat needed for bread did not exist during the beginnings of wheat cultivation. Evidence shows that the first kind of beer, however, was more like a nutritious gruel and had a very low alcohol content.

Humans produced wine during the Neolithic period, even before the domestication of grapes. Theoretically wine was easier to make than beer because merely crushing the grapes started the fermentation process for the wine. Humans improved grape vines through domestication in order to increase production and regulate the taste of the wine. Grape domestication normally occurred in an area where wild grapes already grew.

The cultivators then chose the vines that produced the best grapes and focused on those vines, cloning the best plants to optimize the harvests in the future. Beer, on the other hand, required sprouting or chewing the grain and then spitting it into a container in order to obtain fermentation. Anthropologists have argued that discovering wine gave hunter-gatherers a strong incentive to settle down to tend their vines. In other words, wine making actually led to settlement.

Grapes were not the only fruit humans used to produce wine. One of the most important plants for producing wine was the date palm. Humans began cultivating the date palm around the same time as they did the grapevine. These two, plus olives and figs, constituted the first four cultivated fruits. Some archeologists argue that figs, domesticated around 9500 BCE, could have been used for fermented beverages, since we have evidence that they were used later on for such. All four of these first fruits were definitively under cultivation by the Chalcolithic period, which dated from 3700 to 3200 BCE.

Scholars still debate where the very first wine was made. Wild grapes grew from the east coast of Spain to France, Tadzhikistan, and in valleys in southwest Central Asia. Some of the first kinds of wine came from these wild grapes. Toward the end of the fifth-millennium BCE grape culture spread to the Aegean, Mesopotamia, Syria, and Egypt. Other early evidence for domestic grape cultivation comes from the Chalcolithic period (3700–3200 BCE) and the Early Bronze Age (3200–1900 BCE) in the Levant, Northwestern Iraq, Israel, Lebanon, and Syria, although newer information shows that the first wine came much earlier, around 7000 BCE in China.

Some scholars argue that the very first evidence of wine making in the Middle East comes from an area in Western Iran, called Hajji Firuz Tepe, located in the Zagros mountains. Evidence has been found there that dates to between 5400 and 5000 BCE. Remains from wine have also been discovered in another part of Iran, Godin Tepe, dating from 3500 to 3000 BCE. Other scholars argue that the grape may have been brought to Godin Tepe from the Transcaucasia, the area between Asia and Europe, now the area of Southeastern Turkey, Armenia, and Azerbaijan. Still others argue that the earliest sign of wine making in the Aegean is from the end of the fifth millennium BCE, from eastern Macedonia in northern Greece. These grape pips, dating from 4460–4000 BCE, come from wild grapes or from plants at an early stage of domestication. Researchers also found waste products from wine production at Dikili Tash in Greece indicating that wild grapes were used for wine at the end of the fifth millennium-BCE. Moreover, pottery vessels have been discovered dating back to as early as around 6000 BCE. Therefore, people would have had the means to store juice that then fermented into wine. It is likely that grape growing for wine originated in many areas where a type of wine grape could easily be grown. In addition to evidence of wine production, evidence of alcohol consumption and accompanying feasting is found from the Early Bronze Age. For example, archeologists have found drinking vessels from around 3000 BCE.

Godin Tepe also shows remains of beer-drinking vessels. The beer was likely barley beer, and evidence shows that this was the earliest barley beer made in the world. Moreover, trading and likely political interchange took place between southern Mesopotamia and Godin Tepe because Godin was located on the very important East/West trade route between the Mediterranean and China, the Silk Road. This region is also known for the first writing system, the first code of law, and the first bureaucracy, linking the development of wine and beer production, trade, consumption, and regulation to these important social and political developments in the ancient world.

Moreover, alcohol influenced the development of the ancient civilizations of Egypt, Mesopotamia, China, India, and the Americas. The production and sale of alcohol shaped gender as well as elite and lower-class identities. The consumption of alcohol structured everything from daily nutrition and medicine to social hierarchies and religious rituals, and the regulation of alcohol helped both to regulate trade as it spread and to support governments with taxes.

Two of the first civilizations in the Middle East, Egypt and Mesopotamia, also known as the river valley civilizations, developed along the Nile River and in the area between the Tigris and Euphrates rivers respectively. Egyptian culture was a more uniform culture. Mesopotamia, in contrast, was a disparate civilization, made up of many cultures, including the Sumerians, Akkadians, and Hittites. The characteristics of these two Pre-Classical societies included permanency, regional trade, social hierarchy, governmental regulation, and a religious belief system. The production, trade, consumption, and regulation of alcohol were infused in all of these societal characteristics. The production and trade of alcoholic beverages in Egypt and Mesopotamia facilitated the growth of the economies in those areas. The consumption patterns of alcohol in Mesopotamia and Egypt affected social formation, while the regulation of alcohol shaped political development in those areas.

Egypt

The production, trade, consumption, and regulation of alcohol significantly shaped the growing Egyptian civilization. Production of wine by elites and beer by commoners helped to define class differences. Trade of alcohol by women, both wine in taverns and beer in the market, helped to shape gender ideologies. Consumption of alcohol structured social gatherings, religious rituals, daily sustenance, and the composition of medicine. Social treatises on alcohol singled out particular groups, perpetuating the social hierarchy. Finally, regulations solidified the role of government in the creation of commercial standards, and taxes provided for the growth of government.

The River Valley civilization of Egypt was established after roughly 4000 BCE. Central to the stability of the civilization was its sustenance, especially the excess food production that allowed the civilization to flourish. Part of the food production included wine and beer. Alcohol became so important, in fact, that Egyptians created a god of wine, Dionysus. Egyptians first began purchasing wine from elsewhere before they began producing it themselves. Wild grapes did not grow naturally in Egypt; the dry climate made wine production more difficult. By 3000 BCE, however, vines were distributed throughout the Middle East and the eastern Mediterranean, making wine accessible to Egypt. Early evidence of wine comes from the tomb of an Egyptian king who lived around 3150 BCE; his tomb contained hundreds of wine jars with remnants of resin inside each of them. In virtually all cases, elites, such as kings and priests, cultivated wine in walled gardens, and there existed a royal winemaking industry in the Nile Delta. Domestic grape vines were fairly rare, labor intensive, and took several years to produce, therefore they needed a significant capital investment. In Egypt vineyards likely needed to be irrigated as well. These difficulties in production meant wine was a luxury item. Wine's production and trade as a luxury item helped to diversify the economy in ancient Egypt and established wine use as a notable characteristic of elite culture.

Most Egyptian wines came from the area of the Delta, although little was exported because not enough was produced to export. Egyptians likely produced both white and red wines. Illustrations on tombs from the Old Kingdom show the beginnings of the wine-production industry. Egyptians made grape wine by putting grapes into vats and then treading on them in order to extract the juice. The vats were round in shape and large enough to hold four to six men to stomp the grapes. The vintner sometimes hired musicians to play while the men stomped. The stompers either held onto poles erected above the vats, or held onto the hips of each other to keep their balance. The grapes were about ankle deep in the vats, and the juice flowed out through a bung on the side of the vat into smaller vats. After the workers stomped most of the juice out of the grapes, they put the lees, or the dregs, into a cloth bag, then tied both ends of the cloth to poles and twisted the poles to wring out the last of the juice.

After pressing the juice, the workers strained it through cloth and put it into fermentation jars about two and a half feet tall, the insides of which had been smeared with resin. The resin aided in the preservation of the wine. The mouth of the fermentation jar had a rounded lip and was about 6 inches in diameter; while the body was about 10 inches at its widest. Sometimes the workers heated the jars to speed up the fermentation process. After fermentation, a vintner put the wine into decanters, small ones for religious use and larger ones for daily, household use. He then sealed the containers with straw and clay and stamped them with the official stamps, which had the year of the king's rule, the district, the name of the wine, and sometimes the name of the vintner. Sometimes he poured the wine into skins, especially if the wine was to be carried long distances. Finally, by the time of the New Kingdom (1550–1069 BCE) the vintner impressed his imprimatur, or license, into the stopper. The first imprimatur became more and more detailed as the craft became more professionalized.

After sealing the wine the wine maker then drilled safety holes into the toppers or into the necks to prevent the containers from bursting. He then plugged them with straw, wax, or clay. After awhile he tasted the wine to assess its quality, and then marked the grade on the lids. Wine was labeled good, twice good, three times good, and sweet, twice sweet, and so on. Labeling also told the age of the wine. Other kinds of labeling included wine for taxes and wine for offerings, both indicating that wine had become profitable for the government and important in religious rituals. Finally, the vessels, tapered at the end, were stored leaning and stacked against a wall.

Egyptian wine did not last long; people drank it within a year. It was also very sweet because the sugar content of the grapes was very high. High sugar content occurred because of the dry climate, which meant the grapes were probably shriveled and therefore they could not ferment all the sugar into alcohol and they remained sweet. In addition to regular sweet wine, Egyptians made mixed or spiced wines, flavoring them with juices, herbs, and spices. Egyptians also made palm wine. Palm wine came from oases and palm-growing areas. People tapped into the top of a date palm tree to gather its sap. The sap fermented very quickly because of the hot weather.

Wine was not only made for personal use, but it was also sold in taverns. Most tavern owners as well as tavern employees were women, and many of the women who worked in taverns were prostitutes. As a result, taverns had reputations as houses of prostitution and any woman associated with a tavern was suspect. So as early as ancient Egypt, society began to stereotype as immoral most women who associated with alcohol, especially in public. This same correlation was not applied to men, of course, and elite women, by virtue of their class, escaped the characterization in Egypt.

In addition to wine, beer, too, had an impact on Egyptian society. The beginnings of beer go back to around the fourth-millennium BCE. By 3000 BCE beer was more widespread and in larger production than wine. Beer could be made at any time, unlike wine, which could only be made during the grape harvest. And beer, like bread, could be made in people's homes. Moreover, the grain could be stored and was more portable than grapes. Unlike modern beer, the beer of ancient Egypt was more like food. It was made from either red, white, or black barley, or emmer wheat, and was opaque, thick, and more like soup or gruel. Making barley beer began with moistening barley and laying it out for one day, then moistening it and drying it again while it was in a vessel. After it dried, the beer maker shook it in the sun until it fell apart. Then he or she ground it and made it into loaves adding leaven to make it rise. Workers cooked it for just a little while and then dissolved sweetened water into it and pushed it through a sieve.

Another way to make beer consisted of pouring moistened grain into a mortar, grinding it, adding yeast, then cooking the dough over a slow fire until it was partially baked. Next, the beer maker broke the partially baked bread into pieces and left them to soak in water for several days. He or she then placed the pieces into large human-sized fermentation vats and stomped them into gruel, poured the gruel into a wide-woven basket that was placed over a large jar, and then kneaded it so the liquid could flow through the basket into the jar. Next the maker poured the liquid into large beer jars, sometimes adding dates or date juice to flavor the beer and sugar for fermentation. The beer usually did not have a high alcohol content, perhaps between 4 and 5 percent, although because it was brewed in each home the alcohol content could vary. In the later dynasties, when money came into use, women sold beer in the markets to both men and women. Since women made beer at home for their families, they likely made an excess of beer to sell in the markets. Egyptian society normalized women's roles as beer makers, easily accepting their transition into beer peddlers. The almost exclusive involvement of women in beer production and trade characterized those activities as feminine, creating a defining feature of female gender identity, which in this case was not sexually related.

In addition to influencing gender identity, alcohol in ancient Egypt structured social occasions and religious ceremonies, and prominently figured in daily sustenance and medicine. Elite Egyptians entertained with wine. Many depictions exist of elite banquets where excessive wine drinking took place by both elite men and women. H. F. Lutz's *Viticulture and Brewing in the Ancient Orient* describes a typical party. To begin, a wooden image of a dead person was paraded around the gathering to show that death could come at any time so one should enjoy oneself while it was still possible. Taking their cue from the performance, guests felt free to overindulge in wine. Tomb paintings show that both elite men and women drank to excess; they display pictures of passed out men being carried away by their servants and women vomiting while their heads were held by their female servants. One elite woman was reported to have said "Give me eighteen cups of wine ... don't you see I want to get drunk! My insides are as dry as straw." Society saw wine consumption, even excessive consumption, as a characteristic of the rich, helping to define elite identity, an identity that categorized women by their privilege before their gender.

Wine also shaped Egyptian religion. Many myths surrounded wine in Egypt. Egyptians believed that the reproduction of the vine was the work of the god Osiris, representing his rebirth. Ancient Egyptians commonly offered up wine to the gods. Festivals for the god Dionysus as well as for other gods featured wine. During the New Kingdom when Egypt was very wealthy as a result of Thutmose III, alcohol use during religious festivals soared. The king granted more money to the priests to provide wine for daily temple rituals; and bread and beer were also required twice a day as offerings to the dead god-king at funeral temples. Priests poured wine libations onto the ground as well as drank much of the wine themselves. Staff members of the temples as well as priests and others consumed large quantities of beer in the daily temple rituals as well as in the temple festivals. The annual cat-goddess festival, which drew worshipers from all over Egypt, included excessive alcoholic celebrations by men, women, and children. One of the subsequent kings, Akhenaton, had a yearly festival dedicated to the god Amon for which the king took a state journey to his temple at Karnak. The yearly ritual could last up to a month, and both beer and wine were drunk to excess during the entire festival.

Beer, too, held symbolic meaning in Egypt. For example, the feline goddess Hathor-Sekhmet was supposedly appeased with red-dyed beer in order to save humans from her rage. She was credited with the origin of beer, and her temple was known as the "house of drunkenness." Moreover, Egyptians believed that when men dreamed about beer, each dream held a special meaning. If a man dreamed of sweet beer it was good luck. If he dreamed of bakery beer he would live a long life, or if he dreamed of stored beer he would be healed if sick. If a man dreamed of drinking warm beer he would soon be suffering, or if he dreamed of brewing beer in his own home he would soon be banished from his house. In addition, if a man was having bad dreams he could be cured by rubbing his body with herbs moistened with beer and having a spell uttered over him.

Beer was also an essential part of daily sustenance. Bread and beer were staples for Egyptians from all classes. Beer was even called ancient Egypt's "national drink." It was nutritious; it contained many calories as well as protein, B vitamins, and live yeast. Because it constituted a daily necessity, the government used beer as wages. It paid soldiers through rations of loaves of bread and jugs of beer. Non-military laborers were paid in the same way. A basic wage for an ordinary laborer consisted of ten loaves of bread and anywhere from one-third to two jugs of beer, with an average of about two and a half liters. Higher ranking workers also received bread and beer rations, but in double or triple the quantity. In addition to the army and laborers, priests in temples received an allotted amount of beer for food. Since most beer was drunk for daily sustenance, excess drinking was rare. Beer was considered more of a necessary food than a recreational alcohol. Men ate bread, beer, and onions for lunch. Children and nursing mothers drank beer for health and nutritional reasons.

Hosts commonly provided bread and beer for their guests, and were considered rude if they did not. Offering beer, then, became a symbol of polite society, conferring social capital on those who could afford the gesture. Clearly the wealthy had more ability than poorer people to provide drink to their guests, and thus lack of access to abundant alcohol caused poorer people to have fewer opportunities to become respected members of polite society.

Egyptians also believed in the curative properties of beer and wine. One of the most famous sources for Egyptian medicine, the Papyrus Ebers, which was written about 1500 BCE, is a collection of remedies from as early as 3400 BCE. All of these remedies contained some form of alcohol. One prescription to stop constipation consisted of chewing the berry from a castor oil tree together with drinking some beer. Another prescription for a diuretic called for water from the bird pond, a swill of beer, and fresh milk. Healers could make a purgative from an onion beaten up in the froth of beer, and cure an inflamed abdomen with a mixture of bread of the zizyphus lotus flower, cat's dung, red lead, watermelon, sweet beer, and wine made into a plaster and put onto the abdomen. For problems of the anus, a mixture of cowhorn, pieces of dried oil, and yeast of wine were made into a suppository. To dress a wound, crushed human excrement mixed with the yeast of sweet beer, sefet-oil, and honey were applied to the area. Beer was used to wash down herbs, to rub on the body, and as a mouthwash, an enema, and a douche. Many more remedies existed that included some form of either beer or wine.

Alcohol use in Egyptian society led in some cases to abuse, resulting in socially prescriptive treatises penned by prominent writers and thinkers that pointed to the damage caused by going to beer houses. They also argued against over-indulging in beer and wine, even during times of mourning. For example, Ani, an Egyptian sage, said "Do not pass [thy time] in the beer-house and don't indulge in drinking beer, lest you utter evil speech and don't know what you're saying. Then if thou fallest to the ground and thou breakest the limbs, none reacheth out the hand to help thee. Behold, thy companions! They drink and say: Go home, thou, who has drunk enough!" (as quoted in Lutz, *Viticulture and Brewing in the Ancient Orient*). Moreover, proscriptive works written by Ani and Amenehotep discouraged students from excessive drinking either at home or at inns. It was believed that students would "for-sakest books [and] ... abandon thyself to pleasure." These sages also warned against alcoholism and alcohol-related personality problems. At the same time, however, judgments around alcohol were class specific. Elites looked down upon others who over-indulged, and in particular disparaged tavern keepers. Yet there were many stories of elite banquets after which people had to be carried home by their servants.

In addition to treatises on moderation, the government regulated the quality of wine and levied a wine tax. Inspectors tasted the wines in taverns and markets to regulate the prices and quality of wine. The state also earned substantial revenues from customs duties on foreign wine coming into Egypt. One-sixth of the yield of Egyptian vineyards went to pay taxes except those that were owned by the temples or by the king. These numerous wine taxes were vital to the state treasury as well as to the temples. So the taxes and regulations as well as the production, trade, and numerous uses of alcohol reveal how it permeated all areas of Egyptian society.

Mesopotamia

The production, trade, consumption, and regulation of alcohol in Mesopotamia helped shape many areas in that civilization. Beer production differentiated male and female work roles. In addition, the growing beer trade led to the pro-fessionalization of traders, and the vibrant regional trade in alcohol, especially wine, expanded trade networks. Moreover, alcohol consumption patterns cre-ated class identity, and even differentiated elites from each other. Alcohol was so central to Mesopotamian society that the famous Hammurabic Code of 2225 BCE included many laws regulating the trade.

Ancient southern Mesopotamia was a center of beer-drinking culture. Archeologists have even uncovered an ancient brewery that included tanks for making beer bread. Moreover, jars and drinking tubes for beer were found in tombs, and pictures of beer drinking at banquets and during sexual intercourse were found on cylinder seals. Significantly, one of the first uses of writing in Sumerian culture was the record of a beer recipe, which was written in cuneform around 3500 BCE.

Mesopotamians produced beer from malted barley; they did not have hops. Barley beer was the most common beverage in ancient Sumer because the hot and dry climate was conducive to grain growing. Beer making was very labor intensive, required gender-specific tasks, and coincided with bread making. The beer maker, usually a man, began by crushing grain with a wooden pestle in order to loosen the husks. Then the miller, usually a woman, crushed the grain with a smaller stone. Next, a man mixed the dough by standing in a large vat and kneading it with his feet. Then the dough was made into little cakes, and sometimes dates were added for flavor. The cakes were then allowed to rise. Afterward, another man pressed the dough cakes through a sieve into a large vat, added water, and then poured it into clay jars and sealed them. Over time, brewers changed the ingredients of beer; they began to add spices to improve the taste. The beer was strained to remove sediment and floating grains from it and then many brewers put the beer into leather bags or in clay barrels or jars.

Beer production helped in the development of specialized occupations. Beer making was so individualized that each brewer carried his own unique clay vats with him when he traveled. The cracks in the vats contained yeast, which gave each particular beer its special flavor. Carrying vats also identified brewers by their profession as they traveled. Moreover, beer was so significant in Mesopotamian culture that the brewers' craft was the only one to enjoy divine protection from a goddess – in fact from two female figures – Nin and Siris. Siris was known as the divine patron of the brewer in Mesopotamia.

The Babylonians made both beer and wine, though, and engaged in the alcohol trade. In Babylonia the customer supplied the grain and the brewer supplied the manufacturing equipment, which included the vats, fermenting tubs, barrels, jars, and the brewer's furnace. Babylonians also made wine from date palms. In one method the winemaker scratched the stem of the date plant with a sharp knife and gathered the sap into jars and let it ferment. In another method the winemaker pressed the fresh dates and then left the juice to ferment. Date wine from the stem spoiled within a few hours, but the wine made from the actual dates lasted much longer. Babylonians also made pomegranate wine and liquor from figs. Babylonians made grape wine as well, but produced it only in the dry-farming agricultural areas to the north and west of Babylonia. Unlike beer, though, grape wine could be made only once a year, when the grapes ripened. Wine had a longer shelf life than beer if the wine was kept in sealed jars, which typically held several gallons each.

Since so little wine was produced in Babylonia, most wine came from trade with Syria. The trade in wine helped to develop and expand crucial trading networks in the region as well. In the first-millennium BCE the Damascus region became famous for its wine. This trade increased with the domestication of the camel, and became very important in Mesopotamia along the Euphrates.

Alcohol consumption patterns influenced even more areas in society. Wine was an expensive and rare commodity, which meant that it became an elite drink and its consumption yet another characteristic of the privileged. As a luxury item, wine was served only to the gods and the wealthy. Tablets from the eighth-century BCE reveal the scarcity of wine when noting the wine ration for the royal household to be less than a half pint per person. In areas where vines were easily cultivated, such as Greece, however, wine drinking was more widespread and represented to a lesser degree a class-specific beverage. Yet it was still associated with elites more so than with the lower classes, because even in Greece it cost a regular laborer almost two days' wages to buy one liter.

In Babylonia since grape wine was so expensive poorer people drank cheap date wine. Even into the later Pre-Classical period, during the Hittite Kingdom, 1700–1050 BCE, wine was still used mostly for rituals and festivals, such as for soldiers who were giving their oath of loyalty, for the founding of a new palace, or for supplicating the gods. In the Hittite Kingdom elites drank grape wine and pomegranate wine, both of which were very expensive. Some scholars argue that elites diluted their wine with water, usually half and half, and considered those who did not dilute their wine to be unsophisticated. People diluted their wine likely because the hot climate did not allow for their thirst to be quenched with straight wine, and since potable water was not common, Babylonians believed that mixing water with wine sanitized it and prevented illness. Moreover, elites used wine during the Bronze Age to differentiate status within elite society. Elites utilized wine in "competitive consumption." For example, elites in the Middle Bronze Age competed with each other by throwing lavish, wine-saturated feasts in order to demonstrate their wealth, solidify alliances, and gain the support or loyalty of others.

In contrast to the elite nature of wine, the masses drank beer in ancient southern Mesopotamia. Beer constituted a significant part of the daily diet and was included on the ration lists for palace workers, who received the equivalent of one quart to one gallon of beer per day, depending on their rank. People also drank beer as they socialized in taverns. They drank from a common vat usually through drinking tubes with small perforated holes on the end that acted as strainers to remove solids such as the hulls of the malted barley. Communal beer drinking facilitated camaraderie among patrons, and as drinking it was associated mainly with commoners, it also became a characteristic of lower-class identity.

Alcohol regulation differed by kingdom in Mesopotamia. In the period between 4100 BCE and 3100 BCE, the state controlled the coerced labor that made the beer. In Sumeria the government regulated the quality and measurements of beer. Beer makers had to make no less than the legal amount of beer based on the weight of ingredients given to them by the customer, thus keeping beer makers from cheating the customer. Another regulation stipulated that a barmaid who served watered-down beer would be dunked in water. The Hammurabic Code, created under the Babylonian king, Hammurabi, in

2225 BCE, regulated the proper behavior for tavern owners and those who frequented taverns. For example, the price of beer was set for tavern keepers, who were overwhelmingly women. Regulations allowed credit in the taverns and repayment was a set amount of corn from the customer's harvest. A tavernness had to accept payment for drinks in corn. If she demanded money instead, and the money that she demanded for the drink was greater than the value of the corn, then she would be thrown in the water. Hammurabi also wrote that if a priestess tried to open a tavern, or if she even entered a tavern with the idea of drinking, she was to be immediately burned to death. Moreover, if would-be traitors met in a tavern, and the tavern keeper did not report them, she would be held responsible for their actions and executed. These law codes regulating taverns indicate the role of the government in regulating business, the ubiquity of taverns in Babylonia, as well as the role of taverns as social centers where men gathered and talked politics. Finally, the codes referred to tavern keepers as women, showing that the occupation had become feminized, resulting in gender ideologies that constructed socially acceptable occupations for men and women in Babylonia.

In addition to the Hammurabic code, a later kingdom, the Hittites, created laws specifically to protect the labor intensive and irrigated vineyards. For example, the penalty for the theft of a vine or tendril involved some form of corporal punishment along with the fine of a shekel of silver. There were also fines and punishments for burning down a vineyard, letting one's sheep into a productive vineyard, stealing tendrils from a fenced-in vineyard, or for cutting down a vine. The Hittites also had several laws regulating the price of wine. These regulations reflected the high value of vineyards, and indeed wine, in the Hittite Kingdom.

Jewish society

One of the world's major religions, Judaism, grew out of an area within Mesopotamia. The Jewish people were nomadic, first migrating to an area encompassed by present-day Israel/Palestine and Lebanon, called Canaan, then to Egypt, and then back to Canaan. Judaism followed the Hebrew Bible, in which wine figured prominently. According to the Old Testament (divided and numbered differently than the Hebrew Bible) wine possessed symbolic power, strengthened social relations, and brought happiness. Abuse of wine, however, brought illness, public wrongdoing, and lack of ability to honor God. The Bible praised the moderate use of alcohol, although overindulgence was a sin. To begin with, the Bible mentioned alcohol more than 220 times. Genesis said that God blessed his people with grain and wine, and connected drinking wine with eating food. The Bible also saw wine as a gift from God. Moreover, Psalms stated: "Thou dost cause the grass to grow for the cattle, And Plants for man to cultivate, That he may bring forth food from the earth, And wine to gladden the heart of man, ... " (As quoted in Hewitt, *A Biblical Perspective on the Use and Abuse of Alcohol and Other*

Drugs.) In many places the Bible also equated good hospitality with providing wine for one's guests. Kings served wine to their guests as accorded into the book of Esther: "Wine was served in golden cups of various patterns: the king's wine flowed freely as befitted a king ... " In other places the Bible stated that wine brought happiness. For example, the Book of Judges stated: "new wine ... gladdens gods and men." Song of Solomon stated: "Eat, friends, and drink, until you are drunk with love." Moreover, Jews used wine in all major rituals; circumcisions, weddings, Passover Seder, and Purim – where sanctioned overconsumption took place. Jews gave wine as gifts, used it in celebrations of victory, provided it as a reward for work, and recommended it as a way to honor a king. It was used as an offering to God, a tithe to the church, a gift to priests from parishioners, and a reward from God to his followers.

In many places the Bible warned against using too much alcohol. The story of Lot explained that he drank too much wine, leading him to have intercourse with his daughters. Deuteronomy stated that drunkards were to be severely punished, and Proverbs stated that if one gulped down wine "then your eyes see strange sights, your wits and your speech are confused; you become like a man tossing out at sea ... " Many other passages condemned drunkenness, listing its many ills. It could make one sick, weak, ill, violent, irresponsible, lustful, anxious, and apathetic. It could also lead to a lack of self-control, fights, gossip, poverty, and exile. Most importantly the book of Isaiah admonished that it could lead one to neglect God's work: "[those] inflamed with wine ... have no eyes for the work of the Lord." So the Jewish religion recommended moderation and cautioned against abuse, but more importantly it relied on wine, giving it symbolic power to shape important rituals and celebrations that defined that culture.

China

Alcohol began influencing Chinese civilization earlier than anywhere else in the world. It structured important religious and social ceremonies, established itself as a common medium for healing, and led to significant political turmoil. Legends from the Xia Dynasty, 2140–1711 BCE, explained the beginnings of alcohol in China. One story told of a young woman named Yi Di who tasted fermented grain and subsequently felt elated. She then gave it to Emperor Yu who drank it. He proclaimed that Yi Di must be exiled because of the probable ill effects of alcohol on his kingdom. Another legend told of Du Kang, a young shepherd, again from the Xia Dynasty, who when caught in a rainstorm one day up on a mountain, quickly herded his sheep home and as a result forgot his lunch of cooked and husked sorghum that he had left hanging in a tree. When he returned after a few days the fermented lunch tasted very good and gave him a good feeling. He and his family continued to make alcohol and he has been called the "God of alcohol." These two legends reveal how differently Chinese society viewed women and alcohol versus men and alcohol. The female in the first legend was condemned, while the male in the second legend was rewarded, showing how the cultural meanings of alcohol worked together with gender ideologies to shape gender hierarchies in China.

The actual beginnings of alcohol occurred much earlier than the Xia dynasty. The earliest wine, or fermented liquor, came from China, predating Middle Eastern alcohol by a few thousand years. Archeologists have found pottery shards showing remnants of rice and grape wine dating back to 7000 BCE in Jiahu village in Henan Province. Evidence from a later period shows that fermented alcoholic beverages were also made from millet and rice. Moreover, major excavations along the Yellow River found various kinds of serving goblets that implied the use of fermented beverages during the periods of Erlitou (ca. 1900–1500 BCE), Shang (ca. 1600–1046 BCE), and Western Zhou (ca. 1046–771 BCE).

The Chinese produced most alcohol by using one part black millet and two parts rice mixed together. The mixture was cooked over an open fire in a clay vessel. Workers poured boiling water over rice and added human saliva to begin fermentation. They then let it ferment for five to seven days. In another method workers first milled rice to remove any rough surfaces (in order to make a clearer product), then steamed the rice and spread it out to dry. Next, they made a mash and added ingredients for fermentation. They finally added spices such as pepper to flavor the alcohol. In general alcohol was brewed in the winter and drank in the spring, which leads to the conclusion that it kept for a relatively long period of time.

By the Shang dynasty, which was between 1600 and 1046 BCE, three kinds of alcohol existed: chang, which was an herbal wine; li, which was a sweet, low-alcoholic millet or rice wine; and jiu, which had a high alcohol content of 10 to 15 percent. The later Zhou period, 1046–256 BCE, saw two more kinds of alcoholic beverages called luo, which was fermented from fruit; and lao, which was unfiltered rice or millet wine. The many varieties of wine point to its prevalence in that civilization.

Alcohol shaped religious and cultural ceremonies in ancient China. The Chinese believed that consuming wine allowed them to communicate with the spirit world. Mourners drank to intoxication during burial ceremonies to communicate both with the deceased and with the gods, and alcohol accompanied elites into the next life. Moreover, elites performed elaborate sacrifices that included excessive feasting and drinking, and the king used wine in sacrifices to honor the ancestors.

One of the most important ancient Chinese ceremonies was the ancestor ceremony where wine and food were offered to the ancestors. Patrick McGovern describes this ceremony in *Uncorking the Past: the Quest for Wine, Beer, and Other Alcoholic Beverages*. After four days of fasting a descendent of the deceased, called the shi, was chosen to communicate with the ancestors. Usually the shi was a grandson or a daughter-in-law. After seven days of fasting by the shi there was a feast in the temple for the deceased where the shi drank nine cups of warmed wine. Then the shi offered food and wine to the deceased and afterward ate and drank for the deceased.

Alcohol constructed other rituals as well, and even led to political intrigue. Rites of passage such as manhood and marriage were organized around alcohol. The manhood ceremony featured offerings of alcoholic beverages and food to the ancestors, the mother, and the other relatives and guests at the ceremony. In the wedding ceremony the bride's family offered wine to the groom's parents, symbolizing their acceptance of the marriage. Alcohol became so prevalent in Chinese society that some argue that the downfall of the Shang dynasty was caused by the emperor's perpetual drunkenness. He was reputedly a tyrant who had frequent drunken orgies. Thus he lost the "Mandate of Heaven," or the right to rule, and was deposed.

Alcohol's influence in Chinese culture spread even further. It contributed to the development of Chinese medicine. The ancient Chinese believed in the power of alcohol to heal. For example, Bernard Read in *Chinese Materia Medica* noted that in order to cure apoplexy, fistula, stomach or heart pain, colic, hemorrhoids, worm toxemia, flatulence, and bleeding from the bowel a mixture of pit viper placed in a gallon of wine, which had been buried for a year under a horse's stall, was to be used. Moreover, using donkey's placenta in wine cured alcoholism, and lizard's liver, the skin of a cicada locust, and wine made into a poultice induced abortions, while chicken brains in alcohol and a chicken's claw in wine eased a difficult labor and stopped convulsions by infants. Furthermore, eating chicken intestines with alcohol cured incontinence and frequent urination, and according to Salvatore P. Lucia in *A History of Wine as Therapy*, drinking a combination of 12 herbs, including cinnamon, and ground oyster shells dissolved in warm wine stopped a heart attack. The power of wine to heal, along with its strong symbolism, made it a potent medium in Chinese society.

India

Pre-Classical India, or the early Vedic period, dates back as early as 2500 BCE. During that period Indians produced a fermented alcoholic beverage called soma, which shaped both religious beliefs and cultural practices. Indians equated soma with the gods, and thought of it as a deity in liquid form. Women commonly produced soma in their homes, but the sacred production of soma was highly ritualistic. The roots of a leafless milkweed vine had to be pulled by the light of the moon and then hauled in a goat-pulled cart to a sacrificial place. Priests crushed the vines into a sieve made of wool and then pressed them into a liquid, which was then mixed with either sweet or sour milk or curds and flour. It took nine days to ferment. The Rig-Veda includes many odes to soma (as quoted in Lucia, *A History of Wine as Therapy*):

> O Soma, You have been crushed, you flow as a stream to Indra, scattering joy on all sides, you bestow immortal food. Seven women stir thee with

their fingers blending their voices in a song to thee, you remind the sacrificer of his duties at the sacrifice. Of all the drinks that Indra has, you are the most pleasant and intoxicating. This is Soma, who flows wine, who is strength giving.

This ode glorifies both soma and women's role in its production. Women's connection to alcohol appeared to add to their status in Indian society.

The symbolic power of soma in ancient Indian society led to the belief in its curative powers. The Rig-Veda, one of the sacred texts of Hinduism from the early Vedic period, included medical remedies using soma. Moreover, soma structured many of the rituals in the Hindu religion. For example, soma was used as an offering to the gods, and it was written that drinking soma brought on immortality. Furthermore, it was commonly believed that the gods, especially Indra and Agni, drank soma. In Hinduism ambivalence existed toward soma, however. In some writings it seemed to be accepted, and in others it was not, depending upon the time period. The Bhagaved-gita argued that only those with "demoniac mentality" drank. Ayurveda, a medical practice based on Hindu principles, used alcohol in some of its remedies. So whether or not alcohol consumption was accepted or not remained unresolved in Hinduism. While many contradictions existed regarding alcohol, alcohol consumption and regulation helped to shape society and religion in ancient India.

The Americas

The first known site of humans in the Americas is located at Monte Verde in Chile. It dates back to about 11,000 BCE. While no definitive evidence of alcoholic beverages had been found by the early twenty-first-century, people inhabited the area year round and had access to edible berries and bulrush, both of which could be fermented. Later on, with the domestication of corn, alcohol production became widespread. Corn beer, or chicha, which was made by women, became the most important fermented beverage in the Andean region. There is evidence of pottery dating back to 3000 BCE that was likely used for chicha. Chicha constituted the bulk of daily sustenance for many Andeans. Moreover, they considered it to be sacred, believing it came from the earth goddess. Since only women brewed chicha it became a fundamental part of their identity as women, giving them a role that included not only producing a life-sustaining substance, but also reproducing the very culture of the people.

Conclusion

Production, trade, consumption, and regulation of alcohol helped construct the economic, social, cultural, and political development of early civilizations. First, all these civilizations showed evidence of alcohol production. The virtually universal desire for alcohol from the very beginnings of civilization led to ancient societies creating alcohol out of whatever was available. For example, in Egypt and Mesopotamia grain was plentiful and therefore it was made into beer, which became the most common alcoholic drink in those civilizations. The date palm was also plentiful in those areas and was therefore made into date palm wine. In China rice and millet were readily available and so they were made into wine; in India milkweed was available and so it was made into soma, and in the Americas corn was available and so it was made into chicha. Second, the alcohol trade opened up routes and diversified economic development in Egypt and Mesopotamia, and led to the professionalization of brewers in Mesopotamia.

Third, many cultures, including Egypt, Mesopotamia, India, and the Americas considered alcohol to be a sacred substance and thus ritualized its production in order to reinforce its revered position in society. Fourth, alcohol helped create gender identities. Egyptian society labeled women who sold alcohol in taverns as prostitutes (some, but not all, were), so women's connection to alcohol in that case resulted in a negative gender stereotype. In Egypt, Mesopotamia, and the Americas women brewed beer, thus identifying beer production as feminine and giving women the power to sustain both life and culture. In Mesopotamia male brewers identified themselves as professional artisans as they traveled around, making the professionalization of brewing essentially masculine. In China legends credited a woman in one case, and a man in another, with the discovery of alcohol. The fate of the woman, however, was exile, while that of the man fame and fortune, suggesting that alcohol enhanced male identity but diminished female identity. In all of these cases the origins, production, and trade of alcohol were gendered, helping to define gender ideologies across many civilizations.

Consumption of alcohol helped to define social status, and structure nourishment, medicine, and religious and social rituals throughout the ancient world. First, consumption practices characterized one's place in the social hierarchy. In Egypt and most of Mesopotamia elites had much more access to wine than did the lower classes, thus drinking wine became a characteristic of elite identity. Moreover, the lavish, alcohol-filled parties thrown by elites reinforced their social status. In contrast, in Egypt and Mesopotamia the lower classes drank beer because it was very plentiful; it therefore became part of lower-class culture and identity. Second, in Egypt, Mesopotamia, and the Americas beer was essential to daily sustenance. It was such a staple in the diets of Egyptians and Mesopotamians that it was used as payment for workers and given in rations to soldiers. Third, alcohol helped define medicine. Many civilizations including Egypt, China, and India believed alcohol to be a powerful substance, and used it in almost every cure.

Fourth, alcohol structured social rituals in Egypt, Mesopotamia (including Jewish culture), and China. In Egypt the definition of politeness meant offering alcohol to guests, and in Mesopotamia taverns shaped social life. In Jewish culture alcohol shaped such social rituals as weddings and circumcisions, while in China alcohol structured the ancestor ceremony and marriage ceremonies. Fifth, in Egypt, Mesopotamia, China, India, and the Americas alcohol framed religious beliefs and rituals. Egyptians believed in a god of wine, and that the growth of grapes represented the rebirth of their god Osiris. Alcohol also made up most of their offerings to the gods. In Jewish society wine possessed symbolic power, while the Chinese believed in the power of alcohol as a conduit to the gods, and Indians believed that soma led to immortality. In the Americas Andeans believed that chicha was sacred, given to them by the earth goddess. In all these societies alcohol shaped important aspects of both society and culture.

Alcohol regulation helped standardize trade, define acceptable social mores, and provide governments with essential resources. First, Egypt and Mesopotamia regulated many aspects surrounding the sale of alcohol to ensure fair business practices, giving government an important role in developing a commercial culture. Second, in both Egypt and Mesopotamia (including Jewish culture), prescriptive literature outlined appropriate drinking behavior, especially for certain segments of society, reinforcing social structures and perpetuating social hierarchies. Third, governments came to rely on alcohol taxes as stable income, crucial for governmental stability.

Alcohol gave people the impetus to settle down and form the early agricultural civilizations. Alcohol also shaped the development of ancient societies. People treated it as sacred, believing it to be connected to the gods. It helped signify class and gender identities, as societies characterized the elite and the lower class, as well as women and men in part by their relationship to alcohol. Alcohol structured religious and social rituals as well as daily meals, and defined most medical practice. Finally, its taxes helped maintain and perpetuate ancient governments. Alcohol permeated virtually all areas of the ancient world.

Further reading

Ancient Egyptian Medicine: The Papyrus Ebers. Translated by Cyril P. Bryan. 1930. Chicago: Ares Publishers.

Darby, William, J. Paul Ghalioungui, and Louis Grivetti. 1976. *Food: The Gift of Osiris.* Vol. 2. London: Academic Press.

Davies, W. W. 1905. *The Codes of Hammurabi and Moses.* Cincinnati, OH: Jennings and Graham.

Dayagi-Mendels, M. 1999. *Drink and Be Merry: Wine and Beer in Ancient Times.* Jerusalem: The Israel Museum.

Geller, J. 1993. "Bread and Beer in Fourth-Millennium Egypt." *Food and Foodways.* 5 (3): 255–67.

Hartman, L. F. and A. L. Oppenheim. 1950. "On Beer and Brewing Techniques in Ancient Mesopotamia." *Journal of the American Oriental Society.* 10: 1–55.

Joffe, A. H. 1998. "Alcohol and Social Complexity in Ancient Western Asia." *Current Anthropology.* 39 (3): 297–322.

Lucia, S. P. M. D. 1963. *A History of Wine as Therapy.* Philadelphia: J. B. Lippincott Company.

Lutz, H. F. 1922. *Viticulture and Brewing in The Ancient Orient*. New York: G. E. Stechert & Co.

McGovern, P. E. 2003. *Ancient Wine: The Search for the Origins of Viniculture*. Princeton, NJ: Princeton University Press.

McGovern P. E. 2009. *Uncorking the Past: The Quest for Wine, Beer and Other Alcoholic Beverages*. Berkeley: University of California Press.

McGovern, P. E., E. D. Butrym, A. Nunez, C. S. Wang, M. P. Richards, R. A. Moreau, J. G. Tang, J. Z. Zhang, G. R. Hall, and Z. Q. Zhang 2004. "Fermented Beverages of Pre- and Proto-Historic China." In *Proceedings of the National Academy of Sciences*. November: www.pnas.org cgi/doi/10.1073/pnas.0407921102 (accessed December 13, 2011).

McGovern, P. E., S. J. Fleming and S. Katz (eds.) 1996. *The Origins and Ancient History of Wine*. Amsterdam: Gordon and Breach Publishers.

Paper, J. 1995. *The Spirits are Drunk: Comparative Approaches to Chinese Religion*. Albany: State University of New York Press.

Poo, M.-C. 1995. *Wine and Wine Offering in the Religion of Ancient Egypt*. London: Kegan Paul International.

Purcell, N. 1985. "Wine and Wealth in Ancient Italy." *The Journal of Roman Studies*, 75: 1–19.

Read B. E. n.d. *Chinese Materia Medica*. Shanghai: Henry Lester Institute for Medical Research.

Scheidel, W. and S. von Reden. 2002. *The Ancient Economy*. New York: Routledge.

Steele, P. 1994. *Food & Feast in Ancient Rome*. New York: New Discovery Books.

Tamang, J. P. 2010. *Himalayan Fermented Foods: Microbiology, Nutrition, and Ethnic Values*. New York: CRC Press, Taylor & Francis Group.

Valamoti, M. and M. Koukouli-Chrysanthaki. 2007. "Grape-pressings from northern Greece: the earliest wine in the Aegean." *Antiquity*. 81 (311): 54–61.

Wilson, H. 1988. *Egyptian Food and Drink*. Princes Risborough: Shire Publications.

2   Alcohol and the spread of culture in the Classical Period

In the Classical Period civilizations built upon previous accomplishments in order to form more developed societies and, in fact, empires. These empires spread across many parts of the world. Three empires exemplify the changes that took place during the Classical Period: the Mediterranean, China, and India. In each of these areas there began to be shared language and cultural values. The production, trade, consumption, and regulation of alcohol helped to shape the development of these consolidated civilizations. For example, the ceremonial production process of alcohol in China helped to define culture in that society. In the Mediterranean the trade of alcohol facilitated the spread of Greek and Roman culture. The consumption of alcohol in the Mediterranean, China, and India shaped class and gender roles as well as defined medicine, while the regulation of alcohol helped to moderate public behavior in all of those societies.

Classical Greece and the spread of the Roman Empire

Classical Greece rose after 800 BCE when small city states began to form around the Mediterranean. Roman civilization, which resembled Greek civilization, rose later, around 400 BCE and eventually spread as far as northern Africa and Britain. Alcohol production, trade, consumption, and regulation affected the development of the Greek and Roman civilizations. Production and trade of wine spread Greek and Roman culture across the Mediterranean and even into Africa, and pushed the Roman civilization as far as Britain. Consumption of wine solidified class as well as gender distinctions, and regulation of wine helped to develop social boundaries that came to define both civilizations. Finally, wine taxes remained necessary to support the governments as they continued to spread across the Mediterranean and beyond.

The production and trade of wine took place on the mainland of Greece as well as on the islands of Thasos, Lesbos, and Chios, all of which were known for producing high-quality wines. Grape growers planted vineyards close to waterways because shipping by water was much cheaper than overland shipping. By the beginnings of the Classical Greek civilization wine cultivation had developed into a much more complex process than in earlier periods. By that time, there was specialization within the profession of wine making and it had become one of the three most important trade items, alongside olives and grain. Greeks not only traded wine around the Mediterranean, but also spread its production to other parts of the Mediterranean as well, introducing wine making to parts of France and Italy. Moreover, Greek colonies established in Italy spread the knowledge of viniculture to the Romans. Wine not only brought the Romans Greek technology, but also Greek culture.

Romans also spread wine technology to the areas they dominated. Most of the wine produced in Rome came from large estates worked by slaves. These large estates continually developed new technologies. For example, in order to garner sweeter wines, wine makers left grapes in the sun for five to ten days, thus increasing the sugar content. Some wine makers left grapes on the vine (late harvest) in order to increase the sugar content and produce a sweeter wine. By the first-century CE Romans had developed over 91 varieties of wine, exemplifying the centrality of wine in Roman civilization. Romans spread wine technology to Gaul, Bordeaux, Provence, Languedoc, and finally to Burgundy and Alsace. Romans even produced wine in Britain, though the climate was not as conducive to wine growing as it was in parts of France. By disseminating wine technology, Rome was able to spread its culture throughout Europe.

The popularity of wine throughout the Greek and Roman Empires led to a vibrant trade in wine in the Mediterranean as well as to the overplanting of vineyards in some areas. For example, the founding of Marseille, a Phoenician colony, led to an intensification and diversification of the Mediterranean wine trade. During the fifth- and fourth-centuries BCE, Marseilles had a monopoly on the French wine trade. By the beginning of the first-century B.C.E., however, the Roman Empire had taken over the trade, as viticulture became a profitable business in Rome. Grape growing became even more intense after the eruption of Vesuvius in 79 CE, when not only Pompeii was covered by ash, but many vineyards were also. As a result, many vineyards were planted where wheat had been, eventually causing a shortfall of food and an edict from the emperor against planting any more vineyards. The intense trade in wine certainly helped to spread Roman civilization throughout the Mediterranean, while the choice to plant vineyards over even food demonstrated the critical role of wine not only in Roman culture but also in the economy.

The great Phoenician traders spread wine culture to northwest Africa which was agriculturally underdeveloped, having just emerged from the Neolithic age. During the Greco-Roman period (332 B.E–395 CE) the Phoenicians brought capital, technical expertise, and long-distance trading networks to the area, along with the domesticated grape. Cultivation of wine grapes began between the mid-fourth and the mid-second-centuries BCE. Because grapevines could be transported over long distances if kept moist and cool, the Phoenicians successfully started domestic viticulture in the Maghreb. The arrival of the Phoenicians drew the North Africans into the Mediterranean trading network through wine and thus into the advanced culture of the

Greco-Roman empire. As a result, social complexity followed trade, changing the social and cultural hierarchy of that area.

While production of wine in Greece and Rome clearly indicated its importance in each society, and trade in wine both expanded key trading networks and spread culture, the consumption of alcohol influenced Greece and Rome in even more ways. Consumption of beer and wine in Greek and Roman society helped to differentiate the elite from the lower class. Elite Greeks and Romans equated beer with the lower class. Beer was cheaper to make and was abundant. The majority of the populace consumed beer instead of water, likely because water was not clean. Moreover, beer was a part of daily nourishment for most Greeks, was used in offerings, and was buried with the dead to feed them in the next life. Poorer Greeks did drink wine, but of inferior quality, yet it was beer that structured their lives.

Wine consumption organized leisure, and defined culture, gender, and status. While Greeks of all classes drank wine, all Greek wine was not equal. Some scholars have argued that the ideas of equality in Greece led to the proliferation of wine consumption throughout society. Elites, however, drank the most expensive and high-quality wines as well as defined acceptable drinking habits across society. By the eighth to the sixth-century BCE, feasting and wine drinking were fully adopted into elite male society. Even Hippocrates said: "It is better to be full of wine than full of food." And in the Greek epics, *The Iliad* and *Odyssey*, wine and feasting were central to many parts of the stories.

Elite men drank wine on occasions called symposia. After dinner men gathered, lounged on couches, watched entertainment, and discussed politics. Many of these occasions included sex with prostitutes, young boys, or other men. The only women at these occasions were prostitutes or servants. Women's drinking was looked down upon by men, and women had the reputation of drinking to excess if allowed. Men also believed that women became promiscuous when they drank. Elite men also disapproved of the drinking habits of the lower classes. Moreover, elite drunkenness was acceptable, while drunkenness of the poor was criticized. Elites judged beer drinking or drinking undiluted wine to be uncivilized; both of which the lower classes did. Greeks believed that diluting wine, many times with three-quarters water, and drinking it in a proper setting, such as the symposia, was the only civilized way to imbibe. So while wine was available to all classes, consumption patterns structured elite male leisure, gender roles, social status, and the very definition of civilation.

Wine also shaped Greek medicine. Medical historian Salvatore Lucia wrote that physicians in the eighth and seven centuries BCE proclaimed that wine could cure fatigue, distress, pain, and sorrow, among other things. Moreover, Hippocrates wrote that wine could serve as an important additive to one's diet; it could be used as a dressing for a wound; and it could be used to calm fevers. He also wrote prolifically about the properties of various kinds of wines and how they affected the body. "Soft dark wines … are flatulent and pass better by stool. Harsh white wines heat without drying, and they pass better by urine than by stool. New wines pass by stool better than other wines because they are ... more nourishing ... White wines and thin sweet wines pass better by urine than by stool ... but make the blood weak." (As quoted in Lucia, *A History of Wine as Therapy*.) Socrates, Plato, and Aristotle all wrote about the uses of wine both for medical purposes as well as for the general well-being of people.

In addition to shaping medicine, wine organized religious life in Greece. While wine accompanied most meals in Greece, it was only drunk after it was served to the god of wine, Dionysos. The Greeks held festivals called Dionysia, which were held in winter and spring. These festivals were full of drinking, dancing, and games, and people of all classes attended.

In Rome, drinking behavior was similar to that of Greece, as Romans also consumed prodigious amounts of wine. Wine consumption in Rome shaped elite leisure, daily sustenance, public socializing, medicine, and war. Elites held social events called convivium, much like the Greek symposia, where food and wine were served. Bars were also common in Rome, organizing the social lives of Romans. Wine punctuated Roman meals. Rod Phillips, a wine historian, argues that as the diet in Rome changed from porridge to bread, wine became necessary to wash down the dryer meal.

Romans also believed wine to be essential to health. One of the famous writers of the period, Aurelius Cornelius Celsus (25 BCE–37 CE) praised the health benefits of wine. He wrote that for stomach ailments, one should drink hot wine and then drink light and dry wine. In order to facilitate movement within the digestive tract one should drink sweet wine, and to slow down the digestive tract one should drink harsh or resinated wine. He also prescribed wine for nervous indigestion, jaundice, eye problems, ear problems, and various other maladies. In addition to Celsus, Pliny the Elder (23–79 CE) provided several remedies using wine. One such prescription for "beautiful and virtuous children", noted by Salvatore Lucia in his *History of Wine as Therapy*, called for "ground pine nuts, assorted fruits, honey, myrrh, saffron, yolk of egg, milk and palm wine." Another wine mixture was supposed to tame wild animals if sprinkled upon them. Yet another mixture of saffron and wine was used to alleviate itching and to help as a diuretic.

Moreover, wine was also mandated for the army. Wine, even if of inferior quality, was part of army rations. It was safer than water and soldiers expected to be able to imbibe. Some scholars argue that one of the reasons for the successes of the Roman army was that they carried wine as part of their rations, thus keeping their troops healthy – especially in siege conditions where potable water was extremely scarce.

As the Roman Empire spread into other areas, so did wine consumption habits. In the area of Anatolia wine had become an integral part of the diet by Classical Roman times, and several varieties existed. When the Romans invaded Britain, they created inns, called tabernae, where travelers could stop and imbibe along the roads that the Romans built. These tabernae changed the drinking environment of Britain. They increased wine drinking and acted as important purveyors of Roman culture.

As Christianity spread into Rome, it forever changed Roman culture as well as attitudes towards alcohol. Christianity began with the life of Christ in the Common Era and followed both the Old and New Testaments of the Bible. Like the Old Testament, the New Testament recommended the use of wine, although in moderation. Christians believed wine to be symbolic of Christ's blood, and therefore used it in important rituals. The New Testament section of the Bible both praised wine's benefits, and criticized its harmful effects. In I Timothy the Bible recommended the use of wine to alleviate illness. Jesus shared wine with his disciples at the ritual last supper. And in one of his most well-known miracles Jesus turned water into wine at a wedding feast. In another parable in the New Testament the Good Samaritan used wine and oil to treat the wounds of a Jewish victim he found along the road. While the New Testament lauded the moderate use of wine, it also warned against the excessive use of wine. For example in I Corinthians 11 it stated: "[do] not associate with any one who ... is guilty of immorality or greed, or is an ido-later, reviler, drunkard or robber," clearly equating drunkenness with other serious sins. The warnings against drunkenness came partly from the fear that Christians would partake in the pagan rituals in the cult of Dionysus, practiced by the Greeks, where drunkenness was common.

While wine consumption in Greek and Roman cultures shaped social status and identity, spread culture, and structured the growing Christian religion, the regulation of alcohol defined appropriate civic behavior based on age, status, occupation, and gender. Greek philosophers had much to say about the reg-ulation of wine drinking. Some argued that when drunk in moderation wine was good for a person, it caused laughter and dancing, but it hurt men when drunk to intoxication. It could lead to crime, self-destruction, physical maladies, and the revealing of secrets. Both Philo and Plato agreed that a wise man could drink to excess periodically, as long as his behavior remained respectable. Philo went on to write, however, that temperance and sobriety were much better for both women and men, equating temperance and sobriety with a life of virtue. Plato, too, wrote that temperance on some occasions was very important. For example, he believed that one should only become intoxicated during festivals, but not during marriage ceremonies. He went on to argue that boys under 18 should not use wine at all, those in their twenties should use wine moderately, but those in their forties had the right to drink as much as they wanted. In Plato's final dialogue, *The Laws*, composed around 350 BCE, he outlined the public regulations of drinking in Carthage, which were not uniform across society, but based on one's station, helping to organize social mores in that city. He reported that regulations existed against drinking by soldiers on active duty, city magistrates and judges, ships' pilots, married couples intent upon procreation, all citizens during daytime hours, and all slaves, male or female, anytime.

Moreover, Roman regulations differed for men and women, perpetuating certain gender ideologies. Most women were not allowed to drink wine, and a man could divorce his wife if she became drunk without his knowledge. The

Roman philosopher Pliny the Elder loved wine, but thought women should not drink to excess. His view was shared by most. Some women were even killed by their families for drinking alcohol. Pliny said that the reason men kissed women upon greeting them was to see if they had been drinking alcohol. The rules about women drinking began to loosen around the end of the second-century BCE, however, when wine consumption rose in the general population.

Governments also taxed alcohol, seeing the opportunity to benefit from the high demand. In Plutarch's time, for example, some rulers destroyed personal vineyards in order to make sure that people secured a license to plant grapes. Wine was taxed during the Greco-Roman period (332 BCE–395 CE) in Africa. There were local customs duties and production taxes. The wine tax was to be paid in money, in contrast to earlier periods where it was paid in wine. The wine tax helped maintain and expand the government throughout the empire.

Classical China

During the Tang Dynasty China focused on building up the bureaucracy and the power of the emperor. Part of the construction of classical Chinese culture came from alcohol. Alcohol shaped culture through rituals and festivals, structured society by influencing social mores, and helped define the government's role in the civilization through regulations. When the Tang dynasty conquered Turfan in Central Asia, the most important tributes sent back were grapes and grape wine. The Tang then learned how to make grape wine. Even earlier than the Tang Dynasty, however, the Chinese both fermented and distilled alcohol. Some authors argue that the Chinese were the earliest to distill alcohol. Documents from 116 BCE, the books of Ssu Ma Ch-ien, and documents from 142 CE, the books of Wei Po Yang, appeared to show distillation information. Other authors argue, however, that distillation did not come to China until much later, in the twelfth-century.

The mandated ritualistic production of alcohol perpetuated its privileged place in Classical China. Records from about 500 CE described the proper way to ferment alcohol. Instructions from the Wei dynasty (386–534 CE) gave very specific directions. In August, workers, who had to be male, who were clean, and who had refrained from sex that day could make alcohol. They had to start with 50 liters of steamed, roasted, and raw wheat. A boy had to bring 1,000 liters of water, which no one else could touch. During the making of the alcohol the workers were directed to face west. First, the workers made the mixture of water and wheat into small cakes about two and a half inches in diameter and almost an inch thick. These cakes then dried in a sealed hut for seven days. Next, the workers turned the cakes over to dry for another seven days, after which they put them into a pile. They then took the cakes out of the hut, put them into a clay jar, and sealed the jar with mud to rest for another seven days. Next the workers made holes in the middle of the cakes and strung them up to dry in the sun. The cakes were most likely fermented with saliva. Finally, the workers pressed them with water.

The Chinese also made alcohol from fruit juice. Making alcohol from fruit juice was fairly simple, the fermentation process happened almost automatically if one left the juice alone to ferment. The sugar in the juice, combined with yeast, which could be found on the skins of fruits and in the dust of orchards and gardens, caused the fermentation process to take place.

Much like in the Mediterranean, alcohol consumption perpetuated certain social mores in China. For example, serving alcohol to guests was vital in China during the classical Han period, and hosts always served wine to their guests first, symbolizing respect and propriety. One story told of a man who sold his hair in order to afford alcohol for his guests. Moreover, wine also shaped high culture. Poets, calligraphers, and artists praised the ability of wine to bring out their best work. For example, the poet Wang Ji, of the Eight Immortals of the Wine Cup, wrote the poem: "In spring, pine needles ferment in the wine jugs; In autumn, chrysanthemums float in the wine cups. When we chance upon one another, we would rather get drunk, And definitely will not take up mixing the elixirs." (As quoted in McGovern, *Uncorking the Past*.) Another poet, Li Bai, who was very famous in the Tang Dynasty, wrote many of his poems about alcohol. Many believed that because most of his poems were about alcohol he wrote them while drunk.

Alcohol also figured prominently in festivals, shaping the activities. In the Festival of the Dead, which was two weeks after New Year, alcohol houses organized a parade that included the four levels of prostitutes. The parade also included guilds, merchants, and entertainers dressed as the Eight Immortals of Taoism. Other parade members carried jars of rice wine, which was much more popular than grape wine at that time.

In addition to urban rituals alcohol also structured rituals throughout the empire. Consumption rituals ushered in seasons, emphasized life changes, secured marriage alliances, and signified the arrival of peace across the empire. Alcohol was an important tool in peasant and noble rituals, and in solidifying political alliances. During spring festivals peasants drank prodigiously. Nobles, too, offered alcohol during their own elite ceremonies of passage. In addition, alcohol was central to rites of passage for young women and men. Offerings of alcohol from father to son consummated engagements between men and women. In other rituals, combatants offered a cup of alcohol to an enemy before battle, and after the battle the victors gave alcohol to the defeated. The victors then received the sacred cup of the ancestors. These rituals solidified the triumph of the winners and purged the enemy of the evil spirit that had possessed them to take to battle. After ritual tournaments, such as archery, the losers were offered cups of alcohol first and then afterward the winners drank. Drinking the cup signified the end of the battle and an oath against future attacks.

The Chinese regulated the use of wine and spirits, both legally and socially. For example, the emperor in 147 BCE, King Ti, "prohibited the preparation of certain alcoholic beverages." Around the same time period, one of the earliest Chinese medical texts, *Nei Ching*, from the Han Dynasty, about 200 BCE, warned against drinking at all, arguing it caused health as well as behavioral problems. Another famous precept stated: "The first glass, the man drinks the wine; the second glass, the wine drinks the wine; the third glass, the wine drinks the man." Buddhists banned alcohol, and some historians argue that the spread of Buddhism into China began to curb excessive drinking that had been a problem there in the pre-Buddhist period. Alcohol continued to have a profound effect on society, however, whether through its social and ritual use or through its regulation.

Classical India

During the later Vedic period in India, the highest caste, the Brahmins, led society. Alcohol helped shape many aspects of classical India, including medicine, society, culture, and religion. Indians created many kinds of alcohol. They drank Sura, a liquor made from fermented barley. Indians praised the drink, but also periodically condemned those who drank it. There was also an important drink called Soma, squeezed from a mountainous plant. A third drink during the Classical period was called parisruta and was prepared from fermented flowers or grasses. Fourth, there was a fermented rice drink made with spices. The production of so many kinds of alcohol ensured the influence of alcohol throughout Classical India.

Alcohol influenced the practice of medicine in Classical India. Many of the Classical writings in India showed alcohol to be central to medical cures. The Charaka Samhita, written between 600 BCE and 200 CE was part of the Ayur-Veda, an important Indian medical text. In this text wine was credited with helping with sleeplessness, sorrow, fatigue, digestion, and "cur[ing] the natural flow of internal fluids of the body." (As quoted in Lucia, *A History of Wine as Therapy*.) Later in the Tantras wine was worshipped for its powers to forget one's sorrows and to bring happiness. Buddhist and Jain literature prescribed alcohol to help with digestion, and Hindu literature prescribed wine as an anesthetic for medical operations. Wine was also used to heal animals. For example, wine was used in many remedies to heal elephants, which were sacred to the Hindus.

Alcoholic drinks constituted part of the diet of certain segments of Indian society, as prescribed by the Shastras, which were Hindu instruction books for living. The Tantriks, a group who countered the Vedas, promoted alcohol for medical reasons as well. Sushruta, a surgeon, who lived around the fourth-century BCE, stated that sura (an alcohol) should be used before a surgical operation as an anesthetic. Charak, a doctor, prescribed alcoholic drinks such as soma and sura as well as others to full-term pregnant women, and to women after the extraction of a dead fetus in order to ease pain.

Moreover, alcohol shaped Indian society. Many people consumed alcohol in taverns. These taverns were relatively large, contained many rooms, and some had beds. They were located mainly along trade routes and acted as inns for travelers. Women as well as men drank. It was less common for women, although Brahmin women were afforded more opportunities to embibe.

Alcohol also influenced the development of a major world religion that originated in India; Buddhism developed in India and centered around the teachings of the "enlightened one" or the Buddha. One of the five main precepts in Buddhism banned the use of alcohol. Early Buddhist literature especially forbade monks in monasteries from drinking alcohol. This literature also promoted asceticism, which dovetailed with the absence of alcohol. Despite Buddhist precepts, however, during the Buddhist period in India, around the fifth-century BCE, writings showed that drinking alcohol remained prevalent.

Many sacred texts included sections on the social regulation of alcohol. Many of these texts contradicted each other, however. The Smriti – a law code – stated that the higher castes should not drink wine. Another one of the most famous texts, the *Kama Sutra*, forbade wives from drinking wine, but allowed mistresses to drink wine. The two religious epics called *Ramayana* and the *Mahabharata* exalted wine as a drink for kings, sages, and hermits. Drinking alcohol, however, was one of the seven sins in the Vedas. Drinking was forbidden for Brahmins, elites, and students. In addition, a classic treatise on government, the *Arthashastra*, written by the prime minister under Maurya rule, argued that alcohol had disturbing effects, and forbade the use of it within the army. The government, however, also realized that alcohol taxes were so important to revenues, that curbing alcohol use would hurt the state and alcohol use continued to be widespread in Indian society.

Conclusion

Alcohol production and trade influenced all classical societies. Greece spread its culture into Rome through the wine trade. Subsequently, the spread of Greek and Roman viticulture and trade into newly conquered Northern Africa brought culture and social complexity into that region. Moreover, Romans spread their culture to Britain through the proliferation of tabernae along trade routes in that area. Similar to the Romans in Britain, in Classical India taverns existed along trade routes, which led to the expansion of Indian culture into other societies as well as the integration of other cultures into India. So the spread of alcohol into other civilizations in many cases led the way for the culture to follow.

Consumption of alcohol across civilizations influenced many areas of those societies such as medicine, religion, and class differentiation. First, consumption of alcohol helped to define medicine in many areas. Wine shaped the development of medicine in Greece and Rome as well as India, as it shaped classic treatises on health in all three cultures. Second, consumption of alcohol at religious and social festivals helped to define the belief systems in many cultures. For example, in Classical Greece, Rome, and China, alcohol was a primary ingredient in religious ceremonies and rituals.

Third, in many cultures the consumption of alcohol helped to differentiate among classes. Both Greek and Roman elites held banquets where drinking along with political and literary discussions took place, demonstrating their privileged positions in society. In China, alcohol characterized high culture because of its prominence in poetry and art, and in India the *Ramayana* and *Mahabharata* maintained that wine was for kings, while other treatises forbade Brahmins to drink, helping to define the culture of these segments in society.

Fourth, alcohol consumption influenced gender ideologies, especially surrounding women's sexuality. In Greek culture prostitutes were allowed to drink in the symposia, yet wives were prohibited because men equated women's alcohol use with promiscuous behavior. In China prostitution was associated with wine shops, and the Indian *Kama Sutra* allowed mistresses to drink.

Regulations of alcohol helped to form religions as well as to ensure the order of society. First, one of the five main precepts of Buddhism prohibited the use of alcohol; and while Christianity did not prohibit alcohol, it advocated for moderation. Second, alcohol regulation by the Greeks and Romans helped to keep order in the society through properly prescribing the appropriate relationship to alcohol based on occupation or gender. In Classical China alcohol was regulated in such a way as to instill the benefits of moderation in the populace.

Alcohol shaped many aspects of the world's Classical civilizations. Trade in alcohol brought culture along with it into many parts of the world. Use of alcohol shaped religion, class, and gender. And alcohol regulation influenced governments and religions in all these societies. Alcohol permeated the classical world, finding a place in the social, cultural, political, and economic realms in each society.

Further reading

Granet, M. 1958. *Chinese Civilizaation.* Trans. K. E. Innes and M. R. Brailsford. New York: Meridian Books, Inc.

Hewitt, T. F. 1980. *A Biblical Perspective on the Use and Abuse of Alcohol and Other Drugs.* Raleigh, NC: Pastoral Care Council on Alcohol and Drug Abuse.

Jennings, J., J. Jennings, K. L. Antrobus, S. J. Atencio, E. Glavich, R. Johnson, G. Loffler, and C. Luu. 2005. "Drinking Beer in a Blissful Mood: Alcohol Production, Operational Chains, and Feasting in the Ancient World." *Current Anthropology.* 46 (2): 275–303.

Lemu, B. A. 1992. *Islam and Alcohol.* Alexandria: Saadawi Publications.

O'Brian, J. M. and S. C. Seller. 1982. "Attributes of Alcohol in the Old Testament." *The Drinking and Drug Practices Surveyor.* 18: 18–24.

Prakash, O. 1961. *Food and Drinks in Ancient India: From Earliest Times to C. 1200 A.D.* Delhi: Munshi ram Manohar Lal.

Raymond, I. W. 1927. *The Teaching of the Early Church on the Use of Wine and Strong Drink.* New York: Columbia University Press.

Ssu-Hsieh, C. (of the later Wei Dynasty) 1945. Trans. H. Tzu-Ch'ing and C. Yünts'ung. "The Preparation of Ferments and Wines." *Harvard Journal of Asiatic Studies.* 9 (1): 24–44.

Waltham, C. (ed.) 1971. "Announcement About Drunkenness." In *ShuChing Book of History,* Chicago: Henry Regency Co.

3   Alcohol, cultural development, and the rise of trade in the Post-Classical and early modern world

Dramatic changes characterized many areas in the Post-Classical world. The rise of Islam and its spread across the Middle East and parts of Europe brought trade and technology in its wake. In the Americas vast empires expanded across the continent, creating sophisticated societies in Meso and South America. In the East modern forms of government and society began to develop, while in the West the growth of the merchant class and the rise of technology transformed society. The production, trade, consumption, and regulation of alcohol influenced many of these changes. For example, the production of alcohol in South America by women solidified gender roles in that area. Trade in alcohol across Western Europe facilitated the rising merchant class and the interactions among regions, while consumption patterns in Eastern Europe and Japan delineated social hierarchies in those areas. Finally, regulation of alcohol fostered the development of tax systems in Western Europe.

The Middle East

Islam began to define much of the Middle East toward the end of the Classical Period and beginning of the Post-Classical period. Arab Muslim armies conquered much of the Middle East, including parts of Africa and the Mediterranean. While the entire Middle East was not ethnically unified, Islam served to unite the area and provide the impetus for the spread of culture. Islam began in the 600s with the teachings of the prophet Muhammad, and soon spread throughout the Middle East and Asia. Alcohol regulation became one of the founding principles of the religion. Islam prohibited the consumption of alcohol. A perhaps apocryphal story explained why Mohammed believed drinking should not be tolerated in the Islamic religion. The story related that on one occasion when the prophet's disciples were drinking together, one of them from Mecca stood up and began to recite a rather uncomplimentary poem about one of the disciples from Medina. This resulted in the recipient of the poem hurling a bone at the head of the reciter. Mohammed supposedly asked God, Allah, how to remedy such problems. The result was that alcohol should be outlawed in the religion. Historians have argued that refraining from alcohol was a way for Muslims to distinguish themselves from the Christians who drank wine.

In any event, the spread of Islam across the Middle East and North Africa dramatically decreased alcohol consumption in those areas, but it did not completely erase it. Religious proponents destroyed many vineyards and thus wine consumption necessarily diminished. Sometimes, however, non-Muslims in a religious area were allowed to continue to brew and consume alcohol. And there were still poems that extolled the virtues of wine. In addition, a Persian tradition, for example, allowed for moderate consumption of wine if one was ill. There were other ways around the prohibition of wine by Islam as well. For example, boiling wine or adding salt or relishes to it made it acceptable to drink.

The Quran also mentioned that there were some benefits from wine, and Mohammed claimed that for those Muslims who made it to heaven, wine would be part of the reward. Islamic physicians also used wine to cure ills. One prominent Persian physician, Avicenna (980–1036 CE) wrote that white wine could relieve headaches, and that wine was good for digestion. At the same time, however, he wrote that children should not be given wine and that frequent intoxication was bad for the body, particularly the liver, brain, and nerves. The Quran also noted that wine caused more ills than benefits. Early portions of the Quran mentioned that it was impossible to meditate or pray while intoxicated. Later verses stated that there was a link between wine and a variety of social evils.

Some scholars have argued that the prohibition of wine in the Quran was ambiguous, and that it was not the use of wine, per se, but the use of wine in pagan rituals that was outlawed. Other scholars have argued that rather than being explicitly forbidden like blood or pork or carrion, the Quran maintained that it was the misuse of alcohol that caused severe social problems. It could create divisions among men, and could separate them from God. These historians contend that the prohibition of wine came more from a historical context than divine law. Theocrats in Muslim countries during Mohammed's time did enact controls to regulate drinking. Group pressure was used to curb drinking, and under subsequent caliphates punishments for drinking ranged from between 40 and 80 lashes.

Indeed as Islam spread across parts of the Middle East, Northern Africa, and Europe it changed the drinking habits of the societies there. The absence of alcohol brought on by Islam changed the nature of rituals and ceremonies, as well as social interactions in those cultures. In some regions abstinence did not prevail, however. For example, in Spain wine drinking continued, even in Muslim societies. Similar to the famous symposia of the Greeks, men gathered in the evening and drank, talked, and read poetry. So even in Islam many contradictions existed between the precepts and actual practice. It can be said, however, that the prohibition of alcohol considerably shaped the cultures to which it spread.

Pre-colonial Americas

In the Americas during the pre-colonial period, large sedentary populations grew in Meso-America and in the Andes. Each had their own kind of alcohol based upon the plants available to them. Mexicans drank pulque, made from the agave plant, and Andeans drank chicha, made from corn. In each civilization alcohol figured prominently in daily life, as well as in the cultural construction of gender, social hierarchy, and religion. Alcohol production, consumption, and regulation in the Americas helped define the Aztec and Inca empires. In Meso-America the ubiquity of pulque, even with its long and intense production process, suggests how important alcohol was to that society. The Aztecs regulated its consumption, helping to solidify class and gender distinctions within the empire, and reinforcing the control of the state over its people. Since pulque was consumed during most ritual and ceremonial occasions it helped to define social and religious structures within the empire as well. In Peru, chicha, much like pulque, was important to ceremonies in the Inca empire. Only women produced chicha, so chicha production helped to define gender roles in that culture. Inca leaders regulated chicha use, which became an important tool to strengthen the control of the empire over its conquered areas. In these ways alcohol was central to the development of class, gender, and governmental control in both cultures.

In Mexico, alcohol, in this case pulque, shaped history and religion. According to one folktale, pulque was discovered by a great Toltec noble named Papantzin. Evidence suggest, however, that it was likely used at least 1,500 years before the Toltec civilization. From as early as 200 CE stone carvings showed pulque, although no evidence exists regarding the beginnings of its production. Aztec society linked pulque with fertility, femininity, and agriculture; the goddess of pulque, Mayahuel, was an earth mother who had 400 breasts.

The production of pulque required several years and was very involved. The maguey plant, which was a type of agave plant similar to a cactus, had to grow for eight to ten years in order to mature enough to make pulque. After the plant matured the juice of the plant was extracted over a period of months and stored inside containers inside a tinacal, which was a special building made for that purpose. Pulque was also made by removing the leaves from the agave to get to the heart of the plant. Workers cut the heart into two pieces and slow-cooked it for two or three days in a below-ground earthen oven lined with moist leaves of the plant. Afterwards, the hearts were removed and laid in the sun for several days to dry. After the hearts dried, the pulp was separated from the fiber, and then steeped in water to begin fermentation. The name pulque in Nahuatl means decomposed, or spoiled, which probably relates to the fact that it did not keep long, sometimes only a day after being made.

Consumption patterns of pulque during the Aztec period shaped religion, ritual, social status, and medicine. The Aztecs predominantly used pulque for ritual and medicinal purposes. Only during designated annual ceremonies were people allowed to be publicly intoxicated. For example, annual feasts in honor of the gods as well as harvest festivals called for mass drinking. William Taylor points out in *Drinking, Homicide, and Rebellion in Colonial Mexican*

Villages that other occasions for drinking in pre-colonial Mexico included births, weddings, funerals, and a warrior's rights of passage, all of which justified several days of drinking. During all other times of the year only elites, the elderly, and people who were considered wise were allowed to drink pulque. The majority of the population was rarely allowed to drink. Lower-class women could drink pulque after giving birth, men could drink after strenuous work, and warriors were given pulque after a victory. Drinking pulque on these occasions was allowed because pulque was thought to restore strength. In order to regulate the use of pulque Aztec leaders imposed several punishments for casual pulque drinking, which ranged from having one's head shaved in public, to whipping, or even stoning. These regulations in Aztec society emphasized who could drink and when they could drink, but not how much. Excessive drinking during sanctioned occasions was expected. Taylor points out that "[p]ulque, then, was an important drink ... before the conquest: not really a forbidden drink, but a powerful, almost sacred substance, with unpredictable effects, and generally controlled by rules of periodic, ritual use." Pulque held an important place in the religion and society of the Aztecs and was central in defining how festivals and rituals took place.

In Peru, the first evidence of chicha comes from the period 500–300 BCE. Chicha was generally made from maize, but it could also be made from quinoa, manioc, and peanuts – depending upon the region. The most common kind of chicha was maize chicha, however. Chicha was used in the pre-Incaic empire of the Chimu Indians of Peru. People in that society drank chicha every day as a food-beverage and also used it during ceremonial occasions as well as work parties. Both individual households as well as political leaders used chicha to gather workers.

During the Inca period chicha influenced origin myths, gender idologies, religion, and the spread of culture. The origin myths of the Inca state included chicha. The Incas believed that the four ancestors of the Incas came out of three caves in a mountain called Tambo T'oco. Manco Capac, one of the four men from the mountain, pulled out some corn seeds that he had brought from the cave where he had emerged and then planted the first cornfield in the Cusco valley. Chicha then began to be made from that field. In another myth, Mama Huaco, one of the original ancestors, planted the first field of corn. After she died her body was embalmed and mummified and the people responsible for caring for her mummy made chicha from the corn grown in that field. The chicha was given to those who maintained her cult.

Only women produced chicha, providing a key component in the makeup of female gender identity. Specially chosen women, called mamacona, made chicha for the Inca king. These women were judged the most beautiful in the kingdom and were required to be virgins. They were revered and lived their lives in large, state-run centers made especially for producing chicha and weaving cloth. They procured their grain from tribute to the king and thus had a never-ending supply of maize for their work. Not only did mamacona make chicha for the kingdom, but also individual women made chicha in their homes. Chicha production began when women shaped mouth-sized balls of maize dough and masticated these dough balls until sugar was produced from the starch. To cook the chicha women used large clay pots over open fire pits. A woman heated water in one pot and then poured that hot water over the masticated maize in another clay pot. She then stirred the mixture until it became a paste, which took several hours. The paste slowly separated into liquid at the top and solids at the bottom. Then she boiled more water and slowly added this water to the mixture of masticated corn and water until it produced a cloudy mixture, which she stirred into a soupy consistency. After the mixture rested it separated into three layers. The top layer was skimmed off into a separate pot, as was the second layer. These two layers became chicha after a few days of fermentation. Chicha was opaque and effervescent and tasted a little like apple cider. It usually contained less than 5 percent alcohol, although it could contain up to 12 percent alcohol. Chicha was drunk through straws put into various drinking vessels shaped into llama heads, reed boats, and even the skulls of enemies, all of which held meaning for the Incas.

Chicha also structured the daily lives of the Incas, shaped religious and social ceremonies, and spread Inca culture throughout the empire. Most Andeans in corn-producing areas drank chicha as one of their main food sources. It contained numerous vitamins and nutrients. Inca leaders and their subordinates drank chicha during major feasts and work parties. It was also used in ceremonies of large land holders (patrons) and their workers. Moreover, Incan kings offered chicha to their gods and ancestors. Patrick McGovern in *Uncorking the Past* describes how in a ritual the king poured chicha into a golden bowl located on a throne in the central plaza of the capital. The chicha spilled down the "gullet of the Sun God" into the Temple of the Sun. In addition, commoners drank prodigious amounts of chicha during festivals. Moreover, human sacrifices were "rubbed in the dregs of chicha and then tube-fed with more chicha for days while lying buried alive in tombs." Some authors argue that maize chicha was also crucial in the spread of Incan culture throughout the empire. For example, Inca chiefs gave villagers in far-flung regions of the empire abundant chicha to drink at large banquets held to reinforce the power of the chief. In addition, when Inca representatives stopped along the roads as they traveled, people expected them to provide chicha. In return, the Inca received both the loyalty and the work of the villagers in the Inca's fields. It therefore was the most important piece of material culture that represented and reinforced the social and political hierarchy within the Inca state.

Post-Classical and early-modern Eastern Europe

In Post-Classical and early modern Eastern Europe alcohol swayed the course of religion, defined social status, and structured festivals. When in the tenth-century one Russian state, led by Vladimir, began to move toward a central religion, alcohol shaped the decision. Alcohol was so important in Russian society that Vladimir rejected Islam, for example, because of its proscription against alcohol. The most popular alcoholic drinks in Russia were kvas, which was a rye-based beer, and mead. Elites drank mead, especially in the thirteenth-century when its main ingredient, honey, grew scarce because the bee population died out. As in other areas of Europe, elites also drank wine. Wine was imported to Poland, especially the city of Cracow, which was a trade hub. From here wine was transported to other Eastern European areas and to the Baltic region. The consumption of mead and wine, then, became a way for elites to culturally separate themselves from the rest of the population in early modern Russia and other parts of Eastern Europe.

Peasants drank beer. As in other agricultural societies drinking was a social ritual, based on the agricultural calendar. Binge, or excessive drinking took place during harvest time. Brewing beer was so important to the peasant class, in fact, that even in the times of famine, especially the great famine of 1601, beer brewing continued. Heavy alcohol consumption continued to be emblematic of Russian society throughout the modern period.

Post-Classical and early-modern Japan

Alcohol trade and consumption significantly influenced the development of Japan. During the Heian period, between 794 and 1185 the royal court focused on ultra-polite behavior and luxury. Part of the aristocratic lifestyle was the use of sake, or rice wine, which began to be produced in this period. Political leaders controlled the production of sake, and the royal court designated court brewers to make sake for ritual use. Because it was controlled by royalty and elites, access to sake was one of the factors that effectively separated the classes. Sake production continued to develop between 1185 and 1573, when the court, or shogunate, allowed select families to start independent breweries. These brewing families sold sake at the gates to the temples on market days and competed with each other for customers. Sake became an important commodity, which influenced the development of commercialization in Japan. Ceremonial use of sake helped to structure rituals in early modern Japan. For example, in rural areas most drinking took place during big celebrations where the community made large amounts of alcohol and drank it for days until it was finished. Alcohol continued to shape the Japanese economy and culture as Japan advanced into the modern world.

Post-Classical and early modern West

The West underwent many changes during the Middle Ages and the early modern periods. Improvements in agriculture, expansion of trade, and a rise in technology characterized these periods. Moreover, between the tenth and thirteenth-centuries population levels rose, adding to urbanization. The production, trade, consumption, and regulation of alcohol especially helped to influence the rise and regulation of trade, as well as to shape gender roles, religious practices, and the rules of civic society in Western civilization during the centuries that ushered in the modern world.

Production of wine in Britain increased early in the Post-Classical period. With the introduction of Christianity in Britain in the sixth-century, monasteries proliferated. These monasteries frequently had large vineyards and produced wine and other alcohols. The monasteries made money from the vineyards by renting them out and being paid in wine. The monks also used the wine for prescriptions as the monasteries sometimes became hospitals for the sick. Moreover, monasteries also spread throughout Western Europe creating vineyards as they went, and, as a result, viticulture and viniculture helped solidify the presence of Christianity across Europe.

Not only was wine important in the monasteries, but it also played a major role in accelerating long-distance trade. With the population boom in Europe after 1000 CE elites demanded luxury goods and wine was one of the important luxury items they demanded. The nobility, higher clergy, and wealthier townspeople had a taste for wines. For example, it was not unusual for aristocratic households to spend 30 to 40 percent of their budget on wine. Therefore, from places such as Bordeaux, where vines became more numerous, wine was shipped out to England. French wine tended to last no more than a year and therefore more stable wines from Greece and Italy were also shipped to England. By the early fourteenth-century, wine represented more than 30 percent of English imports and 25 percent of all imports to the Low Countries. The growing demand for wine greatly stimulated commercial viticulture in France, Italy, Spain, Greece, the Mediterranean islands, and parts of Germany. It also led to commercial as well as technological advancements in the industry. In order to facilitate trade, vintners often organized into guilds and imported wine wholesale. In some towns they also monopolized the retail sale of wine, but in general, growing numbers of taverns controlled most of the direct sale of wine to the consumer. This period of increased demand also resulted in technological advancement. Larger wine presses came into use and the technology of growing grapes developed. Viticulturalists began to take greater care in cultivation by loosening the soil around the vines for better water absorption and removing unnecessary leaves to increase yield. Wine, then, helped to intensify long-distance trade throughout Europe as well as to shape elite identity and culture in the early modern period.

While wine was sold to the elite, ale was sold to common people. Ale, made from malted barley, water, and yeast, was the staple drink of the vast majority of those who lived in England, the Low Countries, Scandinavia, northern France, and much of Germany and Eastern Europe. Unlike wine, however, ale was considered a food necessity, not a luxury drink, and it structured the daily diets of most Europeans. Moreover, brewing ale was a household industry, especially in rural areas, and was considered the purview of women. So by the fourteenth-century the majority of those selling ale were women, helping to define female identity during that period. Interestingly, most of the ale traders came from middling to upper-class families. Some poorer women sold ale as well, but usually did not stay in the trade very long, only selling ale when they were in dire straights. The elite female ale sellers, however, remained in their occupation for several years, most more than a decade. Even so, they did not sell ale year round. Rather, ale shops only opened when harvests supplied the grain to women to make ale.

Trade of ale by women continued to spread in the Post-Classical and early modern periods. Brewers sold their ale through alehouses, purchasing their supplies from commercial brewers. Alehouses in rural areas were often extensions of homes, too small to house many people; it was more common for customers to bring in their pail and carry the purchased ale back home to consume. Brewers placed stakes or other signs outside their houses when they had prepared a fresh batch of ale. They also had to display a bush or bunch of ivy on the end of the stake so the local ale-tasting officials knew they could now come to evaluate and price the ale.

In urban areas the establishments were larger and sold ale more consistently. In general, more formal alehouses took shape between the twelfth and the fifteenth-centuries and the quality of the ale improved over that time as well. Before the plague of the fourteenth-century most of the alehouses were transitory in nature. As a result of the plague, however, the trade in ale changed. More people were able to buy ale because wages rose. At the same time, the poorer women who periodically sold ale were not forced into that occupation, so the number of sellers decreased and the occupation became more professionalized. By the 1400s alehouses sometimes provided lodging, food, and entertainment. By the sixteenth-century 86 percent of the drinking establishments in England were alehouses. Even though alehouses were very popular they produced small amounts of ale, and quality still varied from house to house. Ale spoiled within five days or so, thus it had to be brewed quite frequently, and as a result was not a very profitable business. The legally fixed price of ale remained the same from the thirteenth up to the sixteenth-century, even though brewers continually tried to get the price raised.

Tremendous changes took place in the business of fermented grains in the early modern period. The Dutch created hopped beer in the fifteenth-century, so beer made from malt, hops, and water became increasingly popular, eclipsing ale, especially in Holland and Germany. Hopped beer was weaker, more bitter, and less perishable than ale. It was also easier to make in large quantities, and thus more profitable. The addition of hops to ale acted as a preservative; beer brewers could trade their product over longer distances and thus could become highly commercialized.

Hopped beer was brewed and traded by men, which led to identifying the industry as masculine, effectively marginalizing ale women and modifying gender ideologies in early modern Europe. These male beer brewers organized into guilds, unlike alewives who rarely did so. By the sixteenth-century there were large, male-dominated breweries in the city of London. These large breweries began to make huge profits trading beer internationally, opening new markets for European trade. For example, breweries sold beer to Russia in exchange for imported Russian goods that were then sold at higher prices in England. India, too, became a destination for British beer. The international beer industry, then, solidified beer as one of Britain's signature trade items.

An even more monumental change occurred in alcohol production in the early modern period. The process of distilling alcohol (as opposed to the chemical distillation of many other substances) "profoundly influenced the art of distilling" according to R. J. Forbes in *Short History of the Art of Distillation*. Distillers were often connected to vintners or beer makers. Distilling was thought of as a fine art, and distillers kept their recipes very secret. Distilled spirits began to be produced in the West during the early modern period as well. Some historians argue that the Arabs discovered distillation around the tenth-century CE, while others argue that the Chinese discovered them much earlier. Still others argue that distillation began when the Scottish distilled mead in the sixth-century. Distilled alcohol was made from fermented grains, potatoes, and fruits, among other things. Spirits were made in a still, which was an enclosed vessel. It had to have a fire underneath it to start the process. The idea was to separate the liquor (which boiled at 173 degrees Fahrenheit) from water (which boiled at 212 degrees Fahrenheit). The alcohol became vapor and then moved to a final container through a vapor line. As it cooled down, it became a more concentrated liquid, or distilled spirits.

Alcohol made from the distillation of corn in the Low Countries, England, and northern Germany began to compete with wine, which remained expensive. Italian distillers brought liqueurs to Paris as early as 1332. These liqueurs were popular among the wealthy, who expressed their elite culture through its consumption. Distillation spread as far north as Scandinavia. The Dutch, however, were the ones who began to trade distilled alcohol throughout Western Europe. One of the first kinds of distilled wine, brandy, became very popular in Western Europe, bolstering the commercial status of the Dutch who traded it.

As the production of distilled liquor began to spread, more types of spirits were created. In areas where grain rather than grapes grew, beer was distilled into whiskey. Scotland became known for the distillation of whiskey beginning in about the fifteenth-century. In England, gin, flavored with juniper berries, became a popular drink in the slums of London. Much of the distilled liquor in England and Holland was flavored with spices like rosemary, sandalwood, basil, ginger, and cardamom. Both England and Holland were engaged in the spice trade, and so they procured spices from abroad and then used them to flavor the new spirits.

Consumption of wine, ale, beer, and spirits profoundly shaped Western Europe. Wine consumption characterized class identity in many areas in Europe. Wine was the most popular drink of the upper classes, becoming identified with that segment of society. When the middling classes began to gain wealth as a result of commercial development, they strove to emulate elite culture. One of the most easily attainable and observable ways to do so was to drink wine. Moreover, because it was a luxury item it became a favored reward for those who worked for the elite. Artisans as well as laborers received some wine as part of their pay from the elites for whom they worked. Soldiers, too, received a portion of wine as part of their rations.

A majority of the people in the Post-Classical and early modern period consumed ale, however, as it continued to be a very important ingredient in their daily lives. For example, ale was popular at church events. Churches in the thirteenth- and fourteenth-centuries had ale parties to raise money. Villagers made ale, brought it to the function, and the profits went to the church. The leftover ale from the two or three day party went to any of the village bachelors who could still stand. Weddings and funerals always provided ale for the attendees; hundreds of gallons of ale were drunk at these events. Just like in the earlier part of the Post-Classical period, then, alcohol was associated with the church.

People also consumed ale in alehouses. Alehouses were centers of gossip, as well as places where people came to socialize, conduct business, and to discuss literature, art, and politics. As trade increased in Britain, those doing business in urban areas increasingly used alehouses (along with taverns and inns) for business meetings. Members of guilds organized social events in alehouses, and some alehouses became the centers of political activities, housing political clubs. Ale houses or pubs also hosted large celebrations such as baptisms, funerals, and wakes. In addition, brewers made special ales for events and celebrations, naming their batches marriage ale, childbirth ale, journey ale, or Christmas ale.

Ale was still relatively expensive for workers to consume, however. A gallon of ale in the thirteenth-century cost a laborer two-thirds of his daily wages and a craftsman one-third of his daily wages. Poor laborers had access to ale because many landlords included some ale in their wages. And soldiers had access to ale through drink rations. The plague in the fourteenth-century, however, allowed more people access to ale. Because of the decline in the number of laborers, demand for laborers increased and thus wages increased. With rising wages laborers could afford about three times as much ale in 1400 as they could in 1300. By the fifteenth- and sixteenth-centuries, however, hopped beer and gin surpassed ale in popularity with the working classes.

Society continued to believe in the curative properties of alcohol. Apothecaries commonly prescribed beer and spirits to their patients. Moreover, doctors began to prescribe spirits for various illnesses such as diarrhea and typhoid fever, accelerating the spread of spirits across Western Europe in the early modern period. In the sixteenth- and seventeenth-centuries beer was considered a cure for many illnesses. For example, buttered beer was supposed to cure coughs and shortness of breath; and other beers were supposed to cure gout and consumption; and yet another beer, along with other drugs, was used as an anesthetic.

In addition to production, trade, and consumption of alcohol, the regulation of alcohol had an impact on the development of a commercial culture, social development, and government stability in the Post-Classical and early-modern West. Strict regulations controlled the price and quality of wine. In

1330 the London authorities, for example, fixed the price of different qualities of wine; a gallon of the best Gascon wine could sell for no more than four pence, while a gallon of Rhine wine could retail for up to eight pence. In the provinces authorities allowed slightly higher prices in order to cover the costs of transportation. Unfortunately, prices were difficult to enforce, especially during the Hundred Years War, which caused frequent interruptions in supply. Alcohol was not only regulated by the government, but also by the guilds. The Vintner's Company, which was a guild of wine merchants in London, controlled both the wholesale and retail wine trade. The group mandated that wines could only be unloaded off ships by specific workmen, and sold to taverns only in wholesale. The Vintners' Guild also controlled the retail sale of the wine. Many of the regulations by the guilds aimed to keep the quality of wine high. The government also levied taxes on wine, which significantly strengthened the treasury of the crown. Taxes were paid in currency as well as in kind, therefore securing more wine for the royal household.

Much like wine, the price, quality, and measurement of ale were strictly regulated. In England, the government fixed the price of ale based on the changing price of grain from which malt was made. Similar regulations were in force elsewhere in Europe by town decree. Laws limited the price an alewife could ask; if she charged too much she had to pay fines. The quality of ale was regulated by ale tasters, who were appointed or elected in every town and village. Brewers who used impure water or bad malt, who sold ale before the dregs settled or when it was old and spoiled, or who tried to pass off weak ale as a more expensive grade were fined by the local authorities. The measurement of ale was regulated as well. Abuses were frequent, however. Brewers put false bottoms in their measures or used elaborately shaped vessels that held less than the designated amount of ale. As a result, these laws were difficult to enforce. Most brewers found it more profitable to break the laws and pay the fines. By the late medieval period most alewives were paying "pre-emptive" fines to the court for selling ale. These pre-emptive fines eventually became licensing fees charged by the lords.

Governments not only regulated trade and levied taxes, but they also regulated consumption. Expansion of trade in distilled spirits, especially gin, brought about stricter laws aimed to curb drinking spirits in general. Most of the severe problems of drunkenness were associated with spirits. Public drunkenness was punishable in many parts of Europe, setting social standards for a growing European population. In Frankfurt, laws were passed as early as 1360 to regulate the consumption of brandy. Town councils all over Europe raised taxes on spirits as an attempt to curb their appeal. The town of Nürnberg put forth the following edict in 1496. "As many persons in this town have appreciably abused drinking aquavit the town council warns earnestly and they stress that from now on Sundays or other official holidays no spirit shall be kept in the houses, booths, shops or market and even the streets of this town for the purpose of sale or paid consumption." (As quoted in Forbes, *Short History of the Art of Distillation*.) Regulation of alcohol strengthened the role of government in the development of trade, as well as in the development of social mores in the Post-Classical and early modern periods.

Conclusion

Alcohol production, trade, consumption, and regulation changed dramatically over the Post-Classical and early-modern periods, affecting societies in new ways. The production and trade of alcohol influenced gender roles and the spread of culture in several ways. First, the production of alcohol exclusively by one sex helped to distinguish gender roles within societies. For example, inside the Inca Empire making chicha was the exclusive purview of women, categorizing it as feminine. In Britain in the Middle Ages women made and sold ale, idealizing that trade as feminine. Then in the early-modern period in Britain, as beer overtook ale, men stepped into the beer business, excluding women and creating an occupation that became identified as masculine.

Consumption of alcohol shaped many aspects of Post-Classical and early modern societies, including medicine, religion, and class. First, across widely disparate cultures alcohol shaped medicine. Islamic doctors prescribed alcohol, believing in its healing powers, even with the religious edict against its use. Aztec doctor/priests also ordered alcohol for the sick, as that society believed in its curative powers as well. Additionally, in the sixteenth- and seventeenth-century British apothecaries and doctors prepared their medicines using beer and spirits as ingredients. Second, use of alcohol at religious rituals and social festivals helped to define belief systems and mark important events in virtually every culture. The ceremonies of the Incas, Aztecs, Russians, Japanese, and British all featured alcohol. Conversely, yet equally as important, the ban on the use of alcohol in Islam shaped that belief system.

Third, in many cultures alcohol consumption patterns helped to define class identity. In Post-Classical Russia mead and wine characterized elite culture, while kvas beer characterized peasant identity. Alcohol use signified status in Post-Classical Japan where elites drank sake, and in Post-Classical and early modern Britain where elites drank wine and brandy, while commoners drank ale, and later beer and gin. In Aztec society elites had the privilege of drinking alcohol at any time, while commoners could only drink on special or ritual occasions, creating distinct differences between the two groups.

Regulation of alcohol provided governments with a way to control society as well as commerce. The Aztecs strictly regulated alcohol in order to maintain social hierarchy and public order. Islamic governments forbade alcohol as a way to strengthen Muslim identity. The government in early modern Britain regulated alcohol to bring standards to the alcohol business in a growing commercial economy. The British government also regulated the use of spirits to keep public order, especially aimed toward the lower class. Almost universally across cultures, alcohol regulation acted as a particularly invasive way to control the populace, mainly the lower class.

In the Post-Classical and early modern periods production and trade of alcohol spread culture and helped to define gender roles; consumption of alcohol helped to define medicine, class, and gender across many civilizations; and regulation of alcohol strengthened social hierarchy, commerce, and religious identity. In essence, alcohol touched virtually every segment of society, shaping the lives of people in countless ways.

Further reading

Bennett, J. M. 1996. *Ale, Beer, and Brewsters in England: Women's Work in a Changing World, 1300–1600.* New York: Oxford University Press.

Berger, P. 1985. *The Art of Wine in East Asia.* San Francisco: Asian Art Museum of San Francisco.

Bruman, H. J. 2000. *Alcohol in Ancient Mexico.* Salt Lake City: University of Utah Press.

Clark, P. 1983. *The English Alehouse: a Social History, 1200–1830.* New York: Longman.

Forbes, R. J. 1948. *Short History of the Art of Distillation: from the Beginnings up to the Death of Cellier Blumenthal.* Leiden: E.J. Brill.

Hackwood, F. W. 1985. *Inns, Ales and Drinking Customs of Old England.* London: Bracken Books.

Jennings, J. 2005. "La Chichera y El Patrón: Chicha and the Energetics of Feasting in the Prehistoric Andes." In *Archaeological Papers of the American Anthropological Association.* 14: 241–59.

Lucia, S. P. M. D. 1963. *A History of Wine As Therapy.* Philadelphia: J. B. Lippincott Company.

Martin, A. L. 2001. *Alcohol, Sex, and Gender in Late Medieval and Early Modern Europe.* New York: Palgrave (St. Martins).

McGovern, P. E. 2009. *Uncorking the Past: The Quest for Wine, Beer and Other Alcoholic Beverages.* Berkeley, CA: University of California Press.

Moore, J. D. 1989. "Pre-Hispanic Beer in Coastal Peru: Technology and Social Context of Prehistoric Production." *American Anthropologist* 91 (3): 682–95.

Scholliers, P. (ed.) 2001. *Food, Drink and Identity: Cooking, Eating and Drinking in Europe Since the Middle Ages.* New York: Berg.

Watney, J. 1974. *Beer is Best: A History of Beer.* London: Peter Owen.

4 Colonizers and the colonized

Alcohol in the fifteenth- through the nineteenth-centuries

In the 400 years between the 1400s and 1800s two world trends emerged. A world economic system developed, which went hand in hand with European colonization. Called the Atlantic world system by many scholars, the economic structure encompassed multiple continents. Europeans introduced an expanded and intensified market economy. The trade included a variety of goods, and a significant trade good was alcohol. Alcohol played a role in the expanding economies as a sought after commodity and sometimes as currency itself. Several European countries relied on alcohol to pay for hundreds of thousands of slaves from West Africa. The trade in alcohol rather than its production, consumption, or regulation dominated its story in these centuries.

In the other world trend in this period, colonization, the story of alcohol differed. Its production, trade, consumption, and regulation influenced the European colonies and their development. Indigenous demand for alcohol aided in the colonization of North America and Latin America. Alcohol influenced the economic and cultural development of the colonies and new kinds of alcohol, especially distilled liquor, substantially changed the lives of indigenous North Americans and Latin Americans.

European trade

The alcohol trade significantly influenced the growth of the world economic system in the early modern period. European countries earned tremendous profits from the trade. Alcohol was shipped throughout Europe, used aboard ships, and sold to the New World in exchange for everything from timber to slaves. Spain, for example, through exploiting its colonies for silver, was able to inflate the price of wine and earn enormous profits, adding to its already prosperous position. The Portuguese also shipped substantial amounts of alcohol throughout Europe, India, Africa, and the Americas, making them competitive in world trade. Moreover, the promise of alcohol on the arduous voyages successfully enticed Portuguese sailors to board ships. The Dutch traders also relied on alcohol. Like Portugal, the Netherlands plied its sailors with liquor. The Dutch shipped brandy throughout Europe, increasing alcohol consumption in many areas. The French, too, with wine, made significant inroads into international trade. French wine became so well known that people began to identify certain varieties with elites, and other varieties with the lower classes, giving French wine the ability to characterize social status, an ability that has lasted into the twenty-first-century.

In the fifteenth-century Western Europe started exploring and constructed a complex trading and colonial system that would change the face of the globe. The path to exploration had been left open for the Western Europeans by the Chinese, who even though they had had naval and maritime superiority in the fourteenth-century, ceased their movement into trade expansion and instead focused solely on Southeast Asia. Moreover, the breakdown of the Middle-Eastern Caliphates meant that the Middle East was not in a position to begin costly and risky exploration into the unknown.

The Atlantic system, led by European traders, became the center of much of the global trade. And alcohol became one of the important trade goods throughout Europe and from Europe to Africa, North America, and Latin America. Wine as well as distilled liquors were exported throughout the Atlantic system. Countries such as Spain, Portugal, the Netherlands, and France all participated in the trade. Alcohol helped the growth of the economies of these as well as other European countries. Many of these states had a monopoly on the liquor trade and auctioned off the right to distill, produce, and trade alcohol. The winners of the alcohol auctions made sizeable profits in the trade, and each state made considerable profit as well.

During the expansion of world trade Spain exported increasing amounts of wine to Europe as well as to the New World. Part of the reason for Spain's success in the wine trade came from inflation caused by the influx of silver from Spain's Latin American colonies. Inflation brought an increase in the price of Spain's wine and caused a rush to plant vineyards because of the chance to make extraordinary profits from the trade. The wine trade considerably boosted the economy of Spain during the colonial period.

Portugal, too, carried substantial quantities of grape wine on its trading and exploratory ships during colonial expansion starting in the 1400s. Wine lasted a fairly long time and was easily transported. Sailors consumed it and it was a valuable trade item. One of the important wines traded from Portugal was madeira wine, from Madeira island. The madeira wine trade was mainly focused on the Atlantic trade; it went to Britain, the Caribbean, and Portuguese Brazil. The island of Madeira was strategically located between England, the North American colonies, and the Caribbean. Not only did madeira wine go to Europe and the Americas, but it also became an important trade item to India through the East India Trading Company and others in the eighteenth-century. Interestingly, as the ships sailed to tropical ports and temperatures in the hull where the barrels were stored rose to over 100 degrees Fahrenheit, madeira wine improved in quality. So oceanic trade in and of itself actually increased the marketability of this important alcoholic product. In addition to madeira wine, port, a fortified wine from the Doura valley in Portugal, became popular in England during the early eighteenth-century, making substantial income for Portugal. Much like for Spain, commercial alcohol became an important way for Portugal to expand its trade into many parts of the world.

The important shipping giant in the Atlantic World, however, was the Dutch. Not only did they ship their own goods, but also those of other Northern and Southern European countries as well. One of their most important trade items was alcohol. The Dutch became highly involved in the wine trade, not only shipping wine throughout Europe and to the colonies, but also influencing how wine was produced in France, particularly the Bordeaux region. They taught the French to burn sulphur in barrels before filling them with wine. This technique added to the stability of the wines as they were shipped. Dutch shippers also carried brandy from France to England and to other parts of Northern Europe. Brandy became an extremely valuable item of trade. Sailors drank it on ships because it was more easily transported than wine. And it became popular in ports of call as well as in many parts of France. Brandy became the best way to transform otherwise poor-quality wine into a profitable commodity. Moreover, the popularity of brandy increased alcohol consumption across Europe. Shipping brandy and wine bolstered the strong trade position of the Dutch in the colonial period.

France became involved in the alcohol trade as well. Its role in the trade influenced the development of new kinds of wine in France. For example, champagne became popular among European elites during the seventeenth-century, and demand for champagne increased its production. In addition, merchants introduced new kinds of wines by mixing existing wines in order to stabilize them during shipping. As varieties of wines became more recognizable it became more common to distinguish wine drinking between classes. For example, dark red wine was thought to be better for the lower classes, while white and lighter reds were better for elites. Thus trade in wine further defined alcohol consumption patterns, helping to differentiate between classes. The alcohol trade also helped to define the relationship between France and its colonies. France outlawed the importation of rum from the French West Indies as a way to protect the brandy and wine producers at home.

West Africa

As an important commodity alcohol not only helped to shape the trade in slaves from West Africa, but the influx of Western alcohols also transformed drinking habits in ways that would have far-reaching social consequences in the future. Moreover, alcohol made vast profits for those European countries that traded it. Europeans not only traded alcohol for slaves, but also for other important commodities, such as rubber, wax, palm oil, and ivory. These raw materials supplied the beginnings of industrialization in Europe.

Indigenous alcohol was used in Africa, likely since the beginnings of agriculture. Fermented from grains, honey, fruit, palm trees, and milk, alcohol use had been highly regulated by tribal leaders. As early as the fifteenth-century

Europeans began purchasing slaves from Western Africa, trading, among other things, grape wine and distilled spirits such as rum, gin, and brandy. It was distilled spirits, however, that elicited tremendous demand among the Western Africans.

One distilled spirit in particular, rum, became a central ingredient in the famous triangle Atlantic trade. Rum was shipped to the New England colonies in exchange for lumber and grain to be used on the sugar plantations in the Caribbean and Brazil. Caribbean and Brazilian distillers shipped rum to Western Africa to be given as gifts to African kings, and to be used as a secondary trade item for slaves, who then were shipped back to the Caribbean and Brazil. Alcohol became so important to the slave trade that by the late eighteenth-century Western Africa was purchasing almost three million liters of alcohol per year, and by the mid-nineteenth-century almost 24 million liters per year. In the overall Atlantic slave trade in its 300 year history, perhaps 5 to 10 percent of all slaves were purchased with European alcohol.

The Portuguese, especially, relied on alcohol in their trade for slaves in Angola. For example, in the seventeenth-century Portuguese wine was in such high demand by African slave traders that some merchants made up to 500 percent profit in this trade during the 1600s. Moreover, the Portuguese in Brazil began to produce a great deal of cheap distilled liquor from sugarcane, called cachaça, or gerebita, to trade for slaves. This cheap, slave-produced, sugarcane brandy was popular among the slaves in Brazil, and it was popular as a trade item in Africa for more slaves. As a result of the increased Brazilian production of cachaça in the late seventeenth through the early nineteenth-centuries, coastal Brazil gained tremendous power over the slave trade in Angola. Records indicate that 25 percent of the almost 1.2 million slaves sold out of Angola in the eighteenth-century were bought with Brazilian cachaça.

As a result of trading alcohol for slaves, drinking patterns in West Africa changed dramatically. Not only did elites begin to drink European alcohol, but the demand for alcohol also filtered down to the majority of the population, increasing their alcohol consumption and changing the village social dynamics. African leaders no longer controlled alcohol use in their villages. Young African merchants, having earned their own money, gained increased access to the European alcohols, usurping the time-honored power of village elders to control the right to use alcohol.

South Africa

Western Europe not only traded slaves from the coast of West Africa, but it also penetrated South Africa in the period between the sixteenth- and eighteenth-centuries. The Dutch in South Africa began by searching for spices in the sixteenth-century. When they found none, they believed the area to be of little use except to resupply their ships that were headed to Southeast Asia. European immigrants to South Africa realized the value of wine in fueling these trading ships. In the seventeenth-century when Cape Town was founded, transplanted grape vines from areas such as France were soon planted. Again, the grapes were to be made into wine solely to restock ships sailing to Southeast Asia. Due to just a few men, including Jan van Riebeeck and Simon van der Stel, wine growing became popular in South Africa. When French Huguenots immigrated to the area they brought their wine-making expertise and helped the growing industry in Cape Town. Even though the industry was growing, South Africa was not known for high-quality wine. The tremendous demand for wine on the trading and exploration ships, however, fueled the growth of the wine industry in South Africa, helping to shape the economy of that region.

North America

The story of alcohol in colonial North America was one of social, cultural, economic, and political influence. In North America colonists all along the east coast continually attempted to grow wine. They used the liquor themselves, believing that alcohol, especially beer and wine, was essential to their daily lives. Alcohol structured their days; they used beer for food, medicine, and as a medium for socializing. Alcohol not only supplied the lives of the colonists, but it also fueled trade with Native Americans. Demand was so high that Native Americans would trade virtually anything to gain access to it, earning European traders incredible profits. Moreover, as a result of the influx of the previously unknown alcohol, Native American cultural rituals changed, as they began to believe inebriation allowed them to communicate with the spirits.

Both the British and French colonial governments became involved with alcohol, too. Each of them heavily relied on alcohol taxes, yet at the same time, they also tried to control alcohol use, many times as a façade meant to actually control marginalized segments of society. The government focused on public drunkenness and began to highly regulate taverns, correctly believing taverns to be responsible for fomenting political rebellion, since taverns acted as the primary gathering places for men in villages, towns, and even cities. Finally, the French and British governments in Europe vied for the extremely profitable colonial alcohol market, exacerbating their already heated rivalry in the European political arena.

In New England most colonists produced their own alcohol for personal consumption. For example, householders produced their own ale, cider, and brandy. Moreover, because they believed beer to be so important for the health of the colonists, the Virginia colony asked Britain to send over brewers to the colony, and the colony of Massachusetts established its own brewery in 1629. The Puritans in Massachusetts, like the Virginians, believed that beer was essential for the good health of their people. The Dutch in New York and New Jersey also set up breweries as well as taverns, especially in New Amsterdam (New York City). Beer continued to be important in the North

American diet throughout the eighteenth-century and into the period of the war for independence. During the revolutionary period a "buy American" campaign emerged and the constant demand for beer resulted in it becoming one of the targeted commodities to be made exclusively in North America instead of being imported from England.

Beer was not the only preferred form of alcohol in the North American colonies. In the early seventeenth-century North American colonists were urged to produce their own wine. For example, in Jamestown, colonists were required to plant vines and to learn how to make wine. The area was not conducive to wine making, however. The New England colonists started out with the same idea. They believed that because there were so many wild grapes in the area that wine making would flourish. The wild grapes that grew in the New England colonies were not conducive to wine making, however, and the vines that were imported from Europe soon died of various diseases. Colonists in many other areas also tried to make wine and eventually ended up failing. Georgia, South Carolina, Virginia, New Jersey, Louisiana, and Pennsylvania all had failed wine-making attempts. Wine remained so important to the colonists that attempts continued to be made, even though they continued to fail.

Colonists not only produced alcohol for themselves, but they also traded it with Native Americans. As a result of Native American enthusiasm for alcohol the Europeans traded it to them in exchange for their land and other goods such as furs, and sometimes even sexual access to their wives. The Native American demand for alcohol also remained continuous because, unlike other consumer goods, alcohol always needed to be replenished. In fact, the biggest profits for the traders came from trading alcohol, sometimes as much as 400 percent. Not only did the British traders benefit from the trade in alcohol but the French also made extremely high profits from the trade. French trading policies in the North American colonies allowed French Caribbean sugar (desired to be made into alcohol) to be sold at a lower price than British produced sugar, earning profits for the French and fostering the continued rivalry with the British. Even the British North American colonists sold rum made from French colonial molasses to the Native Americans, causing even more competition between the British and French. As a result, those British who owned the sugar plantations in the British Caribbean lost money. The North American colonists continued the practice, however, and made enough money from this trade to buy manufactured goods from England.

Consumption of alcohol influenced the lives of North American colonists as much or more so than production and trade. Colonists consumed alcohol instead of water because the lack of potable water made water an unsafe option. They also used alcohol for medicinal purposes. They used it for fever, indigestion, and general aches and pains. In colonial North America alcohol was also central to nutrition and social functions. Alcohol was so important to the diets of the colonists that George Washington ordered that soldiers be given beer and cider as part of their food rations.

Not only did colonists imbibe, but also Native Americans began drinking after colonization. Native Americans had not been exposed to alcohol before the arrival of the colonists. A perhaps apocryphal story from 1609 tells of Hudson's expedition that came upon Native Americans fishing in the bay of New York. Meeting them on an island, an Englishman offered alcohol (after having drunk the first cup himself), but the chief would not drink it. Instead, a warrior came forward, drank the alcohol, and then passed out. After he woke up he declared it was the best experience he had ever had. The rest of the group then drank the alcohol and they all became drunk. As a result, the Delaware Indians called the place Manahachtanienk, or "the island where we all got drunk." The island was later named Manhattan.

Some Native Americans had used hallucinogenic drugs before the arrival of the Europeans, so they believed that alcohol, too, contained magical powers and the ability to help them communicate with the spirits. Therefore, the goal of consuming alcohol was to become extremely inebriated, and enter into an altered state able to commune with the gods. An account of the time by an English traveler observed that the Native Americans drank in enough quantity to get very drunk. If there was not enough alcohol for everyone in the group to become entirely intoxicated, then some would abstain completely, allowing just a few of the members of the group to experience total inebriation. Some authors have argued, however, that the comportment of Native Americans when drinking came from mimicking the drinking behavior of the Europeans. Whatever the case, alcohol embedded itself into indigenous culture.

Regulation of alcohol also influenced the development of the colonies. Both the British and French colonial governments regulated the alcohol trade. Regulation sometimes reflected the ambivalence of the British and French authorities, however. For example, the British authorities disapproved of the alcohol trade with the Native Americans, while at the same time collecting significant tax revenues from it. Taxes on alcohol helped support colonial governments, especially the growth of infrastructure. The French colonial government approved of the trade with Native Americans in some contexts, but the French clerical authorities disapproved, so much so, that in order to receive absolution for trading alcohol with the Indians one needed to go to a regional bishop or all the way to the Pope. Ambivalence regarding the alcohol trade did not stop Britain and France from fighting over the profits, however.

In 1733, in yet another move in the competition between the British and the French, the British Parliament passed the Molasses Act, which added exorbitant duties on foreign molasses imported into the British North American colonies from the French colonies. The English colonists did not obey this law and continued to purchase cheaper molasses and rum from the French West Indies. In 1764, then, Parliament passed the Sugar Act, which was designed to replace the Molasses Act. The tax on the British colonists for sugar and molasses was lowered, but was more strictly enforced. In addition, other items, including wine (except French wine), were taxed. Parliament justified this act by stating in the act that it needed to increase revenue to the crown in return for protecting the colonies. As a consequence of this stricter law, rum production in the British North American colonies decreased. This resulted in a decline in available currency in the North American colonies, and the decreased ability to buy manufactured goods from England, which, ironically, hurt industries in England where the law was passed. Implicit in the act was a strong anti-French sentiment. The intensity of the fight to regulate the importation of sugar and molasses destined for alcohol production reveals the significance of alcohol as a pawn in the competition between European states to control the colonies in the New World.

Government regulations also covered taverns. Taverns that sold beer were also regulated by the 1630s. The price of beer was fixed and tavern keepers had to have a license. Regulations on producing beer also emerged. For example, it was illegal to brew beer at home; beer had to be bought at taverns. By the eighteenth-century taverns became even more regulated because taverns began to be seen as possible centers of working-class rebellion.

The British government not only regulated the trade in alcohol but also regulated its consumption. Early on alcohol use did not pose any great problem, even though each community had those who were labeled as drunkards. Laws concerning alcohol in the colonies eventually responded to abuses by colonists and Native Americans, however. Parliament gave local North American courts the right to levy fines for public drunkenness. The authorities believed that excessive alcohol consumption led to other crimes such as physical violence, adultery, and even murder. Not only the government, but also the church regulated consumption. The strong social structure of Puritanism worked to control excessive drinking during the first 50 years of the colony in New England. Wine, seemingly, was one of the problematic substances – second only to whiskey and rum. Wine historian Rod Phillips points out:

> In 1645 a definition of excessive drinking was established; half a pint of wine per person on any occasion. … [Moreover,] [i]n 1677, for example, only seven of the twenty-seven men and women licensed to sell alcohol [in Massachusetts] were permitted to sell wine … Laws were also passed to forbid drinking to anyone's health, providing drink as part of wages, and furnishing rations of drink above and beyond wages.

Clearly abuse of alcohol had become something of a problem in the British North American colonies. In addition to wine, however, the increase in the consumption of spirits, especially rum and whiskey, also led to high rates of drunkenness. As a result, stricter regulation was aimed at spirits much more so than ale or beer. Governmental strategies to control the intake of alcohol among the colonists and Native Americans included outlawing its production in many areas. Catholic and Protestant missionaries, as well as the colonists themselves, wanted to control drinking.

Latin America

Alcohol production, trade, consumption, and regulation influenced the development of colonial Latin America in several ways. Latin American-produced spirits drove a good portion of the Atlantic trading system and became the primary trade good for many islands in the Caribbean. Within Latin America the introduction of distilled alcohol forever altered indigenous drinking patterns, social behavior, and culture. The Spaniards introduced distillation into Mexico, stimulating an already growing demand for alcohol among the Native Mexicans. As a result, indigenous consumption patterns radically changed. Whereas alcohol in pre-conquest Mexico had only been available to the general population during festivals and rituals, it was now available all the time; and with the introduction of the Spanish cultural habit of drinking daily, many indigenous over-consumed. The Aztec social mores that had regulated drinking before the conquest no longer existed, so not only did indigenous Mexicans drink more, but more indigenous drank.

Spirits were popular, but native Mexicans primarily drank fermented pluque. As the indigenous population rebounded from the demographic devastation of the conquest, pulque demand skyrocketed. Men especially drank high quantities of pulque, enough for society to equate indigenous masculine identity with alcohol consumption. Moreover, indigenous use of alcohol seemed to provide the most effective way for Native Mexicans to passively resist labor exploitation by the Spaniards. Because of such high demand, the pulque trade provided an opportunity for many to make a great deal of money. The fact that women dominated the small-scale trade while men controlled the large-scale trade began to solidify not only gender identity, but also gender hierarchies within the villages.

Alcohol consumption pattern also signified cultural identity. While native Mexicans drank pulque, Spaniards, who desperately attempted to grow grape vines all over Latin America, demanded wine. Moreover, the Spaniards valued the ability to "hold one's liquor," while many indigenous drank to unconsciousness. In the view of the Spanish, their taste in wine, as well as their supposedly restrained consumption habits, not only set them apart from indigenous culture, but also demonstrated their cultural superiority. Many indigenous also recognized the power of alcohol to distinguish culture. Native Mexicans clandestinely continued to use alcohol in pre-colonial religious rituals, providing a tangible way to maintain their pre-conquest religion and culture. At the same time, the custom of using alcohol in religious rituals and on religious holidays united Catholicism with Mexican religions, allowing Indians to more easily synchronize their religious beliefs with Catholicism.

The colonial governments in Latin America, however, wrestled with the complex role of alcohol in society. Spaniards attempted to limit indigenous consumption, ostensibly to maintain social order, yet in effect to control just another aspect of the lives of the colonized. At the same time that the colonial governments espoused the benefits of moderation with one hand, however, with the other hand they enthusiastically collected substantial alcohol taxes, which they relied upon to fund their colonial project. In essence, alcohol shaped colonial society.

Distilled alcohol became an essential trade item for Latin America in the Atlantic trading system, especially for the Caribbean. Perhaps the most important distilled liquor introduced in the New World was rum. Rum was invented in the sixteenth-century in the Latin American island colonies and was most commonly distilled from sugarcane juice and the scum, or skimmed waste, from sugar production. Barbados by the late 1600s, for example, produced approximately one million gallons of rum, and Martinique produced almost half that amount. The British Caribbean island of Jamaica became the largest producer of rum in the eighteenth-century, and in the 1770s was exporting more than two million gallons per year.

Distilled liquors changed the nature of alcohol consumption in the new world. Its high alcohol content, 40 percent or more in some cases, dwarfed the 2 to 12 percent in the existing fermented beverages, and consumers tended to become much more inebriated than they did on ale, beer, or wine, leading to a tremendous rise in alcohol-related problems such as public drunkenness and violence. Distillers in the Caribbean also made rum for the European colonists who lived on the islands because many kinds of alcohol were too expensive to import from Europe, and the colonists demanded a steady supply of some kind of alcohol.

When Europeans arrived in mainland Latin America they found the indigenous already producing alcohol. In Mesoamerica several kinds of alcohol existed and were used before colonization. All of these were directly fermented from fruit or cacti. One of the most popular drinks in pre-colonial central Mexico was pulque, discussed in the previous chapter. The Spanish introduced distillation technology to Mesoamerica in the sixteenth-century distilling pulque into a spirit called mezcal. The Spanish experimented with several of the at least 200 species of agave in Mexico until they found the best ones to make mezcal.

Mexicans still produced impressive amounts of pulque, however. Elite Mexico City families owned pulque ranches outside of Mexico City and these ranches produced much of the pulque sold in the city. There were also small towns within a 15-mile radius of Mexico City that specialized in making pulque, and for many of these towns pulque was their main source of income. There were peasants who individually became rich off of the pulque trade. Especially by the eighteenth-century there were those who had built up large pulque productions in many villages. This exacerbated social stratification within indigenous society. By the second half of the eighteenth-century Jesuits had founded very profitable pulque haciendas, and after the Bourbon Reforms, elites in New Spain controlled the pulque trade, garnering tremendous profits.

Women dominated the small time trade in pulque. Most of the time it was women who took the pulque from the pulque villages to Mexico City to sell. And in the villages it was women who sold pulque from the doorways of their homes, because of the lack of permanent pulquerías in small villages. The small taverns that did exist were owned by widows. Consequently, women's role as small-time purveyors of pulque not only provided for their economic independence, but also acted as a key component of their female gender identity.

While Native Mexicans focused on the production of pulque, many Spaniards focused on wine. Spaniards not only shipped wine from Spain and Portugal to the New World, but they also began to cultivate wine there. By the 1550s there were vineyards in Mexico, the Andean region, as well as Chile and Argentina. The vines came from Europe because of the lack of suitable vines in the new world. In fact, Cortes, the leader of the conquistadores in Mexico, ordered his encomenderos (those who were given large tracts of land and the labor of the indigenous on that land) to plant grape vines. One thousand grape vines were supposed to be planted for every 100 indigenous workers under the command of an encomendero. Workers grafted European grape vines onto native grape vines in order to create the best possible combination.

Central Mexican viticulture did not work well, however, because of the climate, but Northern Mexico began to be known as a wine-growing region. The missions in California, in particular, began to grow grapes and make wine. So by the eighteenth-century California missions were making thousands of gallons of wine and brandy, although wine making was not a full-scale industry in California until much later. South American climates were also suited to produce wine and these wines circulated throughout Latin America. It was deemed necessary to start viticulture and viniculture in Latin America because shipping wine from Spain was so expensive and there was a high Spanish demand in the colonies. The growing worldwide significance of wine as a status symbol further demonstrated to the Spanish that their taste for wine not only widened the cultural gap between them and the indigenous, but also solidified their racial superiority in Latin America.

Within the Spanish colonies, however, issues over wine production existed. The wine producers in Spain were not happy with wine production in the New World because it competed with the sale of their wine. The Spanish wine growers counted on the colonial markets for substantial profits. The problem became great enough that Philip II of Spain restricted the planting of vine-yards in the New World in 1595. Many colonial wine makers ignored these restrictions, however. Another problem with the growing wine industry, according to Spanish authorities in Mexico, concerned unscrupulous wine sellers who sold wine to unsuspecting Indian villagers in order to get them drunk and cheat them out of their land. The Spaniards could buy indigenous land for much lower than the actual value with alcohol. While wine was not the common alcoholic drink of the indigenous, wine sellers were still successful in their attempts to dupe intoxicated Indians into selling their land. Moreover, because wine had not been a part of the ritual structure of indigenous life before the conquest, the abuse of it was much more common and it caused more social unrest in the villages, especially in the sixteenth- and early seventeenth-centuries when this practice occurred. Consequently, wine production and sale, then, furthered both the Spanish exploitation of the Indians as well as social unrest within indigenous communities.

In Portuguese Brazil, colonization and trade brought new kinds of alcohol to that colony. The Portuguese colonists began planting vineyards as soon as they colonized Brazil in the 1530s. This failed, however, because the climate was not conducive to wine grape growing. In addition, the Portuguese merchants in Portugal did not want the competition for their products. As a result, sugarcane-based alcohol began to be produced. Two very popular types of alcohol made from sugarcane were cachaça and aguardiente. Cachaça was made by fermenting the leftover juices from sugar production. It was then boiled, which increased the alcohol content. These sugarcane-based alcohols became very popular with the slaves in Brazil.

Colonization not only transformed alcohol production, but also consumption. The Spaniards introduced new consumption patterns to the Aztecs because Spanish and Aztec consumption patterns differed. Spaniards not only drank wine on religious holidays, but they also drank wine daily with meals. They did not have the habit of complete drunkenness, however. In fact, the Spanish believed that to call someone a drunkard was considered the worst possible insult one could level against another person. In contrast to the Spaniards, the indigenous Mexicans before the conquest drank pulque mainly for ritual purposes. As a result of the Spanish example, though, alcohol consumption by the indigenous lower classes increased considerably after the conquest. Some sources argue that the Native Americans began to drink daily like the Spaniards, but also continued their former style of drinking, which was drinking until they passed out. The combination had disastrous effects.

In addition, there was an increase in the number of people who drank because the social mores of the Aztecs that prevented many people from drinking had broken down. The numerous Catholic religious holidays and the commercialization of pulque brought on increased abuse as well. Other indications of increased drinking included the creation of taverns and inns in the countryside along travel routes that served pulque and wine, as well as the increased household production of pulque for family use.

People especially drank pulque during the dry season, from October to May, because pulque took the place of water and because the two major Catholic holidays, Christmas and Easter, took place during this period. Many people drank pulque during the day with meals and in the fields while they worked. In addition, the weekly market common in many small towns brought in people from the countryside who used the occasion to drink excessively. The indigenous also drank to excess on Sundays because they thought of Sunday as a religious holiday and because they had the day off from work. People also drank pulque during communal work days, either working in a neighbor's fields or working for the community. Moreover, pulque continued to be used as medicine among the indigenous. Men drank more pulque than women did, which was commonly accepted by the community as a masculine trait. Problems arose, however, when men drank so much that they could not carry out their daily work duties.

Violence also occurred as a result of drinking too much. In some areas drinking preceded many homicides, and in other places it led to fights among villagers. Where violence and drinking mixed to the greatest degree was in and around taverns. These taverns, or pulquerías, were numerous in Mexico City, and offered music, dancing, spicy food, gambling, and prostitution. Social mores seemed to be left at the door of these establishments. Those living in Mexico City drank more often and in larger quantities than did those in the countryside. William Taylor, in *Drinking, Homicide, and Rebellion* notes that in 1783 "the consumption of pulque reached 187 gallons for every adult resident of the city – plus perhaps three gallons of distilled alcohol." Thus new alcohol consumption patterns that included abuse of alcohol exacerbated the social breakdown of the indigenous societies after the conquest. Indigenous drinking became a problem for the Spaniards who sought to control the behavior of the native Mexicans. Spaniards believed that drinking to intoxication led to a breakdown of society because "drunken Indians" were no longer able to be controlled. Moreover, the Spanish, who considered it manly to be able to control one's behavior while drinking, identified drunkenness as a social malady; in a sadly ironic twist, the very drinking patterns introduced by the Spaniards themselves furthered their intense racism against Native Mexicans. Some scholars have argued, however, that indigenous alcohol abuse could be construed as passive resistance against the onerous labor expectations of the Spaniards, who used pulque to entice laborers to build infrastructure, to produce agriculture, and to extract silver.

Even though substantial changes occurred in drinking patterns after the conquest, some continuities remained. Many indigenous village elites continued to practice ceremonies honoring local gods. William Taylor notes the holdovers from pre-conquest drinking patterns. "Animal sacrifices accompanied by community drinking were thought to protect the community from new diseases brought by the Spaniards." So the native Mexicans used pulque in pre-conquest ritual ways, but for new reasons brought on by colonialism. Indigenous leaders also encouraged ritual drinking by commoners as a way to turn them away from Catholic missionary efforts. In addition, pulque continued to be used at marriage ceremonies, at births and deaths, and at harvest ceremonies. However, alcohol also facilitated some syncretism between pre-conquest religions and Catholicism. For example, one group of elite Indians honored the stars by drinking pulque, but on Sunday nights, a Catholic holy day. So in some ways ritual pulque use helped maintain traditional culture in the face of colonialism, but in other ways consumption patterns furthered cultural miscegenation between Indians and Spaniards.

In Latin America the colonial governments had to control much larger centers of population than did the North American colonial governments, and regulating alcohol consumption was central to social control. The colonial Latin American government believed that the indigenous were prone to drunkenness and violent behavior and thus needed special rules regarding liquor. Tensions over regulations arose within the colonial government and between the colonial government and the merchants, however. On the one hand the colonial government relied on high consumption levels for the substantial taxes brought in by alcohol, which also worked in favor of the merchants who just wanted to sell their product. On the other hand the government sought to control Native Mexican behavior through limiting their access to alcohol.

The Spanish king had to repeatedly impose regulations because indigenous alcohol abuse, resulting from the sale of liquor by colonial merchants as well as the church, remained such a problem. In 1524 Phillip II outlawed the sale of any kind of alcohol to indigenous Mexicans. By 1572 the crown tried to control the sale of Spanish wine to Indians by requiring licenses and then by banning the sale of wine to Indians altogether in 1594, 1637, and 1640. The sale of Spanish wine to indigenous villagers continued, however, because of the tremendous profits that could be made. Not only did regular Spanish merchants take part in this trade, but Catholic bishops worked their way into the profitable trade as well. Indigenous village leaders did not sit by passively and allow this influx of wine to ruin their villages' social order, however. Many villages demanded that the viceroy enforce the laws against selling wine to indigenous Mexicans.

William Taylor explains several laws that were instituted to control the pulque trade. In 1579, 1585, and 1586 it became illegal to sell pulque, wine, and maguey syrup except in a few regulated areas in Mexico City. In 1608 the viceroy went so far as to order that only one "respectable old woman" per every 100 Indians could gain a license to sell pulque. Because there was such a large black market in the pulque trade, however, in 1635 and 1639 it became illegal to bring pulque into the city, except during the day. By 1692, however, pulque production was outlawed again because of a Mexico City riot, blamed on "drunken Indians." At the same time, however, the colonial government benefitted from not enforcing the bans on the sale of pulque because of the staggering tax revenues it brought in, which were needed for the growth of infrastructure. The government issued permits to make wine and beer as a strategy to raise tax revenue. The number of petitions for licenses to sell pulque in Mexico City and other populated areas in the sixteenth- and seventeenth-centuries were very high. Once again, however, in the eighteenth-century Spanish colonial officials outlawed pulque because they believed it led to disturbances, although that law lasted only five years. Thus the colonial government remained ambivalent about the sale of alcohol to indigenous Mexicans.

The Spanish monarchy also regulated rum production in its Caribbean colonies. In 1693, all rum making was outlawed in the Spanish colonies. The Spanish officials believed that rum competed too heavily with the Spanish alcohols imported into the colonies. Moreover, these colonial officials were nervous about what they believed to be the overindulgence in rum by African slaves as well as by the indigenous population. They feared that drunkenness would lead to disorder, and could eventually lead to a slave insurrection.

This law was routinely ignored, however, as immediate profits outweighed concerns over potential problems.

In the Andean region the colonial government also regulated alcohol consumption. Chicha, or corn beer, was a staple drink in the Andes. Much like pulque, it had been used for ceremonial purposes throughout the period of Inca rule and before. After colonization, however, the Spanish believed that many problems arose because of excessive chicha use by indigenous South Americans. For example, in 1556, judge Gregorio Gonzales de Cuenca ordered that drinking be stopped. He said:

> Because ... chiefs and leaders used to have 'taverns' and places where all who came to them were given chicha to drink, and it is the cause of the drunkenness of the people, and it occupies many men and women in making the chicha, and it is a thing of bad example, and the said chiefs and leaders spend excessively on it; it is ordered that from now on they (the chiefs) not have such 'taverns' nor public or secret places for drinking ...
>
> (as quoted in Gastineau *et al. Fermented Food Beverages in Nutrition*)

So even though the Spaniards throughout Latin America believed that alcohol caused problems with Native Latin Americans, they used alcohol to further the colonial project as well as to solidify social stratification between the Spaniards and the indigenous. Alcohol played a complex role in Latin American society throughout the colonial period.

Conclusion

In many ways the production, trade, consumption, and regulation of alcohol fostered European success in world trade, helped to solidify the new colonial identities of both the colonists and the indigenous, and structured the ways in which the colonial powers subjugated native North and South Americans. First, both the colonists in North America as well as the indigenous in Latin America fermented their own alcohol because alcohol sustained their nutritional, social, and cultural lives. Second, North American, South African, and Latin American colonists all made repeated attempts at growing grapes for wine because wine not only structured their daily lives, but also seemed to be an essential part of their very identities as Europeans in a foreign land. Third, rum and other liquors fueled the triangle trade in the fifteenth through the nineteenth-centuries, allowing many European states to buy a significant number of slaves because of the high demand for alcohol from African slave traders. Fourth, the colonists in North America and Latin America forcefully sold alcohol to the indigenous, which in North America led to unscrupulous land deals, and in Latin America, social breakdown.

Fifth, alcohol was key in the colonial labor exploitation of both Africans and indigenous Latin Americans. Sixth, Spain, Portugal, the Netherlands, and

France all competed for markets in the lucrative wine trade, which intensified the struggle for power among these European states. Seventh, colonial alcohol producers competed against European alcohol producers for alcohol markets, thus exacerbating the hierarchy that privileged the European states over their colonies.

Consumption of alcohol in the early-modern period disrupted native social structures, created new colonial identities, and created new cultural practices in several ways. First, the introduction of alcohol changed the consumption habits of Native North Americans, West Africans, and Native Latin Americans. In the case of the North Americans they had not previously been introduced to alcohol; in the case of West Africans and Native Latin Americans alcohol consumption had been strictly regulated before contact by indigenous leaders. Thus the tremendous upsurge in drinking caused at best social disorder and at worst social disintegration in all three areas. Third, both in Africa and Latin America the power of indigenous leaders over alcohol consumption diminished, leading to a collapse of the traditional social hierarchy. Fourth, a clash of alcohol cultures led to virtual daily overindulgence by many native North and South Americans. Prior to colonization, Native Latin Americans drank only on ritual occasions, consuming enough alcohol to become completely inebriated and eventually black out. Native North Americans, after the Europeans introduced alcohol to them, also drank to reach complete drunkenness. Yet European alcohol habits called for social drinking on a daily basis. The combination of the two styles led to catastrophic social problems. Fifth, both in North America and in Latin America excessive consumption of alcohol led to violence, which again disrupted social harmony in the population.

Sixth, alcohol use for religious purposes differed between the colonists and the indigenous in both North America and South America. In North America, Protestantism espoused moderation, while Native Americans believed in the necessity of altered states to communicate with the spirits, causing a serious cultural clash of religious practices. In Latin America, however, while the frequency of Catholic holy days led the indigenous to celebrate more often than had been their custom, the similar custom of practicing religion with alcohol allowed the indigenous to more easily accept Catholicism.

Alcohol regulations affected Europe, Africa, and the New World colonies in numerous ways. First, the complex role of alcohol in the colonies led to contradictory policies regarding drinking. On the one hand the colonial governments in North America and Latin America both wanted to regulate the drinking of the indigenous because they wanted to control their behavior. On the other hand, the alcohol business was so lucrative that both governments came to depend upon the taxes garnered from the trade. Second, alcohol regulations were used as a tool in the competition between the British and the French for power both in the colonies and in Europe. Third, even within the Catholic Church in the colonies contradictory approaches to alcohol existed. While Catholics in North America wanted to curb alcohol excesses, the

Catholic Church in Latin America was deeply involved in the alcohol trade, focusing on profits rather than regulation. Fourth, high levels of abuse that seriously disrupted the social order, as well as repeated non-compliance, led to governmental regulations that had to be repeatedly legislated in Mexico, Brazil, North America, and South America.

World trade and colonialism, the two major trends in the early modern period, were significantly influenced by the production, trade, consumption, and regulation of alcohol. The centrality of alcohol in the lives of people across cultures and continents necessitated its daily production by the indigenous as well as the colonists in Africa, North America, and South America. Trade of alcohol provided national as well as individual riches leading to competition among countries and to domestic competition across classes and racial divides. Alcohol also provided Europeans with an effective tool to exploit native West Africans, and North and South Americans, which helped lead to high levels of alcohol consumption by the indigenous in all three areas, causing a breakdown of their social order. Finally, contradictions between governmental regulation and taxation revealed that rather than being immutable, alcohol was a tool on the one hand for social control when necessary, and on the other hand for economic gain when necessary. In all its expressions, however, alcohol played a key role in early modern world trade as well as European colonization.

Further reading

Bennett, L. A. and G. M. Ames. 1985. *The American Experience with Alcohol: Contrasting Cultural Perspectives.* New York: Plenum Press.

Curto, J. 1996. *Alcohol and Slaves: The Luso-Brazilian Alcohol Commerce at Mpinda, Luanda, and Benguela during the Atlantic Slave trade c. 1480–1830 and its Impact on the Societies of West Central Africa.* Phd Dissertation. University of California Los Angeles.

——2006. *Enslaving Spirits: The Portuguese-Brazilian Alcohol Trade at Luanda and its Hinterland, c. 1550–1830.* Boston, MA: Brill.

Gastineau, C. F., W. J. Darby, and T. B. Turner. 1979. *Fermented Food Beverages in Nutrition.* New York: Academic Press.

Hyams, E. 1965. *A Social History of the Wine Vine: Dionysus.* New York: The Macmillian Company.

Jankowiak, W. and D. Bradburd. (eds.) 2003. *Drugs, Labor, and Colonial Expansion.* Tuscon: University of Arizona Press.

Kicza, J. E. 1980. "The Pulque Trade of Late Colonial Mexico City." *The Americas.* 37 (2): 193–221.

——1991. "Drinking, popular protest, and governmental response in seventeenth- and eighteenth-century Latin America." *Contemporary Drug Problems.* 18 (2): 219–36.

MacAndrew, Cr. and R. B. Edgerton. 1969. *Drunken Comportment: A Social Explanation.* Chicago: Aldine Publishing Company.

Scardaville, M. C. 1980. "Alcohol Abuse and Tavern Reform in Late Colonial Mexico City." *The Hispanic American Historial Review.* 60 (4): 643–71.

Taylor, W. B. 1979. *Drinking, Homicide, and Rebellion in Colonial Mexican Villages.* Stanford, CA: Stanford University Press.

5 Alcohol, industrialization, and temperance in the nineteenth- and early twentieth-centuries

Industrialization transformed the world in the eighteenth-, nineteenth-, and early twentieth-centuries. The West led the world in industrialization, which brought with it new forms of labor organization, increased urbanization, and the separation of work from home and leisure from work. All of these changes helped to define the lives of the emerging working and middle classes in particular. Industrialization also transformed the alcohol industry by making it possible to mass produce alcohol. As a result, new forms of production, trade, consumption, and regulation of alcohol influenced the ways that gender, class, ethnicity, politics, and indeed industrialization developed during the eighteenth- and nineteenth-centuries. Most notably, within the arena of alcohol regulation, a powerful and widespread movement, called temperance, developed as a result of the change in consumption patterns. Temperance was one of the most important international social movements of the nineteenth-century, especially in Protestant countries in the West.

Temperance movements in the industrializing West differed based on the religious and ethnic makeup of the countries. Great Britain and the United States were both Protestant countries, yet the large African American population in the United States influenced the development of temperance in that country. Ireland differed from both Britain and the United States because it had a Catholic majority, however, it also was controlled by a Protestant minority that championed temperance. Finally, France was a predominantly Catholic country and one of the world's principal wine-growing areas. It did not have widespread temperance. The non-Western industrializing areas of Japan and Russia did not experience the strong temperance movements characteristic of the Protestant West either.

Great Britain

Alcohol in Britain not only shaped class and gender identities, but also produced a widespread social movement. Mass produced alcohol production pushed out craftsmen and proletarianized the industry. Alcohol establishments, by being essentially segregated by class, also helped to create distinctive class cultures in Britain. Moreover, alcohol venues, namely pubs, acted as the primary social centers for working men, becoming part of a man's masculine identity in the new industrial age. Alcohol consumption also characterized class identity. Cheap gin became identified with the working class. Authorities aggressively regulated the spirit, and temperance movements rallied against it, attempting to control the social lives of the working class in order to insure industry an adequate supply of productive workers, and thus further the development of industry and the concentration of wealth with the owners of capital. Yet at the same time, from the working-class perspective alcohol helped them cope with their difficult lives and ameliorated the social upheavals and social restructuring necessitated by industrialization.

Industrialization transformed the production and trade of alcohol in Great Britain in the eighteenth- and nineteenth-centuries. Large, mechanized brewing houses began to be established, overtaking the cottage industry brewers and changing the beer trade. Large brewing families such as Guinness, Barclay, and Bass emerged during this period and became known as the "Princes of Trade." These large brewers began to sell their beer through a system called tied houses, which they also owned, making them "tied" to the individual brewer, so each house sold only one brand. Brewers expanded the tied system by buying up individually owned taverns or pubs across the country, thus acquiring more markets for their beer. The mechanization of the industry and the tying in of beer pubs, both of which displaced small brewers and began to standardize beer, did not diminish the popularity of pubs in that country, however.

More than simply outlets for beer, pubs developed into social centers for urban working-class men as well as centers for gaming and sports clubs. Cricket teams, football teams, domino players, and other game players met in pubs to talk about the game they had just finished, or to play games with their fellow drinkers. This kind of camaraderie brought men together, reinforcing stereotypically masculine gender roles. If women frequented these establishments they risked being stigmatized as prostitutes. In a few cases, however, pubs had a separate room with a separate entrance where women could drink without being seen by men. Nevertheless, the policies in drinking establishments helped to shape both male and female gender ideologies in the nineteenth-century.

Even though beer remained popular, Britain began to produce large quantities of gin. Gin could be distilled cheaper than beer could be brewed, and thus many brewers turned to distilling. For example, it took from between £2,000 and £10,000 to build a brewery, whereas it took only £500 to £5,000 to build a distillery. Over the eighteenth-century 25 percent of the pubs became gin shops in London. By the nineteenth-century even more alcohol sales focused on gin. "Dram" shops, shops that sold small glasses of spirits called drams, became more numerous as cheap gin rose in popularity with the working class. Many establishments, however, did not obtain licenses to sell spirits, and those that continued to trade in beer alone outnumbered those with spirits licenses. In many cities beerhouses were more popular with working-class men because their beer was cheap, and more importantly, they provided credit.

In addition to providing credit, pubs tried other strategies to maximize the amount of alcohol sold. They changed the layout. Pubs took out all seating, thus encouraging working-class men to crowd up to the bar and quickly order more to drink. These new establishments served no food, had sawdust floors, and only about 10 percent had bathrooms. These changes led to a decline in the respectability of pubs and caused the middle-class to look down upon the establishments and the working-class patrons who frequented them. What is more, virtually all establishments across Britain perpetuated class distinctions. Those of the working class populated the pubs, beerhouses, and dram shops, while those of the middle-class patronized what were called saloon bars, and those of the upper-class frequented private club houses. The separation of drinking establishments by class helped to solidify cultural and social identity among the classes in industrializing Britain.

Alcohol not only influenced identity, but it also shaped the practice of medicine. During the late nineteenth-century in Britain debates abounded regarding the medicinal use of alcohol. Even though the temperance movement was strong, using wine as medicine remained common. For example, a Dr. Francis Anstie wrote a book called *On the Uses of Wine in Health and Disease* in 1877. In this book he explained how wine should be used by those who were healthy and also how wine should be used by those with acute or chronic illnesses. He went on to note that for a healthy young woman a half a bottle a day of light wine was good, or if a young adult was quite active, then a bottle of wine a day was fine. For high fevers he prescribed diluted alcohol, and for typhoid fever he prescribed old sherry. Later books, written around the turn of the century, also lauded the benefits of wine on one's health. For example, these books argued that wine could be used for anemia, gout, and stomach problems.

Society viewed the consumption of spirits, however, in an entirely different light than that of wine. As the working class increasingly consumed more gin in the eighteenth-century the government reacted with stricter regulations. The government deemed gin such a problem that it raised taxes on it in order to slow down its consumption. The government imposed a tax of 20 shillings on every gallon in 1736. In addition, to open a gin shop one had to pay £50. The working class had such an obsession with gin that as a result of gin taxes riots broke out in London. Moreover, people found a way around the new laws. For example, according to John Watney in *Beer is Best: A History of Beer*, clever entrepreneurs set up chemist shops that sold "Cholick Water" that was actually gin. In addition, taverns began coloring the gin and selling it as wine. Another tactic gave gin new names, such as "Ladies' Delight." So despite attempts by the government to curb it, the consumption of gin continued to climb. Abuse of gin became such a problem among the working class in Britain that the government stopped requiring licenses for beer pubs in 1830 as an incentive to create more and cheaper places to drink beer instead of gin. This "Beer Act of 1830" did little to slow gin consumption, however.

Abuse of gin by the working class not only drew the attention of the government, but also of temperance movements. Temperance movements in Britain lauded the "benefits" of beer and condemned the "detriments" of gin as a way to decrease gin consumption. Many temperance advocates wrote poems that extolled the virtues of beer. For example, "Beer! Happy produce of our isle, Can sinewy strength impart, And, wearied with fatigue and toil, Can cheer each manly heart." Conversely, the poems written about gin told another story. "Gin! Cursed fiend with fury fraught, Makes human race a prey, It enters by a deadly draught, And steals our life away." (As quoted in John Watney *Beer is Best: A History of Beer*.) So according to both the government and temperance groups, beer actually helped society whereas gin caused severe problems.

Temperance movements used many tactics to slow down the consumption of gin and other alcohols in the nineteenth-century. Many segments of society joined in these efforts: men and women from both the middle and working classes as well as industrialists participated. Women in the Salvation Army for example formed the Drunkards Rescue Society in 1874 to help individuals with alcohol problems. In another strategy, one temperance group imported a program from Sweden. Called the Gothenburg system, it advocated hiring salaried managers to run pubs instead of owners. It was thought that the managers, seeing no profit incentive in pushing excessive drinking, would better manage consumption. In another approach, reformers advocated adding food back into pubs as well as other forms of entertainment in order to slow down drinking, which, when implemented, did result in lower consumption rates.

In the late nineteenth-century temperance tactics began to change. Instead of focusing on modifying personal behavior and upgrading alcohol venues temperance advocates began to promote wide-reaching legislation. As a result, more and more legislation against alcohol appeared. For example, the Intoxicating Liquor Act, or the Child Messenger Act, outlawed the sale of liquor to children under 14. In addition, the police could now arrest adults who were drunk in public places. In 1914 and 1915 the Defence of the Realm Act was passed, which gave the government the right to regulate the hours of pubs, to inspect breweries and pubs, to buy breweries, and to forbid the sale of certain kinds of alcohol such as absinthe. Finally by 1923 a new law forbade the sale of liquor to anyone under 18 unless that person was over 16 and wanted beer or cider with a meal. So, much of Britain's experience with alcohol in the eighteenth-, nineteenth-, and early twentieth-centuries focused on its regulation, as alcohol control became emblematic of a progressive, well-ordered society, one that controlled the growing working-class.

Ireland

Alcohol consumption in the largely Catholic country of Ireland shaped class, gender, and religious identities, while regulation provided the government with a socially sanctioned tool to control the working class. Alcohol consumption in Ireland skyrocketed in the eighteenth-century. The working class, in an attempt to cope with their lives in Irish urban slums, drank prodigious amounts of alcohol. Moreover, much like in other areas in the West, pubs became male working-class bastions, adding to the new definitions of both masculinity and class, and furthering the separation between work and leisure. Drinking alcohol became something one did outside of work, rather than at points during the workday as had been the case before industrialization. Not only did men drink alcohol away from work, but the increase in the number of urban pubs meant that most alcohol consumption took place in public drinking establishments. The urban working-class led the way in making public drinking a predominant form of leisure.

Whiskey consumption by the working class rose, leading to a flood of anti-whiskey propaganda across society. Both the government and temperance movements attempted to regulate it, and by proxy increase working-class industrial productivity and influence the cultural construction of that class. Alcohol abuse by the urban working class brought on the incumbent problems of violence, absenteeism, and health troubles. Moreover, the Protestant elite characterized Catholics as drunkards, claiming degeneracy of that entire subculture as a result of their alcohol consumption. So Catholics, too, championed temperance as a way to become socially acceptable to the British.

Consumption of alcohol in Ireland, particularly whiskey, jumped in the modern period. For example, in the eighteenth-century the population of Ireland grew by 50 percent, while the consumption of spirits, especially whiskey, grew by almost 750 percent. Whiskey consumption continued to increase in the nineteenth-century with industrialization of the whiskey industry. The mass produced whiskey became more accessible to the working class because it was so cheap. In contrast to the urban working-class, the rural poor still did not have enough disposable income to drink heavily, and the gentry drank wine and not whiskey. These disparate alcohol consumption patterns, then, furthered the cultural gap between the working-class, the gentry, and the rural poor.

Regulation of alcohol in Ireland responded primarily to the problems of whiskey abuse by the urban working-class. The government tried various regulations to slow down its production, including lowering taxes on beer so drinkers would turn to it and away from whiskey. By the 1820s the government established a special police force to catch drunkards; the fines were extremely high. But these efforts did not curb drinking. The government levied higher taxes on whiskey production, which did decrease consumption, but unfortunately also tax revenues. Moreover, there continued to be numerous illegal producers of whiskey who did not pay these taxes. So the government decided to cut taxes on distilleries as a way to curb the illegal production of whiskey and to gain more tax revenues. As a result, many illegal distillers decided to become legal and pay taxes. Tax revenues did increase, although some illegal distilling remained. Ironically the government wanted to decrease working-class whiskey consumption, yet at the same time they relied on extensive alcohol taxes to balance the budget.

In addition to governmental efforts, temperance proponents in the nine-teenth-century also tried to convince the drinking public to moderate their consumption. These movements, which were predominantly Protestant, argued against drinking whiskey, purporting that wine, cider, or beer would be a better choice. Temperance literature claimed that excess whiskey use caused gout, kidney stones, cirrhosis of the liver, asthma, jaundice, poor eyesight, lack of sperm, barrenness in women, and infant mortality. Temperance writers felt they needed to warn drinkers of such extreme effects in order to compete with medical doctors who maintained that spirits could be useful as medicine. Some cur-rent authors argue, however, that rather than having public health in mind the temperance movements had the underlying purpose of controlling the Catho-lic majority in Ireland, who they believed to be the problem drinkers. Protestant temperance movements did further the culture of oppression toward the Catholic majority. Catholics, who made up 80 percent of the population, however, did not comply with the wishes of the temperance groups and continued to drink.

As the century wore on and the temperance strategy of focusing on personal moderation did not work, temperance groups changed their tactics. They worked toward legislative change instead, promoting Sunday closure laws, for example. The legislature did not cooperate with the temperance movements in this particular regard, however, because of the importance of alcohol taxes to the budget.

The Protestant temperance movements were joined by some Catholic tem-perance groups in the nineteenth-century, too. For these Catholic temperance groups, however, the impetus was to free Ireland from the rule of the British. Catholic nationalists believed that to win their freedom they must, among other things, focus on demonstrating a high moral character. One of the ways to do so was to curb alcohol consumption, since alcohol abuse and to some extent even consumption was equated with moral degeneracy. Many Catho-lics believed that England labeled Ireland as a country of drunkards in order to justify their political control of the country.

Temperance did seem to be successful in the long run in Ireland. A larger percentage of the population joined temperance movements in Ireland than did so in England or the United States. Moreover, the consumption levels of spirits by the Irish in the nineteenth-century were lower than that of the Americans. This pattern carried on into the twentieth-century as well. By the 1970s in Northern Ireland, for example, 34 percent of the population abstained, while in Britain only 9 percent abstained. So the stereotype of Irish drunkenness was overrated and perhaps was indeed a myth perpetuated by the British to maintain their power over Ireland.

France

Alcohol, in particular wine, shaped commerce, class, gender, international poli-tics, and government's role in society in eighteenth– and nineteenth–century

France. Wine was the de facto French national drink in the nineteenth-century. Industrialization of the wine trade was perhaps one of the most important areas of modernization, as attempts to broaden wine markets brought on the development of rail networks throughout the country. Moreover, the growth of wealth and the expansion of the industrial upper-class created a demand for fine wines, helping to define elite culture as far removed from that of the lower class. Public spaces serving alcohol also helped to define both gender and class identities. Cafés served both men and women unlike pubs in other Western countries, which served only men. As a result, French women were allowed a broader gender identity. At the same time, however, class specific venues perpetuated distinct differences in class cultures.

Moreover, wine, as emblematic not only of French trade but also of French identity, was used by the British to punish France. The British repeatedly cut off the wine trade with France. In response, the French made sure that wine quotas became central to international treaties with Britain as well as with other countries. Domestic regulation of alcohol in France focused on cafés, cabarets, and taverns. The government feared their role in precipitating rebellion because they were centers of French social life and daily gathering places for many.

Since wine was the predominant alcoholic drink in the eighteenth-century in France, far above beer or brandy, technological advancements centered around wine. In France scientific discoveries in wine spurred industrialization of the wine trade. Louis Pasteur, for example, discovered the best way to store wine for long periods of time: a narrow-necked bottle pointed down so no air could enter. Another chemist, Jean-Antoine-Claude Chaptal, made very important advancements in the production of wine, which also modernized the industry. He popularized using sugar in the process, stabilizing the wine and making it ferment faster. Sugar could also sweeten sour grapes and help make them into good wine. Even with these technological advancements, however, the disease of phylloxera seriously decimated the wine industry in France, as well as across Europe in the mid to late nineteenth-century. The European vines were not resistant to the infestation, and production of wine dropped by 60 to 90 percent. American vines, which were resistant because they had already had the disease, were grafted with the European vines and the vineyards began to recover.

Despite the phylloxera epidemic, the wine industry continued to modernize. Beginning in the 1850s the desire for larger wine markets helped to develop transportation networks to the wine-growing regions. Rail lines spread across the country to the grape-producing areas and helped to grow an internal market. Markets grew across Europe as well. For example, Germany, England, and the Netherlands imported large amounts of French wine. Some winemakers began to produce luxury wines for an increasingly wealthy subculture within France, making fine wine consumption a cultural characteristic of the upper-class. The majority of winemakers, though, mass produced cheaper wine for the lower-classes. During the nineteenth-century not only did wine making modernize, but distillation did as well. Even though industrial development in France lagged behind that of Britain, industrial distilleries remained vital, helping lead the way in French industrialization.

The burgeoning wine industry increasingly relied upon the proliferation of alcohol venues. Much like in other parts of the West the number of drinking establishments rose between the seventeenth- and nineteenth-centuries. For example, in Paris the number of drink shops grew from 3,000 in 1789 to over 30,000 in the late 1880s. The number of establishments across the country rose from approximately 100,000 in 1789 to 500,000 in 1914. One of the most popular drinking establishments was the café. There were different kinds of cafés, those that catered to the working-class, and several that catered to the upper-classes. Cafés were very important social centers for the French. They encompassed the space between private and public life, and exemplified the rise of leisure as a separate activity from work. Both men and women frequented cafés in France thus reflecting a more complicated gender ideology than the traditional nineteenth-century Western belief in the separation of women into the private sphere. Because they were divided by class, however, cafés did perpetuate class differences within France.

In addition to cafés, taverns, called cabarets, arose that catered to the working class. Much like in Britain and Ireland, urban, working-class men escaped from poor living conditions and joined other working-class men to drink and play games. Wine was most often the drink served in these taverns. Because these taverns served men of the same class, they, along with the cafés, helped solidify class boundaries. These taverns almost exclusively catered to men rather than women. If women drank in these taverns they were labeled as prostitutes, thus perpetuating a gender stereotype that automatically equated women's public alcohol consumption with loose morals.

The French also believed alcohol to be effective medically. Wine was used in several kinds of medicines. French doctors and their patients believed that a white wine mixed with juniper berries, squill, digitalis, and potassium acetate would cure heart disease. Wine was used for anemia, eczema, scurvy, and pneumonia. In 1898 Paris hospitals used over three million liters of wine in their cures. Louis Pasteur lauded the positive medicinal effects of wine so much so that in 1903 the French parliament voted to designate wine as healthy and hygienic. As newer more scientific medicines such as aspirin and antibiotics became popular, however, wine began to decline as an official medicine.

Personal alcohol consumption changed slightly in the nineteenth-century. Many in the lower-class in the north began to drink distilled spirits, or what they called "industrial spirits." Even with the increase in the consumption of spirits, though, wine continued to be the most popular alcoholic drink. The majority of peasants in the south of France continued to drink wine because most of the vineyards were located there and therefore wine was inexpensive. As the middle-class in France expanded, both their demand for commodities, as well as their desire to emulate the upper-class, led to an increase in their desire for quality wines. Fine wine consumption perpetuated growing consumerism and furthered the development of separate upper-, middle-, and working-class culture. Another elite commodity, champagne, also became a beverage popular with those in the middle-class who wanted to imitate upper-class lifestyles. The new consumer culture that demanded fine wine and champagne led to a boom in the alcohol advertising industry. For example, the 1855 Paris Exhibition advertised wines not only from France but also from places as far away as Australia. Champagne also became emblematic of the new advertising culture. The labels on the bottles depicted sports, romance, and patriotism – all ways to convince the buyer to consume the product.

Wine became a tool in international relations as well. The wine trade from France was so important that it became embroiled in the war between France and England in the early eighteenth-century. For example, as a result of the conflict, in 1703 the English closed their markets to French wines. French wine merchants, however, came up with alternative ways to get their product to the English consumer. Rod Phillips, author of *A Short History of Wine*, wrote that Bordeaux's wine merchants shipped their wine close to the English coast where English privateers then commandeered the wine, took it to England, and sold it. The privateers received most of the proceeds but likely shared them with the Bordeaux winemakers. There is no hard evidence to prove this theory, but since so much French wine continued to enter England, even though there was a ban on it, the story seems plausible. As the century progressed the wine trade continued to factor into international disagreements. As a result of ongoing tensions between France and England, in 1728 England banned bottled wine, only allowing the less stable barrel wine to be shipped into the country. This law hurt the French winemakers because by the time the barrel wine reached England its quality had deteriorated, thus decreasing French profits.

In the twentieth-century wine continued to be used in political battles. In the First World War the French military provided wine as part of the soldiers' rations during the fighting: they were given up to one liter of wine a day. After the war the French believed that the inclusion of wine in the war effort had helped lead to their success. Moreover, wine was included in international treaties in the twentieth-century. As noted in Rod Phillips' *Short History of Wine*, after the First World War, "the Treaty of Versailles required Germany to import 260,000 hectoliters of French wine each year free of tariffs." So throughout the modern period French wine played a noticeable role in international politics.

Unlike other Western countries in the nineteenth-century, the French government did not regulate drinking to such a great degree. Some attempts at alcohol regulation did exist, however. Temperance advocates in France believed industrial alcohol or spirits caused alcoholism, which was a "new" disease discovered in the mid-nineteenth-century. Moreover, in the late nineteenth-century, as fears of political uprisings grew during the Third Republic, the government increased repression of the café because it suspected cafés and cabarets of being centers of political rebellion. Therefore, nineteenth-century alcohol regulation in France focused on political repression of public spaces where drinking took place.

The United States

Alcohol in the nineteenth-century United States shaped the definitions of leisure, class, gender, and ethnicity. Alcohol consumption rose tremendously in the nineteenth-century. Much like in other industrializing countries, the rise in consumption resulted in part from the working class turning to alcohol to cope with the social upheaval of industrialization. Moreover, the proliferation of saloons facilitated the rise of drinking as the predominant form of leisure. Since most of these establishments catered to men only, and were segregated by class, they helped to define masculinity as well as to solidify working-, middle-, and elite-class boundaries.

Abuse of alcohol also rose in the nineteenth-century. In response, temperance groups spread across the country. Formed by Protestant churches, women, and the middle-class predominantly, these groups made up perhaps the most important reform movement of the era. They sought to "better" the working-class, especially the immigrant working-class, perpetuating ethnic and class prejudices. By the late nineteenth-century temperance groups began to lobby the government to legislate alcohol reform, attempting to co-opt the government into increasing regulations aimed at immigrants and the working-class.

After the turn of the century, temperance groups had succeeded, but like in most countries that tried to legislate prohibition, it did not work. Instead, prohibition led to organized crime, and some argue an increase in alcohol-related diseases. Furthermore, the government began to recognize that an influx of alcohol tax dollars could help bring the country out of the depression.

Industrialization in the United States revolutionized alcohol production. Mechanization of the beer industry in the nineteenth-century perpetuated an increase in the already growing alcohol consumption rates in the United States. In addition to a newly mechanized beer industry, European beer arrived in the United States with the mass immigration of Europeans, especially Germans. Germans brought lager beer to the United States where it began to be produced in the 1840s. By the 1870s lager beer became the most popular beer in the United States, subtly perpetuating cultural miscegenation. The industrialization of the beer industry spread even more rapidly in the late nineteenth century. For example, even though the population of the United States doubled during the period between 1880 and 1910, the production of beer increased four times. Two reasons for the tremendous increase in the production and distribution of beer were refrigeration and the national railroad system.

The number of saloons also rose in the nineteenth-century. By 1870 there were over 100,000 saloons across the country. Many of these saloons were tied to large breweries that came to dominate the industry. Because there were so many saloons, there was stiff competition among them, pushing them to attract customers through illegal activities such as gambling and prostitution.

The sale of alcohol also influenced the advertising industry in the nineteenth century. The alcohol industry began to rely on brand names to sell its products. Most of the advertising for alcohol promoted its health benefits. For example, "Doctor's Special Rum," "The Nourishing Ale," "Hall's Coca Wine," and "Barrett's Stout for invalids" were popularly advertised alcohols. Because the majority of the population was illiterate, advertising took the form of pictures of nurses on the bottles to illustrate their link to health. In addition, the official 1905 *Edition of the United States Pharmacopoeia* included wines and spirits as medicine. By 1916, however, influenced by the temperance movement, the Pharmacopoeial Convention deleted all alcohol from its contents, showing how politics could construct the definition of alcohol.

Along with increased production and trade of alcohol came increased consumption. The consumption of beer dramatically increased during the late nineteenth-century. While statistics from 1863 show that the average per capita consumption of beer was 1.7 gallons, by the 1910s that number had risen to 21 gallons. The growth in the number of saloons partly brought on this increase. Conversely, wine consumption did not rise along with beer. It constituted only 10 percent of the alcohol consumed in the nineteenth-century. Moreover, it tended to be used as medicine or in church ceremonies.

The rise in consumption made drinking the most popular pastime in the United States, defining leisure for many Americans. In agricultural settings before industrialization, people drank alcohol at various times during the day. Work was not separated from home and was bound by agricultural rhythms rather than the clock. During the transition to industrialization family members continued to bring buckets of beer to workers throughout the work day. As industry developed, however, businessmen no longer allowed their employees to drink on the job because of concerns about levels of production. As a result, men stopped by the corner saloon on their way to or from work to drink and socialize with each other. Drinking, then, helped to bracket work and leisure as distinct parts of one's day. The saloon became a focal point for male leisure, helping to create definitions of masculinity that coincided with the new industrial reality. Moreover, by excluding women, saloons perpetuated the stereotype that women who drank in public suffered from loose morals at best, and at worst were prostitutes. The rise of the saloon in the nineteenth-century also helped to shape urban neighborhoods. The corner saloon became a fixture in every urban working-class neighborhood. Furthermore, with the advent of the railroad, saloons appeared along rail routes at railroad stops, helping to define the nature of these stops as social settings rather than merely places to meet trains.

Many different kinds of saloons developed in the late nineteenth-century. Several saloons took out their seats to allow for more customers, forcing men to crowd along the bar, drink quicker, and consume more. In eastern cities many saloons catered almost exclusively to working-class, newly arrived immigrants. The marked increase in immigration by young, single men, especially from Ireland, increased the need for such saloons in their urban slums. Immigrant workers, however, were not the only ones who depended on saloons for leisure. Other groups in society, including the native-born working-class, middle-management, and capitalists all had saloons that catered to them in particular. Working-class saloons were by far the most numerous, however. All these saloons played a major role in solidifying class, gender, and ethnic boundaries in the industrializing United States.

Just as the numbers of saloons and the rates of beer consumption rose in the nineteenth-century, so did the demand for spirits. Statistics show that the consumption levels of spirits by 1830 were 300 percent higher than even those of the late twentieth-century – a highly developed consumer society. This sharp increase reflected the fact that Western grain farmers could more cheaply ship spirits than grain, and thus make more money. Two areas, the western United States and the eastern urban slums, were home to the heaviest consumers of spirits.

The increased use of both beer and spirits and the proliferation of drinking establishments went hand in hand with higher rates of abuse, which, in turn, provoked social and governmental regulation. Social movements aimed at regulating alcohol shaped the nature of nineteenth-century social reform in the United States. Some historians argue that temperance was the largest social movement in nineteenth-century America, larger than even abolition. Temperance movements became so popular that over 500,000 people in the United States pledged temperance or abstinence, and by 1830 over 1,000 temperance groups had been formed. Some temperance groups allowed for medicinal wine, although teetotaler movements did not.

Religious groups, especially the Quakers, were the first to publish anti-drinking tracts. Other religious groups also preached against the "evils" of drink. The American Temperance Society, dominated by evangelical Protestants who had been fired up by the Second Great Awakening, was the first national group. It was founded in Boston in 1826. The most well-known temperance organization was the WCTU or Women's Christian Temperance Union. It had national as well as international influence. The Presbyterian and Methodist Churches also became involved by issuing proclamations against drinking. Many churches at this time also switched to unfermented wine, or grape juice, in their ceremonies because of the temperance influence.

Apart from shaping social reform, temperance movements also influenced the cultural separation of the classes. By the mid nineteenth-century white, middle-class Protestants overwhelmingly supported temperance. They were concerned with the flood of immigration and the drinking habits of those immigrants from Ireland, Scotland, Germany, and later southern Europe. Some historians have argued that the alcohol issue was a way to curb any kind of political power that these new, working-class immigrants might aspire to.

Temperance strategies were numerous. Temperance movements early on urged the government to discontinue its ration to soldiers, and even limit the amount of alcohol soldiers could purchase. Temperance groups also founded temperance towns in many parts of the country, which prohibited drinking within their boundaries. For example, Prohibition Park, New York; Vineland, New Jersey; Harriman, Tennessee; Palo Alto, California; and Demorest, Georgia were all founded as temperance towns.

In the early to mid nineteenth-century the majority of the temperance organizations concentrated on the personal, moral aspects of abuse. Drinkers were seen as morally weak, criminal, or perhaps even insane. Temperance societies wanted to save the drunkard from his problems. Later in the century, however, temperance groups began to focus on prohibition legislation rather than working with the individual drinker. The Anti-Saloon League, a lobby group, put a great deal of pressure on legislatures to pass prohibition. By 1909 seven states had passed prohibition laws and by 1917 half of all of the states had passed prohibition. Seventy-five percent of the states had ratified the prohibition amendment by 1919, and by 1920 the Eighteenth Amendment went into law.

The Eighteenth Amendment legally stopped the "manufacture, sale or transportation of intoxicating liquors." (As quoted in Rothbaum *The Business of Spirits*.) It also had several unintended consequences. It increased organized crime. In fact, some argue that illegal sale of alcohol led to the rise of organized crime in the United States. Also, while some historians argue that prohibition did decrease the amount of alcohol people drank, others argue that it is difficult to know how much people did (or if they did) decrease their consumption because of large-scale bootlegging and the large number of illegal taverns called speakeasies. In some areas the number of bars even increased during prohibition. In New York City, for example, there were twice as many bars during prohibition as there were before prohibition – over 30,000. Moreover, the number of people who died from alcohol related diseases increased during prohibition as well.

By the early 1930s, however, people began to voice their opposition to prohibition. Many groups argued that it violated personal liberties, cost too much to enforce, and led to a big jump in crime, especially organized crime. The government also badly needed the tax revenue from alcohol because of the economic hardship brought on by the depression. Consequently, the Eighteenth Amendment was repealed in 1933. Ending prohibition and subsequently taxing alcohol played an important part in governmental attempts to end the depression.

After the end of prohibition, though, temperance movements did not disappear. One of the most successful social organizations in the twentieth and early twenty-first-centuries has been Alcoholics Anonymous. Rather than advocating for legislative reform, it has worked through meetings that promote the self-restraint of its members. Much like in the nineteenth-century, AA focused on the individual. In contrast to the nineteenth-century, however, it treated alcoholism as a disease rather than a moral failing. The majority in society in the late twentieth century, however, still did not believe in framing alcoholism as a disease.

African Americans and temperance

One of the things that set the United States apart from other Western countries in the nineteenth- and early twentieth-centuries was African slavery and its cultural aftermath. Since temperance was so central in the nineteenth-century, African American responses shed even more light on the role of alcohol in American culture. African Americans involved themselves in the temperance movement as well. Like Catholics in Ireland, many blacks believed that promoting temperance would decrease racism, or dispel the erroneous stereotype that black men were drunkards. In fact, American black temperance advocates were even invited to Ireland to lecture to groups of people on both temperance and abolition. Before emancipation, many free blacks, including leaders such as Frederick Douglass, preached temperance for slaves, infusing anti-alcohol sentiment into the abolition movement. These leaders argued that drinking among slaves dulled their desires for freedom, and thus worked against abolition, while abstinence among slaves would be an effective threat to slave owners. White slave owners also believed in abstinence, but for different reasons. They believed that inebriation among black slaves would lead to rebellion, and thus wanted to curb drinking among blacks. There is little evidence, however, that there were any problems with drunkenness among slaves.

During reconstruction the temperance movement in relation to race changed. Racism increased and the fear of drunken free blacks fed into a growing post-emancipation form of racism. The fear of alcohol consumption among blacks became a tool used during Jim Crow to support racism. In fact, the stereotype of African American alcohol abuse was used in many states to deny blacks their right to vote. African American temperance movements continued to argue against drinking after emancipation, but instead of blaming the drinker for alcohol problems, they blamed the system. Frederick Douglass argued that poverty, racism, and exploitation of the working class led to excessive drinking, rather than the other way around. He also argued that abstinence by free blacks would lead to social betterment. As blacks migrated to northern cities, however, they moved into African American urban communities that had their own, very popular, segregated alcohol leisure industry. So social drinking became a significant part of the cultural identity of northern blacks after the turn of the century. Temperance ideology and alcohol stereotypes, however, continued to influence definitions of race, ethnicity, and class in the United States into the twenty-first-century.

Japan

Two non-Western areas, Japan and Russia, industrialized later than Western countries, yet provide the best comparisons to Western industrialization. Called late-comer industrializers, these two areas also had to respond to changes in alcohol production, trade, consumption, and regulation.

Even though Japan developed industrially, and felt the infiltration of Western culture, it successfully held onto emblematic aspects of Japanese culture through maintaining ritualized drinking habits that structured both festivals and social occasions. Western alcohol, such as beer and wine, however, did flood into Japan with the proliferation of restaurants that accompanied industrialization, spreading Western culture to an elite segment of Japanese society.

In Japan during the Meiji period, 1868–1912, the most important alcoholic beverage was sake. Sake remained dominant during the industrializing period, and even with the rise of mass production, people still brewed sake at home. It was customary for people to drink home-brewed sake during festivals and ceremonial occasions, as drinking remained much more ritualized in Japan than it was in the West. For example, sake shaped marriage rituals. To signify a woman's move from her parents' to her husband's house she took a symbolic last drink of sake with her family before she left. Other ritualized drinking took place at dinner parties. The ritual required the host to offer one filled sake glass to a guest. After drinking the sake the guest would wash out the sake glass in a water basin and return the cup to the host. This went on throughout the dinner party with guest after guest, keeping to the tradition that one never served oneself.

As sake breweries sprang up in the cities people began to buy sake by the bottle and drink more at each sitting, which increased alcohol use. This pattern of heavier drinking spread to the countryside with the opening of village taverns. Moreover, as restaurants spread during the Meiji era, so did the availability of sake when people dined out. Western restaurants spread too. They, however, served beer and wine, which increased the popularity of these Western drinks and became a piece of the cultural Westernization that took place during Japanese industrialization. As a result of increased drinking there arose a Japanese Temperance Society in 1884, but it was not until 1922 that laws forbidding minors from drinking alcohol were enacted. Temperance did not have as much of an impact in Japan as it did in the West, however.

Russia

Alcohol in Russia structured social rituals, influenced medicine and bolstered both the economy and the government. Russians, especially Russian males, consumed large amounts of alcohol, making the alcohol trade one of the most profitable in nineteenth-century Russia. Numerous alcohol rituals structured Russian culture, and alcohol taxes during many decades in the nineteenth-century provided the vast majority of the government's budget. Abuse did lead to a half-hearted attempt at prohibition in the early twentieth-century, which failed because the new communist government could not survive without alcohol tax revenues and because the Russian people depended upon alcohol to structure many parts of their lives.

Vodka was the most important alcohol consumed in Russia during industrialization. Vodka comes from the Slavic word for water, which indicates how common it was in Russian culture. Vodka was introduced into Russian society in the sixteenth-century and continued to be society's preferred drink. Vodka was so popular that it accounted for over 20 per cent of all internal Russian trade in the nineteenth-century. Because it was such a widely desired commodity, its industrial production became an important aspect of industrialization in Russia. With its mass production, vodka consumption levels rose as well. In addition to its economic importance, vodka also played a central social and cultural role in Russian society. Births, deaths, marriages, and other important social occasions were marked with vodka. Russians also believed in the power of vodka to cure ills, using it in medicinal ways such as soaking one's aching feet or rubbing it on one's head for a headache.

The regulation of alcohol in Russia predominantly took the form of taxation. The Russian government relied upon vodka taxes, which provided nearly 10 percent of government revenues in the eighteenth-century, and by the nineteenth-century over 30 percent. Moreover, by the middle of the nineteenth-century, the Russian government was funding most and sometimes all defense spending through vodka excise taxes. In 1894 the government declared a monopoly on the sale of alcohol, indicating its value for the governmental budget. Abuse of vodka rose in the nineteenth-century as well, and by 1914 the Russian government instated prohibition. This lasted until 1923 but only covered the retail sale of alcohol. Alcohol could still be served in restaurants, so prohibition was not as all encompassing as it was in the United States for example. Even limited prohibition failed, however. Russians continued to illegally consume alcohol, and since the government suffered from a precipitous drop in tax revenues, it could no longer support prohibition.

Conclusion

Comparing alcohol across eighteenth- and nineteenth-century industrializing countries in the West and beyond illuminates commonalities brought on by industrialization, but also shows how culture in each society mediated the industrial influence. First, the mechanization of alcohol production and modernization of trade in Britain, France, the United States, and Russia made beer and distilled liquor available to a greater number of people and facilitated a change in the nature of leisure. More alcohol fed the growing demand by the working class, allowing them a social outlet and providing them with the most popular way to cope with the social upheavals of industrialization. Second, industrialization of the production of alcohol also facilitated the rise in consumption across several societies including Britain, Ireland, France, the United States, Japan, and Russia. Increased consumption led to higher rates of abuse, thus alcohol abuse became a significant cultural phenomenon associated with industrialization.

Third, pubs in Britain and Ireland, saloons in the United States, and cafés and cabarets in France all provided a public space to socialize away from home and work. These spaces led the way in solidifying the separation of work, home, and leisure. Fourth, class-based establishments in Britain, Ireland, France, and the United States helped to create distinct working-class, middle-class, and elite cultural identities in all those Western societies. Moreover, in the United

States ethnic prejudice and racism led several working-class saloons to cater mainly to immigrants, and drinking establishments in northern, urban, black neighborhoods to accommodate African Americans alone. Fifth, most of the drinking establishments in Britain, Ireland, and the United States served men and excluded women, creating new definitions of masculinity and indeed appropriate femininity in the industrial period. In contrast, however, in France the café catered to both men and women, which helped perpetuate a gender identity that was more expansive for women than in the other Western, industrializing countries.

While overall alcohol consumption habits changed during industrialization, some forms of alcohol use did not. First, across many societies alcohol continued to be consumed as medicine. In Britain, Ireland, France, the United States, and Russia alcohol remained a key ingredient in medicine as these societies still believed in its curative properties well into the twentieth-century. Second, in the non-Western society of Japan, traditional, ritual consumption practices persisted even in the face of industrialization and Western influence, allowing the Japanese to hold onto their culture in their daily practices.

The virtually universal rise in alcohol use accompanying industrialization brought on higher levels of abuse, which, in turn, led to more social and cultural problems that then gave rise to regulation by the state as well as civic groups. First, the pharmacological effects of spirits over that of fermented alcohol caused greater physical and social problems associated with abuse across many societies including Britain, Ireland, France, the United States, and Russia. Second, governments and reform movements across many societies including Great Britain, Ireland, and the United States mainly focused on abuse by the working-class and ethnic minorities. Reform movements provided a way for middle-class, white reformers to manage their fear of the increase in ethnic immigration and their need to socially control the growing working-class and the ethnically marginalized. Second, governments relied upon the alcohol taxes to make a measurable difference in their revenues. For many countries including Ireland, the United States, and Russia, alcohol taxes provided a significant percentage of all government income. Third, temperance movements were most prevalent in Protestant-dominated societies such as Britain, Ireland (dominated by the Protestant minority), and the United States, while in the non-Protestant societies of France, Japan, and Russia, temperance groups were not as strong during this period. The Protestant ideology of self-restraint fed temperance ideology, which sought to control the seemingly out-of-control drinker, usually belonging to the working-class. At the same time, however, some oppressed groups in societies, for example, Catholics in Ireland and African Americans in the United States, embraced temperance as a tool to prove their respectability to the rest of society. So temperance movements could be used as tools of the socially dominant to further racism and class prejudice, but could also be used as tools of the oppressed to combat prejudice.

Fourth, Western as well as non-Western countries instituted some form of prohibition in the early twentieth-century. Complete prohibition existed in the United States, while prohibition of the retail sale of alcohol existed in Russia. Britain and Japan passed laws barring minors from drinking, and France repressively regulated the café. Yet the centrality of alcohol to society thwarted prohibition efforts everywhere. Fifth, temperance groups in the West professed to care about the health and welfare of the working-classes, yet certain subtexts existed. For example, in France the government feared socialist political movements that arose in pubs and cafés; in Ireland the Protestant minority feared the Catholic majority; in the United States the middle-class feared an increase in political power of African Americans and immigrants; and in all areas capitalists desired more productive workers.

Industrialization in the eighteenth-, nineteenth-, and early twentieth-centuries modernized the alcohol industry. As a result, the new modes of production and trade led to both an increase and a change in the nature of consumption. Consumption patterns shaped leisure as well as class, gender, and ethnic identities. The increase in consumption brought about temperance, and in some cases prohibition, which failed, leading the way to increased acceptance of alcohol consumption in the twentieth-century.

Further reading

Antsie, F. 1877. *On the Uses of Wine in Health and Disease.* London: Macmillan.

Barrows, S. and R. Room. (eds.) 1991. *Drinking Behavior and Belief in Modern History.* Berkeley: University of California Press.

Duis, P. R. 1983. *The Saloon: Public Drinking in Chicago and Boston 1880–1920.* Urbana: University of Illinois Press.

"Ethnography, Alcohol, and South-Central European Societies." 1984. Special issue. *East European Quarterly.* 18 (4): 385–519.

Forbes, R. J. 1948. *Short History of the Art of Distillation: from the Beginnings up to the Death of Cellier Blumenthal.* Leiden: E. J. Brill.

Gordon, E. 1913. *The Anti-Alcohol Movement in Europe.* New York: Fleming H. Revell Company.

Gutzke, D. W. 2006. *Pubs and Progressives: Reinventing the Public House in England, 1896–1960.* Dekalb: Northern Illinois University Press.

Haine, W. S. 1996. *The World of the Paris Café, Sociability Among the French Working Class, 1789–1914.* Baltimore, MD: Johns Hopkins University Press.

Kunio, Y. 1957. *Japanese Manners and Customs in the Meiji Era.* Trans. C. S. Terry. Tokyo: Obunsha.

Malcolm, E. 1986. "Ireland Sober, Ireland Free." In *Drink and Temperance in Nineteenth-Century Ireland.* Syracuse: Syracuse University Press.

Mehta, J. N. n.d. *Alcohol and State Revenue.* New Delhi: All India Prohibition Council.

Okrent, D. 2010. *Last Call: The Rise and Fall of Prohibition.* New York: Scribner.

Phillips, R. 2000. *A Short History of Wine.* New York: Harper Collins.

Rumbarger, J. J. 1989. *Profits, Power, and Prohibition: Alcohol Reform and the Industrializing of America, 1800–1930.* Albany: State University of New York Press.

Watney, J. 1974. *Beer is Best: A History of Beer.* London: Peter Owen.

6 Imperialism and alcohol in the nineteenth- and early twentieth-centuries

The second great wave of colonialism in the eighteenth- and nineteenth-centuries changed the world's political map, especially in Africa, South Asia, and Australia. Industrialization and attendant technological advances in the West facilitated nineteenth-century colonialism. European countries including Britain, France, the Netherlands, Germany, and Belgium all divided up the continent of Africa under their own flags. Most of Africa was colonized in the late nineteenth-century and did not become independent countries until the mid-twentieth century. As an exception, South Africa became independent much earlier than most African countries but remained under oppressive white minority rule until the end of the twentieth-century. On another continent the British began to consolidate their rule in India in the 1700s, which lasted until that country's independence in 1947. In yet another part of the world the British colonized Australia in the eighteenth-century and colonization there lasted until 1901 when Australia became a commonwealth. Colonialism radically changed the lives of the indigenous people in Africa, India, and Australia. In respect to alcohol, new kinds of alcohols began to be produced in the colonies while traditional, indigenous beers continued to be made. The international alcohol trade grew and the alcohol trade within the colonies increased exponentially, which brought great wealth to some and serious social problems to others. Consumption of alcohol both by the colonizers and serious the colonized skyrocketed, resulting in regulations that became one of the tools used by governments to oppress indigenous populations in these colonized areas.

Africa

The very diverse African continent was home to many different modes of alcohol production, trade, consumption, and regulation during the colonial period. Yet similar experiences characterized many cultures. Alcohol structured the lives of native Africans. It anchored their belief systems, sometimes providing the most visible way to retain their native culture in the face of colonialism. Alcohol set in motion work parties, brought together families in marriage, maintained social hierarchies, and defined the daily African diet. Alcohol production constructed gender identity; in most areas of Africa women exclusively made beer, and in other societies only men controlled that task.

As the Europeans infiltrated Africa, alcohol consumption rose. The colonists socialized in white only pubs, publicly setting them apart from and demonstrating their racial superiority to native Africans. The large public works projects such as mining brought together thousands of native laborers, creating a high demand for alcohol. As a result, indigenous women beermakers earned their own money selling to the miners, gaining economic independence from their husbands and upsetting traditional gender roles. In growing urban areas alcohol also defined society's idea of appropriate gender roles. Women's public consumption of alcohol now labeled them as loose or even as prostitutes. The change in alcohol patterns not only disrupted women's roles, but it also upset the male social hierarchy. Young men earned money in the new economy, which gave them access to alcohol, a culturally significant good that had been strictly controlled by elders. Moreover, alcohol ushered in Westernization as native African men began to drink Western beer in pubs as a new form of leisure.

Native African leaders saw new patterns of alcohol consumption as a powerful symbol of colonialism, and as a major cause of the social disintegration that plagued the indigenous populations. They tried, mostly in vain, to regulate it. Colonial governments, however, were lukewarm at best to the kind of alcohol regulations that would result in fewer taxes, since in many colonies alcohol taxes were the largest contributor to their budgets. White controlled governments used alcohol as a powerful tool to subjugate black Africans. The highly regulated black–only beer hall system in South Africa was widely recognized as a pillar of apartheid. It is not surprising, then, that control over alcohol became a major component of many independence movements across the continent.

The production of beer in Africa was so central to native cultures that Africans embedded it in their mythology. Kofyar legends from Nigeria, for example, related that their mythical cultural hero founded villages in the places where he stopped to brew beer. The actual production of beer in Africa goes back millennia. Africans in Western and Southern Africa used two staple grain, millet and sorghum to produce beer. Much later when colonists arrived and began growing a particular kind of corn, or a variety of sorghum, it became an important staple in the production of beer. Keith H. Steinkraus in *Fermented Food Beverages in Nutrition* describes the entire process of making this beer. One first steeped the grain for six to 36 hours, then germinated it by laying it out for four to six days while periodically moistening it. Next the grain was dried in the sun. The producer then made a mash of it by putting it in hot water, which caused it to sour. The mixture was then boiled. Malt was added and then the beer was cooled. It was ready in four to eight hours. Across Africa people brewed beer in similar ways, using a variety of ingredients, and in each area beer provided an important nutritional staple as well as a way to mark social and ceremonial events.

In most areas in Africa women brewed beer. In Zambia, for example, women brewed many types of traditional beers. Women brewed "work beer" for work parties that cleared trees, prepared gardens, weeded, built houses, or thatched roofs. Women also prepared "ceremonial beer" for important transitions in life such as births and deaths. Immediately after death women brewed "first beer". It symbolically cleansed the relatives of the pollution from their contact with the dead. Women then prepared a "second beer" three months after the death. It served to pay respect to the deceased and to determine inheritance. If harvests were bad and beer was in short supply, women might make "secret beer" for a privileged elder of the village who asked for it. Finally, women made "political beer". Those running for office sent this beer around to village leaders in order to garner support. Beer production gave women an essential role in the social, cultural, and political life of the village.

In Tanzania men made beer. Banana beer was the staple beer in this area. Men made banana beer from a particular kind of banana that was ripened by hanging it upside down over the hearth, or burying it in the ground for several days. During that time the fermentation process began. Later, men placed the bananas in dug-out wooden troughs with dried grasses and stomped on them in order to make a mash. The beer makers then added dried sorghum to the mixture, covered it in banana leaves, and left it to ferment for 24 hours. The beer was then ready to drink. Beer making in Tanzania as well as across Africa was a basic responsibility in villages because beer was essential to diets and cultural practices. Therefore, gender-specific production of beer, like in Zambia and Tanzania, helped to define masculine and feminine gender roles. Whoever produced beer not only fed the community, but also reproduced one of society's vital pieces of material culture.

Alcohol as an international trade item dated back to the first interactions between Africans and Europeans. During the 300 years of the Atlantic slave trade European alcohol purchased a significant percentage of those Africans sold into slavery. Alcohol became an even more valuable trade item between Africa and the West during the African colonial period, between the late nineteenth-century and the middle of the twentieth-century. Along with guns, alcohol was one of the commodities that the West, particularly the British, traded for raw materials in Western Africa. African raw materials garnered from the alcohol trade helped further the industrial revolution in the West. Furthermore, the alcohol industry in Western Europe depended upon the colonial markets in Africa in order to survive.

As demand for alcohol in Africa increased during the colonial period, more alcohol began to be produced in the colonies, and sold especially to the colonists. Moreover, alcohol venues, for both domestic and imported alcohol, proliferated. In Angola, for example, alcohol sales provided entrepreneurial opportunities for many colonists. European merchants opened taverns and quickly became rich as a result. Immigrants drank large quantities of alcohol because these taverns were practically the only leisure establishments available for the Angolan settlers. Taverns became so numerous in the nineteenth-century that in Luanda there was a tavern for every 34 inhabitants. In Zambia, like Angola, the alcohol trade exploded. The settlers in Zambia drank copious amounts of alcohol in pubs. In Angola and Zambia, like in many other areas in Africa, alcohol consumption in public establishments became the predominant symbol of leisure for the colonists, mimicking patterns in the industrializing West.

Native Africans, too, were affected by alcohol in the cash economy. In the gold mines of South Africa alcohol itself became currency. The mine owners often paid African workers with domestically produced alcohol. It gave the Boer settlers a market for their grain and provided a cheap way to pay the miners. Using alcohol as pay drastically increased alcohol use by the miners and decreased the amount of income they could bring home to their families, thus hurting their relationships with their families and villages. For many South African miners alcohol shaped their experience in the market economy.

The sizeable increase in demand for alcohol led to the commodification of indigenous beer. In many regions women were the primary producers of beer, so they used their skills to move into the market economy. Therefore, in addition to making beer for ceremonial and social events, they began to make beer to sell. Women had this opportunity particularly in mining areas in South Africa where large populations of single men had currency to buy beer. As women made money they no longer had to depend upon their husbands, who, in many cases, had numerous wives also vying for support. Women spent their newfound earnings on their children. For example, they sent their children to school, influencing the next generation of Africans. Women's involvement in alcohol sales not only allowed their independence from their husbands, but also changed levels of literacy in Africa, especially among girls.

In Zambia, like in South Africa, brewing beer became a way for women to make money. Women sold beer to the locals or to those traveling through the newly constructed roads leading to the mines. Much of their locally produced beer was sold out of taverns called "shebeens." These small, makeshift bars were in a woman's own home, and accounted for most of the alcohol sales in rural areas. Alcohol brought in more revenue than food or other items because it was so popular among the men who were now earning money as wage laborers. Women's economic independence in many areas in Africa rested upon their ability to sell alcohol for money.

Many Africans consumed beer for nutritional reasons. Indigenous beer remained an important dietary supplement for native Africans. For example, sorghum beer augmented the diets of many rural South Africans, especially the lower class. Workmen drank as much as five pints per day. Thirty-five percent of a worker's calories came from locally made beer. The beer contained important nutrients such as thiamine, riboflavin, and nicotinic acid. Even infants in South Africa were fed the dregs of the beer, which contained nutrients as well. In southern Nigeria millions of people continued to drink indigenous alcohol as part of their diets. People drank at least half a liter per day of palm wine because it was such an important part of their nutritional intake. Half a liter contained over 300 calories, vitamins, protein, riboflavin, and vitamin B. In Tanzania, daily moderate consumption of banana beer was considered essential to a balanced diet and was even thought to bring on sexual potency in men. Alcohol as food helped make possible the survival of tens of thousands of Africans.

During colonization the consumption of alcohol by indigenous Africans rose dramatically, however. In Zambia, traditional beer called chibuku began to be mass produced, and along with the proliferation of municipal taverns caused an escalation in drinking. Now strangers were more likely to drink together in taverns, and binge drinking became more common, which many times led to fights. Moreover, new kinds of more potent alcohol, spirits, were introduced in many areas of Africa and thus made intoxication easier. The habit of drinking for leisure by indigenous Africans increased the amounts and frequency of their drinking. As a result, the abuse of alcohol escalated. Many authors argue that alcohol consumption increased during the colonial period because Africans used alcohol as a means of escape from the tremendous social upheaval that colonialism caused in the society.

Not only did an increase in consumption of alcohol by indigenous Africans occur, but also the demographics of those who drank alcohol changed. As young men moved into the cash economy in urban areas they now had more access to alcohol because they could use their earnings to buy it. Moreover, with the mass production of beer, many young men began to drink bottled instead of indigenous beer because it signified one's entrance into the middle class and independence from the male elders in one's home village. In southern Ghana, for example, prior to colonization, male elders controlled the distribution and consumption of palm wine, the primary alcoholic drink and a symbolically powerful example of material culture. Palm wine was essential in many ritual and ceremonial activities within the culture. Elders controlled the land on which the palms grew, and most importantly, they controlled the culturally powerful alcohol produced from it that brought access to women.

Once young men in the villages began to have their own money after migrating to the gold coast to work in the cash economy, they increasingly balked at village rules and began to drink in public for leisure. They were able to challenge the power of the elders in a profound way through their ability to buy and consume alcohol. Moreover, most of the young males migrated only temporarily to the city and then returned to their rural homes with enough capital to buy their own land, and therefore control their own access to alcohol and women. Their ability to consume such a symbolically powerful commodity of their own accord severely weakened the power of the male elders. This generational change in access to alcohol helped to rupture the traditional male social hierarchy in Southern Ghana.

Unlike men, women did not have the option of buying and publicly consuming alcohol for the sake of leisure. Just as in many Western societies if women drank in commercial establishments society assumed they were prostitutes. Husbands and wives rarely drank together in public because it was commonly assumed that when men went out to drink they were often looking for extra-marital sex. Westernization brought with it leisure in the form of drinking in public establishments. Public leisure drinking by men solidified the connection between alcohol and women's socially unacceptable sexual conduct, effectively curtailing women's freedom in urban Africa.

Not all African culture was dominated by Western concepts of alcohol and leisure in the cash economy. In rural Western Africa, for example, the Kofyar, who were farmers in northern Nigeria, continued to define much of their social and spiritual life through the use of beer. In eastern Africa the Iteso tribe of Kenya continued to use alcohol in ritual and ceremonial ways, and in Tanzania, the rural Haya people of the Lesser Kyamutwara Kingdom continued to use banana beer for social and religious purposes. These groups and many more like them continued to use beer as a medium to frame their cultural practices. Many vital and social customs depended upon the use of beer. First and foremost beer remained indispensable for ancestor worship and funeral ceremonies. Second, beer continued to strengthen social, family, and gender hierarchies within villages. Third, beer prevailed as currency in tribute practices, and finally it continued to structure marriage and family ceremonies.

Ritual use of beer dominated the practice of ancestor worship in many African societies. In Nigeria, for example, descendents broke beer jars and blew beer over the graves of their ancestors. In Tanzania every man had to offer beer to the alter of his deceased father before drinking it himself. Moreover, the head of the family offered banana beer to the ancestors in return for the health of his family and the fertility of his wife or wives. Even the king in Tanzanian society ritually provided banana beer to the ancestors. In Zambia a critical rite of passage for a newly married woman included making and then offering to make beer for her husband's and her own ancestors, furthermore during any kind of ritual drinking people offered beer to the spirits before they drank it themselves. In funeral rituals in Zambia an appointed person took a sip of homemade beer in front of the entire village, spit it on the grave, and prayed to the spirit of the deceased for the well-being of the village. All of these societies depended upon beer to shape the most significant of ceremonies in their cultures, those that honored the dead. The Iteso tribe in Kenya gave their deceased five funerals over a period of many years, with beer as a central ingredient in those ceremonies.

Indigenous beer also played a key role in solidifying social hierarchies within the village, the family, and between men and women. In Tanzania a village member, usually the village leader, obligatorily provided banana beer at festivals in exchange for the loyalty of others in the community, reinforcing the village hierarchy. The king of the Asante people in what is now Ghana supplied free alcohol to his people as they celebrated the Odwira festival. The hierarchy in Asante society was loosened because slaves and women drank freely. At the end of the festival, however, social order returned and the elders regained control over who had access to alcohol. The temporary suspension of drinking protocol sanctioned by the elite served to reinforce the normally strict social hierarchy within the kingdom by highlighting the exeptionalism of the festival. Ceremonial alcohol use was one of the predominant ways to keep social hierarchies in balance.

Family, generational, and gender hierarchies were reinforced with the ceremonial consumption of beer. In the Iteso tribe in Kenya families reinforced family hierarchies by drinking beer together. The family sat together around a communal vessel, each with a specifically defined place, and drank beer from shared straws in a predetermined order. When families entertained kin they also had to sit in specific places. Parents and children of the hosts sat on the right side, while grandparents, grandchildren, siblings, and the hosts sat on the left side. In addition, one could not share drinking straws with one's parents-in-law, unless the wife had prepared the beer specifically for her father-in-law and he then asked her to drink first. In Tanzania every man who made banana beer had to offer the first drink of that beer to his father. Generational hierarchies were reinforced through rules surrounding drinking as well. In Kenya, the Iteso tribe demonstrated the high respect paid to elders of the village by the practice of allowing elders to drink beer whenever and wherever they wished. Drinking practices solidified gender differences in many parts of rural Africa, too. In Tanzania, for example, men commonly drank beer out of long-necked calabashes using a reed straw, while women were only allowed to drink beer out of short-necked calabashes and were not allowed to use a straw. All of these highly ritualized customs demonstrated alcohol's crucial role in maintaining social order within communities across Africa.

In many parts of rural Africa the high value of beer made it a kind of currency. In South Africa, for example, within native villages, beer was used to gather work parties for individual or community projects. More workers could be convinced to help when alcohol was the reward, rather than when food was offered. In Nigeria villages paid medicine men with beer. And in Tanzania kings were given beer as tribute. Beer as currency even for kings reflects its status in rural societies in Africa.

Beer also was a vital part of marriage ceremonies and other family rituals. In Zambia, the bride and groom's relatives both poured beer at the entryway to the couple's house to symbolize the coming together of the two lineages, as well as the joining of "field" and "hearth". In Tanzania the exchange of banana beer was expected during marriage negotiations between families. In another family ceremony beer was used to choose a baby's name in the Iteso tribe in Kenya. The family chose a name and then the grandmother tested out the name by offering beer on her finger to the baby. If the baby drank the beer, the chosen name was accepted. If the baby rejected the beer, the process started again. Families depended upon the symbolic power of beer to give power to their important rites of passage. In all of these ways, ancestor worship, social and family hierarchy reinforcement, tribute, and marriage and family rituals, Africans used beer to hold onto their culture in the face of colonialism.

Although traditional patterns of alcohol use persisted in many rural areas, overall drinking increased tremendously across Africa, and, as a result, regulation followed. Africans themselves tried to have the importation of alcohol banned. At the Berlin Conference in 1884 and again at the 1889 Brussels Conference, African leaders lobbied for a ban on alcohol trafficking. At the 1889 conference both the importation of European alcohol as well as the indigenous distillation of alcohol were banned between the parallels of 20 degrees north and 22 degrees south. During the Sixth International Congress on Alcohol Abuse in Brussels in 1897, Bishop Oluwole, representing Nigeria, argued that the importation of spirits was crippling Nigeria. He wanted Nigeria to begin to import more useful items for the development of the country. He argued that alcohol increased crime and brought other social problems to the capital, Lagos. These regulations on alcohol strove to keep native Africans, not European settlers, from drinking. The international community realized the powerful effect alcohol was having on the African people.

The concern over alcohol abuse by native Africans was so widespread that it became one of the major topics in the Peace Accords following the First World War. One of the agreements in 1919 regulated the liquor trade in Africa, both the international trade as well as the manufacture of alcohol in the colonies. The treaty, signed at St. Germain-en-Laye in 1919, prohibited "the importation, trade, and possession of trade spirits of every kind and beverages mixed with these spirits in the entire African continent with the exception of some countries in North Africa and the Union of South Africa." (From Marcus Grant *Alcohol and Emerging Markets: Patterns, Problems, and Responses.*) International leaders chose to control the influx of alcohol into Africa because they recognized the power it had to disrupt the social and political stability on the continent as well as ruin the lives of those who abused it. While perhaps well meaning, alcohol regulations fostered the strict racial hierarchy that developed with colonialism across Africa because these laws were aimed at the native population.

International agreements aside, the colonial governments themselves were ambivalent about the alcohol trade. On the one hand, they gained considerable income from taxes, tariffs, and licenses, on the other hand, however, they, along with Christian missionaries, wanted to control the consumption habits of native Africans. In colonial Nigeria, for example, liquor taxes provided the bulk of the fiscal support for the colonial government, up to 75 percent. Many in Nigeria believed there to be serious problems with alcohol abuse, however. In South Africa early policies allowed for miners to be paid in alcohol as an incentive to continue working in the mines. White South Africans, however, began to believe that alcohol consumption by the workers lowered worker productivity. As a result, in 1897 the government prohibited blacks from drinking alcohol. Some capitalists, however, wanted to be able to entice workers with the promise of alcohol. Consequently, the government passed a law in 1898 allowing native Africans to drink, but only if they were working for a white employer. This law gave whites much more control over the labor of the blacks, the majority of whom wanted to be able to drink. Furthermore, in 1908 the government formed a monopoly on beer, creating a highly regulated beerhall system. Beerhalls became the only legal place where black Africans could drink. High barbed wire fences surrounded many of these beerhalls and native South Africans likened the experience to "drinking in a cage." Moreover, the beer was much more expensive than homemade beer, thus a higher percentage of workers' incomes went to alcohol and not to family necessities.

The beerhalls came to be the preeminent representation of the racist policies of the government. Therefore, rioting against the beerhalls became a direct affront against the government. And people did riot. Not only did they riot, but they also successfully boycotted the beerhalls. In 1929 a year-long boycott by one of the unions caused the government to lose significant income. By mid century the beerhalls were one of the major symbols of apartheid, so much so that in 1976 during anti-apartheid riots many beerhalls were burnt to the ground. Women, especially, rioted against the beerhall system because of the tremendous loss of income they caused. The beerhalls competed with their primary form of livelihood, selling alcohol out of small storefronts connected to their homes.

Eliminating the "shebeens," or the outlets for homemade beer run by women, became another strategy for controlling indigenous alcohol consumption. Women continued to make and sell beer, however, even in the face of continuous raids by the South African police. Many raids on shebeens turned violent. Officials saw their very existence as a major affront to the government. During one raid in 1960 nine policemen were killed and as a result the government outlawed the ANC (African National Congress), the most important bulwark against apartheid. The illegal manufacture and sale of liquor by women in shebeens became a major political statement against the repressive practices of the government. Control over the consumption of alcohol became one of the symbols of freedom by black South Africans.

In Zambia, like in South Africa, the government believed that native Africans needed to be controlled, and they limited access to alcohol to do so. The colonial rulers believed that Africans were prone to drunkenness and unruly behavior, particularly sexually, and thus needed extra rules regarding liquor – especially spirits. In 1930 the Native Beer Ordinance, or the Traditional Beer Act, regulated both where and what native Zambians could drink. The colonial government made it illegal for native Africans to drink any beverage other than home-brewed beer. Moreover, the government prohibited native Africans from making home-brewed beer in urban areas. Instead, the government took over the production of homebrew in the cities, tightening their hold over alcohol even more. Furthermore, the government began to require women who made beer in rural areas to buy special permits. In the cities the government established beerhalls. These beerhalls were meant to control drinking particularly by copper miners who lived in dorms while working in the mines. Away from their families, and with some disposable income, the miners wanted to spend their leisure time drinking. The government, however, sought to extend their control over the miners by regulating their free time. Control over drinking embodied the oppressive racial policies of the colonial government in Zambia.

As nationalist movements rose after the Second World War, however, Zambians began to fight for more autonomy over their own alcohol consumption. The African Representative Council, which was formed in 1946, gave Zambians the right to vote on issues surrounding alcohol. Zambians voted that they should be able to buy European bottled beer and wine. The government implemented the new regulations within two years. Not all laws changed, however. Whites still did not allow "mixed" drinking, which was drinking by blacks and whites in the same place; the women who traditionally made beer still did not have the right to make and sell beer where they pleased; and finally, the hated beerhalls still existed. The changes had made only small steps toward more freedom for Zambians.

The ability to choose what and where they drank was only part of the movement toward personal independence for Zambians. Zambian women fought the colonial government to regain their traditional place as beer producers. Beer making was central to their identity and economic independence. As a result, they created one of the largest pre-independence demonstrations in Zambia, the 1954 beer riots. "More than two thousand women were involved, many with babies on their backs; they were tear-gassed and clubbed by the police for protesting the regulations that prohibited brewing and sale in towns." (In Alan Haworth "Zambia" in *International Handbook on Alcohol and Culture*.) Even after Zambian independence in 1964, however, women still did not have the right to brew and sell traditional beers in town. The new government closed the hated beerhalls, yet ironically, men set up "tea rooms" that sold beer, again usurping the power of Zambian women. Colonization had set in motion the appropriation of traditional power enjoyed by Zambian women. Alcohol production was central to that power. Even after independence the vestiges of colonialism remained in the form of gender bias against women selling alcohol.

Much like similar laws in South Africa and Zambia, the colonial government of Nigeria formulated policies to control alcohol. In 1920 it instated high duties on the alcohol trade and a licensing system for alcohol outlets. Next it called for prohibition in some parts of Nigeria, particularly in the Muslim north. Furthermore, in public establishments the government tried to substitute light beer for the imported high-alcohol spirits. Finally, the government wanted to control the tapping of oil-palm trees used to make palm wine, and to prohibit local distillation of spirits. The government aimed these directives at native Nigerians in an attempt to further control their behavior. These rules lasted until the Second World War when the government legalized the distillation and sale of local alcohol in response to growing nationalist movements. The nationalists subsequently took control of the alcohol trade, which they saw as a major symbol of independence.

In Ghana, indigenous leaders and the British colonial authorities vied for control of alcohol. Alcohol policy became a central bargaining piece between the two groups in their constant negotiations over the extent of colonial rule. Chiefs and other elders concurred with the colonial government that alcohol needed to be regulated, but for two very different reasons. The elders were particularly concerned with the increased availability of it to young men. The availability caused an upheaval in the social order in the villages because young men had previously had little power over their own alcohol consumption. Yet with their move into the market economy they were able to buy their own alcohol without permission from the elders. The government allowed the tribal chiefs some control over access to liquor by younger men as long as the government continued to earn tax revenues from the liquor trade. In this way the goals of the elders, to maintain the social hierarchy, dovetailed with the goals of the colonial government, to profit from the liquor trade. Nevertheless, the elders eventually lost their power. The colonial government still profited from alcohol sales to younger, wealthier men, however.

Some of the largest tax revenues came from the liquor trade in Ghana. In fact, alcohol taxes became crucial to the success of the British colonial government there. To boost tax revenues, the colonial government even allowed an increase in the number of liquor establishments. Ironically, these establishments became centers for political unrest as nationalist groups began agitating for independence. The liquor trade in Ghana financially propped up the colonial government on the one hand, while, on the other hand, alcohol venues became centers for organizations that led to the government's eventual downfall.

India

Colonial India witnessed skyrocketing alcohol consumption as the British brought both their alcohol and their drinking habits with them to the continent. Drinking alcohol, especially Western alcohol, became a symbol of Westernization for middle- and upper-class Indians. While native leaders voiced their concerns regarding rising consumption rates, the colonial government heavily relied on alcohol taxes to fund its treasury. As a result, the nationalist movements toward the end of the nineteenth- and beginning of the twentieth-centuries saw temperance, even abstinence, as a hallmark of the rejection of British rule. Unfortunately, alcohol had become such a central feature of Indian life as a status symbol for the rich, and as a crucial revenue for the independent governments, that its attempted prohibition failed.

The British introduced Scotch whiskey to India during the early colonial period. Drinking it became a status symbol for the rich and Westernized. Western drinking habits became a potent symbol of the British ability to infuse Western culture into the Indian subcontinent and a repudiation of Muslim and Vedic Hindu traditions. Middle-class Indians who were enamored of the British, especially those who were educated in the colonial system, began to drink more alcohol in general. As a result, Indian importation of alcohol increased by 900 percent between 1875 and 1928. The trade in liquors increased so much so that by the late nineteenth-century every village market had a designated space for the sale of spirits.

The British government regulated the skyrocketing trade in alcohol through taxes. When the British gained power in India they promoted the production and trade of liquor because of the profitable tax revenues. In 1773 the state monopolized the liquor trade and by 1790 the state had added an excessive excise tax on alcohol. These high taxes resulted in two outcomes desired by the British: considerably more tax revenues, which they depended upon to run the government, and high liquor prices, which discouraged drinking by all but the upper classes. Throughout the colonial period drinking continued to increase, and between 1891 and 1930 tax revenues on alcohol rose by 800 percent. Throughout the colonial period alcohol taxes made up a sizeable proportion of governmental revenues and contributed in a substantial way to the success of the colonial project.

While the government enjoyed high tax revenues from the alcohol trade, social reformers worried about problems that resulted from alcohol abuse. Both Hindu and Muslim reformists demanded the total abolition of some spirits. Not only did alcohol reform movements have indigenous roots, but they also were influenced by the popular temperance movements in Britain in the late nineteenth-century. In response to such widespread reactions against drinking, the government adopted the policy of restricting the production and importation of some spirits and continued to raise taxes to deter alcohol consumption among the majority of the population, the poor. Reformers were joined by nationalist movements in their concern over alcohol abuse. The Indian National Congress, which was founded in 1885, passed resolutions against excessive alcohol consumption. Its members argued that the British did not have an adequate temperance program in India. Thus the prohibition campaign became central to the platform of the Indian National Congress. In addition, Ghandi, who believed in abstinence, championed the prohibition cause. Ghandi said he believed "drink to be more damnable than thieving and perhaps even prostitution." Alcohol regulation, then, became a cornerstone of the Indian independence movement.

After independence in 1947, India added prohibition to its 1950 constitution. It said "the state shall endeavor to bring about prohibition of the consumption, except for medical purposes, of intoxicating drinks and drugs which are injurious to health." (As quoted in Marcus Grant, *Alcohol and Emerging Markets: Patterns, Problems, and Responses.*) It was up to the individual states to enforce prohibition, however, which was difficult because they had to deal with rampant smuggling. In addition, it was not easy to enforce prohibition with elites who still viewed drinking as a status symbol. Moreover, the states that did enforce prohibition suffered because they lost substantial tax monies, so many states ended it as a result. By the late 1970s most Indian states had outlawed prohibition, mainly because of the loss to their tax revenues. Prohibition as a national cause had come to an end. The realities of state budgets offset any prohibitionist sentiments. For India, alcohol had been significant in many ways. It brought in essential taxes to the colonial government, shaped the platform of the independence movement, and provided indispensible tax revenues to the post-independence Indian government.

Australia

The history of Australia differs dramatically from that of India, even though both were British colonies. Australia started out as a penal colony in the late eighteenth-century, drawing mostly men rather than women to the continent. The indigenous population was quite small, and much of the research on drinking habits and laws have focused on the white immigrant population.

Colonists brought a distinct alcohol culture to Australia, one that has defined national identity into the twenty-first-century. Early on, the British elites consciously separated themselves from the rest of society through their taste for wine and love of viticulture. Pubs, however, became the hallmark of Australian society. Pubs, more so than any other institution, staked out colonial settlements as white society spread inland, defining white life in Australia and bringing Western culture to the interior. Moreover, pubs opened up new gender roles for women who were allowed, even encouraged, to become barmaids, thus separating gender identity in Australian society from that of Europe where women had already been pushed out of the occupation. Pub culture also defined masculinity in Australia, bestowing it on the white men who alone frequented the establishments and emasculating the aboriginal men who were barred. Furthermore, pubs became de facto centers of political power, where white men made virtually all the political decisions excluding women and aborigines from the right to a national identity. Pubs symbolized such power in Australia that the right to finally enter them meant as much to aboriginal and women's rights movements as their eventual right to vote.

Colonization brought viticulture to Australia. The first attempt at producing wine by prisoners came in 1801. It did not turn out well. It was not until a little over a decade later that wine production began to flourish. Several well-known male colonists began to promote viticulture, and by the 1830s Australian wine had made its way to Europe where it was well received. In fact, in many French competitions Australian wine won high marks, much to the chagrin of the French judges who believed the best wine to be from France. Even though wine production continued to develop in Australia, it was not a common drink among the majority of the population. Most colonists, especially the lower classes, imbibed in beer and spirits. The elite minority of the British preferred wine, seeing it as more refined. As a result, wine consumption became a way to separate elite culture from that of the lower-classes in Australian society.

Trade in alcohol became central to the economy and culture in Australia, and pubs were the main outlets for that trade. Pubs were on the forefront of colonization. Pubs carried both the British Empire and British culture to Australia. Before churches or other public buildings, pubs staked out new territory for colonization. As Diane Kirkby wrote in *Barmaids: A History of Women's Work in Pubs* "Pubkeeping had a central place in the process of colonisation." Especially with the discovery of gold in many places in Australia, pubs followed gold miners into the wilderness. Pubs also provided self-employment, especially for women. Even though pub keeping was no longer the purview of women in England, it was in the colony of New South Wales. By the end of the nineteenth-century women commonly held jobs as barmaids in Australia. Women as barmaids participated in the dissemination of European culture, while at the same time staking out an economic place for themselves in the burgeoning alcohol trade.

Regulation of alcohol in Australia became a necessity. In colonial Australia men drank heavily, especially in pubs. These colonists not only drank beer but also spirits, especially rum. As a result, the government as well as social reformers moved to regulate drinking to a greater degree. For example, in 1816, the governor regulated the sale of manufactured beer and spirits. In a move to add more respectability to pubs the government passed a law in 1830 that mandated that pubs also had to be inns, complete with at least two rooms for rent. Pubs became known as both drinking and lodging establishments. In addition to governmental laws, the regulation of alcohol consumption took the form of temperance organizations, of which Australia saw a rise of during the late nineteenth-century. Some authors have argued that the increased immigration of women into Australia and the growth of family life led to a proliferation of these temperance movements. The abuse of spirits was the primary focus of these movements. As a way to curb drunkenness on spirits, breweries were established that brewed beer ostensibly for the health of the colonists. The development of a brewing industry did slowly change drinking habits from spirits to beer, which pleased temperance advocates. In addition to the move from spirits to beer, other ways to curb drinking developed. New forms of entertainment such as sports arose as popular leisure pastimes. Pubs and the masculinity they represented, however, remained the hallmarks of Australian society.

Pubs in colonial Australia were very much bastions of white male culture. Social and governmental regulations supported this fact. Even though most pubs had barmaids, women were shunned from drinking there. If women did drink in pubs men considered them to be "loose". Aboriginal men were also excluded from pubs. Beginning in 1838 the government passed laws that forbade aboriginal presence in and around licensed pubs. Aboriginal men could not obtain alcohol unless it was through the patronage of a white man. The exclusion of aboriginal men denigrated aboriginal manhood to such a great degree because drinking in pubs with other men was a sign of masculinity within Australian culture. Moreover, pubs were centers of power where men discussed politics and business, and thus women and aboriginal men were excluded from these important male power centers.

Australian independence did not bring an end to racist and sexist policies regarding alcohol. Aboriginals and women were still excluded from pubs. Australia's move to commonwealth status came to mean that drinking in pubs not only symbolized manhood and power but also citizenship. Some authors argue that by being excluded from pubs aboriginals and women were disenfranchised and denied a national identity. Eventually, between 1957 and

1975 the states finally accorded aboriginals the right to drink in public venues, and it began to be more common for women to drink in pubs in the later twentieth-century. Access to alcohol was such an important symbol of citizenship to aboriginals and women that as Ann McGrath wrote in her article "'Beneath the Skin': Australian Citizenship, Rights and Aboriginal Women," "The coming of alcohol was perceived by the majority of women and men as the most significant event of their recent times." In other words, more important even than the vote was the ability to drink alcohol publicly. Control over one's own access to it symbolized power, citizenship, and a move toward equality.

Conclusion

Comparisons of the production, trade, consumption, and regulation of alcohol among Africa, India, and Australia shed light on the continuities in European colonialism as well as the cultural distinctions across civilizations. Production and trade of alcohol in all three areas changed with colonization in several ways. First, all three regions began large-scale manufacturing of Western beer, attracting drinkers who wanted to identify with the West, both by drinking Western beer instead of indigenous beer, and by drinking as Westerners did, for leisure in pubs. Second, trade in alcohol became a very significant part of the colonial economy in all three areas. Both international and internal trade in alcohol skyrocketed during colonization as demand from African indigenous mine workers, Westernized Indians, and colonists in all three regions seemed insatiable. This demand allowed indigenous female beer makers in Africa a route to economic independence, dramatically changing indigenous gender roles. In India, the monopoly of the industry by the British colonial government enhanced demand by strongly linking alcohol with the British culture so sought after ambitious Indians. In Australia, the widespread proliferation of pubs in the colony demonstrated the high demand for alcohol as well as alcohol-based leisure, both of which became a defining characteristic of the colony and then the country. Moreover, these fast-multiplying pubs hired respectable young women to be barmaids, broadening the definition of femininity and allowing women a way to gain economic independence.

Consumption patterns in all three areas changed dramatically with colonization as well. First, one's alcohol preference came to define them in colonial society. In Africa young men who moved into the cash economy began to drink manufactured beer instead of indigenous beer, as they strove to be identified as urban, modern, and middle class. In India the British, along with the newly rich, educated, and Westernized Indians publicly displayed their status through their conspicuous consumption of Western alcohol. In Australia British colonial elites took pleasure in wine, which they believed demonstrated their refined culture as separate from that of the beer and spirits drinking masses. Furthermore, the white male population in Australia maintained a sense of exclusivity and privilege through excluding aborigines and women from their pubs. In all three instances alcohol consumption helped to solidify a distinction among classes. Second, drinking alcohol in pubs for leisure and entertainment brought a Western idea of leisure to the colonies. Third, the privilege of legally and rather freely drinking alcohol to socialize in public became an identifying characteristic of masculinity, allowing white men alone the ability to be masculine in Africa and Australia.

Regulation of alcohol provided more than one way to further the colonial project in all three areas. First, in the guise of keeping public order, regulation of alcohol by the colonial governments reinforced racism in Africa, India, and Australia. In South Africa the beerhall system that segregated black South Africans and rigidly regulated their drinking symbolized the oppression of the colonial and then apartheid governments. In India prohibitively high excise taxes on alcohol were meant to control drinking by the lower-classes. And in Australia the government outrightly outlawed drinking by aboriginals. In all three cases alcohol policies furthered racist agendas and came to symbolize the kind of ubiquitous oppression of colonism.

Second, in both Africa and India alcohol was in such high demand that the governments came to depend on its taxes each year. In Africa and India taxing alcohol was so lucrative that governments had little desire to promote temperance. Third, in Africa and India nationalist movements focused on self-determination over alcohol as a symbol of independence. Native Africans struggled for the rights to produce and drink alcohol where and when they pleased. In contrast, the independence movement in India wanted to prohibit alcohol as a repudiation of the Western culture that accompanied colonialism. In all of these ways, alcohol production, trade, consumption, and regulation shaped both the development and meanings of colonialism in the eighteenth and nineteenth-centuries in Africa, India, and Australia.

Further reading

Ambler, C. H. 1987. *Alcohol and Disorder in Pre-Colonial Africa.* Working Papers in African Studies No. 126. African Studies Center. Boston, MA: Boston University.

Bledsoe, C. and G. Pison. (eds.) 1994. *Nuptiality in Sub-Saharan Africa: Contemporary Anthropological and Demographic Perspectives.* Oxford: Clarendon Press.

Bowen, H. V., M. Lincoln, and N. Rigby. 2002. *The Worlds of the East India Company.* Rochester, NY: The Boydell Press.

Bryceson, D. F. (ed.) 2002. *Alcohol in Africa: Mixing Business, Pleasure, and Politics.* Portsmouth, NH: Heinemann.

Carlson, R. G. 1990. "Banana Beer, Reciprocity, and Ancestor Propitiation Among the Haya of Bukoba, Tanzania." *Ethnology.* 29 (4): 297–311.

Colson, E. and T. Scudder. 1988. *For Prayer and Profit: The Ritual, Economic, and Social Importance of Beer in Gwembe District, Zambia, 1950–1982.* Standford, CA: Stanford University Press.

Crush, J. and C. Ambler (eds.) 1992. *Liquor and Labor in Southern Africa.* Athens: Ohio University Press.

Heath, D. B. (ed.) 1995. *International Handbook on Alcohol and Culture*. Westport, CT: Greenwood Press.

Kirkby, D. 1997. *Barmaids: A History of Women's Work In Pubs*. Cambridge: Cambridge University Press.

La Hausse, P. 1988. *Brewers, Beerhalls and Boycotts: A History of Liquor in South Africa*. History Workshop Booklet. Johannesburg: Ravan.

McAllister, P. 2001. *Building the Homestead: Agriculture, Labour and Beer in South Africa's Transkei*. Leiden: Ashgate Publishing.

McGrath, A. 1993. "'Beneath the Skin': Australian Citizenship, Rights and Aboriginal Women" in R. Howe (ed.) "Women and the State", *Journal of Australian Studies*. 37 (June): 99–114.

Pan, L. 1975. *Alcohol in Colonial Africa*. Uppsala: The Scandinavian Institute of African Studies, and Helsinki: The Finnish Foundation for Alcohol Studies: 22.

Steinkraus, K. H. 1979. *Fermented Food Beverages in Nutrition*. Ed. C. Gastineau, W. J. Darby, and T. B. Turner. New York: Academic Press.

Wolcott, H. F. 1974. *The African Beer Gardens of Bulawayo: Integrated Drinking in a Segregated Society*. New Brunswick, NJ: Rutgers Center of Alcohol Studies.

7 Alcohol and globalization, Westernization, and tradition in the twentieth- and twentiety-first-centuries

Toward the end of the twentieth-century globalization transformed the world as post-Cold War contacts among the world's civilizations intensified. Trade, technology, and culture crossed political boundaries with ease. Global cultural transference was perhaps the most insidious aspect of globalization. The flood of culture across the globe was not only made up of Western culture, although that trend still predominated by the turn of the twenty-first-century, but increasingly non-Western cultures as well. Yet nowhere was globalization more readily apparent than in the arena of alcohol. Alcohol became a popular commodity in world trade, effectively spreading both Western and non-Western cultures across the world.

Global advertising promoted the spread of various kinds of alcohols across the globe. For example, because of advertising the world demanded tequila from Mexico, vodka from Russia, rum from the Caribbean, and whiskey from the United States. Wine especially was traded globally through international advertising, and its growing popularity led to its production in many parts of the world away from the most well known center of viticulture, Europe. "New World wines" came from the United States as well as parts of Canada, Australia, New Zealand, South America, and South Africa, to name a few. By 2001 New World wines had seized 35 percent of the global market away from Europe, whereas just 23 years earlier Europe had commanded 91 percent of the world wine trade. These changes in the wine trade represented just one aspect in the globalization of a much larger alcohol trade (from Kym Anderson in *The World's Wine Markets: Globalization at Work*).

Increases in production as well as domestic and international sales of alcohol attempted to meet its growing demand across the world. From the Second World War through the early twenty-first-century global alcohol consumption increased exponentially, especially in developed countries where people had more disposable income. According to Patrick E. McGovern in *Uncorking the Past: the Quest for Wine, Beer, and Other Alcoholic Beverages*, by the early twenty-first-century over "150 billion liters of beer, 27 billion liters of wine, and 2 billion liters of distilled spirits (mainly vodka) were produced worldwide." Alcohol was produced not only for international trade among developed countries, but also for trade to developing countries. Alcohol advertising crossed international boundaries resulting in the introduction of new kinds of alcohols globally. Convenient shipping as well as the ability to produce alcohol in many countries made the prices of alcohol affordable for many consumers across the world.

As consumption levels rose, virtually every society suffered from problems with alcohol abuse. Not only did abuse seriously weaken public health and safety in many countries, but mortality rates also increased, along with increases in liver, heart, and other chronic diseases, including HIV (if one links alcohol to increased dangerous sexual practices). One of the most insidious outcomes of the increase in use and abuse of alcohol, however, was violence. Sociologists argued that several factors led to such violence. One of the most important was the "pharmacological effects of alcohol." Some people, particularly men, when under the influence of alcohol behaved in the following ways: they took more risks, focused on the present instead of the possible results of their behavior, became hyperemotional, suffered from impaired judgment, and inflated their sense of male power. More men than women became violent; younger men rather than older men became violent; and socially or economically marginalized groups were more likely to become violent.

The proliferation of drinking establishments, which reflected as well as fostered the rapidly universalizing consumer culture, led to increased levels of acceptable violence as well. For example, in and around drinking establishments more violence was accepted than in other public venues. "Skid row" bars along with packed clubs fostered more violence, and employees that allowed higher levels of intoxication in effect promoted higher levels violence. Moreover, sexual competition, illegal activities, and "rowdy" music, along with lack of availability of food in the establishments led to more violent behavior. One study of Sydney, Australia showed that 44 percent of assaults and 60 percent of alcohol-related violence (not including domestic violence) occurred around licensed drinking establishments.

The transition of drinking establishments from cottage industries, where the bar owner knew the patrons and had more control over their behavior, to a kind of "night-time economy" based on impersonal control of the environment resulted in higher rates of violence as well. Kathryn Graham and Ross Homel in *Raising the Bar: Preventing Aggression in and Around Bars, Pubs and Clubs* argue that the renovation of run-down areas into large night clubs led to a focus on alcohol-based entertainment in many urban areas. Moreover, young adults under the influence of alcohol, thrown together in these highly sexualized environments brought about higher levels of aggression. The tremendous revenues earned by the clubs, along with the tax revenues gained by governments, contributed to the lax attitudes toward violence that accompanied such establishments. Laws against violence in and around drinking establishments existed, but were routinely ignored. In fact, the kinds of remedies for such socially destructive behavior tended to be directed at individuals. For example, establishments barred individual customers rather than solving the systemic link between alcohol and violence. Violence problems notwithstanding, alcohol grew as a global commodity in the twentieth- and twenty-first-centuries, spreading Western as well as non-Western cultures throughout the world.

Latin America

Worldwide sales of Mexican and Brazilian alcohol in the twentieth-century popularized Latin American culture globally. The growing international demand for culturally specific liquors compelled both Mexico and Brazil to argue for the exclusive rights over the alcohols identified with their countries, thus redefining the meaning of international intellectual property rights. Within Latin America, ceremonial use of traditional alcohols provided indigenous groups with a concrete means to maintain their culture in the face of modernization. Alcohol also shaped masculinity throughout Latin America; society expected that part of manhood included drinking more often and in higher quantities than women. Further shaping male identity, society equated male drunkenness with domestic violence, a widespread and under-documented public safety problem. In these several tangible ways alcohol perpetuated national, ethnic, and gender identities in Latin America.

Brazilian and Mexican alcohols provide examples of globalizing trends in alcohol sales. Brazilian cachaça, a distilled alcohol made from milled sugarcane, and first produced by and for slaves in Brazil in the sixteenth-century, became very popular worldwide toward the end of the twentieth-century. Because it was traditionally very cheap throughout much of the twentieth-century, Brazil's elites dismissed cachaça as a drink of poor Brazilians. During most of the twentieth-century it continued to be made mainly by small producers, but by the end of the twentieth-century large producers entered the market when cachaça became the main ingredient in a mixed drink called a caipirinha. The caipirinha became very trendy in high-class nightclubs in places like Paris and New York. In fact, in the early twenty-first-century cachaça was the second highest selling alcoholic beverage in Germany, just behind beer. And because of aggressive marketing by the Brazilian government it became a favorite drink among Brazil's elite as well.

Its popularity induced many other sugar-producing countries to make cachaça for an international market. As a result, Brazil petitioned the WTO (World Trade Organization) under the Trade Related Intellectual Property Rights agreement (TRIPS) to be the sole producer of cachaça. The Brazilian government hoped that the caipirinha would become Brazil's signature drink – much like the margarita was for Mexico and the mohito was for Cuba. Brazil did not want other countries cashing in on what it saw as a native product.

Like cachaça in Brazil, tequila in Mexico was in the forefront of twenty-first-century global trading trends. Over the twentieth-century it had become a very important export for Mexico. In 1999 alone the United States consumed 80 million liters of tequila. Moreover, Mexico made sure that NAFTA (North American Free Trade Agreement) stated that Mexico alone had the right to make tequila under the intellectual property rights law. The designation of cachaça and tequila as intellectual property became important commodities in international trade agreements, not only influenced how alcohol was traded, but also set a precedent for other kinds of intellectual property to be acknowledged.

World trade in alcohol, however, did not erase traditional forms of alcohol consumption in Latin America. For example, mezcal, a distilled version of the agave based, indigenous alcohol pulque, was still used in traditional ways by late twentieth-century Zapotec Indians living in the state of Oaxaca in Mexico. Zapotecs believed that mezcal should only be used ritually, and the villagers looked down upon excessive use of it outside of festivals and ceremonies. These ritualized drinking patterns date back to pre-colonial Mexico. In addition to the ritualized use of mezcal, the fermented drink, pulque, remained important in the diets of many rural and lower-class Mexicans. It contained thiamine, niacin, riboflavin, pantothenic acid, pyridoxine, vitamin B, and biotin. Per capita consumption of pulque in the late twentieth-century equaled about one liter per day, and even children drank pulque as part of their daily diet. Continuing to drink alcohol in traditional ways helped indigenous Mexicans hold on to their culture in spite of Westernization.

Even though cultural ideology dictated ceremonial use of alcohol for indigenous Mexicans, abuse existed throughout Mexico. In the late twentieth- and early twenty-first-centuries a large percentage of domestic violence cases were linked to alcohol abuse. Other kinds of violence, particularly in and around drinking establishments, brought alcohol abuse to the forefront of the Mexican government's health and safety concerns. The government began to require companies to put warning labels on bottles of alcohol. It also instituted a legal drinking age of 18. By the late twentieth-century Mexico also had a National Council on Addiction, which coordinated efforts to reduce problems with alcoholism. Regulations did not catch up with the problem, however, as alcohol continued to permeate people's lives in Latin America.

Africa

Alcohol in Africa shaped many of the same economic, social, and cultural structures as it did in Latin America. African countries struggled with the infiltration of Western culture and used alcohol in traditional ceremonies to maintain African identity. Moreover, non-cash trade, or gifting of indigenous alcohol continued to structure community hierarchies, and women's exclusive right to produce it shaped beliefs about gender. Women's separate income from their very profitable cottage alcohol industry gave them cash to buy imported goods, entering them into the global consumer society. As domestic alcohol industries modernized and Western alcohol imports grew, conspicuous consumption of these new alcohols provided middle- and upper-class Africans who wished to be modern, urban, and Western a way to display their identity. At the same time, conspicuous abstention provided Muslims and

Protestants with one of the most concrete ways to publicly demonstrate their identity in Africa.

Africa differed from Latin America in its experience with the international trade of alcohol, however. African alcohols were less successful on the international market, and production, trade, and consumption showed a pattern of continuity rather than change. In one example in Burkina Faso women in a cottage industry setting continued to produce red sorghum beer in a customary way well into the twenty-first-century. Beer production remained strictly gender specific. The art of beermaking generally was passed down matrilineally; some female brewers came from a long line of brewers – mothers, grandmothers, and great grandmothers. In these cases a woman might receive help from her female relatives to start or maintain her business.

Producing red sorghum beer was labor intensive and it took three days and at least three women. The women boiled the ingredients the first day for four hours and the second day for eight to nine hours. By the third day the beer was ready to sell to women marketers who then sold it to small taverns or other outlets for resell. These beermakers created networks with the women who marketed the beer to taverns. Not all transactions were cash transactions, however. During the processing of the beer, women often gave some of it away to those who helped make it as payment in kind. Friends and neighbors usually received free beer before the brewer sold it to others. Moreover, a tradition called "lenga" existed, which granted the buyer of the beer a taste before buying it. Elites received a larger "taste" and finally the chief received an entire calabash of beer before he had to buy. In addition to making beer to sell, women in small towns still made red sorghum beer for many ritual and ceremonial occasions. Villagers consumed red sorghum beer for work parties and ceremonies. One of the most important occasions was the memorial festival commemorating one's dead ancestors, which happened several years after the death of the relative. The village always commissioned women to make beer for these celebrations, which were very expensive and elaborate.

While women produced the beer almost exclusively, men grew much of the grain. Early in the second half of the twentieth-century married couples still had separate budgets so a woman could buy grain or malt from her husband and then sell him the beer after she made it, making a profit for herself. Women used some of their profits from selling beer, which could be substantial, to buy imported manufactured items. So even though beermaking and selling remained traditional, its profits brought these women into the international market through their purchases.

Westernization infiltrated Burkina Faso through Catholic missionaries, causing conversion to Catholicism to increase in the late twentieth-century. This cultural change complicated the economic situation for female beer makers. Catholic couples now had joint accounts, rather than the usual separate accounts held before their conversion to Catholicism. In these cases the husband might invest in the business of the brewing wife in order to make more money for the entire family. This new kind of arrangement frequently ended up being disadvantageous for the woman because she no longer sold her product to her husband, and the profits no longer went to her, but to the family unit where the husband held greater power. Moreover, as a result of modernization, women began to be usurped by large producers. Many women ended up merely selling the beer for the large producers rather than making beer for their own small enterprise, taking away much of their economic independence. The move away from cottage industry to large producers also signified the modernization of a significant piece of traditional culture.

Modernization and global trends not only brought changes in production and trade, but also brought changes in consumption of alcohol as well. The global trend of high alcohol consumption in the second half of the twentieth-century held true in Burkina Faso also. In 1970 over 700 million liters of traditional beer was consumed. Traditional beer continued to be an extremely important commodity in the local economies. Change took place in the late twentieth-century, however, because many of the people in Burkina Faso became either Catholic or Muslim. So by the early part of the twenty-first century in the Muslim areas very little alcohol consumption took place. In the Catholic areas people still used alcohol, but for Catholic ceremonies such as name day commemorations rather than for traditional rituals. In this way the change in alcohol consumption habits, brought on by the global spread of religions, signaled a move away from traditional, African culture.

In Burkina Faso an increase in the consumption of Western-style beer transformed the beer market, which had been formerly controlled solely by indigenous beer. Bottled beer became popular in the larger towns where refrigeration was available. In addition, in market towns richer farmers began to drink bottled beer instead of sorghum beer when they brought their goods to market. By the end of the twentieth-century drinking it became a status symbol for the urban elite who could afford to drink the more expensive bottled beer. Westernization in the twentieth- and early twenty-first-centuries made its way into African towns through manufactured beer. Bottled beer consumption further signified one's place in the middle- and upper-classes in Burkina Faso.

Consumption habits in another part of Africa, Zambia, reflected Westernization as well. For example, in the late twentieth-century over 50 percent of Zambians abstained, which could partially be explained by a rise in Protestantism, a Western religion. Just under 15 percent of the population still claimed to be heavy drinkers, however. These heavy drinkers drank two to three times a week and drank to inebriation. Most heavy drinkers were married men over 30 with varied educational and economic status. Since the heavy drinkers were primarily men, alcohol consumption patterns furthered gender differences, but drinking patterns did not seem to further class differences because male heavy drinkers came from all classes and educational levels.

Alcohol consumption habits of rural and urban dwellers in Zambia differed. Rural dwellers more often drank homemade beer. In the city, though, national advertising of manufactured beer influenced the consumption patterns of the urban elite. Elite urbanites almost exclusively drank bottled beer, publicly demonstrating their higher place in the social hierarchy. Moreover, sometimes elites drank international alcohol products and thus were pulled into a globalizing culture through their alcohol choices.

Unfortunately, consumption of alcohol by Zambian men of all classes perpetuated the spread of HIV/AIDS in the late twentieth- and early twenty-first-centuries in that country. Since many men drank in bars without their wives, and reported having sex with women other than their regular partners, there was a strong correlation between the spread of HIV/AIDS and alcohol. As a result of unprotected, alcohol-included male philandering, many women and children contracted a disease that ravaged the country. By the early twenty-first-century, 18 percent of Zambian women were HIV positive. Moreover, many STDs were passed along in the same way. Of those who drank at least once a week, 37 percent had STDs, while of those who did not drink, 23 percent had STDs. Little or no alcohol regulation addressed the problem of the spread of STDs. The meager regulation of drinking in Zambia took the form of employee assistance programs to help staff with alcohol-related problems. The best assurance of abstinence, however, seemed to be participation in Protestantism or Islam, since one's drinking habits overtly signified his or her identity in African society.

Saudi Arabia

In Saudi Arabia the strict ban on alcohol production, consumption, and regulation symbolized the culture's complete adherence to Islam. The rise in illegal production and trade, as well as the increase in consumption in the late twentieth and early twenty-first-centuries, then, represented a small yet noticeable infiltration of Western values and global consumer culture. As abuse rose during the same time period, Western ideology spread, too, as Saudi leaders reluctantly adopted a Western-style treatment protocol and began to define alcohol abuse as a disease, rather than as a failure to adhere to Islam.

Production and trade of alcohol was against the law in Saudi Arabia in the twentieth-century and remained so in the early twenty-first-century. Alcohol traders, however, continued to smuggle it into the eastern part of the country from Bahrain or Jordan where alcohol was available. For example, the Saudi Customs Department reported that it confiscated 88,000 bottles of alcohol in 2010 (Asa Trulsson, "Drugs, Alcohol and Holy Denial," http://www.utrikesper spektiv.se/2011/06/10/stat-och-samhalle/drugs-alcohol-and-holy-denial/, accessed December 14, 2011). Entrepreneurs and individual households also illegally produced many kinds of homemade alcohol, including fermented grapes or dates and a distilled 190 proof spirit called sadiqii.

The unlawful production and trade of alcohol supplied a growing demand in the late twentieth-century. Researchers argued that alcohol consumption began to rise at that time for a number of reasons, all stemming from the tremendous oil wealth that started flowing into Saudi Arabia in the 1970s and 1980s. For example, oil wealth made international travel possible for Saudi elites, who brought back Westernized views of alcohol. Moreover, increased alcohol consumption followed the arrival of the internet, Western movies, global television broadcasting, and the large number of foreign workers who appeared in Saudi Arabia since the 1980s, as signs of Westernization grew. Furthermore, the rapid population growth after the 1970s resulted in a young population who were more influenced by Western culture. In fact, people who had some knowledge of alcohol garnered a certain degree of social capital in personal circles in Saudi society in the late twentieth- and early twenty-first-centuries.

In addition, anecdotal evidence uncovered alcohol use in Western-styled social settings by privileged segments of society. WikiLeaks reported that alcohol could be found at elite parties, and American diplomats told stories of "private" nightclubs that not only served alcohol to both men and women, but also offered dancing to their patrons. Official Saudi consumption rates remained some of the lowest in the world, however, at between 0.25 and 0.6 liters per capita, depending on the source. Drinking also remained such a stigma in the general population that a woman could apply for divorce if her husband drank, and fathers had the right to prohibit their daughters from marrying a man whose father was a known drinker.

The most concrete evidence for rising "unofficial" alcohol consumption arose from statistics on increasing abuse problems. While most Saudi citizens still believed that practicing Islam was the best solution to the problem of alcohol abuse, the Saudi government was forced to provide social services to address the growing problem in the late 1980s. They opened three drug and alcohol treatment hospitals and blanketed the country with a media campaign against drug and alcohol use and abuse. Yet the problem persisted.

By 2003 the WHO (World Health Organization) reported that 24 percent of the patients in one substance abuse hospital had used alcohol and 12 percent had abused alcohol. Virtually all patients in these hospitals were young men, with women constituting only 0.02 percent of the residents. These men, whose average age was 29, cited peer pressure or unemployment as the reason for their addiction. As these statistics on alcoholism came to light, researchers began to examine the social ramifications of alcoholism. For example, a 2006 study on Saudi Arabia correlated alcohol abuse and domestic violence. The study also argued that the continued social stigma around alcohol "exacerbated the effects of alcohol (ab)use within families." (In Abdulaziz A. Albrithen, "Alcoholism and Domestic Violence in Saudi Society.") In addition, because the Saudi government did not officially recognize domestic violence, the problem remained difficult to address.

By the end of the first decade of the twenty-first-century the continued rapid urbanization, modernization, and industrialization had exacerbated alcohol abuse. A 2009 survey of medical students in Riyadh revealed that 75 percent of them believed substance abuse was a problem among young men ages 15 to 30. Furthermore, increased abuse problems made the international news in 2010 when a prominent, UK-educated Saudi doctor and researcher traveled to Detroit, an area with a large Arab-American and Muslim population, to tour one of the oldest alcohol treatment centers in the United States. He sought advice from the directors because he, along with other prominent Saudi healthcare experts, planned to open a 250-bed alcohol and drug treatment hospital in their country. He also had plans to open several more hospitals throughout Saudi Arabia to address the growing addiction problem across the Islamic Middle East. This Western-educated doctor also believed that a 12-step program, modeled after AA, but tailored to an Islamic population, should follow hospitalization.

Even though treatment became available, the government still relied on strict regulation to deter not only alcohol abuse, but also any association with alcohol at all. Even into the twenty-first-century Saudi Arabia maintained the most conservative alcohol laws in the Islamic Middle East. Alcohol policies had always been stringent under the leadership of the Saud dynasty, members of a conservative subgroup of Sunni Islam that believed in a very rigid interpretation of the Quran. Therefore, Saudi law was based on Islam, and the government employed "Islamic police" to rigorously enforce Islamic values. For example, alcohol production or sale resulted in lashings, imprisonment, or even execution. Yet even with these deterrents the production, trade, use, and abuse of alcohol rose in Saudi Arabia in the late twentieth-century. Between 1983 and 2002 alcohol infractions increased by over 300 percent.

After the turn of the twenty-first-century the government seemed to turn its focus from personal use to the production and sale of alcohol. The government now legally ensured treatment for substance abuse sufferers at rehabilitation hospitals, and in 2004, while it blocked the majority of pornography and drug sites on the web, it only blocked one alcohol site out of 60,000. Conversely, it stiffened the penalties for smuggling or selling alcohol, resulting in larger fines, more lashings, longer prison sentences, and higher frequencies of the death penalty. The looser restrictions on personal consumption, however, and the growth of Western-style treatment facilities revealed the government's subtle recognition of a penetration of Western values.

India

As India developed in the later twentieth-century, it began mass production of both Western and indigenous alcohols. Demand for Western alcohol grew as it became a symbol of cultural Westernization. At the same time, many Indians still drank indigenous alcohol, publically demonstrating their desire to preserve Indian culture. Nevertheless, Indian consumption of all alcohols, including indigenous, illegal, and Western jumped in the twentieth-century, indicating India's participation in a global consumer culture as wealth grew in that country. Increased consumption, however, led to increased abuse, which brought on serious public health and safety problems. In response, Western-style Alcoholics Anonymous groups emerged, ushering in yet another Western cultural construct, the disease model of alcohol abuse. Yet the highly contradictory roles of alcohol still plagued India's government, because like many other governments around the world, it wrestled with curbing public over-consumption and its consequences, while at the same time heavily relying on alcohol taxes.

By the late twentieth-century three major kinds of liquor existed in India. First, many Indians still produced indigenous liquor. One of these, called arrack, was distilled from grains, rice, and sugarcane. In addition to arrack, Indians produced several kinds of indigenous palm wine. Both arrack and palm wine remained popular up through the early twenty-first-century. Second, Indians produced a substantial amount of illicit or bootleg liquor. Exactly how much was still unknown by the early twenty-first-century, but it was clear that illegal alcohol production was prevalent. Third, Indians produced "Indian-made foreign liquor," which included Western kinds of liquor such as beer and distilled spirits like whiskey, gin, brandy, and rum. The production of these Western liquors rose by 12 to 15 percent in the 1990s. The popularity of foreign liquor in general, from many areas of the world, brought a global culture to the doorstep of the elite and middle-class Indians who could afford to purchase it.

All classes in India increased their alcohol consumption in the late twentieth- and early twenty-first-centuries. The integration of India into global markets in the latter part of the twentieth-century helped to bring about this change. Many researchers argue that global alcohol advertising urged middle-class Indians, especially, to become less conservative and to take on modern, perhaps more Western values by drinking more liquor. In addition, marketing and mass production of alcohol, and thus its increased availability influenced the rural poor to increase their consumption as well. The poor, however, still had fewer means and thus could not afford the expensive, foreign alcohol. Drinking alcohol, especially Western alcohol, by the elite and middle-classes became even more of a status symbol in the early twenty-first-century. Drinking turned out to be a visible way to set themselves apart from the lower-class.

Along with increased consumption of alcohol came abuse. Popular media at the end of the twentieth-century indicated that problems with excessive alcohol consumption were on the rise. For example, a study in one state found that over 20 percent of the population above the age of ten abused alcohol. Another indicator of increased alcohol problems came from the intake statistics of mental health hospitals. For example, between 1953 and 1965 no patients with alcohol problems were admitted, but by 1994, 25 percent of the patients admitted had alcohol problems. In addition, by the late twentieth-century drivers under the influence of alcohol caused an estimated 25 percent of road accidents.

Governmental regulation of alcohol in India during the late twentieth- and early twenty-first-centuries was checkered. While early twentieth-century independence movements championed prohibition legislation, these laws did not last. The negative tax consequences were too devastating for the states involved. Various states did experiment with prohibition, but by the late 1990s only one state remained dry. As a result, regulation of alcohol took the form of social rather than governmental control as Western-style Alcoholics Anonymous groups multiplied. At first these groups only operated in English, but there was such a demand that they opened chapters in local languages. The spreading culture of Alcoholics Anonymous ideology indicated a penetration of Western values throughout India. Western attitudes toward alcohol in general became emblematic of the Westernization of India in the twentieth- and twenty-first-centuries.

China

In China, the dramatic increases in production, trade, consumption, abuse, and regulation of alcohol in the late twentieth- and early twenty-first-centuries spearheaded cultural modernization and Westernization in that country. Chinese businessmen in particular publicly drank expensive alcohol to flaunt their success. Yet alcohol also helped the Chinese repel aspects of the West, as they continued to use alcohol in traditional social ceremonies and drink the indigenous alcohol baijiu. Chinese society also expected that men drank more than women and tacitly approved of male public drunkenness, illustrating how attitudes about alcohol shaped definitions of masculinity in that country. As alcohol abuse grew, civic responses to the problem took the form of a growing Alcoholics Anonymous movement. This movement ushered in yet another Western ideology, one that both defined alcohol abuse as a disease and used the US generated 12-step program to help.

China, like India, bought more foreign liquor and produced larger quantities of it by the late twentieth- and early twenty-first-centuries. Chinese trade in alcohol rose tremendously with China's move into the international economy. Because of the opening of international markets, the sale of foreign liquors to China doubled in the early 1990s. Not only did sales of foreign liquors rise, but also sales of domestic alcohol products, especially beer, rose as well. By the end of the century China was the second largest beer producer next to the United States. Moreover, the number of drinking establishments skyrocketed. Many scholars argue that advertising played an important role in the increase in Chinese liquor sales. Alcohol producers spent millions of dollars on advertising; by 1995 almost 20 percent of all television advertising was liquor related. Liquor had become a very popular commodity during the globalization of China's economy in the late twentieth-century.

Even though imported alcohol began to claim a larger part of the liquor market in China, many Chinese drinkers still preferred baijiu, a traditional liquor made from sorghum, rice, and unhusked barley. Moreover, the Chinese did not all become modern, Western-style leisure drinkers, rather many still used alcohol in ceremonial ways. For example, at the most important festival of the year, the Chinese New Year, also called the Spring Festival, an alcohol called tusu, which was made from peppers and cypress leaves, prevailed. It symbolized health, luck, and long life. Alcohol remained a central feature of many other rituals and celebrations as well. Alcohol continued to be important in wedding ceremonies for many ethnic groups in China. For example, in one practice the bridegroom's family offered alcohol to the bride's family, and when the bride's family drank the alcohol, it symbolized the solidification of the engagement. Also, during a marriage ceremony the bride and groom drank alcohol out of the same cup, and the groom toasted members of the bride's family and friends. In these ways many Chinese used alcohol to maintain their traditional culture even as China's economy became global.

China's growing economy, which brought on a jump in production and sale of alcohol, also ushered in a dramatic increase in consumption as well as a change in consumption patterns for many Chinese. Political developments also increased consumption. In 1976, with the news of the arrest of the "Gang of Four" at the end of the Cultural Revolution, wine shops quickly sold out of wine. Moreover, alcohol consumption rose by 100 percent between the end of the Cultural Revolution and 1995. A new elite, mainly merchants, began to drink more alcohol publicly, showing off their economic ability to consume. Many kinds of drinking games came into fashion. One such game required the participant to make up a specific kind of poem. If he (most drinkers were men) could not comply quickly, he was forced to take a drink. In addition to playing drinking games these new elites exhibited a high rate of public drunkenness, even though public drunkenness was traditionally looked down upon. Drinking and flouting social norms allowed them to show off their high status. Their relationship to alcohol set them apart from other segments of society, signifying their place in China's new elite class.

Increased alcohol consumption became a leading indicator of China's expanding economy. For example, in 2006 the Chinese made up 20 percent of the world's alcohol consumers. The Chinese also consumed the most spirits by volume, 3.6 billion liters per year. Spirits were very popular in China because their high alcohol content produced more intoxication for the money than did other alcohols. Another pattern surfaced as a result of China's economic growth; the rich Chinese not only drank more alcohol, but they also began to drink more expensive alcohol. These alcohol consumption patterns brought China into line with global cultural trends.

An alcohol abuse problem arose with the overall increase in alcohol consumption, however. More men than women drank and therefore problem drinkers tended to be men instead of women. Those in the middle-classes had fewer problems with alcohol than the elite or lower class. A study of 17 psychiatric hospitals revealed that between 1980 and 1993 the number of patients admitted with alcohol problems increased by 400 percent. By 1995 a whopping 50 percent of the traffic accidents were alcohol related. As a result, social remedies emerged. "Alcohol clubs," similar to Alcoholics Anonymous, were set up to alleviate the increasing problem of abuse. The government also reacted. In an attempt to regulate alcohol consumption the government instituted an alcohol tax. By the beginning of the twenty-first-century the tax was so high that in order to consume much alcohol one had to be relatively wealthy. This tax on alcohol did discourage lower-class drinking but it also furthered the separation of elite culture from that of the rest of society.

The increase in alcohol problems in the late twentieth-century did not mean that China had a high rate of alcoholism compared to other countries, however. By the first decade of the twenty-first-century it was still more common to drink alcohol slowly with meals or on ceremonial occasions. It continued to be common to drink with groups rather than to drink alone, which some authors argue led to less alcoholism. Moreover, a large number of Chinese did not drink at all. One explanation for lower levels of alcohol consumption, according to some researchers, was the flushing response experienced by Asians, which included a rise in body temperature, heart beat, perspiration, nausea, headache, and a flushing of the face when drinking alcohol, which made drinking alcohol less pleasurable. Other researchers argue against this explanation because other Asian cultures such as Japan had high rates of consumption. Even with relatively low consumption and abuse rates, China's new relationship to alcohol signaled its response to modernization and Westernization.

Japan

Skyrocketing alcohol consumption in Japan allowed the Japanese to show their enthusiastic adoption of Western culture, while at the same time alcohol also allowed them to preserve core Japanese values. There was aggressive marketing of not only Western alcohol, but also Western drinking habits, noticeably Westernized Japanese culture. Yet the choreographed ceremonial approach to drinking, even in modern settings, provided the Japanese with a way to overtly adhere to tradition. Moreover, Japan's government benefitted from the high demand through alcohol taxes that appreciably bolstered the national budget, demonstrating alcohol's importance not only to society but also to the political structure that held it together.

The alcohol trade in Japan increased rapidly in the latter part of the twentieth century. The industry modernized and alcohol producers turned to Western-style marketing strategies, which changed drinking culture. For example, by the late twentieth-century beer producers marketed so many varieties of beer that it became more common for drinkers to each order something different in a bar rather than to order one kind of alcohol as a group, as had been the tradition. Alcohol companies continued to strategize about ways to increase individual consumption, which they believed would lead to more drinking. Companies began to market shochu, a traditional, distilled drink, in individual cans in the 1980s. These individual cans became very popular because one company came out with cans of shochu mixed with fruit juice. In addition, sake and beer began to be marketed in single-sized packaging to promote individual choice. One beer company increased its sales of beer because it marketed individual beer cans as masculine. Moreover, alcohol became available in vending machines. Machines stayed open later than liquor stores and opened at 5 am. These trends in alcohol marketing furthered the Western cultural idea of individualism, and thus furthered Westernization.

Following world trends, alcohol consumption increased tremendously in Japan after the Second World War. Between 1950 and 1980 alcohol consumption increased by 800 percent. Some argue that it leveled off in the 1980s. Others argue, however, that it continued to increase through the first part of the twenty-first-century, rising by as much as 1,000 percent overall and 400 percent per capita. Drinking alcohol came to represent one's ability to spend disposable income on leisure activities. It thus became a visible way to separate the rising middle- and upper-classes from the lower-class.

Not only did consumption increase, but tastes in alcohol also began to change. Sake had been the traditional drink of choice, but beer overtook sake in popularity by the late twentieth-century. By the end of the twentieth-century the Japanese drank three times more beer than they did sake. In fact, between the Second World War and the beginning of the twenty-first-century beer drinking increased by 3,000 percent. Whiskey consumption also increased between the Second World War and the first decade of the twenty-first-century. Some argue that it increased as much as 5,500 percent and that by 2010 it made up 25 percent of Japan's alcohol consumption. Others contend, however, that it accounted for much less. Some researchers estimate that alcohol by preference in Japan in 2010 was 66 percent beer, 22 percent sake, 5 percent whiskey, and 4 percent shochu. In any case, as incomes rose and tariffs on whiskey decreased people did consume much more of it. Another new trend that emerged toward the end of the century had people ordering wine more often when they dined out. Moreover, more people drank at home or at sporting events than had traditionally been the case. The addition of new drinking venues as well as the increased consumption of beer, whiskey, and wine furthered the Westernization of culture in the lives of many Japanese.

Even though much drinking behavior changed in the late twentieth- and early twenty-first-centuries, many traditional consumption patterns remained. For example, at social gatherings for businessmen (it was mainly a male drinking culture) it was still common for the employee first to offer a drink, often sake, to his boss. The employee held the drink in two hands while offering it to his boss and the boss received it with one hand, signifying his superior position. After his superior drank, he would offer his employee a drink with one hand while the employee received it with two hands. This etiquette worked the same way when older and younger people drank together on social occasions. Moreover, traditionally at these social occasions one never served oneself, and it was acceptable for men to exhibit drunken behavior while in public. Therefore holding onto traditional drinking habits, even while participating in modern business transactions, was a way to hold onto traditional culture in the face of Westernization and modernization.

Syncretism of cultures existed as well. For example, many people began to drink whiskey, a Western alcohol, yet they ordered it as a group, strengthening traditional group culture. One member of the group would order a bottle of whiskey with enough glasses for everyone, and the whole group would drink the same thing. In this situation, people did not serve themselves either. A waitress or a woman in the group would serve the whiskey. These continuities in drinking patterns helped maintain Japanese culture as Japan's economy went global.

The tremendous increase in alcohol consumption also brought abuse, however. The number of alcoholics in Japan increased from 2 percent of the population after the Second World War to 6 percent in the late twentieth-century. The government continued to regulate alcohol by enforcing its legal drinking age of 20. It also taxed alcohol. In the 1990s alcohol taxes accounted for at least 3 percent of the national budget. There was not a rise of any sort of temperance movement, however, because heavy drinking had traditionally been an acceptable way to relax in Japan.

Russia

The state in Soviet Russia attempted to control all aspects of the production, sale, and consumption of alcohol during its time in power in the twentieth-century. Alcohol demand was already high at the beginning of the twentieth-century and it rose throughout, even though it was highly regulated. Alcohol became the primary coping mechanism during the years of scarcity of consumer and entertainment goods in Soviet Russia. Alcohol continued to dominate the lives of many in the 1990s and 2000s after the fall of the Soviet government. As the economy moved to a free market system, many Russians used alcohol to cope with the severe social and economic upheaval, while the new elite demonstrated their place in the global consumer society by their conspicuous consumption of expensive liquor. Alcohol in the free market also allowed Russia to penetrate the global demand for exotic alcohols after the turn of the twenty-first-century, through its trade in the distinctly Russian samogon, which spread an idealized Russian culture to the West.

During the Soviet years alcohol profits alone allowed the state to maintain fiscal solvency. After the end of Soviet state monopoly on alcohol in the 1990s, the crucial role that alcohol profits had played became glaringly apparent to the new, struggling government. Soviet and post-Soviet regulations on alcohol did not prevent serious problems with abuse, and an unsuccessful campaign against alcohol in the 1980s simply reinforced the centrality of alcohol to Russian society and cultural identity. The extremely high consumption rates of Russian men remained a defining aspect of Russian masculinity, while male alcohol abuse became the number one crisis in public health and safety, especially in the 1990s and beyond.

In the 1920s Stalin mandated a state monopoly on the commodity. He calculated that because of the propensity for Russians to drink, the substantial alcohol profits would be crucial to the solvency of the government. He was correct. In 1940 "there were more shops selling drink than meat, fruit and vegetables put together." (Stephen White in *Russia Goes Dry: Alcohol,*

State and Society.) At the same time, however, the USSR wanted to present a carefully orchestrated picture of life in Russia that did not include any social problems such as alcohol abuse. So by the 1960s the government chose to hide alcohol production rates by grouping them into one category together with ice cream, coffee, cocoa, mushrooms, and spices. Some estimates, however, indicated that legal production of spirits rose by 300 percent between 1940 and 1980, even with a phenomenal 262 percent price increase during the same period.

Price increases did not result from an increase in production costs, however. Instead they represented attempts by the Soviet government to curtail drinking, as well as to bolster the treasury. In fact, some estimates concluded that 92 percent of the purchase price of vodka went to the government, accounting for 13 to 14 percent of the entire state budget. In 1992, however, after the end of the Soviet era, the government abolished its monopoly on alcohol sales. The losses were so great to the financially strapped new government that the Duma attempted to bring back the state monopoly in 2006.

During the twentieth-century, however, legal alcohol accounted for only 60 to 70 percent of all the liquor sold in Russia. Homebrew, called samogon, made up the other 30 to 40 percent of the alcohol produced, bringing in profits to the brewers of as high as 800 percent. The risk to the brewer was great, though, because they could be sentenced to several years in jail if caught. After the fall of the Soviet Union, the new state moved toward legalizing homebrewing in 1992 in an attempt to adequately regulate all alcohol sales. It remained illegal for people to peddle samogon without a license, but in numerous rural villages brewers flouted these regulations. In fact, more people took up brewing and selling samogon. Its sales supported numerous people during the difficult economic times of the early 1990s. It even became a form of currency in some areas. Its price, about 55 percent of the price of vodka, made it even more popular. In 2003 a private company secured a license and began selling samogon legally. The company created its own brand, and even though its samogon sold for three to four times the price of vodka, in 2007 the turnover for the liquor reached five million dollars. This exclusively Russian brand became popular in Russia and by 2011 the company marketed it to the United States as an authentically Russian spirit, even more so than vodka. With the high demand for exotic alcohols in the West, samogon received a positive reception. It made a noticeable impact when a cocktail made from the spirit, called "From Russia with Love" won a prize at the prestigious Ultimate Beverage Challenge contest in 2011.

Alcohol fed an ever-growing consumer demand from the Russian populace over the twentieth- and early twenty-first-centuries. With the exception of the years 1985 to 1988 consumption of alcohol rose steadily. One study found that per capita alcohol consumption increased from 7.3 liters in 1955 to 15.2 liters in 1979. Another study came to a wildly different finding, asserting that the consumption of alcohol increased by an astounding 800 percent between 1940 and 1984. By the 1970s, Russia ranked eighth worldwide in the consumption of all alcohol, and fourth in the consumption of hard liquor. By some estimates, Russians spent between 15 and 20 percent of their disposable income on liquor. By the 1980s a surprising 90 percent of women, who traditionally had relatively low rates of consumption, drank regularly, which correlated with an increase in birth defects. Consumption also increased in other populations as well. By the 1980s almost 80 percent of high school students had tried alcohol. These statistics did not account for the rampant alcohol theft that consistently took place during the Soviet years.

In the new market economy of the early 1990s consumption rates continued to rise. A 30 percent increase occurred within just a few years, perhaps reflecting the social upheavals of the time. Not surprisingly then, by 1993 Russia surpassed France in per capita consumption of alcohol, "with an average consumption of a bottle of vodka for every adult male every two days." (Stephen White, *Russia Goes Dry: Alcohol, State and Society.*) Some companies even paid their workers in vodka because of the shortage of money in early post-Soviet Russia. By 2007, after over 15 years of a new government and economy, consumption rates remained high, at 15 liters per year. At that time the government increased efforts to decrease consumption, and by 2010 the levels dropped to 12.5 liters per year.

High consumption rates led to widespread abuse during the entire Soviet era and beyond. During the early years of the Soviet government, leaders considered alcoholism a hold over from Russia's bourgeois past. But that explanation ceased to hold any credence as abuse rates continually rose throughout the twentieth-century. Alcohol abuse skyrocketed during the 1970s and early 1980s. By the mid 1980s almost 15 percent of the population were alcoholics. Many believed the lack of available alternative entertainment, caused by a government that paid little attention to consumer goods and services, led to the rise.

The abuse spawned myriad social problems. One survey of 500 divorcees showed that almost 40 percent of the complainants cited drunkenness as the problem. In addition, alcohol led to over 30 percent of all auto accidents and 80 percent of all deaths resulting from auto accidents. According to court statistics people under the influence of alcohol committed roughly 74 percent of all murders, 70 percent of all rapes, and 50 percent of all robberies in Russia. Moreover, alcohol abuse caused a considerable decrease in manufacturing output because of absenteeism, especially on Mondays. Workers lost up to 40 days a year of production time because of alcohol abuse. Abuse was so prevalent that during the 1983 Soviet Central Committee meeting it was finally recognized as a serious social problem. When Gorbachev came to power and the government gradually opened up, Alcoholics Anonymous was allowed to start groups within the country. And churches, which were given more rights in post-Soviet Russia, also vocally promoted sobriety.

The post-Soviet collapse of the economy in the 1990s caused an escalation in alcohol abuse and its attendant social problems. By some estimates 30 percent of the population suffered from alcohol problems by 1993. The number of crimes committed while drunk rose, and because, like the rest of the population, 30 percent of the police force abused alcohol, enforcement of the laws deteriorated. Alcohol abuse so deeply permeated society that a marked increase in mortality rates occurred between 1980 and 1994. Life expectancy for men fell from 61 to 57. To address the substantial increase in alcohol abuse in the 1990s, sobriety movements advocated for legislation regulating drinking, but the majority of the public did not support these movements.

Serious social problems continued into the twenty-first-century. In 2002 the WHO (World Health Organization) estimated that 18 percent of Russian men between the ages of 20 and 64 died from alcohol-related problems. By 2005 some studies showed that alcohol-related male mortality rates had risen to 31 percent for those between the ages of 20 and 44. For women of the same age alcohol-related mortality was smaller, yet still a sizeable 20 percent of all deaths. Between 2007 and 2011 most statistics reported male life expectancy to be 60—higher than the age of 57 reported in 1994—yet still resulting in one of the lowest life expectancies in Europe, compared to Germany, for example, where male life expectancy was 77 in 2009. Russian women, however, who had much lower abuse rates than men, lived an average of 73 years. In yet another bleak study it was reported that while 18-year-old men in the West had "a ninety percent chance of reaching retirement age … for young men in Russia the odds are reduced to fifty percent." (Grace Wong, "Russia's Bleak Picture of Health.") These findings caused Russian leaders Vladamir Putin and Dmitry Medvedev to proclaim alcoholism a national security threat in 2011.

The serious alcohol abuse problems also led to a frightening number of alcohol poisonings across Russia. In 2006 over 40,000 people died from alcohol poisoning, compared to 300 in the much more populated United States. The consumption of alternative forms of alcohol, such as cologne, window cleaner, antifreeze, and de-icing fluids, to name a few, led to many of these deaths. Consumption of non-beverage alcohol rose to such crisis proportions that in 2006 the government instituted laws regulating the use of these substances. High rates of alcohol poisoning also came from the Russian habit of binge drinking. There is even a specific word in Russian, *zapoi*, which means "a continuous state of drunkenness over a period of two or more days where the person does not engage in normal social life." By 2008 the number of deaths attributed to alcohol poisoning had dropped to 19,000 because of the efforts of the government to regulate alcohol.

Problems with the regulation of alcohol plagued the Soviet government throughout the twentieth-century. Early on the Bolshevik government attempted prohibition, but it soon failed. So in the 1920s the government resorted to establishing commissions for the treatment of alcoholism. The party also sponsored Anti-Alcohol Societies, to which over 250,000 people belonged by 1929. By the early 1930s, though, the government eliminated a focus on alcoholism and instead concentrated on better living standards for the working class. They did, however, continue to require many abusers to go to rehabilitation centers, several of which resembled prisons.

Finally, toward the end of the Soviet era, the government under Mikhail Gorbachev, himself urged on by his wife and at least two of his close advisors, began a concerted campaign against alcoholism. Starting in 1985 the government formed a temperance society, the state-controlled media published extensive anti-alcohol propaganda, and several governmental and party organizations promoted the campaign. The program included outlawing alcohol at all governmental gatherings, raising the legal drinking age to 21, and increasing fines and penalties for alcohol-related disorderly conduct. Moreover, the government eliminated hundreds of alcohol outlets and increased the price of vodka by so much that it took 19 hours of an average worker's wages to buy a bottle. In addition, the government attempted to eliminate homebrewing. Penalties for the possession of homebrew equipment included up to two years of hard labor and a substantial fine.

The 1985 regulations did bring about change. Crime decreased and public health improved. For example, mortality rates for men dropped considerably. People continued to demand alcohol, however. Customers waiting in lines outside the limited number of alcohol shops numbered in the hundreds in some urban areas, causing Moscow, for example, to assign over 400 police to keep order.

Within three years after the beginning of the campaign, the production of vodka, other liquors, and homebrew began to climb back up to pre-1985 levels. The campaign ended, for all intents and purposes, by 1988, because its supporters in the upper echelons of the party had been replaced, because people turned to dangerous alternatives, and because the decrease in alcohol taxes seriously depleted the treasury. Consumption of state-produced alcohol had temporarily dropped by an astounding 60 percent, but estimates that included the increase in the production of illegal homebrew showed a much smaller, yet still significant, overall decrease of 35 percent.

In the post-Soviet decades of the 1990s and 2000s, the government continued to wrestle with skyrocketing alcohol problems. Between 2009 and 2011, in an effort to curb drinking, the government raised the price of spirits by 10 percent, and the price of beer by over 300 percent. In 2010 the government prohibited the sale of alcohol in Moscow at night. Strict drinking and driving laws were put in place to stop alcohol-related accidents. Until 2011 the law maintained a zero tolerance policy regarding drinking and driving. In 2011 the government raised the legal blood–alcohol content slightly to 0.03 percent because people had complained that even those with hangovers who smelled of alcohol were being pulled over and arrested. Government vigilance did not fade, though, and in 2011 President Dmitry Medvedev signed a measure that would prohibit beer sales from kiosks by 2013, restrict alcohol advertising, and ban alcohol sales between 11 pm and 8 am. The state once again attempted to regulate the most popular commodity in Russia. Yet alcohol's centrality to Russian culture thwarted state efforts.

France

France was one of the wealthiest countries in the world in the early twenty-first-century, housing 39 of the global Fortune 500 companies. The global community, however, associated France with its signature product, wine. Multi-national wine corporations emerged in the 1980s to fill a worldwide demand, and by the turn of the twenty-first-century, the jump in demand by those in non-Western countries boosted wine sales even higher. In almost all societies drinking French wine bestowed prestige on those who purchased it. Within France wine punctuated the daily lives of the vast majority of the population. It structured meals, social events, and cultural rituals. Since wine permeated all segments of society, it was the consumption of other alcohol products, namely beer for the elite and cider for the working class, that signified class status. Moreover, the French identified drinking with masculinity, accepting higher rates of consumption by men as normal. Alcohol abuse by men did lead to higher rates of domestic violence in the late twentieth and early twenty-first-centuries, yet, while they did not condone it, the fact that society was not surprised by this correlation indicated an assumption about alcohol and masculinity.

Like many countries, France increased production of alcohol in the latter half of the twentieth-century. Following the Second World War the wine industry picked up after an earlier downturn. In the late twentieth-century global advertising contributed to its continued success. No longer was wine merely thought of as a part of daily sustenance in the families of the French, but in many areas of the world people thought of it as a status symbol. Consuming fine French wine became another way for the world's rich to demonstrate their cultural superiority.

By the 1980s deregulation in many countries led to another upturn in the global wine business. Global wine conglomerates emerged in the 1990s between French and Australian producers as well as between French and Californian producers. These conglomerates reflected the global nature of wine production at the end of the twentieth-century. Wine sales from France grew again in the first decade of the twenty-first-century because of increased demand from China and Russia for champagne and cognac. The United States, however, continued to lead the world in consumption of alcohol from France. The American market accounted for 22 percent of alcohol sales from France by 2006. France continued to expand its market share of global wine sales in the twenty-first-century. By 2010, for example, France was producing over 23 percent of the world's wine. International wine sales, then, exhibited the very characteristics of globalization that were so prevalent in other industries: deregulation, multi-national corporations, and production for a global market. In many ways the French wine business became an example for the internationalization of other industries. In France, as in other areas of the world, alcohol sales furthered the world trend of globalization.

Within France consumption of wine remained central to the lives of the people. In a survey taken in the mid-twentieth-century, almost 25 percent of the French had drunk some form of alcohol by the age of six, 41 percent by the age of nine, and 61 percent by the age of 12. Most people's early experiences likely entailed wine diluted by water and drunk with meals. By the time they were 18, almost 25 percent of the population had drunk to excess on at least one occasion. There were differences by gender, however. Females drank less than males, and more females abstained completely. Wine consumption in France did decline in the early twenty-first-century, however. For example, between 2001 and 2005 wine consumption in France dropped by 11 percent. Sidewalk cafés that served wine also declined in number as many people drank bottled water or liqueurs and spirits. Nevertheless, by 2007 the French still drank 64 liters a year of wine, much more than other countries.

Wine still remained France's most common drink; 90 percent of men and 56 percent of women drank wine daily by the end of the twentieth-century. Beer, cider, and spirits were consumed, but to a much lesser degree than wine. Yet beer and cider appeared to be class specific. The majority of the beer drinkers in France came from the upper-class, while those who drank cider came from the lower-class. Finally, far fewer people drank distilled spirits, and those spirits usually consisted of some form of brandy as an aperitif.

Many studies showed that abuse of alcohol remained relatively low for most of the twentieth-century in France. For example, in mid century 96 percent of women drank less than 16 ounces a day, while only 40 percent of men drank more than 16 ounces a day; 30 percent of the population did not drink daily. There were differences among classes, too. Agricultural laborers drank much more than other occupations, roughly one and a half times as much as business people. Moreover, as the educational scale lowered, the amount of alcohol increased. At mid century French society was very accepting of drinking, however. Certain specific beliefs contributed to this opinion. For example, people believed that drinking wine was good for those in heavy labor jobs because it was nourishing. They also believed that aperitifs aided digestion, warmed the body, and nicely complimented a meal. Society believed, however, that women should drink less than men. Overall, there was not much evidence that people believed one should not drink.

By the beginning of the twenty-first-century, however, some people argued that problem drinking was becoming a crisis in France. For example, a report written in 2005 by Hervé Chabalier, a prominent French journalist, claimed that France suffered from some serious problems with alcohol, even though society failed to acknowledge it ("'Alcoholism – The Simple Truth' – France." http://www.news-medical.net/news/2005/11/28/14713.aspx, accessed December 19, 2011). He reported that half of all domestic violence cases were associated with alcohol and a significant percentage of traffic accidents were alcohol related. Moreover, he asserted that 10 percent of the population suffered from an alcohol-related disease in the early twenty-first-century, and alcohol caused at least 23,000 deaths per year. He went on to say that the French also suffered from high levels of cirrhosis of the liver, and that France had two million alcoholics.

The French recognized problem drinkers as those who had a strong desire to drink, who had a hard time stopping, and whose drinking caused social or personal problems. Most heavy drinkers drank to excess between meals in cafés. Not all alcohol seemed to lead to problems, however. Many physicians in France did not believe that wine was problematic. For example, the two regions with the highest alcohol-related mortality rates, Normandy and Brittany, also had the lowest percentage of people who drank wine, the highest who drank cider, and the highest who drank distilled spirits. The regions with the highest rates of wine drinkers also had the lowest percentage of problem drinkers. Nevertheless, abuse and its incumbent problems did exist in France, which mirrored many other societies that also had cultures of abuse. Wine remained, however, central to France's cultural identity.

United States

Alcohol consumption in the United States rose throughout the twentieth- and early twenty-first-centuries, contributing to the role of the United States as the quintessential modern consumer society. Beer consumption increased with the introduction of beer cans and bottles in grocery stores, allowing people to drink privately without the social rituals associated with public alcohol venues, thus fostering the individualistic culture of the United States. In the globalized economy after the turn of the twenty-first-century, though, spirits consumption began to rise as global marketing of glamorous foreign liquors cultivated a high-end demand. Exotic spirits bestowed an elitist prestige on those with access to them, and brought especially non-Western cultures to the United States, exoticizing those cultures in the eyes of Americans.

Wine also grew as a status symbol in late twentieth-century America, deriving its demand from predominantly urban areas where people strove to be chic and urbane. Moreover, international marketing of American whiskey to developing countries successfully Westernized the tastes of consumers, providing them with an observable and relatively accessible way to welcome Western culture.

Within the United States alcohol consumption acted as a defining characteristic of identity. More men than women drank, and society defined prevalent alcohol consumption as an acceptable and widespread demonstration of masculinity. High levels of consumption by women, however, did not enhance, and in fact detracted from one's femininity. Moreover, the perceived alcohol habits of American ethnic groups led society to stereotype them, believing that alcohol overuse proved degeneracy, while moderation proved respectability. Abuse in the form of binge drinking by college-aged drinkers, however, somehow became socially acceptable as a normal right of passage.

American society was concerned with abuse, and gave birth to Alcoholics Anonymous in 1935. Alcoholics Anonymous helped popularize the disease concept of prolonged alcohol abuse, influencing the American Medical Association to add alcoholism to its lexicon of officially valid diseases, and indeed broadening the definition of disease itself. By the early twenty-first-century Alcoholics Anonymous had formed groups in the vast majority of countries, creating a worldwide ethos surrounding alcohol.

After the Volstead Act was repealed in 1933 alcohol production began to rise rapidly in the United States. By 1940 the level of beer production, for example, was back to the levels of the 1920s, although it was concentrated in the hands of fewer brewers. The sale of beer continued to increase throughout the war period of the early 1940s even though tin and malt needed for the war effort were scarce. Alcohol sales continued to climb throughout the rest of the twentieth-century and into the twenty-first-century.

Beer, spirits, and wine split the consumer alcohol market. Beer was the highest consumed alcohol at 53 percent, followed by spirits at 31 percent, and finally wine at 16 percent. Beer continued to be the most popular alcohol in the United States throughout the twentieth- and twenty-first-centuries. One reason could be that the price of beer as a percentage of income did not rise between the Second World War and the first decade of the twenty-first-century. Moreover, beer cans were introduced in the 1930s and beer bottles were introduced in the 1950s, so that it became much easier to purchase beer and drink it at home rather than having to go to a tavern to do so. Selling beer in six packs also made it easier to purchase beer for home use. Furthermore, the fact that it was sold in grocery and convenience stores made it easier to purchase and thus even more popular. By the early twenty-first-century 66 percent of all beer was purchased in six packs, whereas in the 1930s, for example, virtually all beer was drunk in taverns.

Spirits remained second to beer in their popularity, even though spirits consumption rose after 2000. For example, per capita consumption of spirits rose 9 percent between 2001 and 2005. And in 2005 alone sales of spirits increased 60 percent. Premium alcohol sales drove these changes. For example, several premium brands took over the top spots from less expensive brands during these years. Spirits companies also used exotic drinks to bring in the high-end alcohol market to the United States and abroad. Various kinds of cocktails such as the cosmo, sour apple martini, and mojito made their associated liquors popular. Other marketing tools such as specific shapes and colors of liquor bottles led consumers to buy more expensive spirits. The spirit that characterized the United States, however, was whiskey. In 2005, for example, whiskey sales rose by 24 percent in Asia, 19 percent in South America, and 89 percent in India, following a worldwide demand for American culture. In the early twenty-first-century these were new developing markets for worldwide advertising. Some researchers argue that part of the reason for the increase in sales both in the United States and abroad was television advertising. Trends in the international sale of spirits from the United States became emblematic of economic globalization in the early twenty-first-century.

Even though wine remained the third most popular drink in the United States, its consumption rose continuously between the Second World War and 2010. Wine became easily purchased by the bottle in many retail venues, which led to increased home consumption. Moreover, in 1991 when US news agencies reported that drinking wine, particularly red wine, could help stave off heart disease, the sale of wine increased 400 percent. It did decrease again after a few years, though. Unlike beer or spirits, drinking patterns for wine differed based on urbanization. By the early twenty-first-century 65 percent of wine was drunk in the largest 50 urban areas. In 2005, however, the Supreme Court ruled that wineries could ship their wine directly to consumers. This ruling began to change the demographics of wine consumption across the country, making boutique wine more accessible to a larger portion of the population. Even with this change, wine remained a status symbol with a largely urban customer base.

While the popularity of beer, spirits, and wine differed, differences also lay in general consumption patterns among people. In the early twenty-first-century in the United States consumption patterns ranged widely based on gender, venue, education, ethnicity, and age. For example, 71 percent of men in the United States drank, while 59 percent of women did. In addition, 75 percent of those with a college education drank while 50 percent of those with less than a high school education drank. Moreover, specific drinking patterns were used by groups to differentiate themselves from other social groups. Kinds of drinking establishments supported these differences. For example, drinking venues catered to specific clientele. Comedy clubs, dance clubs, breweries, martini bars, piano bars, rock music bars, gay/lesbian bars, neighborhood bars, and college bars all catered to specific groups of people.

Perhaps the most significant differences in drinking patterns existed among diverse ethnicities. More importantly, stereotypes regarding the drinking habits of certain ethnic groups served to further prejudice against those groups. Research, too, sometimes perpetuated racial stereotypes against ethnic minorities, especially African Americans, Asian Americans, and Hispanic Americans. By the early twenty-first-century, however, newer research showed that it was difficult to make generalizations about ethnic drinking patterns because tremendous variations existed among subgroups within ethnicities. For example, Mexican-American men had higher rates of heavy drinking as well as problems surrounding alcohol than did Puerto Rican-American men or Cuban-American men. In addition, Mexican-American women had both a higher rate of abstinence and a higher rate of heavy drinking than did Puerto Rican-American women or Cuban-American women.

Within white America many studies in the twentieth-century showed differences among sub-groups. Jewish Americans, for example, had fewer problems with drinking, even though they drank alcohol on social occasions as well as many religious occasions such as Rosh Hashanah, Passover, Hanukkah, Purim, and Yom Kippur. By the end of the twentieth-century, however, there was an increasing problem with excessive drinking among Jewish Americans, although they were still held up as examples of moderation. Other white ethnic groups were stereotyped as having more problems with excessive drinking. According to studies in the first half of the twentieth-century the white ethnic group with the highest percentage of problem drinking was Irish Americans. This research, however, became suspect in the later twentieth-century as prejudice against Irish Americans waned.

In the twentieth-century African Americans were also stereotyped as heavy drinkers. However, research that compared black males to white males showed this stereotype to be false. More black men abstained from alcohol than did white men; 36 percent compared to 26 percent respectively. Black men did drink more heavily in their forties and fifties while white men drank more in their twenties. Still, however, white males in their fifties drank more than black males in their fifties.

Asian Americans were typically stereotyped as low consumers of alcohol in the twentieth-century. As a whole they had lower consumption rates than the national average, but substantial differences arose within the group. Vietnamese Americans, and Chinese-Vietnamese Americans, had the highest levels of drinking, while Chinese Americans had the lowest. Japanese Americans, Filipino Americans, and Korean Americans were in the middle of the range. Japanese-American women had the highest rates of consumption, at 67 percent, while Korean-American women had the lowest, at 18 percent.

Researchers argue that the lower consumption rates of Asian Americans came from the flushing response, which was explained earlier in the discussion of China. Not all researchers, however, agreed with this explanation. Some argued that cultural rather than physiological reasons existed for lower drinking habits. These researchers asserted that Confucian and Taoist traditions that stressed harmony, conformity, and responsibility toward others caused lower consumption rates in first-generation Asian Americans. They went on to show that second- and third-generation Asian immigrants to the United States drank more than their first-generation parents or grandparents. Therefore, they reasoned that socio-logical rather than physiological differences better explained drinking habits.

One of the most widespread myths regarding alcohol consumption in the United States in the twentieth- and early twenty-first-centuries surrounded Native Americans' drinking habits. Native Americans were stereotyped as binge drinkers because of a supposed predisposition to abuse alcohol. Research, however, showed that the stereotype that Native Americans were physiologically and psychologically more apt to drink was false because so many differences in consumption patterns existed among the over five hundred tribes in the United States. Drinking stereotypes in the United States were a powerful tool used to further ethnic stereotypes in the twentieth and twenty-first-centuries.

While not an ethnic group, an important drinking subculture within the United States included youth up to age 25. Young people had specific pro-blems with alcohol. Several research studies in the late twentieth- and early twenty-first centuries focused on underage as well as college-age binge drink-ing as a problem that needed a solution. Binge drinking could cause great harm and even death to those who participated in it. Some argued that binge drinking among youth was inevitable and therefore a policy of trying to curb the problem rather than a policy of trying to eliminate it would be more useful. Overall, drinking among youth decreased in the late twentieth and early twenty-first-centuries, yet binge drinking by those who did drink con-tinued to cause a dangerous problem.

Binge drinking by young adults was only one of the forms of alcohol abuse that occurred in the United States. Alcoholism posed problems both in the twentieth- and early twenty-first-centuries. It afflicted those from dysfunctional as well as those from highly functional backgrounds. A study in the mid-twentieth century concluded that 18 percent of those from dysfunctional backgrounds were alcoholics, while 17 percent of those from functional backgrounds ended up as alcoholics. Alcoholics suffered from many health problems. Researchers knew that excessive use of ethanol, especially in the form of spirits, could cause malnutrition through the maldigestion and malabsorption of nutrients. In a heavy drinker alcohol might be the major form of caloric intake and therefore the drinker might not eat essential foods in his or her diet. Several diseases were associated with excessive alcohol consumption such as encephalopathies, liver problems, heart diseases, and nervous disorders. Deficiencies in vitamin B1 and vitamin B complex, which cause pellagra, dermatosis, digestive disorder, and mental dysfunction were found in heavy drinkers.

During the 1940s in the United States the belief in the disease concept of alcoholism became more widespread. By the first decade of the twenty-first-century the widely accepted viewpoint was that alcoholism was a disease, even though there were still those who believed it to be a personal failing. Within the disease school of alcoholism a question still existed in the early twenty-first-century of whether alcoholism was a mental or physical problem. Some argued that the disease concept was harmful because it implied that a medical "cure" could be found and therefore the psychological aspects were ignored. Others argued that alcoholism was both a physical and psychological disease and therefore required treatment from both fields of healthcare. When alcoholism became accepted as a health problem, or disease, people began to obtain health care coverage for treatment.

By the early twenty-first-century Alcoholics Anonymous was the most widespread organization helping alcoholics. Because there still existed extreme prejudice against alcoholics, the organization focused on anonymity. The AA program was based on a 12-step plan, which included things like admitting lack of control over addiction and making amends for mistakes made while still drinking. Some researchers in the early twenty-first-century, however, argued that AA worked no better than no treatment at all. Moreover, other groups argued that the idea of alcoholism was culturally constructed phenomenon rather than a specific disease. Therefore, because of differing cultural norms surrounding acceptable levels of drinking in the United States, it was ethnocentric to define any certain pattern of drinking as problem drinking. As a result, it became even more complicated to define alcohol issues, making treatment very difficult across ethnicities within the United States. Nonetheless, the Federal Government began to mandate both the availability of treatment programs for alcoholics, as well as their equal treatment under the law. In 1963 and then again in 1968, Congress specifically provided federal support to establish facilities for the treatment and rehabilitation of alcoholics. By 1973, alcoholism was defined as a disability, and alcoholics legally received "reasonable accommodation" at work and in many public places. Finally, in 1990 Congress passed the Americans

With Disabilities Act (ADA), which provided even broader protections for alcoholics who had gone through, or were participating in, alcohol rehabilitation.

Also, for the sake of public safety, the US sought to regulate the sale and use of alcohol after the end of Prohibition. The government limited sales through "blue laws", which restricted the days and times that alcohol could be sold. Moreover, several states passed laws setting the legal drinking age at 21. By 1984 the Federal Government enacted a "national minimum drinking age act," also setting the age at 21 and tying federal highway funds to compliance. By 1988 all states had passed the law. States also concentrated their efforts on drunk driving laws. Indiana passed the first drunk driving law in 1939, setting the blood–alcohol limit at .15. Subsequently, all states enacted drunk driving laws, and by 2004 all states had set .08 as the limit.

While regulation continued to concern the US it also realized the importance of alcohol taxes to the federal budget. One of the reasons the federal government repealed the Volstead Act, in fact, was the promise of alcohol taxes needed to help lift the country out of the depression. Since then the Federal as well as state and local governments have relied on excise taxes. Furthermore, by the end of 2011, after the US suffered a severe recession, several states increased alcohol taxes to make up deficits in their state budgets. Like many countries in the twentieth- and twenty-first-centuries, the US implicitly sought high alcohol sales – thus more tax revenues – far the sake of governmental budgets, blatantly contradicting its support of alcohol regulations for the sake of public safety. These political contradictions merely added to the already complex role of alcohol in economics, culture, and society in the twentieth- and twenty-first-century United States.

Conclusion

In the late twentieth- and early twenty-first-centuries, alcohol fed economic and cultural globalization. First, the international marketing of alcohol from all over the world promoted economic globalization. The rising demand for Latin American cachaça and tequila, Russian vodka and samogon, French wine, and US whiskey opened significant avenues of trade for those countries. Second, the alcohol trade facilitated the movement of Western and non-Western cultures globally. Western culture spread to non-Western areas such as Saudi Arabia, India, China, and Japan through the trade in Western alcohol. Western alcohol smuggled into Saudi Arabia met the increasing demand of elites, especially, to socialize over alcohol, bringing an aspect of Western culture to that country. In India the trade in "Indian-made foreign liquor" such as beer and spirits, and in China a jump in the sales of Western alcohol, provided a means with which to mimic Western culture to the growing number of people who wished to do so. In Japan the introduction of liquor in individually sized containers allowed drinkers to order separately rather than as a group, encouraging a Western sense of individualism. Alcohol production and trade also popularized non-Western culture, as Latin American cachaça and tequila, and Russian samogon spread in the West.

Alcohol consumption patterns helped culturally construct class, gender, and Western and non-Western identities globally. First, drinking patterns defined class identity in such diverse cultures as those found in Africa, Saudi Arabia, India, China, France, and the United States. In several African countries drinking bottled beer instead of indigenous beer signified upper- or middle-class status. In Saudi Arabia the clandestine use of Western liquor bespoke of elite privilege. Moreover, in India consumption of foreign liquors by elites furthered the cultural separation between the upper- and lower-classes, just as in China where drinking foreign alcohol as well as public displays of drunkenness indicated one's higher status within society. In France the upper class and the lower-class both had their signature drinks apart from wine that made up part of their identity; beer for the elites and cider for the lower-class. Finally, in the United States drinking wine became a status symbol, separating those who aspired to be elite from those in the lower-classes.

Third, drinking patterns further defined gender roles in many cultures. For example, men drank more alcohol in virtually every society, including those in Latin America, Africa, Saudi Arabia, China, Japan, Russia, France, and the United States. It became a well-known behavior associated with masculinity. In addition, statistics on Latin America, Russia, France, and the United States all revealed that drinking led to increased male violence, particularly in the home, reflecting society's expectations surrounding men, alcohol, and violence.

Fourth, the consumption of specific liquors bestowed a Western identity upon the consumer. Drinking bottled beer in Africa, Western spirits in India, and beer, whiskey, and wine in Japan overtly signified one's Westernness.

Fifth, the non-Western and rapidly developing societies of Latin America, Africa, India, China, and Japan (although Japan was relatively more developed), all confronted encroachment by an all-pervasive Western culture as they moved into the global economy. In response, many people in those countries maintained time-honored alcohol customs, displaying a visible and symbolic allegiance to traditional values and at least a partial rejection of Westernization.

Addressing the by-products of alcohol abuse in the later twentieth- and early twenty-first-centuries remained a goal of governments as well as civic societies around the world. First, the increase in drinking in the latter half of the twentieth-century resulted in increased alcohol abuse in many societies including Latin America, Saudi Arabia, India, Japan, Russia, France, and the United States. Rising levels of alcohol abuse caused major risks to public health and safety in the twentieth- and twenty-first-centuries. Violence in Latin America, Saudi Arabia, China, France, and the United States; a significant percentage of auto accidents in India, China, Russia, and the United States; skyrocketing mortality rates in Africa and Russia; and increases in mental as well as other chronic diseases in Saudi Arabia, India, France, and the United

States all resulted from alcohol abuse. Yet governments struggled to regulate alcohol. Regulations included such things as mandated legal drinking ages in Mexico, Japan, and the United States. The twentieth-century bore out the fact that prohibition, while perhaps temporarily decreasing consumption, did not eliminate it and instead led to the use of more dangerous forms of alcohol. The almost unanimous inability on the part of governments to have as much control over alcohol as they wanted, demonstrated the continued centrality of alcohol in people's lives. Alcohol's importance was also apparent in governments, as many countries, such as India, China, Japan, Russia, and the US, relied on alcohol taxes to help sustain their budgets. Second, outside of government, Alcoholics Anonymous groups spread out from the United States to virtually every corner of the globe, including Latin America, Africa, Saudi Arabia, India, and China. AA disseminated the Western ideology that alcoholism was a disease and then offered a 12-step plan to recovery. While it adapted to other cultures, AA still brought with it Western beliefs that permeated non-Western societies.

The trade, use, abuse, and regulation of alcohol in the twentieth- and twenty-first-centuries defined people's lives in many ways. Its high demand worldwide opened markets for several countries, earning them both profits from the trade as well as national identities associated with their signature alcohol. Alcohol helped spread Western and non-Western cultures to many parts of the world, while it signified class and social status as well as ethnic and gender identities within societies. Its ubiquitous nature ensured its continued importance into the twenty-first-century.

Further reading

AbuMadini, M. S., Sheikh I. A. Rahim, M. A. Al-Zahrani, and A. O. Al-Johi. 2008. "Two decades of Treatment Seeking for Substance Use Disorders in Saudi Arabia: Trends and Patterns in a Rehabilitation Facility in Dammam." *Drug and Alcohol Dependence.* (97): 231–36.

Albrithen, A. A. 2006 "Alcoholism and Domestic Violence in Saudi Society." PhD Dissertation University of Liverpool.

AlMarri, T. 2009. "Alcohol and Substance Use in the Arabian Gulf Region: A Review." *International Journal of Psychology.* 44 (3): 222–33.

Anderson, K. 1995. *Young People and Alcohol, Drugs and Tobacco.* Finland: World Health Organization.

Anderson, K. (ed.) 2004. *The World's Wine Markets: Globalization at Work.* Cheltenham: Edward Elgar.

Babor, T. F. 1986. *Alcohol and Culture: Comparative Perspectives from Europe and America.* New York: New York Academy of Sciences.

Barr, A. 1999. *Drink: A Social History of America.* New York: Carroll & Graf Publishers.

Blaine, A. (ed.) 1980. *Alcoholism and the Jewish Community.* New York: Commission on Synagogue Relations, Federation of Jewish Philanthropies of New York.

Caetano, R., C. L. Clark, and T. Tam. 1998. "Alcohol Consumption Among Ethnic Minorities, Theory and Research." *Alcohol Health & Research World.* 22 (4): 233–41.

Chaudron, C. D. and D. A. Wilkinson (eds.) 1988. *Theories on Alcoholism*. Toronto: Addiction Research Foundation.

Dorschner, J. P. 1981. *Alcohol Consumption in a Village in North India*. Studies in Cultural Anthropology, NO. 1. Ann Arbor, MI: UMI Research Press.

Eber, C. 1995. *Women & Alcohol in a Highland Maya Town: Water of Hope, Water of Sorrow*. Austin: University of Texas Press.

Ewing, J. A. and B. A. Rouse. 1978. *Drinking: Alcohol in American Society – Issues and Current Research*. Chicago: Nelson-Hall.

Gastineau, C., W. J. Darby, and T. B. Turner (eds.) 1979. *Fermented Food Beverages in Nutrition*. New York: Academic Press.

Gefou-Madianou, D. (ed.) 1992. *Alcohol, Gender and Culture*. New York: Routledge.

Giesbrecht, N., R. Room, E. Oesterberg, J. Moskalewicz, and M. Cahannes (eds.) 1983. "Consequences of Drinking, Trends in Alcohol Problem Statistics in Seven Countries." Papers associated with Alcohol, Society, and the State – a report of the International Study of Alcohol Control Experiences, in collaboration with the World Health Organization Regional Office for Europe. Toronto: Addiction Research Foundation.

Graham, K. and R. Homel. 2008. *Raising the Bar: Preventing Aggression in and Around Bars, Pubs, and Clubs*. Portland, OR: Willan Publishing.

Grant, M. 1998. *Alcohol and Emerging Markets: Patterns, Problems, and Responses*. Philadelphia: Brunner/Mazel.

Grant, M. and J. Litvak. 1998. *Drinking Patterns and Their Consequences*. Washington, DC: Taylor & Francis.

Hao W., J. Derson, S. Xiao, L. Li, and L. Zhang 1999. "Alcohol Consumption and Alcohol-Related Problems: Chinese experience from Six Area Samples, 1994." *Addiction*. 94 (10): 1467–76.

Hauge, R. 1984. *Alcohol and Crime*. Strasbourg: Council of Europe.

Heath, D. B. 1987. "Anthropology and Alcohol Studies: Current Issues." *Annual Review of Anthropology*. (16): 99–142.

——2000. *Drinking Occasions, Comparative Perspectives on Alcohol and Culture*. Series on Alcohol in Society. International Center for Alcohol Policies. Ann Arbor, MI: Sheridan Books.

Helzer, J. E. and G. J. Canino. (eds.) 1992. *Alcoholism in North America, Europe, and Asia*. New York: Oxford University Press.

Hiramani, A. B. and N. Sharma. 1988. *Health and Youth in India*. Delhi: Agam Prakashan.

Jones, A., W. D. Connor, and D. E. Powell (eds.) 1991. *Soviet Social Problems*. Boulder, CO: Westview Press.

Kirkby, D. 1998. *Barmaids: A History of Women's Work in Pubs*. New York: Cambridge University Press.

Kueny, K. 2001. *The Rhetoric of Sobriety: Wine in Early Islam*. Albany: State University of New York Press.

Lehto, J. 1995. *Approaches to Alcohol Control Policy*. Copenhagen: World Health Organization.

Leon, D. A., V. M. Shkolnikow, and M. Mckee. 2009. "Alcohol and Russian Mortality: A Continuing Crisis." *Addiction*. 104 (10) (October): 1630–36.

Lin, T. and D. T. Lin. 1982. "Alcoholism among the Chinese: Further observations of a low-risk population." *Culture, Medicine and Psychiatry*. 6 (2): 109–16.

Manheimer, A. (ed.) 2007. *Alcohol*. New York: Thomson Gale.

Maternovsky, D. and M. Sysoyeva. 2011. "Medvedev Signs Law Restricting Russian Beer, Alcohol Sales." *Bloomberg News.* http://www.bloomberg.com/news/2011-7-20/medvedev-signs-law-restricting-russian-beer-alcohol-sales-1-.html (accessed September 2, 2011).

McDonald, M. (ed.) 1994. *Gender, Drink and Drugs.* New York: Berg.

McGovern, P. E. 2009. *Uncorking the Past: The Quest for Wine, Beer and Other Alcoholic Beverages.* Berkeley: University of California Press.

Michalak, L. and K. Trocki. 2006. "Alcohol and Islam: An Overview." *Contemporary Drug Problems.* 33 (4) (Winter): 523–62.

Minai, K. 1986. *Trends in Alcoholic Beverage Consumption in Postwar Japan: An Analysis and Interpretation of Aggregate Data.* Singapore: Department of Japanese Studies National University of Singapore.

Peele, S. and M. Grant. 1999. *Alcohol and Pleasure: A Health Perspective.* Philadelphia: Brunner/Mazel.

Pernanen, K. 1991. *Alcohol in Human Violence.* New York: The Guilford Press.

Phillips, R. 2000. *A Short History of Wine.* New York: Harper Collins.

Roberts, B. D. 2000. "Always Cheaply Pleasant: Beer as Commodity in a Rural Kenyan Society." In *Commodities and Globalization, Anthropological Perspectives.* A. Haugerud, M. P. Stone, and P. D. Little (eds.) New York: Rowman & Littlefield.

Room, R. 1984. "Alcohol and Ethnography: A Case of Problem Deflation?" *Current Anthropology.* 25 (2): 169–91.

Rothbaum, N. 2007. *The Business of Spirits: How Savvy Marketers, Innovative Distillers, and Entrepreneurs Changed How We Drink.* New York: Kaplan.

Saul, M. 1981. "Beer, Sorghum and Women: Production for the Market in Rural Upper Volta." *Africa.* 51 (3): 746–64.

Single, E., P. Morgan, and J. de Lint (eds.) 1981. *Alcohol, Society, and the State: The Social History of Control Policy in Seven Countries.* Toronto: Addition Research Foundation and World Health Organization.

Smith, S. R. 1992. "Drinking Etiquette in a Changing Beverage Market." In *Re-Made in Japan.* J. J. Tobin (ed.) New Haven, CT: Yale University Press.

Snyder, C. R. 1958. *Alcohol and the Jews: A Cultural Study of Drinking and Sobriety.* New Haven, CT: Yale Center of Alcohol Studies.

White, S. 1996. *Russia Goes Dry: Alcohol, State and Society.* Cambridge: Cambridge University Press.

Wong, G. 2009. "Russia's Bleak Picture of Health." CNN.com/health. May 19. http://edition.cnn.com/2009/HEALTH/05/19/russia.health/index.html (accessed September 2, 2011).

Zhang, F.-P. 1982. "Drinking in China." *The Drinking and Drug Practices Surveyor.* 18: 12–15.

8   Conclusion

Continuity rather than change characterizes the story of alcohol over time and across civilizations. From even earlier than the beginnings of agriculture to the twenty-first-century alcohol shaped the cultural, social, political, and economic spheres of societies. It structured rituals and celebrations. It spread culture, and it also preserved culture in the face of social and political change. Alcohol furthered social differences such as class, ethnicity, and gender, and it prompted one of the most important social movements of the nineteenth-century in many Western countries, temperance. Alcohol regulation effectively controlled segments of society, and its taxes bolstered governments by bringing in significant revenues. Colonial governments used alcohol as a tool to further oppress the colonized, and the colonized used alcohol to resist oppressive governments. Finally, through trade, especially international trade, alcohol helped economies flourish. In essence, alcohol defined cultures, signified social differentiation, funded political structures, and stimulated economic development.

Alcohol possessed symbolic meanings from the time of the ancient civilizations into the twenty-first-century. In virtually every society it was central to rights of passage and it shaped important rituals. It symbolized the hospitality of hosts, the coming together of families in marriage, and the passing of life into death. Moreover, alcohol held symbolic meanings in the world's organized religions. Its use shaped the way religious ceremonies took place in Judaism and Christianity, and its regulation defined the fundamental principles of Islam and Buddhism.

Alcohol was a medium through which culture spread, or conversely, a medium to maintain traditions in the face of cultural infiltration. The expansion of alcohol into new areas changed social interactions and rituals. For example, the classical Greeks extended their culture to the colonies in Italy through viticulture and viniculture. In the late Classical and Post-Classical periods organized religions across the globe used alcohol to solidify their cultural impact by either introducing new alcohol rituals or by banning alcohol outrightly. In pre-colonial Latin America the Incas successfully co-opted conquered groups by establishing their own corn beer, or chicha, rituals in the newly conquered areas.

In modern world history Western culture permeated non-Western cultures through alcohol. For example, in the sixteenth-century Spanish drinking habits migrated to Latin America with colonization, not only changing indigenous cultures but also causing social unrest. In the nineteenth-century Western alcohol customs infiltrated Africa through colonization, transforming indigenous life and in some cases causing social breakdown. In both cases, however, indigenous groups did not completely succumb, rather they continued to practice alcohol traditions as a way to stave off Western cultural influences. In the twentieth-century, US culture permeated Japan through new drinking practices, while at the same time the Japanese used Western alcohol to continue established cultural traditions. Finally, in the late twentieth-century the culture of alcoholism as a disease spread from Western to non-Western societies such as China and India, augmenting their definitions of disease.

Alcohol helped shape societies. It was a vital nutritional ingredient in the daily lives of most agriculturally based groups, and it helped define medicine in many societies from the Pre-Classical period up through the twenty-first-century. One of the most important social roles that alcohol played, however, was to signify or sometimes even grant status within societies. In ancient and Classical civilizations people gained status through providing alcohol for feasts, which gave them tremendous social capital. In Classical Greek society elites especially labeled people based on the type of alcohol they drank. Drinking diluted wine, according to elites, distinguished them from others, while drinking beer and undiluted wine demonstrated one's lower class status. Alcohol consumption patterns continued to denote class in modern history. Wine, for example, was a status symbol in many societies. In colonial Latin America elite Spaniards flaunted their status by drinking wine, while the indigenous lower classes drank pulque. In early-modern Britain elites drank wine and the lower classes drank ale, and in nineteenth-century Ireland the gentry drank wine, while the lower-classes drank whiskey and beer. In the twentieth and early twenty-first-century West, wine remained a status symbol. Other alcohols, too, were used to display status in the twentieth- and early twenty-first-centuries. In modern India, Western whiskey was a status symbol, and in modern Africa drinking bottled beer became a sign of middle-class status. In the twenty-first-century West, drinking exotic indigenous alcohols from non-Western countries conferred a status of exclusivity on the usually young, urban professionals who drank them.

Drinking privileges and venues also separated elites and commoners. For example, the ancient Egyptians and later the pre-colonial Aztecs both allowed elites the privilege of drinking to excess, while they punished commoners for such behavior. In the twenty-first-century the Chinese began to accept public drunkenness by elites even though such behavior violated social mores. Drinking venues in modern societies also furthered the differentiation among classes. This was especially true in the West. In nineteenth-century France cafés specialized in serving either the elite or the working-class, and in industrializing Britain private clubs served elites while many pubs catered only to the working-class. Separation of drinking venues by class continued into the twenty-first-century.

Other social differences were defined by alcohol consumption patterns as well. During the formation of Islam Muslims visibly set themselves apart from Christians by abstaining from alcohol. Christians, too, created new alcohol rituals to set themselves apart from pagans. People continued to use alcohol in modern history to prove social differentiation, and even to reinforce stereotypes. In the twentieth-century United States, for example, mainstream beliefs about ethnic drinking patterns fueled prejudice. Negative stereotypes of Irish Americans, African Americans, and Native Americans were justified by labeling them as alcohol abusers, while positive stereotypes of Asian Americans were furthered by the belief that they were prudent in their alcohol consumption habits. It was true that each ethnic group represented certain trends in alcohol consumption, yet within ethnic groups widely varying alcohol habits existed. Moreover, in the twentieth- and early twenty-first-century United States various subcultures used alcohol venues to affirm their shared identity. Gay and lesbian bars, college bars, country and western bars, and neighborhood bars all exemplified this pattern.

Alcohol reinforced and at times defined gender identity. Both alcohol production as well as consumption patterns helped to strengthen gender roles. In many agricultural societies women were responsible for producing alcohol. In pre-colonial Incan society, for example, only women made chicha. Since chicha was a sacred element, as well as central to daily nutrition, making it strengthened women's status in that society. Moreover, as civilizations developed into market societies and alcohol became a commodity, women kept their roles as alcohol producers and began selling it, gaining some economic independence as a result. For example, in medieval Britain many women made their livings by producing and selling alcohol. The same was true in Latin America and Africa. In many cases, however, with the onset of mass production, the alcohol trade moved away from cottage industry and became a big business. Men took over its production and sale, identifying the industry as masculine, and economically marginalizing many women as a result. This happened in early-modern Britain and later on in many parts of Africa. In parts of Latin America, however, chicha remained popular, and its production stayed predominantly in the hands of women in cottage industry, showing that in the areas where an indigenous alcohol culture remained, women continued to hold economically strong roles by selling alcohol.

Many cultures, however, severely limited women's access to alcohol. In Rome, for example, during the Greco-Roman period men were said to kiss their wives upon arrival for the sole purpose of detecting alcohol on their breath, and some women were even killed by their families for drinking alcohol. In Classical India the *Kama Sutra* forbade wives to drink alcohol, but allowed mistresses, whose sexual reputation was already tainted, to do so. Modern societies, even into the twentieth-century, virtually banned women from drinking in public venues. Those who did risked being labeled as prostitutes. Societies imbued alcohol with so much power to define women that association with it could ruin or even kill a woman.

Men's gender identity was defined by their relationship to alcohol as well. In Australia up until the late-twentieth-century, pubs were bastions of white male power as well as centers of political activity. Pubs epitomized masculinity, and acted as centers of political power in that country, effectively emasculating aboriginal men who were banned from them, and excluding aborigines as well as women from politics. In the late twentieth-century, however, it became legal for aborigines to drink in pubs and more acceptable for women to do so. Acquiring these rights was so momentous that women viewed their ability to finally enter pubs as even more important than their right to vote. Beliefs surrounding alcohol and gender began to shift toward the end of the twentieth-century, but older stereotypes likely still influenced male and female behavior. In the United States, for example, at the end of the twentieth century 71 percent of men drank while 59 percent of women did so.

Reinforcing and sometimes creating identity was not the only way alcohol influenced society. Alcohol prompted a powerful, international social movement in the nineteenth- and early-twentieth-centuries. Temperance arose largely in Western, Protestant countries ostensibly as a response to the upsurge in alcohol consumption brought on by the tremendous social changes accompanying industrialization. It became, however, an effective means for the powerful as well as the oppressed to further their social and political agendas. For example, in nineteenth-century Ireland the Protestant minority used temperance ideology to justify their political and social control over the marginalized Catholic majority, who they deemed irresponsible drunkards. In the United States widely held temperance beliefs gave the elite and the middle class a moral rationale for the poor conditions of both ethnic minorities and the urban working class. They labeled these marginalized groups as alcohol abusers, successfully deflecting the focus away from structural inequality. Marginalized groups also embraced temperance, however. Catholics in nineteenth-century Ireland and African Americans in the nineteenth-century United States both advocated for temperance within their own groups as a way to prove their high moral character, thus justifying their arguments for equality.

Governments, too, used alcohol to further their agendas. Virtually all governments regulated alcohol in some way. Alcohol regulation, however, became more than a means to protect public health and safety. It played three important roles in society. First, governments used liquor laws as a tool to reinforce the social hierarchy, directing most of the regulations at the lower classes and the socially marginalized. Liquor laws effectively controlled the behavior of these groups and reinforced their lack of power. For example, the Aztecs highly curtailed the consumption of alcohol by commoners and punished them severely if they did not comply. In colonial Latin America the Spanish government repeatedly passed laws to regulate indigenous drinking. The same was true in industrializing Britain where the government regulated gin consumption, a favorite of the working-class, and in nineteenth-century Ireland where the government regulated whiskey, also a drink of the lower class. Second, governments regulated alcohol venues as a way to maintain political control. Governments from Mesopotamia, to the colonial Americas, to nineteenth-century France all believed that drinking establishments were dangerous centers of political intrigue, fearing that political agitators gathered in these places to foment rebellion.

Third, even though governments regulated alcohol, they also took advantage of its popularity. Some of the same governments that attempted to limit the consumption of alcohol by the lower classes also used it as a way to induce that same segment of society to work for the benefit of the government. In sixteenth-century colonial Latin America and in nineteenth-century colonial Africa, for example, the governments paid indigenous workers in alcohol to work in the mines and to build large infrastructure projects. Moreover, many governments brought in significant tax revenues from the alcohol trade. These monies provided the means for the growth and maintenance of their political structures. For example, alcohol taxes played a large role in sustaining the governments of ancient Egypt, early-modern Britain, colonial Latin America, nineteenth-century Russia, and twentieth-century colonial Africa. By the nineteenth-century, Russian alcohol taxes accounted for 30 percent of their total tax revenues, and in twentieth-century colonial Nigeria alcohol taxes accounted for 75 percent of that government's revenue. These many regulations as well as taxes show that governments recognized the power of alcohol and its venues to destabilize as well as sustain political and social structures.

Indigenous groups struggling for political autonomy also understood the power of alcohol in politics. They believed that gaining control over alcohol use symbolized independence. This was the case in India in the nineteenth and early-twentieth-centuries where the independence movement pushed for prohibition, which was seen as a break away from the British colonial alcohol culture, and in South Africa later in the century where native Africans rioted to abolish the beerhall system, a hated symbol of apartheid.

In many societies alcohol played a role in their economic success. In these societies alcohol accounted for a sizable portion of trade, and sometimes even drove economic growth. In ancient Mesopotamia, for example, the wine trade was predominantly responsible for developing crucial trading networks. In Europe in the early-modern period wine accounted for 30 percent of all English imports and 25 percent of all imports to the Low Countries. Moreover, during the formation of the modern world system wine was a valuable commodity for the powerful Dutch traders, and its widespread demand allowed Portugal to expand its trading networks to many parts of the world. Furthermore, the African demand for alcohol during the Atlantic slave trade helped to make that system work. For example, it paid for 25 percent of all the slaves from Angola. Even after the end of the Atlantic slave trade Europe sold alcohol to Africa in exchange for raw materials crucial to European industry. In the late-twentieth- and early-twenty-first-centuries alcohol became important in international trade agreements. Mexico in one agreement and Brazil in another demanded sole ownership of the names of popular liquors that had originated in their countries. Their success set precedents for international laws regarding intellectual property rights. Finally, in the late-twentieth century the value of alcohol as a commodity could be seen in the significant advertising space it commanded. In China, for example, alcohol producers spent almost 20 percent of all their television advertising budgets on liquor ads.

Alcohol has had a presence in almost all civilizations. Its physiological properties as well as its symbolism have smoothed the path for human interactions in cultural, social, political, and economic settings. It has shaped cultures both where it has been used and where it has been banned. Control over its use has provided social as well as political power. And its economic value has made it an important commodity in the domestic as well as the international trade of many societies. Its meanings as well as its uses have been myriad, making its influence omnipresent in human history.

Bibliography

AbuMadini, M. S., Sheikh I. A. Rahim, M. A. Al-Zahrani, and A. O. Al-Johi. 2008. "Two Decades of Treatment Seeking for Substance Use Disorders in Saudi Arabia: Trends and Patterns in a Rehabilitation Facility in Dammam." *Drug and Alcohol Dependence* (97): 231–36.

AlMarri, T. 2009. "Alcohol and Substance Use in the Arabian Gulf Region: A Review." *International Journal of Psychology* 44 (3): 222–33.

Ambler, C. H. 1987. *Alcohol and Disorder in Pre-Colonial Africa.* Working Papers in African Studies No. 126. Boston: African Studies Center, Boston University.

Ancient Egyptian Medicine: The Papyrus Ebers. 1930. Trans. C. P. Bryan. Chicago: Ares Publishers.

Anderson, K. 1995. *Young People and Alcohol, Drugs and Tobacco.* Finland: World Health Organization.

Anderson, K. (ed.) 2004. *The World's Wine Markets: Globalization at Work.* Cheltenham: Edward Elgar.

Babor, T. F. 1986. *Alcohol and Culture: Comparative Perspectives from Europe and America.* New York: New York Academy of Sciences.

Barr, A. 1999. *Drink: A Social History of America.* New York: Carroll & Graf Publishers.

Barrows, S. and R. Room. (eds.) 1991. *Drinking Behavior and Belief in Modern History.* Berkeley: University of California Press.

Bennett, J. M. 1996. *Ale, Beer, and Brewsters in England: Women's Work in a Changing World, 1300–1600.* New York: Oxford University Press.

Bennett, L. A. 1984. "Ethnography, Alcohol, and South-Central European Societies." A dedicated issue of articles in the *East European Quarterly* 18, no. 4.

Bennett, L. A. and G. M. Ames. 1985. *The American Experience with Alcohol: Contrasting Cultural Perspectives.* New York: Plenum Press.

Berger, P. 1985. *The Art of Wine in East Asia.* San Francisco: Asian Art Museum of San Francisco.

Blaine, A. (ed.) 1980. *Alcoholism and the Jewish Community.* New York: Commission on Synagogue Relations, Federation of Jewish Philanthropies of New York.

Bledsoe, C. and G. Pison. (eds.) 1994. *Nuptiality in Sub-Saharan Africa: Contemporary Anthropological and Demographic Perspectives.* Oxford: Clarendon Press.

Bowen, H. V., M. Lincoln, and N. Rigby. 2002. *The Worlds of the East India Company.* Rochester, New York: The Boydell Press.

Bruman, H. J. 2000. *Alcohol in Ancient Mexico.* Salt Lake City: University of Utah Press.

Bryceson, D. F. (ed.) 2002. *Alcohol in Africa: Mixing Business, Pleasure, and Politics.* Portsmouth, NH: Heinemann.

Caetano, R., C. L. Clark, and T. Tam. 1998. "Alcohol Consumption Among Ethnic Minorities, Theory and Research." *Alcohol Health & Research World* 22 (4): 233–41.

Carlson, R. G. 1990. "Banana Beer, Reciprocity, and Ancestor Propitiation Among the Haya of Bukoba, Tanzania." *Ethnology* 29 (4): 297–311.

Chaudron, C. D. and D. A. Wilkinson. (eds.) 1988. *Theories on Alcoholism.* Toronto: Addiction Research Foundation.

Clark, P. 1983. *The English Alehouse: a social history, 1200–1830.* New York: Longman.

Colson, E. and T. Scudder. 1988. *For Prayer and Profit: The Ritual, Economic, and Social Importance of Beer in Gwembe District, Zambia, 1950–1982.* Standford, CA: Stanford University Press.

Crush, J. and C. Ambler (eds.) 1992. *Liquor and Labor in Southern Africa.* Athens: Ohio University Press.

Curto, J. 1996. *Alcohol and Slaves: The Luso-Brazilian Alcohol Commerce at Mpinda, Luanda, and Benguela during the Atlantic Slave trade c. 1480–1830 and its Impact on the Societies of West Central Africa.* PhD Dissertation University of California Los Angeles.

——2006. *Enslaving Spirits: The Portuguese-Brazilian Alcohol Trade at Luanda and its Hinterland, c. 1550–1830.* Boston, MA: Brill.

Darby, W. J. P. G. and L. Grivetti. 1976. *Food: The Gift of Osiris.* Vol. 2. London: Academic Press.

Davies, W. W. 1905. *The Codes of Hammurabi and Moses.* Cincinnati: Jennings and Graham.

Dayagi-Mendels, M. 1999. *Drink and Be Merry: Wine and Beer in Ancient Times.* Jerusalem: The Israel Museum.

Dietler, M. and B. Hayden. (eds.) 2001. *Feasts: Archaeological and Ethnographic Perspectives on Food, Politics, and Power.* Washington, DC: Smithsonian Institution Press.

Dorschner, J. P. 1981. *Alcohol Consumption in a Village in North India.* Studies in Cultural Anthropology, No. 1. Ann Arbor, MI: UMI Research Press.

Duis, P. R. 1983. *The Saloon: Public Drinking in Chicago and Boston 1880–1920.* Urbana: University of Illinois Press.

Eber, C. 1995. *Women & Alcohol in a Highland Maya Town: Water of Hope, Water of Sorrow.* Austin: University of Texas Press.

Ewing, J. A. and B. A. Rouse. 1978. *Drinking: Alcohol in American Society – Issues and Current Research.* Chicago: Nelson-Hall.

Forbes, R. J. 1948. *Short History of the Art of Distillation: from the Beginnings up to the Death of Cellier Blumenthal.* Leiden: E. J. Brill.

Gastineau, C., W. J. Darby, and T. B. Turner (eds.) 1979. *Fermented Food Beverages in Nutrition.* New York: Academic Press.

Gately, I. 2009. *Drink: A Cultural History of Alcohol.* New York: Gotham.

Gefou-Madianou, D. (ed.) 1992. *Alcohol, Gender and Culture.* New York: Routledge.

Geller, J. 1993. "Bread and Beer in Fourth-Millennium Egypt." *Food and Foodways* 5 (3): 255–67.

Giesbrecht, N., R. Room, E. Oesterberg, J. Moskalewicz, and M. Cahannes (eds.) 1983. *Consequences of Drinking, Trends in Alcohol Problem Statistics in Seven Countries. Papers associated with Alcohol, Society, and the State – a report of the International Study of Alcohol Control Experiences, in collaboration with the World*

Health Organization Regional Office for Europe. Toronto: Addiction Research Foundation.

Gordon, E. 1913. *The Anti-Alcohol Movement in Europe*. New York: Fleming H. Revell Company.

Graham, K. and R. Homel. 2008. *Raising the Bar: Preventing Aggression in and Around Bars, Pubs, and Clubs*. Portland, OR: Willan Publishing.

Grant, M. 1958. *Chinese Civilizaation*. Trans. K. E. Innes and M. R. Brailsford. New York: Meridian Books, Inc.

——1998. *Alcohol and Emerging Markets: Patterns, Problems, and Responses*. Philadelphia: Brunner/Mazel.

Grant, M. and J. Litvak. 1998. *Drinking Patterns and Their Consequences*. Washington, DC: Taylor & Francis.

Gutzke, D. W. 1996. *Alcohol in the British Isles from Roman Times to 1996: An Annotated Bibliography*. Westport, CT: Greenwood Press.

Hackwood, F. W. 1985. *Inns, Ales and Drinking Customs of Old England*. London: Bracken Books.

Haine, W. S. 1996. *The World of the Paris Café, Sociability Among the French Working Class, 1789–1914*. Baltimore, MD: Johns Hopkins University Press.

Hao Wei, Y. Derson, S. Xiao, L. Li, and Y. Zhang 1999. "Alcohol Consumption and Alcohol-Related Problems: Chinese experience from Six Area Samples, 1994." *Addiction* 94 (10): 1467–76.

Hartman, L. F. and A. L. Oppenheim. 1950. "On Beer and Brewing Techniques in Ancient Mesopotamia." *Journal of the American Oriental Society* 10: 1–55.

Hauge, R. 1984. *Alcohol and Crime*. Strasbourg: Council of Europe.

Haworth, A. 1995. "Zambia." In D. B. Heath (ed.) *International Handbook on Alcohol and Culture*. Westport, CT: Greenwood Press.

Heath, D. B. 1987. "Anthropology and Alcohol Studies: Current Issues." *Annual Review of Anthropology* 16: 99–142.

——2000. *Drinking Occasions, Comparative Perspectives on Alcohol and Culture*. Series on Alcohol in Society Published by the International Center for Alcohol Policies. Ann Arbor, MI: Sheridan Books.

——(ed.) 1995. *International Handbook on Alcohol and Culture*. Westport, CT: Greenwood Press.

Heath, D. B. and A. M. Cooper. 1981. *Alcohol Use and World Cultures: A Comprehensive Bibliography of Anthropological Sources*. Bibliographic Series No. 15. Toronto: Addiction Research Foundation.

Helzer, J. E. and G. J. Canino. (eds.) 1992. *Alcoholism in North America, Europe, and Asia*. New York: Oxford University Press.

Hewitt, T. F. 1980. *A Biblical Perspective on the Use and Abuse of Alcohol and Other Drugs*. Raleigh, NC: Pastoral Care Council on Alcohol and Drug Abuse.

Hiramani, A. B. and N. Sharma. 1988. *Health and Youth in India*. Delhi: Agam Prakashan.

Hyams, E. 1965. *Dionysus: A Social History of the Wine Vine*. New York: The Macmillian Company.

Jankowiak, W. and D. Bradburd. (eds.) 2003. *Drugs, Labor, and Colonial Expansion*. Tucson: University of Arizona Press.

Jennings, J. 2005. "La Chichera y El Patrón: Chicha and the Energetics of Feasting in the Prehistoric Andes." *Archaeological Papers of the American Anthropological Association* 14: 241–59.

Joffe, A. H. 1998. "Alcohol and Social Complexity in Ancient Western Asia." *Current Anthropology* 39 (3): 297–322.

Jones, A., W. D. Connor, and D. E. Powell. (eds.) 1991. *Soviet Social Problems.* Boulder, CO: Westview Press.

Kicza, J. E. 1980. "The Pulque Trade of Late Colonial Mexico City." *The Americas* 37 (2): 193–221.

Kirkby, D. 1997. *Barmaids: A History of Women's Work in Pubs.* Cambridge: Cambridge University Press.

Kueny, K. 2001. *The Rhetoric of Sobriety: Wine in Early Islam.* Albany: State University of New York Press.

Kunio, Y. 1957. *Japanese Manners and Customs in the Meiji Era.* Trans. C. S. Terry. Tokyo: Obunsha.

La Hausse, P. 1988. *Brewers, Beerhalls and Boycotts: A history of Liquor in South Africa.* History Workshop Booklet. Johannesburg: Ravan.

Lehto, J. 1995. *Approaches to Alcohol Control Policy.* Copenhagen: World Health Organization.

Lemu, B. A. 1992. *Islam and Alcohol.* Alexandria: Saadawi Publications.

Leon, D. A., V. M. Shkolnikow, and M. Mckee. 2009. "Alcohol and Russian Mortality: A Continuing Crisis." *Addiction* 104 (10) (October): 1630–36.

Lin, T. and D. T. Lin. 1982. "Alcoholism among the Chinese: Further observations of a low-risk population." *Culture, Medicine and Psychiatry* 6 (2):109–16.

Lucia, S. P., M.D. 1963. *A History of Wine As Therapy.* Philadelphia: J. B. Lippincott Company.

Lutz, H. F. 1922. *Viticulture and Brewing in The Ancient Orient.* New York: G. E. Stechert & Co.

MacAndrew, C. and B. R. Edgerton 1969. *Drunken Comportment: A Social Explanation.* Chicago: Aldine Publishing Company.

Malcolm, E. 1986. *"Ireland Sober, Ireland Free" Drink and Temperance in Nineteenth-Century Ireland.* Syracuse, NY: Syracuse University Press.

Manheimer, A. (ed.) 2007. *Alcohol.* New York: Thomson Gale.

Martin, A. L. 2001. *Alcohol, Sex, and Gender in Late Medieval and Early Modern Europe.* New York: Palgrave.

Maternovsky, D. and M. Sysoyeva. 2011. "Medvedev Signs Law Restricting Russian Beer, Alcohol Sales." *Bloomberg News.* http://www.bloomberg.com/news/2011-7-20/medvedev-signs-law-restricting-russian-beer-alcohol-sales-1-.html (accessed September 2, 2011).

McAllister, P. 2001. *Building the Homestead: Agriculture, Labour and Beer in South Africa's Transkei.* Leiden: Ashgate Publishing.

——2006. *Xhosa Beer Drinking Rituals: Power, Practice and Performance in the South African Rural Periphery.* Durham, NC: Carolina Academic Press.

McDonald, M. (ed.) 1994. *Gender, Drink and Drugs.* New York: Berg.

McGovern, P. E. 2003. *Ancient Wine: The Search for the Origins of Viniculture.* Princeton, NJ: Princeton University Press.

——2009. *Uncorking the Past: The Quest for Wine, Beer and Other Alcoholic Beverages.* Berkeley: University of California Press.

McGovern, P. E., S. J. Fleming, and S. Katz. (eds.) 1996. *The Origins and Ancient History of Wine.* Amsterdam: Gordon and Breach Publishers.

McGovern, P. E., E. D. Butrym, A. Nunez, C. S. Wang, M. P. Richards, R. A. Moreau, J. G. Tang, J. Z. Zhang, G. R. Hall, and Z. Q. Zhang. 2004. "Fermented Beverages of Pre- and Proto-Historic China." *Proceedings of the National Academy of Sciences.* November. www.pnas.org cgi/doi/10.1073/pnas.0407921102 (accessed December 16, 2011).

McGrath, A. 1993. "Beneath the Skin: Australian Citizenship, Rights and Aboriginal Women." In R. Howe (ed.) "Women and the State", *Journal of Australian Studies* 37 (June): 99–114.

Mehta, J. N. n. d. *Alcohol and State Revenue.* New Delhi: All India Prohibition Council.

Michalak, L. and K. Trocki. 2006. "Alcohol and Islam: An Overview." *Contemporary Drug Problems* 33 (4) (Winter): 523–62.

Minai, K. 1986. *Trends in Alcoholic Beverage Consumption in Postwar Japan: An Analysis and Interpretation of Aggregate Data.* Singapore: Department of Japanese Studies National University of Singapore.

Moore, J. D. 1989. "Pre-Hispanic Beer in Coastal Peru: Technology and Social Context of Prehistoric Production." *American Anthropologist* 91 (3): 682–95.

O'Brian, J. M. and S. C. Seller. 1982. "Attributes of Alcohol in the Old Testament." *The Drinking and Drug Practices Surveyor* 18: 18–24.

Okrent, D. 2010. *Last Call: The Rise and Fall of Prohibition.* New York: Scribner.

Pan, L. 1975. *Alcohol in Colonial Africa.* Vol. 22. Uppsala: The Scandinavian Institute of African Studies, and Helsinki: The Finnish Foundation for Alcohol Studies.

Paper, J. 1995. *The Spirits are Drunk: Comparative Approaches to Chinese Religion.* Albany: State University of New York Press.

Peele, S. and M. Grant. 1999. *Alcohol and Pleasure: A Health Perspective.* Philadelphia: Brunner/Mazel.

Pernanen, K. 1991. *Alcohol in Human Violence.* New York: The Guilford Press.

Phillips, R. 2000. *A Short History of Wine.* New York: Harper Collins.

Platt, B. 1955. "Some Traditional Alcoholic Beverages and Their Importance in Indigenous African Communities." *Proceedings of the Nutrition Society* 14: 115–24.

Poo, M.-C. 1995. *Wine and Wine Offering in the Religion of Ancient Egypt.* London: Kegan Paul International.

Prakash, O. 1961. *Food and Drinks in Ancient India: From Earliest Times to C. 1200 A.D.* Delhi: Munshi ram Manohar Lal.

Purcell, N. 1985. "Wine and Wealth in Ancient Italy." *The Journal of Roman Studies* 75: 1–19.

Raymond, I. W. 1927. *The Teaching of the Early Church on the Use of Wine and Strong Drink.* New York: Columbia University Press.

Read, B. E. n. d. *Chinese Materia Medica.* Shanghai: Henry Lester Institute for Medical Research.

Roberts, B. D. 2000. "Always Cheaply Pleasant: Beer as Commodity in a Rural Kenyan Society." In A. Haugerud, M. P. Stone, and P. D. Little (eds.) New *Commodities and Globalization, Anthropological Perspectives.* York: Rowman & Littlefield.

Room, R. 1984. "Alcohol and Ethnography: A Case of Problem Deflation?" *Current Anthropology* 25 (2): 169–91.

Rothbaum, N. 2007. *The Business of Spirits: How Savvy Marketers, Innovative Distillers, and Entrepreneurs Changed How We Drink.* New York: Kaplan.

Rumbarger, J. J. 1989. *Profits, Power, and Prohibition: Alcohol Reform and the Industrializing of America, 1800–1930.* Albany, NY: State University of New York Press.

Sadoun, R., G. Lolli, and M. Silverman. 1965. *Drinking in French Culture.* New Brunswick, NJ: Rutgers Center of Alcohol Studies.

Saul, M. 1981. "Beer, Sorghum and Women: Production for the Market in Rural Upper Volta." *Africa* 51 (3): 746–64.

Scardaville, M. C. 1980. "Alcohol Abuse and Tavern Reform in Late Colonial Mexico City." *The Hispanic American Historial Review* 60 (4): 643–71.

Scheidel, W. and S. von Reden. 2002. *The Ancient Economy.* New York: Routledge.

Scholliers, P. (ed.) 2001. *Food, Drink and Identity: Cooking, Eating and Drinking in Europe Since the Middle Ages.* New York: Berg.

Single, E., P. Morgan, and J. de Lint. (eds.) 1981. *Alcohol, Society, and the State: The Social History of Control Policy in Seven Countries.* Toronto: Addition Research Foundation and World Health Organization.

Smith, S. R. 1992. "Drinking Etiquette in a Changing Beverage Market." In J. J. Tobin (ed.) *Re-Made in Japan.* New Haven, CT: Yale University Press.

Snyder, C. R. 1958. *Alcohol and the Jews: A Cultural Study of Drinking and Sobriety.* New Haven, CT: Yale Center of Alcohol Studies.

Ssu-Hsieh, C. (of the later Wei Dynasty) 1945."The Preparation of Ferments and Wines." Trans. H. Tzu-Ch'ing and C. Yünts'ung. *Harvard Journal of Asiatic Studies* 9 (1): 24–44.

Tamang, J. P. 2010. *Himalayan Fermented Foods: Microbiology, Nutrition, and Ethnic Values.* New York: CRC Press, Taylor & Francis Group.

Taylor, W. B. 1979. *Drinking, Homicide, and Rebellion in Colonial Mexican Villages.* Stanford, CA: Stanford University Press.

Valamoti, M. and M. Koukouli-Chrysanthaki. 2007. "Grape-pressings from northern Greece: the earliest wine in the Aegean." *Antiquity* 81 (311): 54–61.

Waltham, C. (ed.) 1971. "Announcement About Drunkenness." In *ShuChing Book of History*, Chicago: Henry Regency Co.

Waltham, C. and Legge, J. 1971. "Announcement About Drunkenness." In *ShuChing Book of History.* Chicago: Henry Regency Co.

Watney, J. 1974. *Beer is Best: A History of Beer.* London: Peter Owen.

White, S. 1996. *Russia Goes Dry: Alcohol, State and Society.* Cambridge: Cambridge University Press.

Wilson, H. 1988. *Egyptian Food and Drink.* Princes Risborough: Shire Publications.

Wolcott, H. F. 1974. *The African Beer Gardens of Bulawayo: Integrated Drinking in a Segregated Society.* New Brunswick, NJ: Rutgers Center of Alcohol Studies.

Zhang, F.-P. 1982. "Drinking in China." *The Drinking and Drug Practices Surveyor* 18: 12–15.

Index

109, 124, 130; Classical world 25; drinking establishments 78–9, 130; Egypt 7–10, 12, 20; European 39–40, 41; France 117, 124; French wines 47, 48, 69, 71; Greece 25, 31–2, 130; India 31, 92, 107, 124; Ireland 67, 130; Japan 38, 44, 77; Latin America 130; Mesopotamia 12, 14, 20; Mexico 55, 58; Rome 25, 26, 31–2; Russia 38, 44, 112; Saudi Arabia 104, 105, 124; United States 72, 124, 132; West Africa 49; Zambia 103–4

fermentation: banana beer 83; beers 2, 9–10, 13; chemical processes 1; chicha 19, 37; Chinese legends 16–17; Chinese techniques 17, 28–9; Egyptian techniques 8–10; Indian history 18–19, 30; Mesopotamian techniques 13; pulque 35; wines 2, 5–6, 8–9, 13, 17
Festival of the Dead, China 29
Forbes, R. J. 41, 43
France: alcohol abuse 125; alcohol production and trade 78, 130; colonial government 50, 52, 81; problem drinking 118–19; uses and regulation of alcohol 68–72, 79, 133; viticulture 39; wine consumption 117–18; wine trade 48, 61, 68–9, 71, 116–17; wine varieties 47

Gandhi, Mohandas 92
gender roles: Africa 81–3, 86–7, 90, 95, 101–3; alcohol production and consumption patterns 131; ale production and trade 39–40; ancient world 7, 20, 21; Australia 93, 132; beer production and trade 10, 13, 20, 40, 82–3, 90, 95, 102; Britain 63–4; chicha production 35, 36–7, 44; China 17, 20; Classical Period 23; consumption patterns 124; Egypt 7, 10, 20; elite women 10; France 68–9, 70, 79, 117–18; Ireland 66; Latin America 100; Mesopotamia 13, 15, 20; Post-Classical and early modern West 38, 44–5; pulque production and trade 35, 54, 56; South American production, consumption and regulation 33, 35; tavern keepers 15, 20; trade by women 7; United States 72, 74, 121, 132; wine consumption 10, 23, 25, 27, 32
Germany 81

Ghana 85, 86, 90, 91
gin: alcohol content 3; class identity 44, 64; consumption 41, 42, 44, 64, 65–6; production 64, 107; regulation 65–6, 132; temperance movements 66; trade 43, 49
globalization 98–100, 123–5
Godin Tepe 6, 7
Gonzales de Cuenca, Gregorio 60
Gorbachev, Mikhail 114, 115
Graham, Kathryn 99
Grant, Marcus 88, 92
grapes 5–6; domestication 5–6, 8; wild, 5, 6, 8, 51
Greece, classical 3, 6, 14, 23–8, 31, 130
guests 10, 11, 16, 18, 20, 29

Hajji Firus Tepe 6
Hammurabic Code 14–15
Hathor-Sekhmet 11
Haworth, Alan 90
Hewitt, T. F. 15
Hinduism 19, 30, 91, 92
Hippocrates 25
Hittite Kingdom 14, 15
HIV/AIDS 99, 104
Homel, Ross 99
hops 40
Hudson, Henry 52

Inca 3, 35, 37, 131
India: alcohol abuse 125; alcohol consumption and trade 91–2, 95, 110–12, 124; alcoholism 130; ancient 3, 7, 18–19, 20, 21; beer imports 40; Classical 30–1; illegal liquor production 107; prohibition campaign 92, 133; ritual use of alcohol 21; soma 18–19, 20, 21, 30; Westernization 106–8, 124
industrialization 63
Ireland: alcohol consumption and regulation 66–7, 130, 132; alcohol taxation 79; Catholics and Protestants 63, 67–8, 76, 79–80, 132; temperance movements 68, 132
Islam (Muslims): in Africa 104; in India 91–92; medical use of alcohol 34, 44; prohibition of alcohol 33–4, 129, 131; Russian rejection of 37; Saudi Arabia 104–6

Jamaica 55
Japan: alcohol abuse 125; alcohol consumption 110–12, 124;

THE REAL ESTATE
INVESTOR'S GUIDE TO
FINANCING

Insider Advice for Making
the Most Money on Every Deal

David Reed

AMACOM

American Management Association
New York • Atlanta • Brussels • Chicago • Mexico City • San Francisco
Shanghai • Tokyo • Toronto • Washington, D.C.

Special discounts on bulk quantities of AMACOM books are
available to corporations, professional associations, and other
organizations. For details, contact Special Sales Department,
AMACOM, a division of American Management Association,
1601 Broadway, New York, NY 10019.
Tel.: 212-903-8316 Fax: 212-903-8083
E-mail: specialsls@amanet.org
Website: www.amacombooks.org/go/specialsales
To view all AMACOM titles go to: www.amacombooks.org

This publication is designed to provide accurate and authoritative
information in regard to the subject matter covered. It is sold with the
understanding that the publisher is not engaged in rendering legal,
accounting, or other professional service. If legal advice or other expert
assistance is required, the services of a competent professional person
should be sought.

REALTOR® is a registered collective membership mark that identifies
a real estate professional who is a member of the NATIONAL
ASSOCIATION OF REALTORS® and subscribes to its strict code of
ethics.

Library of Congress Cataloging-in-Publication Data

Reed, David, 1957 Oct. 1–
    The real estate investor's guide to financing : insider advice for
making the most money on every deal / David Reed.
        p.   cm.
    Includes index.
    ISBN-13: 978–0-8144–8061–8
    ISBN-10: 0–8144–8061–6
    1. Real estate investment—Finance.   I. Title.
HD1382.5.R424   2008
32.7'2—dc22
                                    2007034441

Printed in the United States of America.

Printing number

10   9   8   7   6   5   4   3   2   1

I dedicate this book to Jim and Glenda Nees for all they've done for both me and my family. Thank you.

Contents

Acknowledgments

I personally thank my former editor at AMACOM, Christina Parisi, who helped guide me through my first six books. *The Real Estate Investor's Guide to Financing* is our last project together. You've been absolutely wonderful. I also give thanks to Kirk Tuck at Kirk Tuck Photography in Austin, Texas, for his outstanding work. What a talent. Thanks also to Blanche Evans at *Realty Times* who is always there for me to talk real estate.

Basic Finance for the Investor

While there are certainly plenty of real estate books on the market that specialize in real estate investment, those same books fall short when it comes to one of the most important aspects of real estate investing: financing.

Buying real estate as an investment can bring great rewards. Holding real estate and watching its value rise over the long term is a nice way to retirement for many people.

One of the advantages of real estate can also be a disadvantage, however. It's not a liquid asset. You can't get your money out of it as easily as you can get money out of an ATM. If it's a stinker, you have to sell it, and that takes time and it takes money.

You can't just change your mind because of a heavy dose of buyer's remorse, take your receipt for your investment condo back to the store, and get your money back after saying something like, "Well, it was the wrong size, and my aunt gave me one for Christmas."

Real estate investment needs commitment. You need to decide that it's right for you before you get involved.

There are two different types of investors: those who buy and hold, and those who buy and sell quickly, a process that is often called *flipping*. Flippers attempt to find bargains, fix them up, then sell them for a profit. And these two types of investors are not exclusive; you can both be a flipper and hold for the long term.

Flipping brings a whole new element to real estate investing compared to simply holding onto property for a long period of time, then either selling it when you think you've made enough money or keeping it and passing it down to your grateful heirs.

Flipping requires more than just buying; it requires you to know how to make repairs on a home and evaluate how much of a return in the form of increased value those repairs would generate. Or maybe the issue isn't just increased value but simply making the place livable.

Flipping requires different financing strategies from those used for long-term investments. Any real estate investment book you read concentrates more on either finding, fixing, and flipping real estate or finding and keeping real estate while paying little attention to the financial aspect—perhaps one of the most critical pieces of the real estate investment puzzle.

Getting the wrong financial package can wipe out your profits, hold you back from selling because of lack of equity, or perhaps require you to sell for more than the market will bear because of the bad loan you got when you bought the property in the first place.

If you're a flipper, financing is critical. If you're long term, financing is also critical, but at least in long-term deals you can always refinance the property down the road if you made a bad loan choice in the beginning. We'll discuss refinancing investment properties in detail in Chapter 4.

But then again, because you're reading this book, you won't be making those mistakes, now will you?

One advantage that a long-term investor has is the ability to buy in other markets.

Let's say, for instance, that your local real estate market is humming right along. You know that you can find a property, fix it up, and sell it for a profit. Or maybe your market is really moving and you can find a piece of property that takes absolutely no work (or very little), and because of the real estate demand in your area, you know you can make another 10 percent on your investment.

You know you can do this because you know your market. You know the neighborhoods. You know the contractors who work on your properties, or if you do most of the rehab yourself, you can drive to the job site every day.

That's not true if you're buying in Texas and you live in California. Yes, you can fly in and look at properties, but if you want to fix and flip, you've got a brand-new problem. How do you find someone you trust to be the contractor while you're a couple of time zones away? How do you monitor the contractor's progress?

How do you pay the workers, and how do you make sure they're not sitting around drinking beer all day long while you're frantically trying to get your contractor to return your voicemails?

The truth is, you can't. If you're a flipper, then a long-distance rehab project may not be for you. In fact, if you were planning on making $20,000 on a nice little flip, then all the labor, plane fare, and headaches won't be worth it at the end.

Yes, you can be a long-distance flipper if the properties you're buying don't need any work and you think you can sell them quickly and for a profit. Yet, you're not local. You're not the only real estate investor, and there will be local professional investors who can sniff out a flip a lot more quickly than you can simply by being where the property is. By the time you've found a potential investment, gotten on the plane, and rented a car to look at your potential investment, if it was such a good deal, it's probably been snatched up while you were checking your bags.

I will note that sometimes faraway investors can have the upper hand

when they're in a part of the country that is doing better economically than the locale they want to invest in.

For instance, a town may have experienced some huge layoffs as a result of downsizing, creating a significant economic hit. If you are living in an area that is not depressed, you may have more disposable income and be able to buy a house for less than market value.

But even then, as a flipper, if you invest in a depressed area, who are you going to sell to—another flipper? If the local economy you're buying into is in the middle of some major economic upheaval, then home buyers aren't exactly going to be lining up along the street waiting to bite on that "bargain" house you found. Many of the people in the town where you found your bargain have, unfortunately, been laid off.

Being a long-distance flipper, then, is a challenge. You don't know the area as well as the locals do, you can't monitor your project efficiently, and it's hard to find buyers in a depressed market.

On the other hand, such opportunities bode well for long-term investors. If you see that a certain area outside where you live is going through some difficult times, you can find a bargain house and hold onto it, waiting to sell until the economy recovers.

I own a home in Austin, Texas, that I bought in the late 1990s. The seller was an investor from California who had bought the house some 10 years earlier—right in the middle of the S&L debacle. Combine that crisis with an oil and gas industry that was suffering through perhaps one of its most trying times, and you can see why real estate in Texas was depressed.

The investor bought in 1988 during an economic downturn in Texas and sold 10 years later, doubling his money, after the economy recovered. He was long term.

Not just that, but the property I bought was listed as a "fixer-upper" that needed some "tender loving care," meaning that it had its challenges. In fact, the California owner had never lived in the property but had rented it to various people for the entire decade.

When I bought the house, it needed some work. The carpet was old,

the tile in the kitchen area was coming up, and the entire house needed some significant updating—Significant with a capital S.

My wife and I had been looking in that particular part of Austin for nearly a year, trying to find the perfect deal. We had seen so many similar houses that we knew immediately that the property was a steal. The property had been listed, and within 24 hours of its original listing, it had had three offers—all from locals.

We not only offered the asking price but also bumped it up by a few thousand dollars (because we knew we had found a bargain) and won the bid. We bought the home, completely remodeled it, and turned it into a very nice piece of property. We still own the home today, and the property has appreciated nearly fourfold since we bought it. And I doubt that we will ever sell it. Okay, we will, but not for a long, long time. I know the area, and it's a keeper.

Sometimes people get into real estate investments by accident. For instance, you find a house you really, really want to move into, but your current property isn't selling for what you'd like to sell it for, so you keep it and rent it out.

Or perhaps you inherited a property from a relative and decide to keep it long term and not sell right away.

Occasionally life simply causes you to get into real estate when you had no initial motivation to do so. You'd never thought of it, and now you're in it. And you find out you like it!

The Pros and Cons of Being a Landlord

First and foremost, the landlord owns the property and collects (hopefully) the rent each month. The landlord is also at the bidding of her tenants when it comes to repairs and maintenance of the property.

This doesn't mean day-to-day maintenance. A landlord may not be responsible for a clogged sink, but he might be responsible if the clogged sink is due to tree roots from outside the house invading the outdoor plumbing.

Typically, if something goes wrong, you as the landlord have got to fix it. If it's an emergency situation or something that makes the property uninhabitable or dangerous, not only may the terms of the rental agreement require you to fix it, but local or state laws may also require that you fix it.

Think fallen tree limbs knocking down power lines or a flood from a broken pipe. Or suppose there's no heat in the winter or cool air in the summer because of a poor heating or cooling system.

This means that you've got to have some money handy, or at a minimum a few credit cards or trade lines opened up at Lowe's or Home Depot. When your tenants squawk, you'll need to have whatever they're squawking about fixed, and pronto.

Being a landlord also means collecting rents on time; after all, if one of the reasons you want to buy investment property is to have the tenants pay your mortgage for you, then it stands to reason that you'll want to be paid on a regular basis.

That's also one of the advantages of holding: having someone else pay your mortgage for you while your asset appreciates in value. Let's look at an example of how that works.

You want to buy a duplex for $200,000, and you put 20 percent down. You finance the property at 6.50 percent for 30 years, so the monthly payments you make to the mortgage company come in at around $1,250 per month, including taxes and insurance.

Rents in that neighborhood go for about $900 per month per unit, so your duplex brings in about $550 per month over and above your payments. That's not counting regular maintenance, but you're still ahead.

Now let's also assume that property in that area is appreciating at a rate of about 5 percent per year.

After five years, you've made just over $33,000 in additional income. Your tenants have paid for your investment by more than making your payments each month. Your property has also appreciated to $255,250.

The total value of your holdings = $40,000 down payment + $55,250 appreciation + $33,000 income. That's a $128,250 equity position, or a gain of $88,250. Plus, if you invested that $33,000 in income at a 5 percent annual yield, you probably made even more.

These are the kinds of numbers you need to keep in your head when you get a call at 2:00 a.m. from your tenant complaining that there is no hot water. Besides wondering what she's doing up at 2:00 in the morning needing hot water, you have to answer her call.

What makes for a good landlord? Easy: A good tenant living in a good property.

If your tenant pays his rent on time, then you'll have enough money to pay your bills on time. If the property you own and rent out is in good shape and is not inclined to disrepair, then you'll spend less time fixing hot water heaters and maybe more time making how-to-get-rich-quick infomercials while sipping margaritas.

Take the Headache Out of Being a Landlord

Another way to be a good landlord is to have someone else be a landlord for you by using a property management company. Most property management companies have some sort of affiliation with a real estate company, if they are not owned outright by such a company.

These firms do all the dirty work for you. They keep up the property for you, they collect the rent, they send out repair companies to fix that bad hot water heater, and they screen tenants. They charge a fee for all this, of course. But still, property management companies do this for a living, and they both have experience in daily property management and have built relationships with other affiliated services, such as carpenters or repairmen, who work for them and offer discounts for their services as well.

All of this is your call, of course, but as you acquire more properties, you're going to need some help, so either you can hire some staff to do

the work for you and work at this full time, or you can have another company do the daily tasks for you.

I know a lady who owns multiple properties and has one neat handy-man whom she employs full time and who does nothing except be on call when her tenants have a problem. She owns houses and apartments and duplexes, but she has a guy who works directly for her who goes out and fixes things when they're broken. Needless to say, he's busy. But he works directly for her. She doesn't have to share him with any other property owners, as she would if she hired a management company.

There's also an in-between. You can have a management company just collect the rent while you take care of repairs, or you can have the management company find renters for you while you take care of any-thing or everything else. It all depends on your agreement and your schedule. It's up to you.

Or you can hire somebody you know and trust with all your heart—your spouse, or your son or daughter, or really anyone you know well. But being a landlord means managing and maintaining your asset. Your renters won't be there forever, so it's up to you to keep the property in good shape for the next tenants and to establish a reputation for being a nice landlord who fixes stuff when it breaks.

Setting Up the Utilities

There's something else to consider when renting property, and that's the utilities. Who takes care of the electric bill, the water, the phone, the cable? That can depend on the type of property you own, such as a single-family unit or a multifamily property like an apartment building.

You can set up any arrangement that you want, but to avoid the hassles of paying utility bills and monitoring their usage, you can simply have the tenants pay their own way when it comes to things like water and sewer or oil and electricity.

If your property is an apartment building and the units don't have

separate metering, then you may not have that luxury, so instead you can divide the total unit cost of utilities equally among the number of apartment units and consider that per-unit cost when determining rental rates.

Both utilities and maintenance are costs of owning and need to be considered when setting rental rates. After all, you're in this to make money, not lose it, right?

Setting Rental Rates

The easy way to set rental rates is to figure out how much the property costs you each month in terms of mortgage payment, taxes, and insurance plus maintenance and any utility costs, then charge more than that each month. Before you buy, you should find out what similar rentals in the area are going for. Without knowing this, you won't know whether you will be able to rent the apartment at a rate that will make you money. You can find this out yourself by monitoring the rental rates listed in the paper and online, or you can get a list of comparable apartments from a local Realtor.

Let's look at our duplex again and now add repairs and utilities.

Monthly payment	$ 1,250
Repairs (per month)	$ 100
Water/sewer	$ 75
Total	**$ 1,425**

With this example, anything above $1,425 is what you would make as a profit. This doesn't count intangible expenses such as your worrying about that hot water heater breaking this year or the time and effort you spend managing the property or even the cost of hiring a property management firm.

But with this method, you add your monthly expenses and simply charge more. If you want to make $500 per month on top of the $1,425,

your monthly rent would be $1,925. Or divided by two so you can split that duplex profit between the two units, your monthly rent for each side of the duplex would be $962.50.

That's how much you would charge each tenant if you wanted to make $500. Do you want to make more than that? Then charge more. Do you want to make $1,000 more each month? Then sock it to your tenants.

Of course, sometimes you can't do that. What you want to charge in rent and what you can realistically get are two entirely different things. You can really charge only the maximum that the market will bear.

Let's look again at the duplex. In most places where you find one duplex, you'll find another. And perhaps another. That's because the area has been designated, or zoned, by the city or locale as being able to have duplexes, triplexes, and fourplexes. You usually won't find a bunch of single-family residences with one duplex sandwiched among them.

That means that before you buy that duplex, you can see what other duplexes are renting for. If other duplexes are renting their units out for $1,000 per month, then you can expect to get $1,000 per month out of your property as well.

That's all things being equal, of course, such as square footage, number of bedrooms, and the condition of the property. If you want to charge $1,500, you certainly can, but if other units in the area are charging only $900, you won't get any takers. Maybe you can spice up your offer with some free cable TV, or a hot tub, or something else, but there's a difference between what you want to charge and what the market will allow you to charge.

When Should You Buy?

There are "hot" real estate markets and there are "cold" real estate markets and there are "steady" real estate markets.

There can also be hot markets and cold markets in the same city or

town, and this can depend upon a variety of factors. In fact, one hot market could be the next cold market, and vice versa.

For example, I know of a public school district that won a couple of "teacher of the year" awards. Suddenly people realized that instead of paying for private schools, they could get a solid education for their kids in a public school. This neighborhood had previously languished for years with regard to real estate values, but it suddenly became very popular.

Now, that school district suddenly created a hot real estate market where there had been none before. This part of town was once shunned, but now, because of the "free" public education, people were moving into the district, paying more for homes than the same homes had sold for just a few months earlier, and driving up prices.

The area was hot. Property values increased. Market rents went through the roof. And the people who had originally bought those homes in that once-downtrodden neighborhood, who had newfound cash that they hadn't had before, sold and moved into bigger houses in other parts of town. They had lived in that neighborhood for years, their kids had grown up and moved on, and now they had newfound wealth through nothing more than market appreciation.

The buyers won and the sellers won.

In both an up market and a down market, different buying strategies emerge and also make the financing aspect even more important.

The Strength of the Market Will Determine What Financing You Should Get

When you're buying in a strong market, you're probably looking at other economic factors for that area that indicate strong economic growth for a long period of time. For example, suppose employers are moving into an area and building new plants. This indicates that people will be moving into the area to be near their work.

When there are indications of a strong market, you should seriously consider holding properties for the long term and therefore look for long-term financing that makes sense. We'll examine in detail which financing types to choose for different holding periods in Chapter 4.

Buying in a growing market may also mean that you intend to buy low and sell high on a relatively short-term basis, such as two or three years. You're betting that your property will appreciate over that period, and you want to unload your appreciating asset a few short years down the road.

Buying in a booming market, where home prices are appreciating at a rapid clip, say 10 to 20 percent or more per year, might even mean selling the property a few months after you bought it. If you anticipate turning a property that quickly, your financing package for that property is key to your profit.

Even in new construction, when home sales are white hot, you can buy a home or a condo that's currently under construction and has not yet been completed, and then turn around and sell that condo to someone else for a still higher price.

This phenomenon doesn't happen very often, but it happens in extremely hot markets. Solid growth and speculative buying can ignite a sales frenzy where new construction can't keep up with the demand. Professional real estate investors can spot this trend and buy early, selling the real estate to someone else for a profit without ever having seen the house or condo completed!

On the flip side, should you buy in a down market? Or should you buy in a market that hasn't yet hit bottom but may be on its way?

Certainly not if you're a flipper, right? Unless you can find some wildly distressed property and a true diamond in the rough, you're taking a big gamble if you're flipping in a down market. If nobody's buying, then who are you going to sell to?

If you're a long-term investor, then buying in a down market makes sense. Prices are lower, and real estate always comes back unless you're talking about Chernobyl or somewhere with similar long-term issues.

Just as there are dips, there are also rebounds. Financing for the long term is essential in a down market; you shouldn't consider short-term notes for this kind of market. This is why you sometimes hear the phrase "real estate is local," meaning that one area can be hard hit with tough economic news while another part of the country is literally booming.

If the national economy is in the doldrums with only pockets of stout economic activity, then there's another byproduct of that gloom: lower interest rates. We'll closely examine how interest rates move in Chapter 5, but overall, mortgage rates will be lower in times of slower economic activity than in times of strong economic activity.

In this scenario, you're really getting the best of both worlds by buying a property at depressed prices in an economy that offers lower rates.

In the long run, however, most housing markets are neither boom nor bust, but simply "steady as she goes." So do you wait until there's a slowing economy to find deals? Of course not; real estate investing is not all about buying in a hot or cold cycle, but about understanding the type of investor you'd like to be, then methodically going about executing your plan.

Then, of course, there's a third choice: Do nothing at all. If you can't find a property to buy and you can't see how you're going to make any money at it, then don't feel compelled to buy something unless the math works out.

I recall a reporter who wanted to do a story on investment properties. She called me up one weekend afternoon and wanted some information about how to finance investment properties.

In particular, she wanted to know what to do if the investment properties she saw were too expensive to buy and she couldn't get them to cash flow each month. How was she going to get around that particular little problem?

As a matter of fact, she confided, that person was her. She was looking into buying real estate as a long-term investment to help with her daughter's college and her own retirement, but she couldn't find anything to buy.

The rents being charged in the area she wanted to invest in weren't high enough to offset the mortgage payments. She called me to see if I had some magical financing trick that could keep her monthly payments low enough so that she could buy the property and make money each month.

The fact of the matter was, she couldn't. She didn't have much, if any, money to put down, but she still thought it was a good idea to invest in real estate. Her direct question to me was: "What should I do?"

I said, "Let me make sure I understand your situation. You want to invest in real estate for the long haul to help pay for college and retirement later on in life as your kids get older and you retire. You also don't want to put any money down on any of these properties. The rents in the area you want to invest in aren't high enough to offset the monthly payments, and you want to know how to get around that. Is that about right?"

"Yes, exactly." She said.

"Well, if you can't afford it and you can't cover the monthly expenses and you don't have any money for reserves, then the answer is to do nothing."

She was somewhat surprised at that and was taken aback a little. "Huh," she said, "I guess I didn't think about that."

But you should. If you can't make the deal work, no amount of creative financing can help. Maybe you should just wait. Or perhaps you shouldn't invest all your money in one big deal but should get your toes wet first.

For instance, suppose you have $100,000 you'd like to invest. Do you want to leverage all your money into one big property or split that money up among several different properties? Or maybe just buy one small property at first? Buy the small property at first. Get your toes wet before jumping in.

Yes, you could make a lot more money on one big transaction, but won't get much sleep at night as you hope that your acquisition price,

rehab costs, and selling price all work out as planned. If they do, congratulations. If not, you made a big mistake. How do you know what types of properties to buy? We'll discuss various property types in detail in Chapter 2, but really you should think less about the type of property in which to invest and more about profit.

One of the easiest ways to determine if a house might be a good investment is to compare a property that's on the market with recent sales in the area by calculating the price per square foot.

Price per Square Foot

You'll need access to your local Multiple Listing Service (MLS) for this, either by having your real estate license or having a Realtor perform a search for you. Such a search is commonly called a comparative market analysis, or CMA. A CMA is a detailed evaluation of a property's potential selling price. Among the data that a CMA will provide is a cost per square foot number.

If a property sold for $200,000 and the home is 2,000 square feet, then the cost per square foot is $100. If another house in the same neighborhood sold for $250,000 and is 2,500 square feet, the property again costs $100 per square foot.

Now suppose the property you're considering buying is listed for sale at $225,000 and is 2,500 square feet, or $90 per square foot.

Unfortunately, in reality, comparing price per square foot won't be this easy, as sales prices, square footage, and the condition of the various properties are all likely to be different.

And don't just compare two houses; compare as many as you can find that were sold within the previous 12-month period; anything that was sold longer ago than that wouldn't be considered a "recent" sale, and there could have been external market factors then that are nonexistent now. At a minimum, try to get five recent sales in the neighborhood

where you want to buy, then compare cost per square foot. You do this by averaging the costs per square foot of all the properties in your CMA, then compare that number to the figure for the property you're considering buying.

House 1	$106.00
House 2	$109.00
House 3	$ 101.00
House 4	$ 99.00
House 5	$ 97.00
Total	472 ÷ 5 = $102.40 per square foot

Now let's say you found a house that is selling for $189,200, or $86.00 per square foot, and the house is similar in size to the ones listed in your CMA, or 2,200 square feet. Based on your average of $102.40 per square foot, the home should sell for $225,280. The difference is a potential $36,080 gross profit.

Verify Your Numbers

If, however, a home is "supposed" to sell for $225,280 based upon price per square foot averages, then your next question is: Why is it listed at only $189,200? There are two likely possibilities:

Distressed sale

Condition of the property

Distressed Sale

A distressed sale occurs when the owners either are forced to sell or want to sell quickly for other reasons. Perhaps the home is going into foreclosure and the sellers need to sell fast, so they drop the price below market. I've seen properties sold below market because the couple who

originally bought the home are now getting divorced and want to sell their home, cash out, and move on.

Condition of the Property

This means that the property is in less than ideal selling condition and needs repairs or significant updating to compete with other properties in the neighborhood—so-called fixer-uppers.

In either instance, you need to find out why the property is selling below market, and you can do this by talking to the sellers or the listing agent selling the home. If there is a foreclosure or divorce looming, then that will explain the reduced price. You can quickly pop in, buy the house, and sell it at a profit.

If there are repair issues, you can inspect the home with a professional inspector and review the Property Disclosure Form, which is a document that lists all the things that might be wrong with the property, according to the seller. This document is not an option, it's a requirement, and it helps you determine how much it would cost to bring the property up to scale with other properties in the neighborhood.

After the inspection and the review of the Seller's Disclosure, you need to consider how much it's going to take to repair or renovate the home to make it marketable at closer to the $102.40 per square foot average.

Calculating Returns

If the property does need some work, your next step is to find out how much it's going to cost to repair; if you're not a general contractor, then you need to find one and become best friends. A contractor is a critical part of your team, as we explore in more detail in Chapter 3.

After you present your inspection and disclosure report to the contractor, it's determined that you will need to replace the carpet and update

one of the bathrooms, plus you want to add a nice new deck for the backyard.

Replace 1,500 square feet of carpet	$ 6,200
Upgrade guest bathroom	$ 9,400
New deck	$ 7,100
Total	**$22,700**

By adding these costs to the purchase price of $189,200, you get $211,900. That's the amount you'll need to get to break even. Almost.

When you buy and sell real estate, you'll encounter a whole host of closing fees to people from title insurance companies to appraisers to lenders—well, to a lot of people. We'll discuss closing costs in detail in Chapter 6, but they're something that needs to be deducted from your gross profits as well.

Total costs from rehab	$22,700
Closing costs to buy and sell	$ 10,500
Total costs	**$ 33,200**

There's one more thing, interest costs. Depending upon which type of financing you choose, your interest payments could be anywhere from $940 to $1,377 per month. Assuming that it takes you three months to acquire, rehab, and sell the property, then interest costs could be as low as $2,820 or as high as $4,130.

Let's say you chose the wrong type of financing (conventional 30-year fixed), which increased your costs by $1,377. Add the $4,130 to $33,200 and you have a final cost of $37,330.

You have determined that with the new carpet, deck, and bathroom remodeling, you can charge on the high end per square foot for your investment, or $107 per square foot; $107 times 2,200 square feet is $235,400.

Sales price	$ 235,400
Less:	
Acquisition price	$ 189,200
Costs	$ 37,300
Profit	$ 8,900

Or $10,210 if you selected the correct financing option. Is $10,210 over 90 days enough for you? No? Then flip more than one house during that period.

You're not buying to flip? Then you should have chosen the higher interest payment.

It's time to figure out the best ways to finance your real estate so that you can make more money, sleep at night, and always know that you're on the right financial track. Good financing makes for good investments. Bad financing leads to nightmares . . . or worse.

Types of Investment Property

So you want to invest in real estate. But what kind of real estate? A cute little bungalow down the street? A duplex? A fourplex? A condo? An apartment building? Raw land? Spec construction?

Different types of property require different financing options, and certainly there is no "one size fits all" approach to real estate finance. Buying an empty lot will require a different strategy from buying a condo downtown. Most real estate investment books that you read give only a passing reference to financing, when in fact how you finance the property is just as important as what you pay for it.

If your mortgage payments outstrip the income from the property, you're going negative each month and perhaps relying only on some real estate losses to help you out come income tax time.

But different types of real estate offer different financing opportunities.

Raw Land

There are two types of real estate: improved and unimproved. Raw land is, of course, unimproved. This means that no structure has been built on the land to "improve" it.

(Some could argue with this term, saying that some land needs to stay pristine, and I completely agree with them. I know of some absolutely beautiful pieces of property that have no "improvements" like a big house and a swimming pool but do have acres of grass, trees, and a fishing pond.)

For purposes of real estate investment, however, this type of property is typically bought to buy and hold as is, to build a new home on the property, or to subdivide the property into individual lots and develop it with brand-new houses.

Acreage that is being held and not being improved by adding a house to it requires some special financing, and there aren't too many avenues of finance from which to choose. Such land is usually more than 25 acres and is outside of a city or town.

Raw land also doesn't change hands very often. It's not like a four-bedroom duplex right next to a college dorm, where there might be a lot of demand for it. People generally buy homes more often than they buy unimproved property.

Raw land can also be more difficult to evaluate from a lending perspective. Because such large acreage purchases don't happen very often and are by their nature remote, lenders can't compare similar sales as easily as they can do with houses.

In fact, most lenders who do finance raw land won't touch it unless it has already been subdivided and has utilities in place. This also means that such loans are short term, such as 12 to 18 months, while the land is awaiting a new home to be built on top of it.

If the raw land has no such plans or utilities in place, it's perhaps one of the most difficult pieces of real estate to make a loan on. If the buyer goes bad on her loan and the bank is forced to take the land back, it is often sitting on a white elephant that it can't get rid of.

To offset such risk, a raw land lender will ask for as much as 50 percent or more down before making a loan decision. If there are development plans in place, then that down payment requirement can be lowered significantly to closer to 20 or even 10 percent, given a strong borrower.

Still, if the land doesn't appear to have any development potential, the bank is lending more on the strength of the borrower and much less on the asset.

Another consideration regarding raw land is that it's usually surrounded by other raw land. That means that if you want to sell the acreage to a potential buyer, then your offer will have to be better than all of the other raw land deals that surround you.

If you're going to develop the land by putting in utilities and roads and subdividing it, then that's a different story and becomes easier to lend on, but if you're buying raw land as speculative, then be prepared to put a lot of money down for it relative to the sales price and have lots of patience.

This is definitely an investment that you should plan to hold for a long time.

New Construction

New construction investment can be in the form of financing the costs of building the unit itself, such as hammers, nails, paint, and labor, or financing that includes not just those items but also the acquisition of the lot as well.

This form of investment property may or may not have a buyer when the unit is completed. If it does not, the investment can be called purely speculative, or a "spec" home.

If you own the land that the home is going to be built on and you get construction financing for the house, the lot that you own is automatically considered your equity in the deal, meaning that when you apply

for a construction loan that requires a 10 percent down payment, instead of your bringing cash to the table, the construction lender will use the value of the lot as your down payment.

Let's say you get some bids to build a 3,000-square-foot home on a half-acre lot that you own. The lot is worth $150,000, unimproved.

Bids to build the house come in right around $1.50 per square foot, or $450,000 in value when the home is completed.

By adding your lot value of $150,000 and the completed value of $450,000, you have a total value of $600,000. If your construction lender is requiring a 20 percent down payment to finance your construction, 20 percent of $600,000 is $120,000, so you've already covered that down payment requirement through the $150,000 equity position you have in the lot.

That's assuming that you own the lot free and clear. You must deduct any notes due on that lot to determine your finished equity. If your lot is valued at $150,000 and you have a $50,000 note against it, your equity position is only $100,000.

Therefore, if the construction lender requires 20 percent down on that same deal, you still need $120,000, but you have only $100,000 in lot equity, so you will in fact need to come to the construction lender with another $20,000 to get your construction loan.

Construction lenders value new construction using an "as built" approach. There really is no value in the home—not much, anyway—until it's finished. When a bank makes a determination of the value of your home and how much to lend on it, it sends an appraiser out to the job site with a set of plans; the appraiser then makes a value determination based upon the house being completed, and the bank issues a construction loan based upon the house being already built.

When the home is finally finished, the bank will send the appraiser out one more time to make sure the house is finally 100 percent complete. At this stage, when the home is finished, you will need to get a permanent mortgage to replace the construction loan. Note that the term

permanent doesn't necessarily equate to "long term"; it means only that its job is to replace the temporary construction note.

Construction loans are short term and cover only the hard costs of building and soft costs such as building permits and inspections. At the conclusion of construction, a permanent mortgage will replace the shorter-term note.

That is, unless you've already sold the property while the house is being built and so won't need permanent financing. If you haven't found a buyer for your spec house, then you'll need to arrange some sort of financing to hold onto the property while you're trying to sell it.

In the case of spec houses, you really need to have your ear to the ground. When you start construction, depending on the type and size of the house, it could be a year out before it's done. You need a pretty good crystal ball for that.

And you may also need some experience with spec houses in the past before a bank will finance one for you. The bank doesn't want the spec house. If it did, it would build one of its own. The bank wants your money.

When you build on spec and you are an investor, you can anticipate making a higher down payment in the form of lot equity or cash and potentially paying a higher interest rate associated with non-owner-occupied properties.

Investment Property Versus Second Homes

There is a clear distinction in lending between investment properties and second homes in terms of classification of occupancy type. When you complete a loan application, one of the areas it asks you to complete is whether or not you're going to live in the property as your primary residence . . . your home.

Occupancy is one of the risk factors that lenders use to evaluate a loan. The three occupancy classifications are primary, second home, and

investment property. Investment property is considered to have the highest risk of default to a lender of the three types.

A second home is considered the second of the risk groups, and the primary home is considered to have the lowest risk. The difference between a second home and an investment home is usually about 3/8 to $^1/_2$ percent in rate, or about 1.5 to 2.00 points.

On a $400,000 deal, 2 points works out to $8,000. Or an increase in rate of $^1/_2$ percent means that that same $400,000 loan went up about $125 per month, every month. Over the course of a 30-year loan, that's a lot of money—about $45,000.

A second home is a home that is not rented out by the owners but is used as a vacation home or a getaway spot for the owner. A second home is typically out of the immediate geographic area and is often in a vacation or resort spot, such as in the mountains, on the beach, or stuck far away from civilization.

An investment property is a rental. It can be in a vacation area or in the mountains, but from a lender's perspective, if the property is rented out more than two weeks during the entire year, the home isn't considered a vacation or "second" home but is a rental. That means higher rates, perhaps a larger down payment, and higher costs.

How does a lender determine whether the property in question is a second home or an investment property? There is no exact formula, but the underwriter who reviews your loan will use a little common sense.

If the property is across town, then it's not a vacation home. There is no reason to go on vacation to get away from it all if it only takes a 30-minute cab ride. If the property is in an area where the underwriter feels it's "just not right" that someone would have a second home, he'll ask questions.

If you live in Tulsa and you want to buy a second home in Little Rock, you may need to provide an explanation letter that says something like, "We love Little Rock and always enjoy making the short drive to Hot Springs to watch the races."

But that still might not pass muster. If the underwriter sees that the property you're going to buy is occupied by renters and not the owners,

then you may find that the underwriter will have a little squabble with you.

Second homes make more sense if you live in Sioux Falls and are buying in Corpus Christi, Texas, or if you live in Phoenix during the winter and spend the summer in Colorado.

When you are dealing with an underwriter, the burden of proof is on you—the underwriter doesn't have to make the case.

In fact, lenders can actually send a representative to the property after the loan is closed and knock on the door and see who answers. If it's not you, and it's renters, you're busted. The lender has the right to call in your loan. Don't try to disguise an investment property as a second home; it can get you in trouble.

When lenders face additional risk, they offset that risk with other factors, such as a higher down payment (equity from the borrower), higher rates, or some combination thereof.

This is because if a borrower who owns three properties, an investment home, a vacation home, and a primary residence, falls on hard times, the lender knows it's the primary home that will be the one she holds onto.

A rental property could be sold or even foreclosed on before someone will let go of his house or second home.

Even when refinancing a second home, the underwriter can ask for tax returns and look for "rental income" on those returns to determine whether the property is indeed a vacation home or a rental.

Real estate investment property and a vacation home are two distinct types of investment, and lenders will pay close attention to how you check the box on the application that asks which type of property you're buying and getting financing for.

Single-Family Residences

A single-family residence (SFR) is a house. No, it doesn't have to have a family in it, but that's the definition of a house from a lender's perspective.

This type of property is eligible for the best financing terms. Although an investment property will have a 3/8 to $^1/_2$ percent higher rate than a primary residence, it will still have better mortgage terms available than most other property types.

This type of property is the easiest to qualify for a loan on, easiest to underwrite a loan on, and easiest to sell when you are ready to do so precisely because there are more of these properties than any other type and almost every mortgage program designed for residential real estate uses the SFR as its standard collateral model.

When you see interest rates advertised in the newspaper or on the Internet, they are for this type of property.

Duplexes

A duplex is two separate units that are connected. Each side has its own living areas, kitchen, bedrooms, and baths and has a separate entry. The units are also almost always metered separately, but they don't have to be.

Separate metering allows you as the landlord to have the tenants pay their own utilities instead of you paying the utilities for them. There really is no way to discover who is using more water or who is using less electricity if the duplex has just one meter for each utility.

A duplex enjoys the same mortgage choices as a single-family residence does. You can also rent out one side of the unit and live in the other, meaning that the renter next door is typically making your house payments.

For example, suppose a duplex sells for $185,000. Using a 30-year fixed rate at 6.50 percent and 20 percent down, the monthly payment would be $935, plus taxes and insurance.

By renting the other half of the duplex for $1,200 per month (assuming market conditions support that price), you're living on the other side of the duplex mortgage-free—at least as long as you have a tenant next door and as long as she's paying you on time every month.

There's one difference between SFRs and duplexes: Whether you live in one of the sides or not, the duplex will usually be priced as an investment unit, meaning that your rate will be 3/8 to $^1/_2$ percent higher than if you bought a SFR and lived in it.

It may not seem fair to charge you investment rates while you're living in the property, but that's how these loans are priced.

Another feature of a duplex is that the maximum conforming loan limit is higher than for a SFR.

Any loan amount above the conforming figure is called a "jumbo" mortgage and typically carries an interest rate about $^1/_4$ percent higher than conforming loans.

However, a duplex has a higher loan limit to still be conforming, about one-third higher than the SFR limit. These limits will change each year, based upon the previous year's increase in average home prices.

Triplexes

This is the same idea as a duplex, only there are three connected units and not two. Just as the conforming loan limit increases with a duplex, it also increases with a triplex by about another.

Fourplexes

This is the same idea as a duplex and a triplex, but with four attached units and a higher maximum conforming loan limit at $801,950. Often a triplex or a fourplex can be called a 1–4-unit structure yet still have only three or only four units.

Multifamily Properties

A multifamily project is five or more units, but it is most easily described as an apartment complex. Instead of getting financing for each individual unit, you will invest in the entire apartment complex.

Depending upon the sales price of the apartment building, you may be able to get financing just as you would for any other residential real estate by completing a residential loan application. Normally such loans will cap out at $1.5 million, and the lender will ask for a minimum of 20 percent down.

If you want to borrow more than $1.5 million, then you'll step out of the residential mortgage arena and straight into commercial financing packages.

Commercial Financing

Commercial financing for residential real estate typically requires 20 percent or more down; the terms are typically three, five, or seven years and are based upon the prime rate plus 1 to 3 percent. There is also an additional aspect of commercial financing called the debt service coverage ratio, or DSCR, which is calculated this way:

$$\text{DSCR} = \text{net operating income} \div \text{debt service.}$$

Debt service is the principal and interest payments on the note used to buy the apartment. Net operating income is the income minus all expenses associated with keeping up the building (net income). Therefore, the DSCR is net income divided by the mortgage payment on the loan.

The required DSCR is normally 1.2 to 1.3; it is rarely below that. A number above 1.0 represents a positive cash flow. If the DSCR is 1.3, then for each dollar of the mortgage payment on an apartment project, the prospective lender wants to see an additional 30 cents in net operating income.

Commercial financing is underwritten using entirely different formulas and is reviewed by commercial loan officers.

If the apartment complex you want to buy costs $1.5 million or less,

then there are loan programs based more closely on the individual, just as with any other residential real estate loan.

Condominiums

A condominium, or "condo," is a structure in which the owners own the interiors of their units individually and share the outside or common areas with all the other owners in their condominium association.

The most common type of condominium resembles an apartment building, but with the apartments being owned rather than rented. The owners have complete control of the interior of their unit, but everything else is commonly owned.

If there is a common area like a swimming pool or a workout room, then all the tenants own an equal part of that swimming pool or workout room. Condos can be large or small, and they can be attached to one another like apartments are or be detached units that don't share the same walls.

Condos are governed by a Homeowners' Association, which sets certain bylaws that condo owners are expected to follow.

Condos are divided into two types: warrantable and nonwarrantable.

A warrantable condo means that it meets the property guidelines established by Fannie Mae, Freddie Mac, or the Federal Housing Administration (FHA). Fannie Mae is the nickname for the Federal National Mortgage Association (FNMA), and Freddie Mac is short for FHLMC, or the Federal Home Loan Mortgage Corporation.

Fannie Mae and Freddie Mac are entities owned by the federal government, yet they are publicly traded on the stock market. The purpose of each of these government-sponsored enterprises (GSEs) is to provide liquidity to the mortgage market. We'll examine why this is important in more detail in Chapter 5, yet a condo that is warrantable meets these guidelines.

This makes the loan terms more favorable. A nonwarrantable condo

is a condo that does not meet one or more of Fannie Mae or Freddie Mac's condo requirements.

A warrantable condo is one where:

All phases have been completed.

The common areas are 100 percent complete.

Ownership has changed hands from the developer to the Homeowners' Association.

No one individual owns more than 10 percent of the project.

The condos are occupied primarily by the owners.

A nonwarrantable condo means that one or more of these requirements has not been met.

All Phases Have Been Completed

A condominium project can be built in phases. Instead of building 300 units at the same time, a developer could build the units in phases. In new construction, no one can move into a unit until that unit is completed. When an SFR is done, the owners can move in or rent it out, but not until it's 100 percent complete.

If a builder waited until all 300 units were complete, he would have to wait a long time to get his money back. Instead, he may build in phases, with 100 units being completed in Phase 1, 100 more units in Phase 2, and finally another 100 units in Phase 3.

This way he can build and sell, build and sell. For a condo to be warrantable, all phases must be completed. To get the very best lending terms, the buyer of a condo might have to wait until all phases are done in order to qualify for a Fannie Mae or Freddie Mac loan.

Common Areas Are Complete

The common areas are the sidewalks, the parking lot or garage, the landscaping, and even the pool or workout facilities. Common areas are

owned by all the tenants equally and are kept up by the Homeowners' Association using the dues paid by the owners to the Homeowners' Association.

All common areas must be completed before a condo can get warrantable status. Confirmation of 100 percent completion comes during a final inspection done by your appraiser. Sometimes your condo may be done, but these areas aren't complete.

But before a condo is warrantable, the appraiser must verify that everything has been completed according to building specifications.

Ownership Must Change Hands From the Developer to the Homeowners' Association

During construction, the developer owns the project and controls its daily operations. But once the units have been completed, the developer must legally transfer the ownership to the homeowners.

No Single Entity Can Own More than 10 Percent of the Project

If there are 100 units, no one person or business entity can own more than 10 units. Again, the appraiser will typically ask the Homeowners' Association for this information and verify its accuracy. One of the association's many functions, especially early in a new condominium project, is to complete these homeowners' questionnaires for prospective lenders.

Most Units Are Occupied by the Owners

Finally, a warrantable condo project is primarily owner-occupied, meaning that while there may be renters in the condo project, they must make up no more than 40 percent of the total number of units.

If any of these conditions are not met, the condo is nonwarrantable. The condo could have every other warrantable property, but if the ownership hasn't legally changed hands from the developer to the Homeowners' Association, then everything stops. This doesn't mean that you can't get financing on your investment condo; it simply means that you can't get conventional financing.

Another way to get competitive financing is if the units have been approved by the Federal Housing Administration. The FHA has its own condominium guidelines, and if the project has been audited and approved by the FHA, then the condo automatically qualifies for FHA pricing, which is just as competitive as conventional pricing on Fannie Mae and Freddie Mac loans.

If you're looking to invest in a condo project and want to know if it's been approved by the FHA, the listing agent will typically have that information. If not, the Homeowners' Association will have it, and if you're still running up against a wall, the FHA has a special web site listing FHA-approved condominium projects at https://entp.hud.gov/idapp/html/condlook.cfm. Simply search for a particular condo project or by state or by address.

Nonwarrantable pricing is higher than warrantable, often nearly $1/2$ percent higher than a conventional or FHA mortgage product, and this can make a real difference if cash flow is tight for a particular investment.

There is a way to turn an investment condo into a primary residence condo, allowing you to get the best terms available, but this works only when a family member will be living in the unit and will also be on the note and on title. This is sometimes called a "kiddie condo," where mom and dad buy a condo and put their son or daughter on the note as well as having him or her live there.

This is a very popular structure in college towns, where students can live in property their parents own while they go to college, then the parents can either sell the condo for a profit when the student graduates or keep the unit and continue to rent it out.

This strategy will usually work only with FHA loans because most

other loans require a review of the employment, credit, and debt ratios of the person occupying the condo. Conventional lending on a kiddie condo will work, but only if the student can show some income and meets certain ratio requirements along with mom and dad.

Often the problem is that the student doesn't make enough money to help with the mortgage payments. If the student is working part time and makes about $300 per month and the condo payments are $2,000 per month, then it's doubtful that a lender will allow the student to go on the note in order to get the more favorable owner-occupied rate.

That's not the case with FHA loans, as there is no requirement for the owner-occupant (student) to show income to help qualify, as long as the student goes on the note and title at the same time that mom and dad bought the condo.

If you want to explore this option, first visit the FHA web site that lists FHA-approved projects, then take the next step about qualifying. This is by far the most popular method of kiddie condo financing.

Note: To have received FHA approval, the units must also be warrantable under conventional standards. The FHA doesn't warrant properties much differently from Fannie Mae or Freddie Mac, yet its owner-occupant guidelines are different for purposes of loan terms.

You can also make an investment property out of an owner-occupied property if you move into it first, then move out later if that's what you decide. If you decide to move to Lincoln, Nebraska, and you buy a house, move in, and work, then that's an owner-occupied home.

If later you decide to move out but keep the property, the lender doesn't call you back and make you pay a higher rate just because you moved out. In fact, many people actually get started in real estate investment under such circumstances. By accident.

Say you bought a house and lived in it for a while, and then you either got transferred or decided that Lincoln was too cold in the winters for you, so you think about selling. But either you can't get the price you want or you can't sell fast enough or you simply want to rent out the

house, thinking that one day you might move back, so you keep the house and rent it out instead, moving on to a warmer climate.

Suddenly, you now own investment property at owner-occupied terms. You're not obligated to redo the entire loan to make it an investment property. You simply moved out.

One thing you cannot do, however, is move in, then move out the next day. Or the next week, or maybe even the next month, for that matter. When you check "owner-occupied" on your loan application, your new lender will soon verify that you in fact do live there after you close.

If your unit is rented out to someone else, the lender could call in the note and redo it. You fibbed in order to get a better rate. However, if you can prove that you fully intended to live in the property, but external forces such as a job change or illness or some other emergency forced you to move, you could claim a hardship.

Turning owner-occupied property into investment property is usually not something that's planned; it's just something that happened later on down the road.

Unusual Properties

Finally, the last type of properties to invest in are ones that I call "weird" properties. This can mean a property that is physically different in type or one that is dissimilar to other properties in the area, or both.

Got a good deal on a geodesic dome? You know, those weird-looking things that look like a geometry set gone bad? Did you fall for the salesman's pitch that geodesic domes provide more comfort and more space and last longer than traditional homes, and they're the wave of the future? Typically the future hasn't arrived, and your real estate investment may hit a snag if the lender you want to have finance the property can't finance it because yours is the only geodesic dome in the neighborhood.

Lenders like a certain level of conformity. Conformity shows that

there is a demand for a particular type of property, and if there's a demand, then if the lender ever has to take back the property, there's an apparent market for it. It "fits in."

Geodesic domes don't fit in. In fact, the only place they fit in is someplace where there are lots of other dome enthusiasts. That's where you're most likely to find domes: with other domes. Even then, lenders will balk. You can get financing on domes, but not the best. There's just not enough demand for them to command a competitive mortgage rate. Log cabins? See geodesic domes.

Unusual properties don't necessarily have to be physically all that different; it's just that there aren't exactly similar sales in the area.

I financed an entire subdivision for a builder who had gotten himself into hot water. He had an idea for building some unique student housing in a college town that would be inexpensive to build and inexpensive to buy, and that would generate cash flow for his investors immediately.

He drew up plans, made the pitch to his bank, and got a construction loan to build these new cash cows. The concept was brilliant: He designed four-bedroom houses where each bedroom had its own bathroom, but they shared a central living area and kitchen.

The buildings were very much like dormitories, but with only four units. The demand for student housing was there, as this college was booming and was running out of space for its students, and most of the available housing was either older apartment dwellings or single-family houses.

Now, four students would pay rent on one house and live in a brand-new neighborhood instead of in some tacky old apartment building. In addition, the builder constructed these units more cheaply by using modular housing instead of traditional "stick-built" houses.

Modular housing meets the very same building code standards that regular housing does, yet the "parts" are built off-site and put together on-site. The walls, the roofs, and the bathrooms are prefabricated—everything is prebuilt at a factory.

The houses looked the same and were built the same; the only differ-

ences were the color of the houses and the roof. Other than that, they were identical, built from materials that had already been made at a pre-fab factory.

In other words, they were extremely cheap to build, yet they still met the same rigorous building codes as a standard house. Not to be confused with manufactured housing, modular housing provides value with solid construction.

The builder pitched his project to different people he knew, and the units were 100 percent sold before construction ever took place. It was a real "no-brainer."

He completed the project and began to transfer ownership of the houses to the buyers. There was one big problem, though: No one would lend on them. No one could get financing. He was stuck. The bank wanted his money, but he didn't have it—it was tied up in his modular home project.

Why would no one lend on these houses? They were weird. They were four-bedroom, four-bath houses (that's different already), and they also had a unique construction: modular. Okay, they weren't weird in the literal sense; they looked like any other house, only nicer because they were brand new. There simply were no other houses in the area that would be considered similar to these units. There were no comparable sales, or "comps." There were absolutely zero four-bedroom, four-bath houses with one central living area built entirely using modular construction.

So the developer called me on the phone one day: "David, I need your help."

We met for lunch, and he showed me his plans. He had contracts for 48 houses at $125,000 each, and he couldn't close on any of them.

I reviewed the project and came up with a plan. We found one person who would pay cash for his unit; that gave us a comparable sale inside the new development. Next, I found lenders who would make loans for modular housing. Then we closed four of these loans with one lender before we went on to the next lender. Why did I do that?

It's an investment term called *exposure*. A lender
more than 10 percent of any new development. We had
ent lender each time we closed four deals.

And because these units were a bit out of the ordinary,
tive, or "alt," financing. Alt financing is typically anythi͟   ͟ ͟ot
conventional or government; it is used to make loans on properties that
Fannie Mae, Freddie Mac, or FHA won't do.

These loans are made under different terms, mind you. Typical alt
financing can be between $^1/_2$ and 1 percent higher than the rates reserved
for conventional products. The developer almost lost his entire development to his bank before he got his financing arranged.

You need to pay close attention to what available financing packages,
if any, are out there that you can use. If there aren't any, regardless of
how enticing the investment is, you won't get financing for it, and you
must either pull equity out of other properties or pay cash.

In general, rates can change depending upon property type, as indicated by this chart.

Property Type	Base Rate	Min. Down
SFR	6.25%	0%
SFR rental	6.625%	10%
Duplex	6.625%	10%
1–4 units	6.625%	20%
Kiddie condo	6.25%	0%
Investment condo	6.625%	10%
Alternative	7.25%	10%
Multifamily*	10.25%	20%

*Based upon a *Wall Street Journal* prime rate of 8.25 percent
plus 2 percentage points.

The Players

More than ever, the people and players you associate yourself with both during your property search and throughout your loan closing can affect the profitability of your investment.

It's critical that you know not just who each of the players is, but who each one is in relation to your investment. Some you can negotiate fees with, while others will be an integral part of your real estate team, helping you to find and acquire the right property while still making the numbers work. After all, that's what it's all about, right?

We'll identify the various people in the real estate transaction, explain their function, note their average costs, and label them "critical," "important," or "necessary."

Critical Players

The Lender

This is where you get the money; it is obviously a critical piece of the transaction. But going to your lender doesn't necessarily mean that you'll

automatically get the best deal; your best deal may not come from a lender at all, but could very well come from someone who doesn't make the mortgage but simply arranges the financing for you. This person, a mortgage broker, has the ability to search various lending programs for you to find the most favorable financing terms that meet your requirements.

There are two basic sources of money: mortgage bankers and mortgage brokers. Mortgage bankers are entities that lend their own money, while mortgage brokers do not lend their own money but find money for you.

Mortgage bankers come in all shapes and sizes. Every retail bank you see on the street corner has a mortgage banking operation. A bank may not only have your checking account, your car loan, and your credit card (all different divisions of the same bank), but also have a dedicated business line that makes mortgage loans, collects the mortgage payments, and performs other mortgage-related functions. Mortgage bankers approve the loan directly and typically have a bit more latitude when they make a lending decision.

On the other hand, a mortgage broker may have a particular advantage in the mortgage world: choice. Almost every bank and mortgage company you've ever heard of (and plenty more that you haven't heard of) operates a wholesale mortgage business. A wholesale mortgage business works a bit differently from a retail mortgage lender in that a wholesale lender's customer is not the buyer but the mortgage broker.

Wholesale lenders have account representatives, or salespeople, who do nothing but call on their various mortgage brokers and get more mortgage brokers to do business with them.

When you walk into a bank or a mortgage company, you'll notice lots of employees, desks, telephones, and light fixtures, and there will also be things you won't see, such as wages, insurance coverage, and employment taxes. These are hard costs, costs that a mortgage company must pay while still making a profit doing so if it wants to stay in business very long.

Wholesale lenders, while they have employees, do not set up offices that take loan applications from consumers. Instead, they visit mortgage brokers, who already have offices and employees and all the other associated expenses of running an office, and find brokers who will market their mortgages for them.

In return, the wholesale lender offers the mortgage broker a reduced rate on its mortgage programs, which the mortgage broker "marks up" to retail level. Therefore, a mortgage broker is not necessarily more expensive than a mortgage banker, although it can be if the broker marked up the mortgage too much.

A typical markup from wholesale to retail is about $1/4$ percent in interest rate or about 1 discount point. A discount point, or point, is 1 percent of the loan amount, or $2,000 on a $200,000 loan.

Wholesale lenders compete for the mortgage brokers' business just as lenders compete for yours. Each day, wholesale lenders compile their rate sheets and e-mail or fax them to their mortgage brokers. Each day, mortgage brokers review those rate sheets trying to find the absolute lowest interest rate for that day, hoping to find the best possible deal for their borrowers.

Another distinction a broker has is the ability to not just compare mortgage rates but also find unique or niche mortgage loan programs that not all lenders have. A lender could offer a special program for investors that requires zero money down. Not many lenders offer such a program; in fact, there is no conventional or government product that offers such terms. But there are programs that do just that.

A mortgage broker can search through his bevy of lenders and find a mortgage program that not many of them have. In fact, if you see advertisements in the newspaper or on the Internet showing loan programs that seem a bit unusual, they're probably from a mortgage broker.

Not only do brokers attempt to find you the best rate, but they may also help you find a unique program that fits your requirements, as I was able to do for the modular condo investor mentioned in the last chapter.

Note: If a mortgage broker does find a zero-down investor loan, it has

to get that loan from a wholesale lender. And if it gets the loan from the wholesale lender, you can bet that the wholesale lender's retail mortgage banking operation has the exact same zero-down program.

The advantage for you is that you don't have to make phone calls all day long or search the Internet for unique loan offerings; a mortgage broker does that for you and most likely knows exactly where to get niche products with little effort, all at competitive prices.

That's why, depending upon which source you use, mortgage brokers originate about two-thirds of all mortgage loans today. That's a lot, and it's a huge leap from when mortgage brokers first became mainstream in the early 1990s.

Bankers, on the other hand, offer more control over your loan. That means that when problems arise, the banker can address those problems directly without having to go through the various channels that a broker must use.

Bankers can make lending exceptions on loan files, exceptions that might mean stretching a lending requirement. Bankers are also more advantageous when it comes to "hands-on" loan programs such as renovation or construction loans.

During the process of a remodeling or new construction, lenders do periodic reviews of the progress of the property before doling out additional construction funds to the builder as the work progresses. Mortgage brokers won't be around for that; they're off getting other loans.

Bankers can also be just as competitive as brokers can, generally anyway. I've been both a mortgage broker and a mortgage banker, and I enjoyed being a broker, but I really enjoy being a banker primarily because it gives me the ability to step in when a mortgage problem arises and take care of the issue directly instead of passing the problem up the ladder and waiting for someone else to fix it.

There is one more possibility: a mortgage banker that also acts as a mortgage broker. For an investor, this is quite possibly the best of both worlds. A banker can lend out of the bank's own funds, approving loans using previously approved lending guidelines, but if an investor needs a

mortgage program that the banker doesn't personally have, the banker can also find other wholesale lenders he is already signed up with and use their products to fund the loan.

I recently closed a loan for a client in Austin, Texas, who wanted a zero percent down investment condo. My conventional loans via Fannie Mae, Freddie Mac, or FHA didn't offer such a product, but another wholesale lender I use occasionally did offer it. I simply sent the loan package to the wholesale lender, and it approved the loan.

National mortgage bankers won't also broker. If they can't do the deal, they'll either try to talk you into something else or pass altogether. If you want a banker who is licensed as a broker as well, you're looking for a local or regional mortgage banker.

It's difficult, if not impossible, to tell whether someone is a banker or broker just by the name. Many names, such as First Southwest Capital, could be used by either a mortgage banker or a mortgage broker. Often you must simply ask the company whether it's a banker and whether it also brokers when needed.

States have different licensing requirements for mortgage brokers and mortgage bankers, so you can log onto your state's web site, search for mortgage licensing, and look them up. However you find out, finding a mortgage banker with broker capabilities is a pretty strong start.

When you find your lender of choice, keeping that lender in your portfolio helps you when you find additional properties that you want to buy. Often, lenders can simply open up your old loan file and copy some of the old data into a new loan application for you to sign. This is much easier than applying over and over again each time you find a property that you want to buy.

You're also establishing a long-term relationship that's built on trust. When you have such a relationship, you can spend less time searching for the ideal loan and more time on finding ideal properties to buy.

Mortgage lenders get paid as a result of their loan officers finding mortgage loans, and they split the loan proceeds with the loan officer. A typical commission on an individual loan is somewhere between 1 and 2

percent, and the lender and the loan officer will divvy that up between themselves.

Mortgage lenders also make money by charging you "junk fees," which can range anywhere from $300 to $1,000 or more. We'll discuss closing costs and loan fees in more detail in Chapter 6.

The Loan Officer

Your lender will also be the employer of your loan officer. Whether you are using a mortgage broker or a mortgage banker, it's your loan officer who will work with you in finding the proper mortgage. You're not working with a mortgage "company"; instead, you're working with a person who either works for or owns that mortgage company.

Your loan officer will quote rates, quote fees, compare programs, and identify lending opportunities that you may not be aware of. Your loan officer will be your most trusted financial adviser as it pertains to financing real estate.

A bank, a mortgage banker, a credit union, and any other mortgage company is only as good as its front-line people—the loan officers.

This can be particularly true of major mortgage bankers and retail banks that advertise heavily, touting their neat investor loan products. It really comes down not necessarily to the bank, but to the experience of your loan officer.

It's critical that you choose a good lender. It's also critical that within that lender, you choose an experienced loan officer and stick with her.

Think about that for a second. You walk into your bank or credit union or your favorite lender's web site and see all these great ads with cool marketing phrases and just the right colors to make you want to do business with that mortgage company.

But guess what? All those posters in the lobby or the online ads are worthless if your loan officer doesn't get the job done.

A bank can have the biggest advertising budget in the world but also

have a bunch of rookies who do nothing but take loan applications and have little experience in mortgage lending.

The lender is the one who holds the purse strings, approves the loan, and issues your closing papers. Lenders may lend locally, across the state, or across the country.

Because of state and federal lending laws, a company that lends nationally is typically a federally chartered bank or a mortgage banking operation with licenses and operation in all 50 states.

If you invest locally, or at least in your own state, then almost any loan officer can help you. If, however, you want to broaden your horizons and invest in other parts of the country, you'll want to find someone who can lend pretty much anywhere.

You won't always be that lucky, but that's the ideal: to find one loan officer who can work with you anywhere.

I recall a client who lived in California and wanted to purchase an apartment building in Galveston, Texas. He called me; I said I could do what he wanted. He also had some properties in Texas that he wanted to refinance; I could do that also.

Then he asked about Nevada, because he had some stuff that he needed help with there also. And Hawaii. I wasn't licensed in Hawaii and couldn't help with that, but I could help with Nevada. So he contacted another mortgage company that was licensed to lend in Hawaii.

That meant that he had to have more than one application at different lenders and had to provide duplicates of everything to both me and his Hawaii company. Had I been able to lend everywhere, he wouldn't have had to duplicate all of his efforts and could have established a working relationship with just one person who had his personal goals in mind. But it doesn't always work out that way.

There is one other difference you need to be aware of: Loan officers get paid differently at different lending institutions.

Mortgage brokers work for themselves. Or at least they're loan officers who work at a mortgage brokerage operation and typically lend only

in their state. Mortgage bankers also work for their company and can often lend in their state and perhaps a few others.

Do your homework and try to find a loan officer who can meet your investment requirements while always being on the lookout for your mortgage fitness.

Mortgage fitness can mean refinancing when the time is right. Or a new loan program may become available that you need to be made aware of. You're investing in real estate, not investing all your time in keeping up with mortgage rates on a daily basis. A trusted loan officer will do just that for you.

If your investment goals take you beyond your local borders, then in a perfect world, finding a loan officer who can lend anywhere you want to buy is a plus.

The Contractor

When you find a property that you want to rehab, the contractor is a key element; he provides advice on how much your project will cost and how long the remodeling will take.

Finding a good contractor is done through referrals, and fortunately, when researching a contractor, his abilities are easy to discern from the work he's done on other properties.

Begin by asking friends, family, your lender, your Realtor, or anyone else you know who might have had experience with remodeling or who knows a contractor firsthand.

You want your contractor to be able to not only provide quality work but also perform that work within the specified time frame. Time is indeed money, and if you go past a projected completion date, you'll be paying another month's worth of interest charges that you didn't antici-pate, eating into your profit margins.

You also need someone who can accurately predict how much a proj-ect will cost. If you budgeted $10,000 for a bathroom remodeling and it comes out at $13,000, then you're again losing income.

Your ideal contractor will be able to provide accurate quotes on both time and expense as well as be able to begin and finish as planned. Often you'll find that good contractors are booked up way in advance of when you need them. Apparently they're good enough that their schedule is packed solid for several months, so you need to look elsewhere.

Once you do find a contractor that you can count on, you should do whatever you can to keep her in your camp, and in yours alone.

The Realtor

This person's job is to find properties that fit your criteria. And let me add one important point here: Realtor is a licensed trademark of the National Association of Realtors. Someone who gets his real estate license and becomes an agent is not necessarily a Realtor.

A Realtor is someone who is a member of the National Association of Realtors and who adheres to its strict code of ethics. A Realtor is a dedicated professional. I'm not saying that someone who is not a Realtor is not dedicated, just that agents who are Realtors have pledged themselves to a higher level of education, professionalism, and ethical business practices. Use a Realtor and not just a licensed agent.

Or more specifically, use a Realtor who represents you, the buyer. The listing agent is the one who puts the property up for sale. The listing agent is not on your side; the listing agent is on the side of the seller. You want a buyer's agent when you're purchasing properties.

You can certainly begin buying investment properties on your own, and in fact that might be how you buy your first property, but you won't have the access to new properties that become listed that a Realtor does.

Properties are typically listed in a system called the Multiple Listing Service, or the MLS. The MLS is a database where Realtors share information about new properties for sale.

I recall that many years ago, when my mom was a Realtor, agents would keep their own listings on index cards or in a property book. As

Realtors went out and found properties to sell, they would enter those properties in the listing book or write them down on cards.

Each week, various Realtors would meet over coffee or at a lunch or a business meeting and share their new listings with one another. It would go something like this:

"I have a new three-bedroom house on one-half acre that is all brick and has a brand-new pool. The owners are asking $49,000 for it, and it was just listed last week."

Remember, there was no such thing as the Internet back then, right? Eventually, though, personal computers became more common, and the property information was kept in a centralized database and accessed using DOS-based programs.

Nowadays, the database is on the Internet, and as Realtors post new listings, they become available to other Realtors almost immediately. In fact, some Realtors' web sites let you key in your search parameters and will notify you when properties that meet your needs are listed.

You can certainly start this way, but solely from a property search standpoint, it's the Realtor who can sniff out potential listings before they even come on the market. That's one of his jobs, the good ones anyway.

Good Realtors are constantly searching for new listings; that's where real estate really gets started—by finding people who want to sell. You need a good Realtor who is always on the lookout for potential investments that fit your profile.

For instance, you may have determined that you want to invest in a town where you know that the local chamber of commerce has been courting major industry for the past couple of years. You decide that it would be a good time to invest in single-family houses designed for people who will transfer into that area.

You tell your Realtor that you're on the market for three- or four-bedroom houses, about 10 to 15 years old, and under $185,000 where you could get some serious cash flow from renting them.

A Realtor becomes your bloodhound, looking for properties that

come up before they ever hit the market. And that's what you want. A Realtor will scour the neighborhood you're interested in (and surrounding ones) for three- or four-bedroom homes under $185,000 by sending out mailers, going to functions, and essentially letting the world know that she has a serious (and secret) buyer who is looking to buy—right now.

The clear advantage is that you can find property before it ever hits the MLS. You certainly don't want to get into a bidding war or find a house that suddenly has multiple offers. No, you want your Realtor to find those properties for you. That's one of his jobs. It's a critical function.

A Realtor will also guide you through the negotiation process and help you with your offer. Unless you're a seasoned veteran of the real estate business, the Realtor can help you with an offer, make sure there aren't any "gotchas" in the contract, and help you with other affiliated partners such as inspectors, insurance companies, contractors, and lender referrals (just to name a few).

Your Realtor has his pulse on the real estate community, full time.

When you are buying the property, a Realtor doesn't cost you anything. A Realtor usually gets paid a percentage of the listing agent's commission, so the seller usually pays the Realtor.

When a listing agent lists a home, the seller and the listing Realtor agree upon a commission. For instance, say the seller and the Realtor agree that the Realtor will get 4 percent of the sales price of the home. On a $500,000 property, that would be a commission of $20,000.

The listing agent will put the property in the MLS and will also post what amount of commission she will pay other Realtors who bring a qualified buyer to the closing table. Often this commission is split 50/50, but the split can be just about anything the listing agent and the seller agree upon.

If the listing agent agrees to split her commission 50/50 with another Realtor if he brings a buyer, in this case the buyer's agent (yours) will get 50 percent of $20,000, or $10,000. You don't pay your Realtor to find

properties for you; the listing agent does so out of the commission she earned from the seller.

Now, $10,000 is a lot of money, and if you're a serious investor, you can bet that your Realtor will constantly be searching for more $10,000 paychecks—properties for you that meet your exact specifications.

If you consistently use a Realtor to find properties for you, you can also negotiate the commission she gets by having her pay some of your closing costs at the closing table. If your Realtor gets paid $10,000 on each transaction and you've bought five properties in the previous year, then ask what type of contribution she can make toward some of your closing fees, such as inspections, appraisals, or even discount points to buy your mortgage rate down.

If a Realtor is making $50,000 per year from just one client (you), you're certainly within your rights to ask for some help with your expenses on occasion. This is something that's negotiable. It may not always happen, but if you promise all your business to one Realtor, you should expect some discounts. And you can get these discounts when you decide to sell property as well as when you buy it.

When You're Ready to Sell

Unless you're an active Realtor as well, you'll need a solid Realtor to help you when you sell the properties you've invested in.

A listing agent's primary responsibility is to you and you only. His priority is you and finding the best offer for your properties when you decide to cash in. You can certainly sell properties on your own, but if you're not a professional at it, then you need to find a good Realtor.

A listing agent will work with you to determine the potential market value of the property you're going to sell. A listing agent will go to all the Realtor meetings, promote your property to as many eyes as he can get in front of, and attempt to get you top dollar.

Listing agents don't make money until they sell, which is quite a

motivating factor. They make their commission from selling your property. Commissions are negotiable and are between you and the Realtor. There is no set standard for Realtors' commissions.

However, when you find a good listing Realtor, you should be able to negotiate a competitive commission if you dedicate your business to her.

You can use the same Realtor for both listing and buying properties. In fact, this might be the best deal of all, as your Realtor will be dedicated to you on both sides of any transaction and will see you as a major income stream. If she messes up, she's lost your business. If, however, she does well, you should keep her.

Your Realtor and you should be the closest of buddies. Find a good one and keep her.

Important Players

Loan Processor

Your loan processor is the person who will shepherd your loan application through the mortgage approval maze. The loan processor works for the mortgage company where you get your loan, but he also works directly for your loan officer.

Your loan goes through a process, from beginning to end. The beginning is essentially when you fill out your loan application, and the end is when money is transferred from the buyer to the seller. A lot happens in between those two points, and it's your loan processor who guides the ship to safe harbor.

Your loan processor will talk or otherwise communicate in some fashion with every single person or party who is involved in your loan application. Who they all are really depends upon which part of the country you live in or the property you're buying is located, but your processor talks to all of them.

The processor will contact your insurance agent for evidence of insurance coverage. Your processor will contact the title insurance agent

for title insurance. Your processor will also contact the attorney, the appraiser, the inspector, the surveyor—anyone and everyone who is involved with your loan. Your processor is the person responsible for making sure that your loan has all the required documents included for loan approval.

You need to know your processor intimately. It's your loan officer who finds your financing, but it's your processor who makes sure that everything is in order before your loan goes to final approval from the underwriter.

In fact, once you choose a loan program, your loan officer will most likely be out looking for more business. That's part of her job. But after the purchase contract is signed, it's the processor who will be your new best friend.

When there are loan questions that need to be answered or gaps that need to be filled before a loan is funded, your processor will contact you directly. If there's a question about some tax returns or insurance coverage, you'll be speaking with your processor.

Your processor will work with your Realtor and your attorney and your closer to get your loan documents to closing.

Loan processing fees typically run about $300 to $400 per loan file. You'll pay this charge when you go to the closing table as part of your lender fees. We'll discuss ways to avoid lender fees in Chapter 6.

Appraiser

The appraiser is the person who helps determine the market value of the property you're buying. The appraiser will take a copy of your sales contract and make a physical visit to the subject property.

An appraisal is divided into two basic valuation parts: cost approach and market approach.

The cost approach takes the value of the lot, adds estimated hard costs, typically based upon a dollar amount per square foot, and estimates how much the unit would cost if you built it from scratch.

However, lenders do not rely on the cost approach, but rather on the market approach.

Lenders will review an appraisal to make sure the property they're making a loan on conforms to other properties in the area. One way to make a lender lose sleep is to finance a property that is totally out of step with the neighborhood, such as a one-bedroom, 800-square-foot house that is surrounded by four- to five-bedroom 4,000-square-foot houses.

An appraisal will examine at least three sales of properties in the general area where you're buying that have taken place over the previous 12-month period and compare those sales to your prospective purchase.

Market value, in essence, is the highest price you were willing to pay compared to the lowest price the seller was willing to accept. All other things being equal.

Other things being equal means that the property was not sold under duress, as when the seller wanted to sell quickly to avoid a foreclosure or there was a divorce and the couple simply wanted to get rid of the property at any price.

But without a duress sale, the market forces gather together and form a market price. The appraisal attempts to justify that price based on similar sales in the area.

It's likely that you will never meet your appraiser; you'll only receive a copy of the report. You won't necessarily establish a relationship with an appraiser; those relationships are typically established between a lender and the appraiser.

On the other hand, I know of investors who do call on an appraiser in special circumstances when they have a question about a speculative project. I have an acquaintance who is a builder who builds homes on his own on speculation that he will be able to sell the home for a certain price.

When he wants to know whether a house he wants to build will sell for a certain amount, he'll call his appraisal contact and run the scenario by her. There was a nice big lot here in Austin, Texas, that was in a very desirable location.

The builder wanted to buy the lot, raze the house that was sitting on the lot, build a huge new house, and sell it for about $2.5 million. That was at the high end of anything in the area, as the neighborhood contained lots of smaller, older homes that would fetch nowhere near that amount.

He contacted the appraiser and showed her his plans for building, and the appraiser went to work and decided that, yes, according to his plans and specifications, he just might get $2.5 million. The builder took her advice, built the home, and sold it for $2.3 million.

Your appraiser might also do something that you don't expect: value the property at less than what you offered for it.

Lenders base their loan decisions on the lower of the sales price or appraised value. If you make an offer of $200,000 on a property and it's accepted, but the appraisal comes in at $190,000, then you have an immediate problem.

Because the lender will base its loan valuation on the $190,000 appraisal and not the agreed-upon price of $200,000, it's you who will have to make up the difference. If you wanted to put down 10 percent of the sales price for the loan, you'll have to come in with 10 percent of $190,000 plus the difference between $200,000 and $190,000.

The loan is based on $190,000, meaning that you'll have to come in with $19,000 for the down payment and $10,000 for the difference between the sales price and the appraised value. If, of course, you feel strongly enough to go through with the deal.

Most contracts that you offer (and you need to make sure that this wording is in the contract) state that the deal is off if the appraised valued does not meet the sales price. This gives you an out if the appraisal comes in low.

On the other hand, if the appraisal comes in higher than the sales price, you don't automatically get the increased equity. If you bought the home at $200,000 and the appraisal comes in at $210,000, don't get excited. While it's nice on paper, your loan will be based on the $200,000 figure.

On another note, that value will remain in play for at least the first year of ownership. You can't buy a property for $10,000 under the appraisal, then refinance a few weeks later and pull equity out of the property based upon the higher appraisal number. Lenders will require that the lower of the appraised value or sales price be the determining loan value for at least one year.

When either of these events occurs, there's something amiss somewhere. If your appraised value comes in too low, then perhaps you paid too much. If it comes in too high, the seller didn't sell for enough (and you win!). Such variances occur only rarely, but they do occur; you just have to know that from a lending standpoint, the appraisal attempts to support your contract using comparable sales in your area.

Appraisals cost $350 for loans around $500,000 and more for properties that sell for more than that.

Underwriter

Your underwriter is another person that you'll probably never talk to, but she is important in that her job is to make sure that your loan application conforms completely to the loan you're applying for.

This means that everything you put on your application regarding your income, employment, and assets must be verified by the underwriter. The underwriter puts her name on the line, stating that your loan conforms and is approvable. If the loan ever goes bad, it's the underwriter who must explain what happened.

Mortgage loans are made in accordance with a set of previously established lending standards, be it a conventional Fannie Mae or Freddie Mac format or Federal Housing Administration, Veterans Administration (VA), or some other organization's lending rules.

When you apply for one of these loans, everything has to be in conformance with the rules. If the rules say that your total house payment must be no more than 33 percent of your gross monthly income, the

underwriter will literally make those calculations on his own, confirming that indeed your income is in line with the loan rules.

If the loan requires you to have $10,000 in the bank somewhere, the underwriter will ask to see bank statements reflecting $10,000. A common underwriting requirement for real estate investors is that they have been landlords or otherwise self-employed for at least two years in order to qualify for certain loan programs.

In this case, the underwriter will look for a Schedule E from your tax returns or a letter from an accountant who has prepared your tax returns in the past declaring that you have been self-employed for two years or that you have owned investment properties for the past year or whatever the loan requires.

The underwriter can seem picky at times because she asks a lot of questions, but really she is simply making sure that your loan is in compliance with the lending guidelines.

The underwriter is the person who will give the thumbs up or thumbs down when reviewing questionable documentation.

There are loan requirements and there are loan guidelines. Guidelines means that there's some latitude. Requirements means that there's no variance from the lending script.

A good example of a loan requirement is that a self-employed borrower needs to have been in business for two years. I've had clients who have been in business for one year and ten months who simply had to wait. There was no variance in the rules: It was two years, period.

A guideline is something like a debt ratio. A debt ratio is the number arrived at when you divide monthly debt payments by gross monthly income. If your monthly debt payments are $5,000 and your gross monthly income is $15,000, then your ratio is $5,000/$15,000 or 0.33, or 33 percent.

If the ratio guideline is 33 percent and your ratio comes in at 37 percent, your loan may not automatically be declined. This isn't a requirement; it's a rule of thumb. If the underwriter feels that other parts of

your application merit a guideline waiver, she can approve the loan with the higher 37 percent ratio, disregarding the 33 percent number.

Underwriters work directly for lenders; you do not pay them directly.

Inspector

A home inspector is an important piece of the equation in that the inspector goes over your property with a fine-toothed comb looking for structural defects or evidence of infestation with pests such as termites or other wood-eating insects (like my sister-in-law).

An inspector is different from an appraiser, who helps justify the market value. An inspector will look for things that are wrong with the property you're buying. While the paint job is nice and the roof looks okay, the inspector will crawl through the attic inspecting things that you'll probably never see or even know they're there.

An inspector will flip light switches to make sure they work, flush toilets, and even inspect sewage lines that run across your property line to make sure there are no leaks. If you're investing in an older home, an inspector will ascertain that the electrical and other utilities are up to code. An inspector will find things that neither you nor the appraiser can find and is an important party when you're buying property.

Your inspector should be an integral part of your real estate transaction, and if you establish a solid relationship with one, she can be an invaluable resource when you're determining whether or not a property is worth investing in from a structural standpoint.

An inspector should be an independent third party, not a general contractor who specializes in remodelings. An inspector should be someone who is trained to look for problems or potential problems, not someone who identifies those problems and also fixes them. That could lead to some self-serving actions.

Inspectors are trained to find problems and potential problems that the casual eye wouldn't catch. I recall a client who bought an investment

condo in downtown Austin, Texas, and had just made an offer that was below the asking price but was almost immediately accepted.

Fast-accepted offers are not necessarily a sign of a problem with the property, and in this case it was simply a great deal in a hot market. But accepted it was.

She called me for financing and needed to rush, but I suggested that before we did anything further, such as ordering an appraisal, she should have the property inspected. She did so, and the inspector came up with a couple of things that she would never have noticed, but that revealed some issues.

The biggest problem the inspector found was that there was some water leakage from the master bathroom into the master bedroom. Even though there was carpet on the master bedroom floor, he suspected water damage.

How did he know? Certainly the carpet would hide any water leaks and was in fact doing such a good job of hiding them that even the seller wasn't aware of any water problems. But the inspector caught it.

At the bottom of the wall between the bathroom and the bedroom, he saw that there was a slight separation between the baseboards and the wall, about a foot long, while the rest of the baseboards were stuck solidly against the wall. It wasn't a huge separation, probably no more than an eighth of an inch or so.

The inspector looked a little more closely at the electrical outlet positioned right above the separation; he pulled out the socket and saw that the sheetrock was falling apart. He pulled up the carpet directly underneath the outlet and saw some obvious signs of mildew. He pulled up the carpet even further and saw that there was evidence of water leakage from the master shower through the wall and into the master bedroom.

This was a condo on the third floor, so there was no way to know if water damage had affected the unit below the one my client was thinking of buying. She contacted the people who owned the condo right below hers.

There was no water damage on the lower unit's ceiling, but she was

concerned about the structure of the floor in the master bedroom. Water-sogged wood supports can be a problem, and there was no way for her to know how long the water leakage had been occurring. The inspector said that even though the wood was now dry, there was no guarantee that it would not happen again, nor any indication of how long ago the last leakage had happened.

My client withdrew her offer, and rightfully so. But had she not had a competent inspector, she would never have known about the water problem, and perhaps would have faced a future legal issue with the people who lived below.

Inspections, unlike appraisals, are not a lending requirement. Lenders don't require that you get a physical inspection of the property; it's typically up to the buyer. But if there is any money better spent, given the peace of mind that an inspection offers, I don't know about it.

How do you find a good inspector? I'd start with the ones your Realtor recommends. People who solicit Realtors' business know that they'd better do a good job or that Realtor won't refer them any more.

Perhaps more important is the experience your inspector has. Certainly you need to find out how many years your inspector has been inspecting, but there are also two other organizations that you need to be aware of: NACHI and ASHI.

NACHI is the National Association of Certified Home Inspectors, and ASHI is the American Society of Home Inspectors. While there are local and state licensing requirements, these two destinations require the inspector to have a higher level of experience as well as requiring him to attend certification and continuing education classes to keep his skills sharp.

When considering potential inspectors, either of these two certifications should be a requirement.

While physical inspectors for structural issues may not be a lending requirement, some states do require an inspection for pests, namely termites.

There's not a lot to elaborate about a termite inspection other than if

the inspector sees evidence of any termite damage, old or new, then the lender will in fact require a complete inspection to show that there are no termites in the structure.

In fact, even in states where a termite inspection is not required, many people still order one. And it's a good call in areas where termites live. But when a lender sees a termite report that says, "Evidence of infestation: Yes," then the loan process slows down a bit until the termite issue is resolved.

Inspections generally cost approximately $400; this amount is typically not negotiable and is paid at the time of service.

Necessary Players

Attorney

Depending upon where you live or where the property that you want to buy is located, you might be surprised that an attorney is not a critical or important piece of the puzzle.

But an attorney's function varies depending upon the state in which the property is located. In California, attorneys are not involved in any way, unless someone wants to have his contract reviewed for his personal benefit. However, real estate contracts are normally dictated by the state agency governing real estate, so most of the legalese has been gone over so many times that a legal review is usually not needed.

In Illinois, however, attorneys are required; they handle the contract review for the buyers and sellers and hold the real estate closings. In Texas, attorneys have a limited, yet required role, as their legal blessing is needed on every set of home loan documents printed in the state of Texas.

Attorneys are an important piece of the transaction, and they're necessary where they're required. You probably won't have a bevy of real estate attorneys in your Rolodex, so you'll probably get your lawyer contacts from your Realtor.

I can hear a litany of lawyers reading this section screaming at me and telling me how important they are, and yes, when they're important, they're important, even if they're not required. And yes, there are also clients' interests involved, especially when issues such as limited partnerships, trusts, corporations, or other nonindividual entities investing in real estate come up. But overall, lawyers are needed when they're required and that's all.

Attorney's fees vary by region and customary charges and often can't be negotiated; a common range is $200 to $500.

Title Insurance Agent

Title insurance is a requirement on every loan that involves a lender. Title insurance is an insurance policy that protects the owners and lenders from previous claims to the property. Title insurance can be provided by a title agent or sometimes by an attorney, again depending upon where the property you're buying is located.

But they all provide one thing: title insurance.

Specifically, what is title and why should you care about it?

Title is evidence of ownership or an interest in property. If someone is "on title," then that person has a legal interest in the property, meaning that she probably owns some part of it or otherwise must be compensated when the property changes hands.

Lenders make loans on property only when they're presented with a title that's "clear." A clear title means that when the property changes hands from the seller to the new buyer, there are no other parties who could make a claim to the property.

For instance, suppose you buy a duplex in New Orleans, close on the deal, and begin to live happily ever after, collecting rent that more than pays for your mortgage. One day you open your mailbox, and there's a letter from a lawyer telling you that she represents a long-lost heir to the duplex you just bought and that you owe that heir money.

Not only that, but you may not even legally own the property.

Title insurance pays for such occurrences. A title insurance agent will research all previous owners and claimants, also making sure that there are no other liens on the property from home remodelers who never got paid or from back property taxes that remain delinquent.

If there is a previous claim on the property, you might be in trouble. But title insurance insures against such claims. That's why lenders not only like title insurance but also require that their interest (the collateral) be protected from any unknown "Uncle Harry" who feels that 15 years ago, he was cheated out of the duplex you purchased.

Assuming that Uncle Harry was right and he did have a claim, title insurance would pay off Uncle Harry, and you'd still own the duplex.

Let's assume for a second that you bought a property outright with cash and no financing. You'd still want to buy a title insurance policy, not only to protect yourself during the time you own the property, but also to protect yourself when you sell the property to someone else down the road.

Title insurance agents get paid by their company and not by you, but title insurance, like any other insurance policy, can be paid by either the buyer or the seller.

Closer

Your closer is the person who is responsible for overseeing the legal transfer of property from the seller to the buyer, and who physically makes sure that all required legal and loan documents have been signed as they're supposed to be signed.

The closer can be an attorney, a title agent, an escrow officer, or anyone else who is legally authorized to monitor closing transactions.

Lenders not only send your closing papers to your closing, but also send a list of "lender's instructions" that tell the closer exactly what needs to be signed, and where and when, before money changes hands.

Lender's instructions could include such things as "sign this piece of paper," "make copies of a driver's license and a passport," or "send us a

legible copy of the original sales contract." They really can include anything the lender requires, but it's the closer who makes sure that everything is done exactly as the lender requests.

When your closer does what he's supposed to do, he's given a code
number, commonly called a "funding number," that unlocks the money
the lender has deposited in the closer's vault.

It's important that your closer does everything that the lender
requires. Otherwise you could have a loan that's not yet settled but is
accruing interest, or you could possibly lose the investment altogether
because the closing did not take place exactly how and when it was supposed to.

Closers charge what's customary in the region, but typically a closing
costs a couple of hundred bucks. The fee is not usually negotiable, and
the closer is often selected by the seller or the seller's listing agent.

Surveyor

A survey is a physical description or a map showing the exact location of
your structure on the property. A survey will show the boundaries of
your property, setbacks, and all permanent improvements. Permanent
improvements are things such as fences, sidewalks, your house, a storage
shed, or a pool.

A survey done as a map looks like any other map, but it is a legal
representation of your property. A survey may also be in written format,
where the legal property description is done by a method called *metes and
bounds* and reads more like a geography lesson.

A description of your property would be something like, "4 miles
east of XXX, 253.4 feet from SYZ . . ." Some states, such as California,
don't use survey maps but instead use the metes and bounds description
included in the title report.

A survey will also show any easements that run through your property. An easement is the legal right of a third party to access your property; they are typically limited to utility companies, telephone companies,

and the cable guy. When the water meter reader needs to read your water meter and it's in your backyard, the water company has a legal right to walk into your backyard without permission to read your meter. An easement allows for that.

There could be a utility pole planted squarely on your property that belongs to the electric company. During an electrical outage, the electric company can walk across your property to fix it.

Don't worry about easements. They're necessary, and usually they're not an issue. However, you do need to look at a survey to see exactly where the easement is issued. An easement will have a definite location on your property (where the utility line runs or the cable is connected).

Often a problem arises when you want to build on your property, especially when it comes to fencing or other boundaries. Let's say you don't build a fence, but you would like to put up a row of evergreen trees as close to your property line as possible to help deflect wind in the winter and to keep your nosy neighbors from watching you do whatever you do.

You must make certain that those trees aren't on your neighbor's property.

Once you've assembled a team of experts working for you, the next step is to consider the financing options available.

CHAPTER 4

Loan Types for Investment Property

Just as there is a myriad of loan programs for a primary residence, so too there is an endless supply of loan choices available to the real estate investor. Investment property real estate loan types can include the following:

Six-month CD ARM

One-year Treasury ARM

3/1 hybrid

5/1 hybrid

7/1 hybrid

Interest only

30-year fixed

15-year fixed

CHAPTER 4

Loan Types for Investment Property

Just as there is a myriad of loan programs for a primary residence, so too there is an endless supply of loan choices available to the real estate investor. Investment property real estate loan types can include the following:

Six-month CD ARM

One-year Treasury ARM

3/1 hybrid

5/1 hybrid

7/1 hybrid

Interest only

30-year fixed

15-year fixed

And that's just for starters. Each individual loan program can also have several interest rates from which to choose, depending upon how low you want your rate to be and how many discount points you want to pay—or not pay.

Investment property loans also have additional down payment requirements as well as certain stipulations concerning the number of properties owned, levels of documentation required, and experience as a landlord.

Each and every loan officer, especially a mortgage broker, will receive loan program rate sheets each and every day, either from his company's loan pricing department or from wholesale lenders who work strictly with mortgage brokers.

We'll discuss loan pricing and interest-rate adjustments in greater detail later in the chapter, but all in all, mortgage lenders really aren't very different from one another. In fact, if it weren't for their marketing departments, they would be nearly identical, as each lender will usually have the same loan programs as its competitors do.

But lenders have to appear different to their loan officers and their customers by presenting as many loan possibilities as they can come up with. I recall that when I was working with a major bank, our mortgage department would issue rate sheets that were seven pages long with no less than eight different loan programs on each sheet. That's at least 56 different loan programs. Now add the rate variables with each loan, usually about eight different rate and point combinations, and the result was nearly five hundred loan program and rate possibilities.

That's ridiculous, in my opinion, but it's common nonetheless. In an attempt to appear different, a lender will offer variations on a single loan product to make it appear that it has something that another lender does not have.

Rarely, if ever, will this in fact be the case. Lenders base their loan programs on the very same indexes. Thus, 30-year fixed-rate loans from Lender A and Lender B are based on the same number. A one-year Trea-

sury ARM will be based on the one-year Treasury. There aren't several versions of that; there's only one one-year Treasury.

Lenders can also take a particular loan program and give it a special name, again trying to appear different. For example, instead of being called a 40-year fixed, a loan that is amortized over 40 years could be called a "payment stretcher," or a loan that is amortized over 15 years could be called an "interest saver" or some such moniker instead of a 15-year fixed. Just understand that lenders simply don't have any corner on the loan program market.

Therefore there really are only two types of loans, not five hundred. Those types are fixed-rate and adjustable-rate.

Fixed-Rate Mortgages

Fixed-rate loans have one interest rate over the entire life of the loan and can be paid off, or amortized, over almost any predetermined period. Most fixed-rate mortgages are for 30 years, but these mortgages can also be packaged in 5-year increments from 10 to 50 years. A mortgage company may be quoting you only 30-year and 15-year increments, but it can certainly offer you anything in between as long as it's in a 5-year increment. But you may have to ask for them.

Fixed-rate loans are designed for long-term holding or to capture the bottom of interest-rate swings. Fixed-rate loans are good investment tools because you will never have to wonder what your payment will be 5, 10, or 20 years down the road.

A fixed rate also helps stave off any future inflation effects on your payment. If your monthly payment today is $1,000 in today's dollars, it will always be $1,000, regardless of how the dollar is devalued in the future as a result of inflationary pressures. You're locking in low rates and keeping your payment exactly the same.

The longer the term of a fixed-rate mortgage, the lower the payment, but also the more interest you pay in total. Shorter terms have lower rates but also increase your monthly payment, affecting your cash flow.

A common rate variance between 10- and 40-year loans looks like this:

Loan amount: $200,000

Term	Rate	Payment
10 years	5.75%	$2,195
15 years	5.75%	$1,660
20 years	5.75%	$1,404
25 years	6.00%	$1,288
30 years	6.00%	$1,199
40 years	6.125%	$1,117

Notice that as the loan terms increase, the rate increases slightly, but because of the period the loan is repaid over, the monthly payment is lower.

To see how important the loan term is on a fixed-rate loan, let's now look at monthly cash flow based upon a $1,500 rental income. We'll leave out taxes and insurance in this equation just to show the effect of rate and term.

Term	Rate	Payment	Rent	Profit (Loss)
10 years	5.75%	$2,195	$1,500	($695)
15 years	5.75%	$1,660	$1,500	($160)
20 years	5.75%	$1,404	$1,500	$ 96
25 years	6.00%	$1,288	$1,500	$212
30 years	6.00%	$1,199	$1,500	$301
40 years	6.125%	$1,117	$1,500	$383

Let's now look at the interest paid over the life of each loan term.

Term	Rate	Payment	Total Interest Paid
10 years	5.75%	$2,195	$63,400
15 years	5.75%	$1,660	$98,800
20 years	5.75%	$1,404	$136,960
25 years	6.00%	$1,288	$186,400
30 years	6.00%	$1,199	$231,640
40 years	6.125%	$1,117	$336,160

There is a definitive trade-off between term and payment. You want cash flow on your properties, so you need to have your rent exceed your own mortgage payment. But you also don't want to extend the loan term so far to increase cash flow that you'll hardly make a dent in your principal balance, at least until the latter years of the fixed-rate loan.

This is because at the beginning of each fixed-rate loan, most of the payment goes toward interest, with the remainder going to the principal of the loan.

In all likelihood, you won't keep a property 20, 30, or 40 years. You might, but it's not likely. Longer amortization periods keep your original loan balance intact, and when you sell the property, you won't have the advantage of a fully amortizing loan that has gradually paid itself down. A 40-year or even a 50-year note is available, but I don't suggest using one of these unless you really, really have to keep that payment down. And if that's the case, there are other options that can accomplish the same thing while avoiding long-term interest.

Using that same example, let's look at what the loan balance would be halfway through those loan terms:

Term	Rate	Payment	Midpoint Balance
10 years	5.75%	$2,195	$114,243
15 years	5.75%	$1,660	$121,453
20 years	5.75%	$1,404	$127,919
25 years	6.00%	$1,288	$135,700
30 years	6.00%	$1,199	$139,083
40 years	6.125%	$1,117	$154,479

The difference is staggering. With a 40-year loan, after 20 years you still owe $154,479; you have paid down the original balance by only $45,527. At the opposite end of the spectrum, after 5 years, a 10-year loan has been paid down by nearly half; you've paid off $85,757.

There is a balance; the combination of best rate and best term could

be a 20- or 25-year fixed-rate loan, provided, of course, that you can still achieve positive cash flow on your unit.

Another consideration is whether or not to pay down the interest rate to make it go even lower.

Rates can be "bought down" by paying points, or discount points. A point is 1 percent of the loan amount and typically buys down an interest rate by $1/4$ percent. Again, using the same example:

Loan amount: $200,000; 1 point = $2,000

Term	Rate	Payment	Rate	Payment	Savings
10 years	5.75%	$2,195	5.50%	$2,170	$25
15 years	5.75%	$1,660	5.50%	$1,634	$26
20 years	5.75%	$1,404	5.50%	$1,375	$28
25 years	6.00%	$1,288	5.75%	$1,258	$30
30 years	6.00%	$1,199	5.75%	$1,167	$32
40 years	6.125%	$1,117	5.875%	$1,083	$34

You can see the interest savings for each loan term, but you had to pay $2,000 in points. How do you determine whether or not to pay points?

You take the monthly savings with the lower payment and divide it into the cost of the point. The result is the number of months it will take to recover that point in terms of cash outlay.

Loan amount: $200,000; 1 point = $2,000

Term	Rate	Payment	Rate	Payment	Savings	Return (months)
10 years	5.75%	$2,195	5.50%	$2,170	$25	83
15 years	5.75%	$1,660	5.50%	$1,634	$26	76
20 years	5.75%	$1,404	5.50%	$1,375	$28	71
25 years	6.00%	$1,288	5.75%	$1,258	$30	66
30 years	6.00%	$1,199	5.75%	$1,167	$32	62
40 years	6.125%	$1,117	5.875%	$1,083	$34	58

Points are typically tax-deductible because they are a form of prepaid interest; you pay the lender interest up front in the form of a point and write it off just as you would mortgage interest.

I've never been a big fan of points; the return is just never that great, and I could do lots of things with that $2,000, like make improvements, invest it, or simply use it to pay down the loan balance.

What if you can't make any of the payments work? What if the market rent for the area is only $1,000 per month and the lowest you can get your monthly payment is $1,112? Then you need to reconsider the investment.

Are you buying in a depressed area where there are lots of rentals and few renters? Does the area have any long-term prospects of recovering, leading to increasing rents along the way? Do you anticipate significant near-term appreciation?

If any of these answers is "yes" or "probably," then you could take a small loss, but only if you can afford it and have certain reasons why you'd want a loss on a rental property. Your CPA needs to be consulted in such cases.

Adjustable-Rate Mortgages

Adjustable-rate mortgages, or ARMs, are so called because they can and do adjust, or change, at some point over the life of the loan. Fortunately, you know in advance both how and when the adjustment will be made.

An ARM has three components: an index, a margin, and caps.

The index is the starting point for figuring an ARM rate. An index can be any agreed-upon number, but common ARM indexes are:

One-year Treasury bill (Treasury Constant Maturity, or TCM)

Three-month Treasury bill

Six-month Treasury bill

Six-month LIBOR

One-year LIBOR

11th District Cost of Funds Index (COFI)

The next component of an ARM is the margin, or the amount in terms of percent added to the index. The final number, when the index and the margin are added, is called the *fully indexed rate*, which is what your monthly payment will be based upon.

For instance, you have an ARM based on a one-year Treasury bill and you get a notice in the mail from your lender telling you that your note can adjust in two months based upon the then-current one-year Treasury bill rate plus your margin. Common margins are 2.25 to 2.75 percent.

Two months later, the lender looks up the yield on the one-year Treasury bill, and it's 5.75 percent. Add your margin of 2.50 percent and your new rate will be 5.75 percent plus 2.50 percent, or 8.25 percent.

The final component of an ARM is the cap. An ARM will actually have two types of caps, an adjustment cap and a lifetime cap.

An adjustment cap is a consumer protection feature that limits how high your rate can go at any one adjustment. Common caps are 1 percent for every six months or 2 percent annually.

In the example listed earlier, if your initial rate was at 5.00 percent but the new fully indexed rate was 8.25 percent, that would be a significant payment change—so much so that it could create a payment shock sufficient to either suddenly make the investment unaffordable or reverse your cash flow to the negative.

On a $200,000 loan amortized over 30 years, a rate of 5.00 percent would yield a payment of $1,073, while the new rate of 8.25 percent would give you a payment of $1,502. That's $429, or an increase of nearly a third. That's hardly something you could adjust your rental income to compensate for, even if the markets were willing.

But because of the adjustment cap of 2 percent, while your true rate would be 8.25 percent, it wouldn't go more than 2.00 percent above the

previous rate of 5.00 percent. It's capped. Now the new payment would be based upon 7.00 percent, or $1,330. That's an increase, but not as great a one.

Now, all things being equal, another year passes and it's time to adjust once again. If the index is still at 5.75 percent, you would add your margin of 2.50 percent and the fully indexed rate would again be 8.25 percent.

This time, however, your 2.00 percent cap won't protect you; your rate will go from 7.00 percent to 8.25 percent for the remaining year. One note: Just because an ARM can adjust doesn't mean that it will always adjust. It most likely will, but it doesn't have to. If year to year the index is 5.75 percent, then the fully indexed rate will always be at 8.25 percent.

The final cap component is the lifetime cap. The lifetime cap is the maximum the rate can ever go to throughout the life of the loan. A common lifetime cap is 6.00 percent. If you started at 5.00 percent, then your rate would never be above 5.00 percent plus 6.00 percent, or 11.00 percent. That's regardless of what your index does—even if your index hits 20.00 percent.

Your ARM will typically adjust with your index period. An ARM using the one-year Treasury bill will adjust once per year, while an ARM with a six-month index will adjust every six months.

Every ARM works the same way: Your index is identified, and the margin is added to find your new rate, taking caps into account.

When do you take an ARM and when do you take a fixed-rate product? In these two examples of fixed-rate mortgages and ARMs, the ARM rate was actually higher when it was fully indexed. This doesn't happen very often, but it can happen.

ARMs typically start out with a lower "teaser" rate. This teaser rate is an enticement to get you to take the ARM. A teaser rate could be 3.00 percent, for example; that's what your payment would be based upon for one full year on a one-year ARM.

For the same $200,000, the payment using 3.00 percent is $843.

That's significant, and that's why people select an ARM: to get the lower rate. Talk about significant cash flow.

In this instance, you would want to use an ARM if you were planning to hold the property short term, say for a year or two, or less. If you're going to buy a property to fix and flip, it's an ARM you want to look at first.

But let's say that you're looking at an investment property and you intend to keep it for several years—which is better for you, a fixed-rate loan or an ARM?

Essentially, take an ARM when rates are at relative highs and take fixed rates when rates are at relative lows. We'll discuss how rates are set in more detail in Chapter 5, but historically this is how you should look at loan types.

When rates are at relative highs, it's not the time to look at locking in long-term rates, since history shows that rates could soon move downward. And adjustable-rate mortgages can also move down just as they can move up.

By selecting an ARM when rates are in a high cycle, you'll both be locking in a lower "teaser" rate at the outset of the loan and potentially watching your index soften to a new low each year, with your monthly payment following it.

Then, as rates begin to bottom out, you can always refinance your mortgage into a fixed rate and lock in low rates for the future.

When rates are at relative lows, then forget about ARMs entirely and lock in the low rates.

There's no absolute forecasting of anything, other than death or taxes, I guess. This is especially true of interest rates and property values. However, using the past as a guide can help you predict the future.

One of the best resources I've found that tracks historical interest rates is an online site called www.hsh.com. This is the place to go to find rate patterns for almost every imaginable index, and I refer people to it frequently. This site has been documenting and reporting rate histories

online longer than anyone else that I know of. You should bookmark the page.

Sometimes the fully indexed rate is higher than available fixed rates. This isn't a common scenario, but it happens; it is called *inversion*, where the yields on shorter-term holdings are higher than those on longer-term ones. This isn't normal in the marketplace. Typically a yield on a shorter-term investment will be lower than that on a longer-term one because the long-term investor wants to be paid more for tying his money up for so long. That's why six-month CDs pay more than three-month CDs.

When fully indexed ARMs are higher than the fixed-rate product, it's important to take a fixed rate, because, all things being equal, the ARM will eventually be higher than the fixed rate, and soon. That is, unless you're flipping quickly and you're certain that you'll have sold the property before an adjustment is made to your rate.

Interest-Only Loans

A feature available with both adjustable- and fixed-rate mortgage financing is called "interest only," or IO, loans. IO loans give the borrower the option of paying simple interest on the loan at any time, without paying anything toward the principal.

This can be a double-edged sword. While a 40-year fully amortized loan takes a long time to pay down the loan balance, an IO mortgage takes even longer—in fact, it would never pay the principal down.

The payment on an IO loan is calculated simply by multiplying the loan amount by the rate, then dividing the result by 12 to get a monthly payment.

The payment on a 30-year $200,000 loan that is fully amortized at 6.00 percent is $1,199. An IO payment at 6.00 percent on $200,000 is 6.00 percent × $200,000 ÷ 12, or $1,000 per month. An advantage with an IO loan is that if your property is currently vacant or otherwise not producing any income, then you can elect to make an interest-only payment to help offset the monthly loss.

Then, when you get another tenant or you begin receiving income again, you can revert back to the fully amortized payment of $1,199. An IO loan gives you some flexibility.

IO loans are not limited to fixed-rate loans; they can also be used for ARMs as well. If a fully indexed ARM rate is at 5.50 percent, then the fully amortized payment would be $1,135 on a $200,000 loan but only $916 with an IO.

One word of warning when considering an IO: Make sure you have some equity in the property going in or otherwise obtain additional equity through a sale, because an IO loan won't pay anything at all toward your loan balance unless you make extra payments yourself.

This is especially true with the temptation of zero-down loans. Buying investment property with zero down should be considered only by those holding for the long term. Why? Because of closing costs and associated costs to sell a property. We'll discuss costs in more detail in Chapter 6, but closing costs must be considered when selling and buying investment property.

For example, suppose you found a house that you wanted to buy at a bargain, hold for a few months while you do some touch-up work, then resell.

Purchase price	$ 200,000
Repairs/touch-up	$ 5,000
Acquisition costs	$ 5,000
Cost basis	**$ 210,000**

Acquisition costs are the closing costs involved when you bought the property. Standard closing fees on real estate investments will include appraisal charges, credit reports, lender fees, inspections, attorney fees, title insurance, and more.

You're now into this unit for $210,000. You'll need to sell it for that plus a bit more just to break even, right? Actually, no. Because when you sell, you'll also incur a new round of closing costs.

Unless you're a Realtor, you'll want to have a professional list and sell your property for you. Maybe you agree to pay your Realtor $8,000 as a listing commission.

You will also have attorney charges, some title and escrow fees, and a host of other closing costs associated with selling a home. Let's add another $3,000 of closing costs to the Realtor's fees and you're now at $11,000 to sell.

You now need to add the $11,000 to the $210,000 in order to break even. This doesn't count the miscellaneous hours you "donated" to the project that you didn't count as a hard cost.

Now you're at $221,000 to break even. But you're not investing in real estate to break even, are you? Goodness knows, you don't need the practice, right? A zero-down loan means that you don't have any equity to work with, and if you can't sell at the price you need to sell at, then it's possible that you'll be forced to either wait until you can get the price you need or bring money to the closing table.

Zero down means you must be certain of your future value; otherwise, you'll be paying closing fees out of your own pocket. A down payment would give you wiggle room. Zero down can mean writing a check when you sell a property. And an IO loan means that you've paid absolutely nothing toward the loan balance to help reduce your liability (that is, unless you paid extra on the loan while making an IO payment).

You can always make additional payments on almost any type of real estate financing. Rarely will you find a prepayment penalty, and when you do, it's either because you're buying a property with damaged credit and need a subprime loan (see Chapter 7) or because you elected to take a prepayment penalty to get a lower initial rate.

Prepayment penalties for those with excellent credit make an occasional entrance into the mortgage market, then escape for a few years, then come back. Why would someone ever take a prepayment penalty on a loan? To lower her payments.

Prepayment penalties come in two types: soft and hard.

A hard prepayment penalty means that if you pay so much as $1

additional toward the principal, then you may be subject to as much as six months' worth of mortgage interest as a penalty for paying ahead on your note. Hard penalties are mostly associated with subprime loans.

Soft penalties can sometimes be found as an option on mortgages for those with good credit. A soft penalty will let you pay additional principal on the mortgage, but no more than 20 percent of the principal balance during any successive 12-month period. Soft penalties usually expire after two or three years.

The rate with a penalty is sometimes as much as $1/4$ percent lower than the current market rate. If you're looking at a term longer than two or three years on an investment property and a prepayment penalty is offered, then it's something you might consider.

A soft penalty still lets you pay extra (quite a bit extra, I might add), but it asks that you don't retire the whole mortgage with one big lump sum during the first 24 to 36 months. Most soft penalties also give you a reprieve if you sell the property, which would retire the note, instead of keeping the property and writing a check to the mortgage company to pay off the outstanding note.

Prepayment penalties aside, you can always pay extra toward a principal balance. But depending upon whether you have a fixed-rate loan or an ARM, the loan reacts differently when you pay extra.

With an ARM, you reduce the monthly payment, but with a fixed-rate loan, you reduce the term.

Using a 30-year fixed rate of 6.00 percent on a $200,000 loan, your loan would fully amortize in year 30. But if you paid extra each month on your mortgage, then your loan term would be shortened while your payment remained the same.

On the flip side, with an ARM, when you make an extra payment, your term remains the same, yet your monthly payment drops.

With a fixed-rate loan, there are certain patterns of prepaying, with the most common one being a biweekly program. With a biweekly program, you pay part of your mortgage every other week instead of once per month.

That means that you make 13 payments per year, or one extra payment per year.

On a 30-year loan, that typically knocks about 9 years off of your loan term, but what it really does is "piggy bank" your equity payments in your investment.

There are companies that specialize in setting up a biweekly system for you, for a fee; they usually auto-debit your account every other week and apply your extra payments and regular payment when they're due—on the first of each month.

But there's no reason to pay a fee when you can do this yourself. In fact, the easiest way to accomplish the very same thing is to take one month's payment, divide it by 12, and add that amount to each month's regular mortgage payment.

When you do that, you're making 13 payments per year and knocking 9 years off the term. And it's easier to do and less painful. After all, who wants to write a check every other week for a mortgage payment? Not me.

ARM loans accommodate extra payments by reducing the payment while keeping the loan the same. This is also called *recasting*.

When you make an extra payment on an ARM, when the adjustment period comes up, the new loan payment takes the new lower loan balance (that you paid down), then amortizes it over the remaining loan term.

If you originally had a $200,000 30-year ARM at 5.00 percent and you paid $10,000 extra in year one of your 30-year note, when your payment adjusted, it would recast at a reduced principal balance over 29 years, again at 5.00 percent should the index remain the same.

In this example, after the first year, the principal balance would naturally be $197,049 with a monthly payment of $1,069. But by paying $10,000 extra at or before the recast time one year later, the payment would drop to $1,014. However, you'd still have 29 years left.

Paying extra on a fixed-rate loan reduces the term. Paying extra on an ARM reduces the payment. This is important when considering loan

types as well, just as it is important when reviewing loan rates compared to their history.

If you're aggressive in paying down your mortgage balances and rates are at relative highs, you'll get a boost with an ARM in the form of increased cash flow each month through both declining rates and recasts.

With fixed-rate loans and an aggressive paydown, you want rates to be at relative lows, and you need to understand that you're shortening the loan term by paying down the loan more quickly.

Hybrids

Another consideration is what you'll do when your well-laid-out plans just don't pan out. What if you bought a property that you intended to sell soon, but suddenly the market turned real south and you're stuck?

I mentioned that there are only two loan types, not 500. Okay, maybe there are two-and-a-half. The other one's a hybrid. A mortgage hybrid is a cross between a fixed-rate mortgage and an ARM. Okay, technically it's an ARM, but a hybrid performs like both a fixed- and an adjustable-rate mortgage.

A hybrid is fixed at the outset for a preset period of time. The most common hybrids are designated as 3/1 and 5/1 hybrids. A 3/1 hybrid is fixed for three years, then turns into an ARM, while a 5/1 is fixed for five years, then turns into an ARM.

Hybrids are a good choice because they start out with a lower rate than fixed-rate loans and keep that fixed rate longer than an annual or six-month ARM. It's sort of a best-of-both-worlds thing.

They're a neat gig, I think, and they have their place. Hybrids are really ARMs, and they have some features that can be dangerous, but if you're trying to decide between a fixed-rate mortgage and an ARM, and you're not certain, then a hybrid might be your best choice.

Since hybrids are in fact ARMs, they also have an index, a margin, and caps, and they use the exact same indexes, margins, and caps that regular ARMs do.

Hybrids normally offer initial rates about $^{1}/_{2}$ percent lower than fixed-rate mortgages and about $^{1}/_{2}$ percent higher than the teaser rate on ARMs. They're a nice fit for short-termers. If you're flipping, maybe a hybrid isn't for you, but it just might be if the future of real estate isn't set in stone—and really, when has it ever been?

What are the dangerous features of a hybrid? There's an additional cap called an initial cap.

An initial cap is the first adjustment that can be made after the initial fixed period. Many hybrids have a 5 percent initial cap rather than the 2 percent cap associated with a typical ARM.

That means that if you started at 4.00 percent on your 5/1 hybrid, but rates moved up considerably during that period, then you could be hit with a 9.00 percent rate after 60 months.

That aside, the hybrid does give the sense of security that comes from simply knowing what your rate will be over a specific period of time.

You won't be surprised at what your rate adjusts to because you'll be following the interest rates, watching to see if rates are moving up and you're in for a rate adjustment that you'd rather not have.

If this is the case—you see rates moving up and your adjustment is coming up—you can always avoid that adjustment by refinancing.

Refinancing

A refinance is nothing more than replacing a current loan with another one, and you can refinance for a variety of reasons.

Let's say your hybrid has been very nice to you over the past four years, but you also notice that your index has crept up to 6.00 percent and your margin is 2.75 percent. With your 5.00 percent initial cap, your rate will most likely go to 8.75 percent from your neat little 4.00 percent rate. Your payment will nearly double.

But because you were on your toes, you recognized this beforehand and applied with a mortgage company for a new loan. When rates are

trending upward, almost all indexes will follow. This means that if ARMs are going up, then fixed rates usually are as well, unless there is rate inversion, which is unusual.

You have a choice to make: Do you want to refinance into another hybrid ARM? If so, your rate would be in between those on a fixed-rate mortgage and a one-year ARM—higher than the rate on the ARM, but lower than that on the fixed-rate mortgage.

When deciding which type of loan you want to refinance into, you should use the same logic as when you got the original loan. If you're holding long term, take a fixed-rate loan; for a shorter term, look at an ARM or a hybrid.

When you refinance out of an ARM or a hybrid that's about to adjust, you're avoiding that huge interest-rate adjustment that's coming up. Refinancing is simple; in fact, it's easier than the financing you got when you originally bought the property, primarily because there's no sales contract you have to perform to, such as closing by a certain date or making certain repairs.

Another reason to refinance is that rates have gone down, not up. In fact, this is the most common reason why people refinance: because rates have dropped below what they're currently paying and they want a better rate.

Refinancing because rates have dropped should be done only if you're planning to hold onto the property at least long enough to recover the closing costs that will be involved with any mortgage loan.

How low do rates have to go to make it profitable to refinance a mortgage? A common myth is that rates need to be 2 percent lower than the rate you currently have, but that 2 percent "rule" simply makes no sense.

Instead of targeting a specific rate, target your closing fees compared to the new payment.

It's important to remember that mortgage acquisition costs should be kept as low as possible, which means avoiding things like discount points or origination charges. Recall that paying $2,000 on a $200,000

loan lowers your interest rate by only $^1/_4$ percent or so and that your payback period is around five years.

What if you paid a point on a hybrid or a fixed-rate loan and then refinanced three years after the original note? That means you've lost the benefit of the lower payment you bought at the beginning of the original mortgage. No one can accurately predict the future, but you can certainly have some contingency plans.

One of those contingency plans is to keep mortgage costs low so that you can more easily benefit from refinancing.

For example, suppose your current 30-year fixed rate is at 6.875 percent on a $200,000 note. Rates have dropped to 6.00 percent, and you're considering refinancing. First, compare your current monthly payment with the proposed new one. Here, 6.875 percent on $200,000 is $1,313 per month, while 6.00 percent on $200,000 is $1,199. You'll first notice that a change from 6.875 percent to 6.00 percent is nowhere near 2 percent, right? But you can also see that there is a difference of $113 in the monthly payment. That's like raising your rent, but you didn't have to.

Next, take a look at your closing fees. Say your closing costs for title insurance, appraisal, attorney, and everything else come to $3,000. Now divide that $113 into the $3,000 and you get 26. That's 26 months to recover your investment of $3,000 in closing costs.

You get an immediate benefit from the lower monthly payment, yet you have to consider that it cost you money to do so; in fact, it cost you $3,000. As long as you're keeping the property for 26 months, refinancing is probably a good idea. If rates drop only $^1/_4$ percent, from 6.875 percent to 6.625 percent, the payment only goes to $1,280, or a savings of just $32. That's 93 months, which is far too long.

Another advantage with refinancing is that refinancing loans allow you to roll closing costs into your loan amount, something that you couldn't do when you bought the property. From a cash flow perspective, rolling closing costs into your loan keeps money in your pocket while reducing the monthly payment on the loan. It does add to your loan, so

your payment will go up, but not by much. A $203,000 mortgage at 6.00 percent has a payment of $1,217, or an additional $18. Not a bad leverage, don't you think?

One main consideration when refinancing investment properties compared to refinancing a property you live in is that with a refinancing, you need some equity. Even if you acquired the investment with a zero-down mortgage, a refinancing typically requires at least 5 percent in equity, with most asking for 10 percent.

This is another good reason to be careful before buying with zero down.

That means that the maximum loan amount on the $200,000 duplex you bought must be 90 percent of $200,000, or $180,000. After a few years, it's likely that your property will have appreciated to the point where you have a 10 percent equity position.

Some investors buy what they think is a steal, hoping that it will be appraised for far more than what they paid for it. That can work, but it can work only after the first year. Lenders make mortgage loans based upon the lower of the sales price or appraised value.

If you bought some property and it was appraised at $200,000 but you paid $100,000, you don't automatically have $100,000 in equity—at least, not in terms of getting financing. The lender will base your loan on the $100,000 price, not the $200,000 appraised value. If you decide to refinance after 12 months, then if the appraisal still comes in at $200,000, you're fine.

This process is called *seasoning*, meaning that your value has been set in stone for 12 months. Seasoning applies to all properties, not just investment ones, but I emphasize it here because many investors buy with zero down hoping that the property will appreciate quickly.

Refinancing also provides an opportunity to pull equity out of the investment in the form of cash, called a *cash-out refinance*. While limits on cash-out refinances for investment properties typically stop at 75 percent of the value for conventional loans, if you have some equity that you'd like to pull out for whatever reason—for home improvements or

to pay bills—you can borrow more than your current loan balance plus closing costs and get a check at closing.

For example, suppose that your property is appraised at $200,000, you owe $100,000, and you want to pull out $25,000 in cash.

Appraised value	$ 200,000
Current loan	$ 100,000
Closing costs	$ 3,000
Cash out	$ 25,000
Final loan amount	**$ 128,000**

If your initial rate was 6.875 percent, your payment on $100,000 would be $656, while the new lower 6.00 percent rate gives you a payment of $599, or a difference of $57. When you divide the $56 into the $3,000 closing costs, the result is 53 months, much longer than the previous example. But you reduced your monthly payment while at the same time accessing equity from the investment property.

This is another example of why you should pay little attention to how much rates have to drop in order to refinance and focus more on the actual numbers. Interest rates are factored into a loan amount, while closing costs are fixed.

If you refinance an $800,000 property and rates go from 6.875 percent to 6.00 percent, the payments change from $5,255 to $4,796, a savings of $458 per month. You'll recover your closing costs rather quickly at that rate.

The larger the loan amount, the sooner it will take to recover fixed closing costs.

Refinancing and pulling cash out should be done simultaneously, meaning that you shouldn't refinance a property just to get at some cash. It's an expensive proposition. Instead, consider pulling cash out of an investment property only if you were going to refinance the property anyway. There are cheaper ways to get at equity that don't have such high closing costs.

Equity Loans

An equity loan can be a line of credit or a single loan that is placed upon a property at little or no cost to you. If your property is appraised at $200,000 and your loan balance is $100,000, you could place an equity line of credit typically up to 80 percent of the value of the home, on the property at rates $1/4$ to $1/2$ percent higher than those on equity lines for a primary residence.

If there are any fees, there will typically be a government recording fee, but often a bank will waive all fees as long as you use the equity line at least once during a 12-month period.

When you refinance a mortgage loan, you'll have to qualify all over again. I know it might seem a bit redundant, but you are in fact getting a brand-new loan, perhaps from a new lender, and you'll be underwritten just as if it were a brand-new purchase.

This means that from a financial and/or credit perspective, things could have changed. If your credit has been hurt since you bought the property, you can anticipate a little more scrutiny. Or if your income has changed for the worse, then again you may find it more difficult to qualify for the new loan, whether or not you have made timely payments on the previous mortgage.

Or perhaps you've added to your investment portfolio and are now carrying additional mortgages or other debt, and so you might be facing some debt ratio concerns.

There are several sources for investment loans, but you need to understand the background of mortgages so that you'll understand how different loan programs view your financial status when reviewing your loan application to buy investment property.

Mortgage lenders make money by making loans. A mortgage company can have a bunch of money in the bank to lend out, or, more likely, it can have a credit line it can draw on as it places a new mortgage.

Say you just bought a rental house and borrowed $150,000. The lender will approve your loan, transfer the funds from its credit line to the seller's account at closing, and give you a mortgage to pay back.

If a lender has a $50 million credit line on which to draw, once that lender has issued around 300 more $150,000 loans, it will start to run out of money to lend. After all, with no more money, there are no more loans.

The lender can decide whether it wants to keep your loan and collect the monthly interest or to sell your loan to someone else, like another mortgage lender or Fannie Mae or Freddie Mac. Selling in this fashion is selling to the secondary market.

Smaller, independent mortgage lenders will almost always sell your loan before you ever make your first mortgage payment. That lender needs to free up its credit line, and quickly, in order to make more loans. Selling loans one by one is called *flow* selling, and it is so called because the lender uses it to keep its cash flow going.

Other banks and mortgage bankers will stockpile loans, then, when the balance has reached a certain point, sell an entire pool of loans to another investor; again another bank, a mortgage banker, or another secondary market player; this is called *bulk* selling.

But to do either type of sale, the loans must adhere to a strict set of guidelines.

Fannie Mae and Freddie Mac were both formed for the same purpose: to provide lenders with liquidity when they need it. Liquidity means more cash on hand that they can lend. Specifically Fannie Mae and Freddie Mac's purpose is to foster homeownership, but they do so by helping lenders make loans by providing them with more cash in exchange for the loans they have already made.

When you hear the term *conventional mortgage*, it means that the mortgage lender is responsible for issuing the mortgage loan and will take the heat if the loan goes bad. However, when a lender makes a conventional mortgage loan, it does so using secondary guidelines, or those set forth by Fannie Mae and Freddie Mac.

These guidelines are vast, but typical lending rules ask that the loan be at or below a certain dollar limit, that the borrower's debt ratios be in

a certain range, and that the borrower verify his own funds to close on a home loan.

These underwriting criteria cover absolutely everything from what may or may not be on a title report to how many homes must be analyzed on an appraisal. In return for making loans that fit these lending rules, lenders can sell these loans to Fannie Mae or Freddie Mac or even to other lenders who might wish to buy loans and collect the interest instead of going out and finding brand-new ones.

The secondary market turns mortgage loan programs into a commodity; one 30-year fixed-rate loan is underwritten to the very same standards as another 30-year fixed-rate loan, and so the two loans are exactly alike.

And when there's a lot of one thing, there's tremendous price pressure to keep rates competitive. Lenders can get cutthroat when it comes to pricing a mortgage loan, and consumers don't have to wonder whether one loan is wildly different from another loan down the street—it's not, because it's underwritten using the very same set of rules.

Conventional loans, being the most common, are your best deal in terms of rate and fee structure. Conventional loans will have the lowest rates of any available loan product for investors.

That having been said, there are other guidelines that you must adhere to in order to qualify for investment properties.

- Number of properties owned

- Previous landlord experience

- Adherence to debt ratio guidelines

Number of Properties Owned

Fannie Mae and Freddie Mac have different guidelines when it comes to the number of properties you can own that have mortgages on them. Fannie Mae limits you to ten financed properties, whereas Freddie Mac limits you to four financed properties.

Note here that this doesn't mean that Fannie Mae won't make any more mortgages to you if you own 10 properties; you can own 20 or more, but the limitation is on the number of properties that currently have financing on them. Having 10 properties with loans on them means that you have to look outside conventional loans.

Fannie Mae is much more liberal than Freddie Mac with regard to the number of properties with mortgages on them that you can own. Conventional loans also ask for a minimum of 10 percent down for investment properties. Remember that neither Fannie Mae nor Freddie Mac actually approves the loan; the lender does. It's just that the lender approves the loan under Fannie Mae or Freddie Mac's guidelines.

Previous Landlord Experience

Another interesting twist in underwriting for conventional loans is that in order to use rental income from the unit(s) being purchased to qualify for the mortgage, the buyer must have two years of landlord experience.

This is important when you are buying multiple properties at once or in a short period of time. Sometimes an investor will buy several properties, but her current income levels can't support the new mortgage payments required on the investment properties.

In these instances, the rental income from the property to be acquired needs to be used to help qualify the purchase.

Adherence to Debt Ratios

For example, suppose an investor makes $8,000 per month. Typical lending guidelines ask that the borrower's debt ratio be around 40 percent, meaning that the total monthly debt divided by the gross monthly income should be close to 0.40, or 40 percent. But the investor sees a new property that has just been listed; it's a $200,000 duplex that brings in $3,000 per month in income.

The investor's current ratio is right at 40 percent; his total monthly

obligations, including his primary residence plus his other properties, are $3,200 per month, and $3,200 divided by $8,000 is 0.40, or 40 percent.

The new mortgage payment on the $200,000 house with a 30-year, 6.50 percent rate plus taxes and insurance comes to:

Principal and interest	$ 1,264
Taxes	$ 165
Insurance	$ 80
Total PITI	**$ 1,509**

Adding $1,509 to the current debt load of $3,200 makes the new total debt load $4,709. With an income of $8,000, the ratio would be $4,709 divided by $8,000 or 0.59. While this is not a death knell, unless the borrower has some significant outstanding factors like credit scores in the high 700 or low 800 range or a lot of money in the bank, this loan might not be approved.

This transaction needs the $3,000 per month income in order to fit the 40 debt ratio guideline. Adding the $3,000 makes the ratio $4,709 divided by $11,000 = 0.42, which is much closer to the target and probably approvable.

If this is the investor's first purchase, however, and he has no landlord experience, he can't use the $3,000 to help him qualify. If this is not his first investment purchase and he has had two years of landlord experience, then the future rental income could in fact be used and the deal could close.

How does a lender know whether or not you've got experience at owning investment properties? It will simply ask for two years' previous tax returns and look on Schedule E of those returns to see if there are any entries for rental income.

Qualifying for conventional financing is sometimes more difficult than qualifying for other loan types in the market, but it should be your first source because of the lower rates.

Calculating Rental Income

Another underwriting quirk in investment property lending rules is how rental income is calculated for purposes of qualifying.

A lender can take the income information right off of tax returns, or the lender can simply take the gross monthly rent, multiply it by 0.75, and use the lower amount. Why would a lender reduce your monthly rent for qualification purposes?

There are two reasons: One, the property may not always be rented out, so there will be a vacancy factor, and two, the property will also need maintenance and repairs, and these will have to be deducted from your gross proceeds.

For instance, suppose your mortgage payment on a rental is $1,100, including taxes and insurance, and your rent is $1,300, so the income from the rental that a lender will use is 75 percent of $1,300, or $975.

Now, instead of showing a positive cash flow, you're actually being hit with negative rent. Subtract the mortgage payment of $1,100 from the adjusted $975 and the result is ($125). Not only will the lender not give you any income for that rental property, but it will add the $125 to your monthly debt load, much as it would do if you had an automobile loan or credit card payment.

Alternative Lending

What happens if:

You own more than 10 properties with mortgages on them?

You don't want to put any money down?

You need to use rental income to qualify, but you don't have the required experience?

You go outside of conventional lending to another, increasingly common loan type called *alternative* lending.

Alternative, or "alt," lending is an increasingly large pool of loans offered by various lenders and mortgage brokers all across the country that make loans that do not fit the current Fannie Mae or Freddie Mac guidelines.

Alt loans are made in a similar fashion to any other loan: You apply at a mortgage banker or broker, document the file, get approved, and move on. Alt loans are also sold to investors on the secondary market to increase liquidity, just like their conventional cousins.

However, alt loans reach outside the conventional box and offer a whole new array of lending guidelines that do not conform to Fannie Mae or Freddie Mac's. The catch, of course, is slightly higher rates. Not a lot, but some.

Alt loans also place more emphasis on adjustable-rate mortgages, and although alt loans do come in fixed-rate varieties, the differences between a fixed-rate alt and a fixed-rate conventional loan can be considerable, so most people who choose alt financing take a hybrid.

For instance, a common alt versus conventional comparison would look like this with 20 percent down:

	Fixed 30	Fixed 15	5/1 hybrid
Conventional	5.875%	5.50%	5.75%
Alt	6.375%	6.00%	6.125%

That's nothing to sneeze at; still, alt lending isn't that far out of the mortgage picture, and odds are that you'll use an alt at some point when your requirements fall outside the lending guidelines for conventional loans.

Alt loans have a base rate and then make adjustments to that rate depending upon various parameters, such as loan size or credit score or the degree of documentation. We'll discuss documentation in more detail in the next chapter.

For example, an alt product for a 5/6 hybrid might start out at 6.00 percent; the lender will then make adjustments according to its pricing matrix.

Table 4-1 shows a standard alt matrix for mortgage loans:

See the adjustments? It's extraordinary. There are 256 potential adjustments to one loan program. For instance, in this chart, if you wanted an investor loan of $650,000, you were prepared to provide all your documentation, including tax returns, your credit score was 668, and it was an interest-only loan, you would add a total of 2.625 points to the base rate.

Since 1 point usually equals $1/4$ percent in rate, 2.625 points would increase your rate by about 5/8 percent, from 6.00 to 6.625 percent. Or you would simply pay the 2.625 points (which if you followed my advice, you wouldn't do).

Alt loans are not necessarily designed for people with bad credit. However, there is another group of loans called "alt A–," which stands for alternative A minus, that indicates a lower credit grade than a standard alt or alt A loan.

Not all alt lenders offer alt A– programs, but most do. Just don't confuse an alt loan with something designed for people who have harmed their credit.

Financing the Multifamily Property

Loans on multifamily properties are different from both conventional and alt loans. A property is considered to be multifamily if it has more than four units. While conventional loans can be used to finance up to a fourplex, when you go beyond that, the property falls into a new category. A multifamily property is most often an apartment building.

A multifamily property is considered a commercial property; hence, it requires commercial financing. Commercial financing is much different from conventional or alt financing and is based as much on the cash flow of the property as it is on the creditworthiness and equity position of the borrower.

Commercial financing also has higher rates, is often shorter term if

Table 4-1. An Alt Matrix for Mortgage Loans

	N Series Alt A Adjustments to Price for FIXED and ARMS							
	<= 60%	60.01 to 70%	70.01 to 75%	75.01 to 80%	80.01 to 85%	85.01 to 90%	90.01 to 95%	95.01 to 100%
Loan Amt: $40,000–$49,999	2.000	2.000	2.000	2.000	2.000	2.000	2.000	2.000
Loan Amt: $50,000–$99,999	0.750	0.750	0.750	0.750	0.750	0.750	0.750	0.750
Loan Amt: $250,000–$417,000	-0.500	-0.500	-0.500	-0.375	-0.375	-0.375	-0.000	-0.000
Loan Amt: $417,001–$650,000	0.000	0.125	0.250	0.250	0.250	0.250	0.500	0.500
Loan Amt: $650,001–$1,000,000	0.250	0.375	0.500	0.750	n/a	n/a	n/a	n/a
Loam Amt: $1,000,001–$1,500,000	0.750	1.000	1.125	n/a	n/a	n/a	n/a	n/a
Loan Amt: $1,500,001–$2,000,000	1.000	1.250	n/a	n/a	n/a	n/a	n/a	n/a
Cash Out (not available in Tx on PR's)	0.000	0.250	0.375	0.625	0.750	1.000	1.250	n/a
2nd Home	0.250	0.500	0.625	0.750	1.000	1.250	1.250	n/a
Investor	0.500	0.750	1.000	1.250	1.500	1.625	n/a	n/a
2 units	0.000	0.000	0.125	0.250	0.375	0.375	0.500	n/a
3–4 units	0.250	0.500	0.625	0.875	0.875	1.000	1.125	n/a
Condo <= 4 floors	0.000	0.250	0.375	0.500	0.500	0.500	0.500	0.750
Condo >4 floors	0.250	0.500	0.750	1.000	1.000	1.000	1.000	1.250
Non Warrantable Condo	1.000	1.000	1.125	1.250	1.375	1.500	n/a	1.000
Full Documentation	-0.250	-0.125	-0.125	-0.125	0.000	0.250	0.625	1.000
Stated Income / Verified Assets (SIVA)	-0.125	0.125	0.250	0.375	0.500	0.750	1.125	n/a
Stated Income / Stated Assets (SISA)	0.000	0.375	0.500	0.625	1.000	1.250	1.625	n/a
No Income / Verified Assets (NIVA)	0.000	0.250	0.500	0.750	0.875	1.125	1.625	n/a
No Income / No Assets (NINA)	0.000	0.375	1.000	1.500	1.750	1.750	2.000	n/a
No Doc (NINANE)	0.000	0.375	1.000	1.500	2.000	2.000	2.250	n/a
Fico >= 720	-0.375	-0.250	-0.250	-0.250	-0.250	-0.250	-0.250	0.000
Fico 680–719	-0.125	0.000	0.000	0.000	0.000	0.000	0.000	0.000
Fico 660–679	0.000	0.250	0.250	0.000	0.500	1.000	1.000	n/a
Fico 620–659	0.500	0.500	0.500	0.500	n/a	n/a	n/a	n/a
CLTV >95%	0.250	0.250	0.250	0.250	0.250	0.250	0.250	0.250
DTI >50%	0.000	0.000	0.000	0.125	0.250	0.375	0.500	n/a
40 due in 30 (Fixed)	0.375	0.375	0.375	0.375	0.375	0.375	0.375	0.375
Interest only (Fixed)	0.375	0.375	0.375	0.375	0.375	0.375	0.375	0.375
Interest only (Arms)	0.250	0.250	0.250	0.250	0.250	0.250	0.250	0.250
Ono Texas Property	0.250	0.250	0.250	0.250	0.250	0.250	0.250	0.250
Escrow Waiver	0.250	0.250	0.250	0.250	0.250	n/a	n/a	n/a

you work directly with a commercial bank, and is most often tied to the prime rate plus a margin.

Lenders making multifamily, or apartment, loans look at a number called the DSCR, or debt service coverage ratio. That number also has a benchmark, and that benchmark is 1.2.

The DSCR is calculated by dividing the net income by the debt service. The debt service includes not just the loan payment, but also taxes, insurance, and other day-to-day expenses that the property requires in order to operate. A number below 1.0 means that the property is losing money. Anything above 1.0 means that the property is making money.

For instance, take an apartment building that has 12 units and generates $18,000 per month. Next, take the costs associated with operating those units, divide that into the income, and you get your DSCR.

Management expense	$ 1,000
Taxes	$ 3,000
Insurance	$ 1,500
Maintenance and repairs	$ 2,000
Utility payments	$ 3,000
Security	$ 1,000
Total expenses	**$ 11,500**
Net income	**$ 6,500**
Debt (mortgage)	**$ 3,500**
DSCR	**1.85**

In this example, the lender sees a positive cash flow; next, you need to qualify from a borrower standpoint, which means providing tax returns, assets, and credit reports.

When you invest in residential real estate, the lender values the property but doesn't concern itself with the income unless the income is needed to help you qualify. With a commercial loan, both you and the property must meet certain lending guidelines.

Commercial rates are higher, but then again, commercial properties

shouldn't be compared to residential properties because they really are two different types of real estate.

A fixed rate for an apartment building might be 10 percent or more, compared to a fixed rate in the 6.00 percent range for residential real estate. Most often, though, multifamily investors elect to go with a shorter-term loan program, such as a hybrid, that offers lower rates, then refinance later on down the road when the loan begins to adjust.

Most short-term financing will come from a retail bank, although there are mortgage brokers who can also broker commercial loans. In fact, your mortgage broker has access to a niche area of commercial lending: commercial loans that fall between $100,000 and $1.5 million.

Many commercial lenders won't touch anything "that small." I know that sounds a bit odd—$1.5 million being labeled as "small"—but commercial loans are typically much larger than that.

Loans that fall into that range are called "small commercial" and often resemble residential loans when it comes to loan approval.

In fact, many of these small commercial lenders don't require a DSCR at all, but instead review only your loan application and credit profile.

Commercial loans also always require a down payment. You will not find 100 percent commercial financing; in fact, most lenders require at least 20 percent down. Commercial loans are also more expensive in terms of acquisition cost.

Appraisals can cost $1,500 or more compared with about $350 for a residential appraisal. Points and origination charges are almost always charged; in fact, I don't recall seeing a commercial loan without points. There is no such thing as a "no-closing-cost" multifamily loan.

All that having been said, however, multifamily investments can provide some serious cash flow, so if you're ready to play the commercial game, find a good management company to help run the complex, get the loan, and start making money.

Changing Investment Strategies

What if you bought a property intending to flip it, but you find that you can't sell it for a variety of reasons, and you decide or are forced to hold? If you took a short-term note and are left holding the bag long term, then you may be affected by the type of loan you took out.

For example, suppose you bought four duplexes in a town where a new factory had just announced it was moving in. This was a great deal, especially since the area had been so economically depressed that housing prices were at their low point.

But you also knew that you wouldn't be the only one to recognize this fact, and so you quickly snatched up some real estate before everyone else did. And you bought it close to where the new factory was going to be built.

You didn't intend to hold onto these properties, because you figured you could make a quick $40,000 selling them to other investors who were holders.

You acquired these properties using interest-only, short-term financing with zero closing costs. Fortunately, you put 10 percent down.

Why are you fortunate that you put 10 percent down?

Because six months later, the new factory deal fell through because the town the factory was moving to decided against providing relocation incentives to the new company.

Now you have four duplexes and four mortgages. But since you put 10 percent down, you also have some equity. Lenders need 10 percent equity in order to refinance a residential rental. And you will want to refinance into a fixed-rate loan before your adjustable-rate mortgage moves up at its next adjustment period.

This is key with investment financing: Have some equity going into the property, and keep your closing costs to a minimum. Pay no points, pay no origination charges, and, in most cases, pay little or no closing costs.

This strategy, explained in more detail in Chapter 6, gives you more flexibility should things happen to your best-laid plans.

Rent Loss Coverage

Your financing package may include a provision for rent loss coverage. Some loan types require such coverage and some do not; this can depend upon several variables for both conventional and alternative loans.

Credit scores, equity position, and number of properties owned can all contribute to the requirement for rent loss coverage.

Rent loss coverage is a form of insurance—issued as a supplement, or "rider," to your hazard insurance policy—that is designed to pay the mortgage should the property be damaged to the point where tenants can't live there, and therefore no one is paying you any rent.

Let's say the house was damaged by fire or the roof was damaged to such an extent that it had to be replaced or some other disaster occurred that made the property uninhabitable. While the property was being repaired, you wouldn't have to pay the mortgage payments out of your pocket; instead, the insurance policy would pay them for you.

Rent loss coverage does not pay the mortgage just because you can't find renters, a situation that is sometimes called a "casual" rent loss. It's a hard policy that pays the note during times of unit repair.

| C H A P T E R 5 |

Interest Rates and Rate Strategies

In a sentence: If rates are high, your profit will be low. You also need to know which type of loan to select for your properties based upon recent trends and forecasts. Sometimes it might be better to hold off on a purchase because of interest-rate conditions. And you certainly need to know when it's profitable and when it's not profitable to refinance your properties.

That's easy enough, right? There's no science to that. But knowing when to buy based upon the cost of money can be just as important as the cost of acquiring the property itself. Knowing how rates are set, how they move, and how they're quoted by your loan officer can mean the difference between getting qualified and gaining positive cash flow and either being declined or losing money every month on your rental property.

When rates are at their relative highs, it may not be a good time to invest in real estate if the higher rates have a negative effect on your cash flow.

It's easier to first explain how mortgage rates are not set. Your mortgage rate is not established by the Federal Reserve. Nor is it set by the 10-year Treasury.

This may come as a surprise, but it's important that you understand this concept, because as you're deciding how to pay for a property, rates are moving while you're thinking. Really.

Rates are set by lenders each and every business day, typically right around 11:00 EST. Why at this time? That's when all the economic news for that day has been released and mortgage companies have had time to digest all the new data.

Mortgage rates are tied to specific indexes; for fixed-rate loans, for instance, the most common is the Fannie Mae mortgage bond. Mortgage bonds are a trading commodity just like any other financial instrument. Investors invest in mortgage bonds every day, and the demand for these bonds from those investors causes prices to rise and fall.

And when there is more demand for anything, that means that the price goes up, right? The very same thing happens with mortgage bonds, but with interesting results: As the price of a bond goes up, mortgage rates go down. Just as with any bond.

First, though, how does demand affect the price of a bond?

Bonds are fixed investments. They don't change in value. If you pay $75 for a $100 bond that matures in 10 years, then you're going to get a guaranteed return. It's not a real sexy return, 33 percent appreciation over 10 years, but it's still a solid return.

Now compare a bond with another common investment, a stock from a publicly traded company.

If you found a stock priced at $75 today, would you expect only $25 in profit in 10 years? Probably not. Stock prices are based more on the profitability of a particular company, and stocks do not have a guaranteed return the way a bond does.

So why do people invest in bonds? There is a guarantee in bonds where there is no guarantee in stocks. And both are traded every single second of the trading day between buyers and sellers on Wall Street.

In strong economic times, investors put their money in stocks, anticipating higher profits from the companies they invest in and pushing up the prices of those companies' stocks. In recessionary periods, companies can lose money, driving the price of their stock down.

If you bought stock in Widget Company for $25, and Widget Company suddenly sold a million widgets to a new customer, you could see that stock price go from $25 to $50. If you owned 10,000 shares of Widget stock, you just made $250,000—at least on paper (if you didn't cash in).

But suppose you find out the next week that the company that Widget sold all its stuff to had gone bankrupt and couldn't pay Widget its money. Widget is out of inventory and out of cash, and it has no more customers to sell widgets to.

The stock then drops from $50 per share to $1 per share. Since you owned 10,000 shares, last week you made $250,000, but this week you lost $490,000. Quite a week, wouldn't you say?

Bonds, however, do not have that volatility. Whatever price you bought your bond at, you're guaranteed a return. Bonds are boring, but they're predicable. Stocks can be exciting, but they're anything but predictable.

During economic boom times, when everyone is rosy on the economy, more money flows into the stock market and out of bond markets because of the likelihood of greater returns. Yes, making $25 over 10 years isn't a great return, but it's a heck of a lot better than losing $490,000.

And during times of economic weakness, investors take money out of stocks and put them in safer investments, like bonds—all sorts of bonds, including mortgage bonds.

As demand for bonds increases, the prices of bonds move up. As demand for bonds softens, their prices move down. But the yield on your original purchase price (profit) remains the same. This is the function of rate and yield. Stay with me here, because unless you understand these dynamics, you can find yourself bamboozled by a shifty loan officer who

is quoting you higher rates when rates should be lower. And locking in a higher rate can cost you each and every month.

Understanding these dynamics also means that when rates are moving up, you may want to wait to buy a property, or that you may select an ARM over a fixed-rate mortgage when rates are at relative highs.

If you don't understand how mortgage rates move, then you really shouldn't be investing your money in real estate. As with any other investment, if you don't understand the acquisition cost, you can't evaluate the true profit.

It works like this: Let's say a bond is priced at $100 and yields 6.00 percent a year over five years. After five years, your $100 is now worth $134. Sure, there might be some more exciting prospects than making $34 over five years, but bonds offer security and not excitement.

Mortgage bonds are also traded throughout the day, and lenders peg their daily interest rates to the exact same index and have some very smart people at their company who do nothing but watch the price of mortgage bonds all day, hoping to predict the future of mortgage rates at the same time.

How do the prices of mortgage bonds affect rates? Let's say there are suddenly signs of an economic slowdown. Unemployment reports are showing more and more people out of work, and the gross domestic product, or GDP, is slowing down or perhaps even showing negative growth.

When investors see these data, they may pull their money out of the stocks they had invested in so that they can keep their profits, but they don't want to just park that money in a cash account somewhere. They buy bonds while they weather out the economic storm.

Now, if more and more people want to buy the very same bond, it's going to drive the price of that bond up. The 6.00 percent return will remain the same, but the bond price moves up, to $101, for instance. It may even move higher if continued economic news is being released and more and more investors push up the price of mortgage bonds because of their safety.

If you pay $103 for that same bond, your return will be $31, not $34, as a result of the rise in price. Therefore, as the price of a mortgage bond increases, mortgage rates go down.

Conversely, signs of economic strength will hurt mortgage bond prices and drive rates up. Less demand means that sellers of bonds will reduce their price to attract buyers. Less demand and lower prices mean higher rates ahead.

But to be ahead of the game, you need to know what the Fed is or is not going to do at its next meeting. While no one really knows this until after the fact, watching economic indicators and key indexes can help you determine when to lock in an interest rate and when to stand pat. Some of the most significant economic reports that will affect your interest rate are:

- Employment   Higher employment = higher rates

- Factory orders   More factory orders = higher rates

- Hourly earnings   Higher wages = higher rates

- Gross domestic product   More factory output = higher rates

- Consumer confidence   Greater confidence = higher rates

- Nonfarm payrolls   More people on payroll = higher rates

- Durable goods orders   More goods ordered = higher rates

Of course, the opposite can happen; rates will be lower if employment is lower and not higher, if factory orders are down and not up, if earnings are lower and not higher, and so on.

Another bedeviler of the economy is inflation. If you're guaranteed $134 on a $100 investment, you'll want to compare the value of the estimated return in current dollars versus future dollars.

Inflation eats away at profits. If there's an annual inflation rate of 5.00 percent, then that $100 you thought you had after one year is now

only worth $95. Yes, you got your $134 return after five years, but the dollar had devalued since you bought the original bond and the money just isn't what it used to be.

That's also a key concern that the Fed has: keeping inflation in control.

The way the Fed keeps (or tries to keep, anyway) inflation under control is by controlling a pivotal index, called the federal funds, or fed funds, rate. When the Fed holds its regular meetings, this is the number it adjusts; it doesn't adjust your mortgage rate.

The Fed adjusts the fed funds rate because that affects the cost of money at its most basic level—when banks borrow short-term money (as in overnight) to keep their reserves in line.

Throughout the day, a lender will not only make loans, but also cash checks or receive card payments. At the end of the day, however, the bank is required to have a certain amount of money in its vaults.

If a bank lends out all its money, so that when you go in to cash a check, it doesn't have any money, then there'd be quite a ruckus, don't you think? This is the purpose of reserves.

The fed funds rate hit an historic low in 2001, when the rate actually hit 1.00 percent. Think of that for a moment: an interest rate of 1.00 percent. That was a time when the economy wasn't doing all that well and the Fed wanted to help stimulate the economy by lowering the cost of money.

By lowering the cost of money to a bank, the Fed can encourage that bank to make more loans—cheap money, right? Conversely, when the economy is overheating or has the potential to overheat with low unemployment numbers, high wages, and a solid GDP, the Fed will begin to increase short-term rates to discourage banks from making loans.

Banks make loans to businesses so that they can hire more people or make more widgets, and the better business is, the more money companies might want to borrow.

There is a constant ebb and flow in the money markets, and this is

something you need to understand so that you can catch mortgage rates at the most opportune time—or at least get as close as you can.

Economic Indicators

It's important that you understand what will worry the Fed one way or the other. Essentially, if anything shows positive growth for the economy, then the Fed will be looking at raising the fed funds rate. While it rises by only $1/4$ to $1/2$ percent at a time, this is still a significant increase in the cost of funds.

Economic reports are released throughout the business month and there are a number of them, but the ones that have the most impact on interest rates are:

Unemployment report

Consumer Price Index (CPI) and Producer Price Index (PPI)

Gross domestic product

Factory orders

Retail sales

Consumer confidence

Personal income and personal spending

Chicago Purchasing Managers' Index

Productivity

Unemployment Reports

This report is one of the most influential economic reports released. It is released the first business Friday of each month, and it shows three key elements:

The unemployment rate

Nonfarm payroll

Wages

The unemployment rate is stated as a percentage and is perhaps the most widely published number coming from this report. For instance, an unemployment rate of 5.565 percent would mean that of all the available workers in the United States—those who are either working or actively looking for work—5.565 percent are currently out of work but are looking for work.

The nonfarm payroll number is the most important number of the three; it compares job growth from month to month in a numerical format. The nonfarm payroll number might show that 400,000 new jobs were created during the previous month.

Now, 400,000 new jobs is a significant number, indicating a growing economy with a bunch of new people with fat paychecks entering the labor force. This could mean that the Fed will increase the fed funds rate at its next meeting.

A meager job growth number (say, 50,000) or negative job growth, where the economy actually pares employees, would indicate a likelihood of a Fed decrease in interest rates.

The wage number also can indicate whether or not working employees are making more money than they did the previous month. More money in someone's pockets means that that person is likely to spend that money on something like a new big-screen TV or a new car. More demand for consumer products can drive up prices, meaning more inflation down the road.

In this example, the Fed would consider raising interest rates to cool off the economy.

Consumer Price Index and Producer Price Index

This is a month-to-month comparison of the prices people pay for goods from one month to the next. It is an initial indicator of possible inflation.

If more people are buying more products and businesses find that they can charge more, then the Fed will keep a keen eye on this number.

The Consumer Price Index, or CPI, measures the prices people pay at the retail level—at your grocery store or hardware store.

The Producer Price Index, or PPI, measures the wholesale prices at which businesses sell to one another.

There are a couple of volatile components in these indexes, with the two biggest being food prices and energy prices. Both can make wild swings from month to month, so they're often removed from the index.

If there's an oil pipeline shutdown somewhere and the price of a gallon of crude suddenly spikes, that doesn't necessarily indicate that the economy is growing as a result of demand for goods and services.

No, in this case the price of oil went up simply because of a one-time event. Food prices can behave similarly. A sudden cold snap could hit Florida or California, for instance, and wipe out much of the orange crop, reducing supply significantly and raising prices.

Neither of these one-time events is indicative of inflation caused by increased demand; the price rise is due to external forces that have nothing to do with consumer interest. That's why this more volatile "food and energy" component is often removed from the CPI and PPI number for analysts to digest.

Gross Domestic Product

The GDP number is the total cost of goods and services produced in the United States. Everything. Shoes, gasoline, automobiles, airplanes—everything is added up and tallied. This report is issued quarterly.

The GDP number shouldn't have very many surprises in it, since many of the data are tallied monthly. However, there can be surprises, and when there are, the markets can get hit pretty hard one way or the other.

A surprising number would indicate that either significantly less

goods were produced than anticipated or significantly more goods were produced than anticipated.

Factory Orders

This monthly number shows activity on a wholesale basis and logs purchase orders from the previous month by various businesses and service providers.

More factory orders indicate a strengthening economy, leaning toward higher rates.

Retail Sales

This is another month-to-month report that gathers all the sales data from all retail outlets in the United States. Retail sales include food, clothing, entertainment, plasma-screen television sets—everything that consumers can buy in the open market.

This report can also be affected by seasonal factors and is adjusted accordingly. For instance, retail sales in December are always stronger than retail sales in July because people buy lots of presents in December.

Retail sales are also compared on a yearly basis, with February of this year being compared to February of last year. There is also another retail sales figure called "same store sales" that looks at retailers, such as Home Depot, and compares retail sales numbers for the current month to those from one year ago for all stores that were open during both periods.

Higher retail sales indicate a growing economy, and, of course, slower sales mean a slowing economy.

Consumer Confidence

This report also has a significant effect on interest rates. Confident consumers buy more things and put more things on credit cards, as they have a mindset that everything is coming up roses and they will be able to pay the bills.

Consumer confidence also affects other reports, such as retail sales, home sales, and almost anything involving the retail sector.

When consumers lose confidence in the economy, the economy begins to shrink, carrying with it the likelihood of lower rates in the future.

Personal Income and Personal Spending

Personal income is tracked to anticipate higher retail spending. The more money people have, the more they'll spend. Personal income growth is also a measure of inflation. If people make more money, that's because their employers are forced to pay them more as a result of a tight job market.

The employers must then pass that additional labor cost through to the price of their goods and services, affecting inflation.

Both personal income and personal spending increases can cause interest rates to rise and produce a double-whammy of inflation and economic growth.

Chicago Purchasing Managers' Index

The Chicago Purchasing Managers' Index (PMI) report is a nationwide tally of business and factory purchasing agents, asking them how much stuff they bought in the previous month.

This could include widgets to make other widgets, automobile tires to put on new cars, or just about anything that a business buys to build things with.

When a company orders 100,000 new tires from a tire manufacturer, one can conclude that the automobile manufacturer is getting ready to produce a lot of new cars.

A strong PMI shows a strengthening economy, which can result in higher rates.

Productivity

Productivity is a measure of the output of consumer goods and services as it relates to how much is produced per capita. That means that people make more stuff or serve more people with the same or less effort than they used to.

Having more products or more services produced by the same group of producers available on the market helps to keep costs down and is a key component in the rate mix.

These reports are released over the period of a month and then are repeated the following month. And sometimes there's a frenzy. One report may show strong economic growth, while a subsequent report can indicate a slowing economy.

For instance, retail sales could show a month-to-month decrease, yet 350,000 new jobs were added in the economy. Conflicting reports will make for a choppy market.

Still further, a report could indicate no change whatsoever. The trend could be sideways!

Do you need to spend sleepless nights wondering what the unemployment rate for the previous month will be? Of course not. But you do need to keep an ear to the ground regarding the economy in general, and if you notice that the economy is beginning to show some signs of weakness (over an extended period, such as three to four months), be prepared to refinance your properties to lower your rates or wait a month or two to buy another rental.

How Interest Rates Move and How They're Set

If you don't know how rates move and how they're set, you're missing out on a key component of your real estate investment strategy. Interest rates can change without warning, and if you miss an opportunity to lock in interest rates while they're at their bottom, you'll pay for that

nonchalance each and every month as you make your mortgage payments and deposit your rent checks.

The Fed reacts slowly to all these economic reports. There will be no knee-jerk response from it with regard to adjusting rates. In fact, the Fed meets only every six weeks or so and rarely has an emergency session.

Thus, the real reason to follow these economic reports is to get an idea of what the Fed might do at future meetings. If there are continued signs of an economic slowdown, then mortgage bond traders, and other bond traders, will begin to increase their holdings of mortgage bonds.

That means that the prices of mortgage bonds will be higher, resulting in lower mortgage rates for consumers.

If the economic reports indicate a healthy, growing economy, then more money will be pulled out of bonds and put into the stock market, lowering bond prices and increasing mortgage rates.

That's why, when the Fed has a meeting and announces that it has adjusted the fed funds rate by $1/4$ percent one way or the other, you won't see wild interest-rate swings; in fact, there probably will be no rate swing at all because the Fed moves have been not only anticipated but also priced into the mortgage rate.

If you base your investment strategy on what the Fed does instead of what it might do, you're way behind the curve. You need to make your real estate investment decisions based upon the same anticipation that mortgage lenders have.

That's why by the time the Fed does anything about interest rates, there's little immediate effect on the mortgage market. Lenders are pretty good at anticipating Fed moves and have a bevy of people who do nothing but set interest rates.

Mortgage rates can change throughout the day as a result of the reaction to market data that are released. Rates can also change because of noneconomic and political factors, such as overseas turmoil, wars, or political unrest that might affect the growth of the U.S. economy.

Mortgage rates can change throughout the day, as mortgage companies follow the markets all day long and react to them if need be.

For instance, it's 11:00 a.m., and the nonfarm payroll numbers come in just as expected, so the mortgage bond markets don't react. Rates are stable for that day. So far.

Later that afternoon, a report is issued showing that the new home construction numbers are below expected levels, and a Fed governor somewhere announces that he sees reduced signs of inflation. A Fed governor can be at a luncheon somewhere, and everyone hangs on his every word to get a hint of what the Fed is thinking.

Two things have happened since the release of the rates for that morning: New home construction is down, indicating a possible slowdown in the economy, and the Fed sees no inflation problems down the road.

Or so lenders guess. In this instance, it is likely that a rate change would be in order for that day, so the lenders resend all their interest rates to their loan officers and mortgage brokers, who are excited that rates have gone down 1/8 percent since early morning.

The next day, existing home sales are released, showing strong sales in various parts of the country: Sales "exceeded analysts' expectations," and home prices are higher than what everyone thought they would be.

Guess what? Seeing signs of a pickup in the economy, lenders consider the state of the economy all over again, now thinking that the Fed may be considering a rate increase instead of a decrease at its next meeting.

So rates go up from the previous day.

I know this sounds a little hectic, but that's how it's done each and every day. It's also important to understand this when you compare one lender to the next, trying to find the very best interest rate.

Since lenders follow the same economic data and price their loans against the very same mortgage bond, that should also tell you that lenders' rates are essentially the same. One lender can't be at 6.00 percent while everyone else is at 7.00 percent. This can't happen, and now you know why. If someone is advertising a rate that seems too good to be true, it probably is.

That's also another good reason to shy away from unsolicited advertisements from lenders or loan officers that you've never heard of. One lender can't have some special rate that no one else has.

And it's also a good reason to use some of the referrals your friends or Realtors have given you. When companies that you've never heard of are asking for your business, what other way do they have to get your business than to offer some unbelievably low rate?

Instead, what you'll end up with is a bait-and-switch tactic: "Oh, that loan special was over last week, but let me tell you what I've got now, blah, blah, blah." This happens every day, so beware.

Your job is to secure the most competitive financing you can get, but if you can combine competitive loan pricing with competent service from your loan officer, well, that's the company you want to establish a relationship with.

But there's one important point to remember here: Lenders don't set interest rates; ultimately, the loan officer will.

I know that sounds incongruous with what I said earlier about lenders setting mortgage rates at 11:00 and so on, but what the lender does is set base interest rates for its loan officers to quote to its retail customers.

How Loan Officers Quote Rates to You

Most mortgage loan officers get paid on commission. So what a loan officer does each day is collect its lender's rate sheets from that morning and use them to quote you, the consumer, an interest rate that is competitive with the market and low enough to entice you to do business with that lender.

On a $200,000 mortgage loan, a lender might make 1 percent, or $2,000. The loan officer will get part of that, usually 50 percent, although megaproducers will command a much higher percentage of that profit because of their ability to find more loan business.

The rate sheet given to the loan officer looks something like this:

30-year fixed-rate loan

Rate	Points
5.00%	2.00
5.25%	1.00
5.50%	0.00

The lower the rate, the more points you'll have to pay. The higher the rate, the fewer points you'll pay, if you pay any at all. The choice of rate/point combination will ultimately be yours.

But what the loan officer is looking at is not your rates, it's his rates before he adds his commission on top of that and makes a quote to you. If the loan officer wants to make 1 point total on this loan, he'll quote something like this to you:

30-year fixed-rate loan

Rate	Points
5.00%	3.00
5.25%	2.00
5.50%	1.00

That's how it works. If the loan officer wants to try to make 2 points off of you, she'll add 2 points to the rate. Or if you don't want to pay any points at all, your rate will be increased accordingly, normally by $1/4$ percent for each point the lender makes.

This is from a mortgage banker. A mortgage broker will get similar rate sheets, but he will get them from a multitude of wholesale lenders who are soliciting that mortgage broker's business. A mortgage broker might look at a dozen or more rate sheets every day, scouring them all for the absolute best deal.

But the secret is that since the mortgage lenders all base their prices on the same mortgage bond, the mortgage broker is looking for a variance in the price, not the rate. A mortgage broker might be able to find

an interest rate that is 1/8 percent better, meaning about $^1/_2$ point in discount.

That's an extreme example, as lenders usually aren't that far apart (although sometimes they can be). But if the broker can find a lender that offers that extra $^1/_2$ point, odds are that he'll keep that $^1/_2$ point in additional revenue on top of the 1 discount point he already plans to make.

We'll discuss in detail how to negotiate closing costs in Chapter 6.

With these two factors in mind, it's now important to understand both who sets the rates and where those rates come from. That means if you call one loan officer in the morning and call two others later that afternoon, you might find that the prices from the afternoon loan officers are a bit lower than the price you were given early in the morning.

It's quite possible that rates have moved during the day and that the rates in the afternoon were in fact a little lower. If you think that's the case, and perhaps even if you don't think that's the case, you should contact the morning loan officer and give her the opportunity to requote.

How do you know if there's been a price change during the course of the day? It's hard. Unless you subscribe to such data, it's difficult to get your finger on live mortgage bond pricing.

You might find mortgage bond prices listed in the *Wall Street Journal* the next day, but that's already old news and is of no use when you are wondering which rate and lender to choose.

There are mortgage bond reporting services that feed mortgage companies live data from the places where mortgage bonds are traded. This service isn't cheap for a lender or loan officer, and the price is so high that subscribing to it is not feasible for a consumer. Loan officers can pay $2,000 or more per year for such data. It wouldn't be worth it to you to pay that much.

Instead, try to track a couple of numbers that, while not specifically giving you interest-rate movements, can give you a general idea as to how the market is doing.

Macroeconomically, when the Dow Jones Industrial Average is doing

well, it's likely that longer-term fixed-income securities like the 10-year Treasury aren't doing so well. Remember, when the economy looks rosy, people often pull money out of notes and bonds and move that money into stocks.

And vice versa. If the Dow is doing poorly and Treasuries are doing well, it's likely that mortgage bonds are performing favorably for you. That information is available almost anywhere on business news channels or the Internet.

Keeping Your Loan Officer in Check

You'll use this information to make sure that the loan officer who is quoting you rates is giving you the correct information as to why the rate you were quoted went down. Or up.

If your rate quote unexpectedly increases, you need to ask why. A competent loan officer will be able to answer this question, but the loan officer may say something like, "Well, the unemployment report came out and it was down/up."

You can certainly check that, but you can also check to see how the general markets are reacting. If the stock markets and bond markets are marching in tune in their respective directions, and this doesn't jibe with what you're being quoted, simply ask, "What is the Fannie Mae mortgage bond doing today?"

If you ask that question, you can be guaranteed that your quoting loan officer won't be playing any rate quote games with you. You have just shown him that you know how rates are set, so he shouldn't try to play such games with you.

This whole scenario, however, doesn't include everyone. Just because the economy overall isn't performing well doesn't mean that there aren't areas that are booming or that have lower-than-average real estate prices.

Interest Rates Are National

As an investor, if the national economy is soft and rates in your area are moving down right along with it, you need to remember that real estate is local, meaning that what's cooking in Queens may not be all that desirable in Detroit.

Interest rates are set using the very same index by lenders all across the country; there aren't different rates for Florida and for Wyoming, for instance—the rates are national. That means that if rates are low and your area is soft, you might want to be on the lookout for other parts of the country where real estate is selling because of local activity.

You can have a market that is experiencing it's own "mini-boom" while at the same time enjoying lower rates as a result of the national economy's being slow.

If you're a flipper, this is an ideal market for you, as you're able to invest at lower rates and still turn a profit later on down the road because the real estate market is hot.

The next piece of the rate puzzle is to guarantee, or "lock in," your rate quote.

Locking In Your Rate Quotes

Nothing is guaranteed. I can quote you an interest rate of 3.00 percent, but if I can't guarantee it, it's worthless, isn't it? Of course it is. That's why you need a lock agreement—to hold the lender's feet to the fire.

Interest rates can be guaranteed, but not forever. Most interest-rate quotes, for instance, are for a 15- to 30-day period. Longer lock periods are available, but it's not the lender who pays for the longer guarantee; it's you. For each additional 30-day period beyond the initial 30-day lock, you can expect to pay another $1/4$ discount point.

If a 30-year fixed rate is available at 6.50 percent for 1 point, if you want to lock it in for 60 days instead of 30, it will be quoted to you at

6.50 percent plus 1.25 points. Or, since rates generally move $^1/_4$ percent for each point paid or not paid, you can simply increase your rate to 6.75 percent, still pay only 1 point, yet have that rate guaranteed for 60 days and not 30.

Lenders will also typically be willing to lock you in for 90 days, but if you want a lock period longer than that, most lenders will ask that you pay them a 1 percent origination or commitment fee up front. Why?

When you lock a loan with a lender, the lender in turn locks your rate request in its pool of mortgage funds. The lender has reserved some money with your name on it at a particular interest rate. If you lock with a lender and your deal falls through for whatever reason, the lender will typically lose some money on the deal.

When lenders reserve money for you and the lender breaks the lock, it can cost the lender a small fee or lost interest from you, or both. Lenders charge commitment and origination fees up front to help keep consumers from locking in a rate when they are not yet committed to any particular lender. Lenders don't like to tie up their money unless they have a committed client.

Longer-term locks should be used only for construction properties to replace a construction loan, or for a property that's not yet finished but soon will be. When you shop for a rate, you may not have the luxury of comparing too many lenders all at once. When you find a property you want to buy, you'll typically have 30 days or so in which to close the deal. This means you don't have the time to get lenders to compete for your loan; you need to decide on a lender, make an application, and move on.

You'll want to have selected a lender a minimum of three weeks before you close your deal. Anything shorter than that and you can run the risk of not closing on time because you were still rate shopping.

Refinancing, on the other hand, gives you a little more leeway and strategy when it comes to interest rates. There is no time frame in which you must perform; you can apply at a lender somewhere, maybe open up a title report and pay for an appraisal, but you can wait, and wait, and wait until your magic rate arrives.

If you've already determined that refinancing a property is a good thing, as explained in Chapter 4, then, while you can wait around because you have that right, three things can happen:

Rates go down while you're waiting.

Rates go up while you're waiting.

Rates do nothing while you're waiting.

And each of these possibilities has its own risks.

Rates Go Down While You're Waiting

If you locked, this means that you locked at the wrong time. If you were smart and did not lock, but "floated" your loan rate, then you won. If you locked in with a lender, you can't call up the lender and ask for the new lower rates. The lender won't honor your request.

So you have a couple of choices: Do you swallow and take the rate you locked, knowing that rates have moved downward at other lenders (and also the one you're at because you locked), or do you try to negotiate or move to another lender?

First, if rates have moved down by $1/4$ percent or more, you'll find you have a little more negotiating power. Lenders realize that if you move to another lender, you are taking a risk, as rates could move up again while you are doing so and it's possible that you could lose a sure thing.

If rates move by 1/8 percent or less, or only by $1/4$ to $1/2$ point, don't expect your locked lender to budge. If rates move more than that, threaten to move your loan to another lender. Lenders are well aware of rate moves and their consequences and will try to accommodate your relock request.

Remember, though, that when you lock in an interest rate, you should be relatively confident that it's a good move. You've already run the numbers and decided that current market rates are a good idea for you. Anything else on top of that is gravy.

If you lock and rates go down, you can threaten to pull your loan or you can accept the rate that you locked in, knowing that you got a good thing.

Rates Can Go Up While You're Waiting

This probably means you got greedy. You had already determined that the new lower rates would benefit you and your properties, but you wanted to squeeze out that last extra 1/8 percent because, well, all the economic reports pointed toward still lower rates.

The problem with that scenario is simply that things happen. No one knows where interest rates are headed; they can only make educated guesses. And people a lot smarter than you are watching rate moves like a hawk. At least, a lot of people who think they're smarter than you are watching. You are reading this book, after all. That's the risk of waiting. You had a good thing, didn't take it, and lost the opportunity. If you have several properties that can benefit from new, lower rates, you missed out big time.

If you're ever wondering whether or not it's a good time to lock, I always tell my clients this: Assume that whatever rate lock decision you make will have been the wrong one—which way would you rather be wrong?

Would you rather be wrong in locking in an acceptable rate now and enjoying the benefits for years to come, or would you rather be wrong in having an acceptable low rate but rates moved up on you while you were waiting—forever?

I thought so.

Rates Do Nothing While You're Waiting

Let's say that rates have moved to a point where you save $500 per month on your properties. You have five properties, and you will save $100 per month on each should you refinance. But instead of locking that in, you

try to save another 1/8 percent, say from 6.00 percent to 5.875 percent on a $200,000 loan.

That's about $15 on each loan. You're already ahead by $500 by refinancing, but you wait one more month to see if rates drop further. They don't. So you wait one more and they still stay the same.

So far, by waiting, you've lost $1,000. You had $500 per month guaranteed, but you wanted a little more. You had significant gains in your pocket, yet greed got the best of you.

There are risks in all three scenarios, and you can harm yourself further simply by trying to make it just "this much more."

You can't be a serious real estate investor without keeping a keen eye on how the cost of your money is set. As rates move one way or the other, so should your investment strategy. Being able to anticipate rate swings instead of reacting to them will yield untold profits—not to mention helping you sleep a little better at night.

Investment Properties and Closing Costs

Investment properties carry the same typical closing costs as primary single-family homes do, but they also have some particulars that you need to be prepared for, as well as knowing how closing cost quotes work and how you can get through all the smoke and mirrors associated with interest-rate quotes and closing charges.

Interest rates and closing costs are the biggest shell game in the business.

Each time you finance a property, your loan officer is required to provide you with a Good Faith Estimate of Settlement Charges, or GFE, within three days after you send in your application or apply online, or immediately if you provide a loan application to a loan officer in person.

The GFE is a document that shows you all of the potential charges you might incur during that particular real estate transaction, whether that lender charges those fees or not.

For instance, even though the lender won't be acting as an attorney or performing any legal services for you, the loan officer is still required

to give you an estimate, "in good faith," of what he thinks an attorney will charge for your transaction.

The same sort of cost estimate will be provided for other third parties as well, such as for title insurance or a rental survey.

Because real estate is local and is governed and licensed differently in different states, closing fees aren't universal. Standard closing costs for loans in Oklahoma will be different from those found in Florida, for example. That said, here is a list of expected closing costs:

Origination	1% of the loan amount
Point(s)	1% of the loan amount
Appraisal	$ 350
Rental survey	$ 100
Credit report	$ 15
Inspection	$ 200
Underwriting	$ 350
Processing	$ 400
Flood certificate	$ 65
Document prep	$ 100
Settlement/escrow	$ 200
Title search	$ 150
Loan documents	$ 250
Attorney	$ 250
Title insurance	$ 800
Notary fees	$ 25
Tax certificate	$ 40
Recording	$ 100
Survey	$ 400
Pest inspection	$ 100

Again, this is a rough list. Some people will notice that title insurance is very low—or very high. Or that there is no intangible tax or property transfer tax or some other fee. It's simply impossible and confusing to list all the fees that could pertain in all locales, but this is a good summary of the closing costs I've seen from California to Florida.

You also need to ask for the GFE when getting interest-rate quotes from different loan officers. When you get your rate quotes from Lenders A, B, and C, also ask for their Good Faith Estimates as well.

Here's where things can get interesting.

You will undoubtedly see three different rate and fee quotes from the three lenders. I know this sounds ridiculous, but it also points out how fractured the real estate finance business can actually be, with so many players having to provide their very own piece of information or service and mailing an invoice for that piece of information or service.

Loan officers who have been around for a while can rattle off these various fees in a matter of seconds, but other loan officers may use the Good Faith Estimate to try to make their rate quote appear better than their competitors'.

Let's say you want a 30-year rate quote on $200,000 that would be good for 30 days. You might get something like this:

Lender A	Lender B	Lender C
6.00%, 1 point	6.00%, 1.25 points	6.00%, 1 point

So far, it seems pretty easy, right? Lender B appears to have the worst offering, while Lenders A and C are tied.

However, you decide to query further and get a Good Faith Estimate from Lenders A and C, leaving Lender B out in the cold, since she was higher to begin with.

Lender A provides his estimate:

Appraisal	$ 350
Credit report	$ 15
Underwriting	$ 500
Processing	$ 400
Flood certificate	$ 65
Origination charge	$ 2,000
Total	**$ 3,330**

Lender C provides his estimate:

Appraisal	$	350
Credit report	$	15
Underwriting	$	800
Processing	$	600
Administrative	$	400
Flood certificate	$	65
Origination charge		2$ 0
Total	**$**	**2,230**

That's a difference of $1,100. Lender C wins, right? Well, maybe. You left Lender B out in the cold when you shouldn't have. When you called for rate quotes, you asked only for a rate quote; you didn't ask for a list of the lender fees that go with it.

If you went back and asked Lender B for her Good Faith Estimate, it would look like this:

Lender B

Appraisal	$	350
Credit report	$	15
Underwriting	$	100
Flood certificate	$	65
Origination charge	$	1,000
Total	**$**	**1,530**

Lender B now beats Lender A by $1,800 and Lender C by $700. Yes, the interest rate at Lender B is 1/8 percent higher, but the monthly payment at 6.00 percent is $1,199 and that at 6 1/8 percent is $1,215, only $16 higher.

If you divide that $16 difference into the $700 in closing costs savings, you'll get the number 43. That's 43 months that it would take to get

the full advantage of the 6.00 percent rate and additional $700 in costs compared with $700 less in costs and a slightly higher payment.

Lender B has the better deal.

That's why interest-rate quotes need to be examined with a fine-toothed comb, even if you've got a seasoned veteran you're working with. Lenders can quote lower rates yet offset them with higher lender fees such as "underwriting" costs or "processing" fees.

Let's take it a step further. The previous example showed only lender fees; it didn't show title or attorney or anyone else's charges. So let's look at those now:

Lender C

Settlement or closing fee	$ 200
Title search	$ 200
Document fee	$ 250
Attorney fee	$ 175
Title insurance	$ 800
Recording fee	$ 100
Survey	$ 400
Total nonlender fees	**$ 2,125**
Lender C fees	**$ 2,230**
Total fee quote	**$ 4,355**

Lender B

Settlement or closing fee	$ 150
Title search	$ 200
Document fee	$ 250
Attorney fee	$ 250
Title insurance	$ 800
Recording fee	$ 85
Survey	$ 400
Total nonlender fees	**$ 2,135**
Total lender fees	**$ 1,530**
Total fee quote	**$ 3,665**

Lender A

Settlement or closing fee	$	50
Title search	$	50
Document fee	$	150
Attorney fee	$	50
Title insurance	$	399
Recording fee	$	50
Survey	$	100
Total nonlender fees	**$**	**849**
Total lender fees	**$**	**3,380**
Total fee quote	**$**	**4,229**

Suddenly, Lender A is slightly better than Lender C and, while still not better than Lender B, much closer.

Can you see the big problem here?

Lender A "low-balled" all third-party fees in order to make his quote look more attractive. The problem with this is: Lender A has absolutely no control over nonlender charges. He can quote pretty much anything he wants to because at the closing table, those fees will be what they're supposed to be and not what the misleading loan officer is quoting.

If you have different lenders' rate quotes along with their respective Good Faith Estimates, you should pay little, if any, attention to the non-lender fees. They will be what they will be, and if you see this kind of discrepancy, simply pick up the phone and call the attorney or the title company and ask it directly what it charges.

Types of Closing Costs

There are two groups of closing fees: recurring and nonrecurring and lender and nonlender.

We've just seen the differences between a lender and a nonlender fee quote. Recurring charges are charges that will occur again and again, such as your property taxes, hazard insurance, and mortgage interest,

while nonrecurring charges are one-time charges associated with that particular transaction.

Low-balling of closing costs is not limited to nonrecurring fees. It can also be done with property taxes or hazard insurance.

Recurring charges can also be an issue when you are deciding whether or not to take an "escrow" or "impound" account, or the T and I in PITI. Most parts of the country call these escrow accounts, but in other parts of the country, the term *impound* is used to describe the very same type of account.

When you establish an escrow or impound account, you're paying one-twelfth of your annual tax or insurance bill each month. At the end of 12 months, you've accumulated enough to pay your property taxes and insurance when they are due.

This is convenient, and you never have to worry about whether your taxes or insurance has been paid. And escrow and impound accounts are an option only when you have a minimum of 20 percent equity in the deal.

If you put less than 20 percent down in the purchase, then escrow accounts are required; if you put down more than 20 percent, they are an option. Are escrow accounts a good thing?

Having escrow accounts will affect your monthly cash flow. If you collect $1,500 per month in rent and your principal and interest payment is $1,200, then you have cash flow of $300 per month.

If you escrow and add insurance and taxes to that—say, $50 per month in insurance and $150 per month for property taxes—you now have cash flow of only $100 per month, as PITI is now $1,400.

It's your call really. I'm of the opinion that it really doesn't matter whether you choose to have or not to have escrows, although others will disagree with me, claiming that you could put that monthly escrow amount into an interest-bearing something or other or into a reserve account for normal repairs and maintenance on the unit, and they'd be right.

It's just that the difference is so slight, since you will have to pay

taxes and insurance on the property; it's just a matter of whether you do it every month and help ease the burden come tax time or you choose to sequester the funds somewhere else and let them earn some interest.

Refinancing and Escrow/Impound Account Strategy

There's one interesting feature about escrow accounts when it comes to refinancing.

When you refinance and replace your current mortgage with another mortgage, you'll also do the very same thing with the escrow account that you have with your current lender. Escrow accounts can't be transferred from one lender to the next; you have to pay for a new one, then wait to get your old escrow funds reimbursed.

This can require a sizable amount of money if you're refinancing toward the end of the year or just before your hazard insurance policy expires. This can be even more true if you're refinancing several properties at once.

Let's say your taxes of $150 per month and insurance of $50 per month have been put in your escrow account and it's close to the end of the tax year, yet your current lender hasn't paid taxes yet or renewed your policy.

After 10 months of insurance, that's $1,500 plus $500, or $2,000. You must come to the closing table with that amount of money, either in the form of a cashier's check or by rolling those escrow funds into your new loan. If you have five properties that you're refinancing, then that's $10,000 that you need to reconcile.

When you close on your units, your old lender will send you, in a separate check, the funds in your old escrow accounts, which add up to the amount you just provided for the new loans. This refund process doesn't take very long; normally you get your funds back within 30 days.

If you'd rather not tie up your cash for this long or add it to the principal balance of your new loan, you may decide to waive escrows on the new loans entirely. This way, you keep the $10,000 and still get the

$10,000 that you currently had in the old escrow accounts, and you pay the taxes and insurance directly.

Waiver Fees

One note: There is a fee called an *escrow waiver fee* or *impound account waiver fee* that is equal to $^1/_4$ point of your loan amount. If you decide to waive escrows, be prepared to pay this charge. It can sometimes be negotiated away, usually at the discretion of the loan officer you're working with.

In reality, the escrow waiver fee doesn't disappear; the loan officer pays for it out of her own loan commission.

It's common to see people refinance investment property without escrow accounts toward the end of the year, then, after the first of the year, when taxes and insurance have been paid, contact the lender and sign up for escrow accounts. Lenders like people to have these accounts. It makes for less risk of defaulted payments on property taxes and insurance, so much so that lenders will hit you with that escrow waiver fee if you waive them.

In Chapter 3, we reviewed some of the players in the real estate transaction and discussed which ones had negotiable fees and which ones did not. The fact is that since closing costs and customs can vary from region to region, there is no one "standard" set of closing fees.

As a result, there are no strict lists of negotiable fees. In fact, even if a fee were negotiable, do you think the company would advertise it as such?

"Hi, we're ABC Appraisals, and our fee is $400, but of course we'll come down if you want us to." Think that'll happen? Nope. If it did, then ABC probably wouldn't be as profitable as it would like to be.

Government fees can't be negotiated, title fees and closing fees usually can't be, and inspection and survey costs usually can't be. But there's no reason not to call these folks up and ask, right?

If you're an active real estate investor who will need these services

over and over again, then you can find some discounts if you promise to do business with that person or company exclusively.

The best way to keep tabs on closing costs is to keep copies of previous settlement statements from previous purchases area by area. Keep Texas settlement statements separate from Florida settlement statements. That way, if there's a fee that doesn't seem quite right, you can pull out the old settlement statement and compare the old one with the new one.

Title insurance is also a moving target. Some states do not allow title insurance discounts, and if they do allow them, all title companies must charge the very same fee. There are states in which title insurance discounts are available if you use them for a refinancing and if you used that title company for the last transaction on the same property.

Other states allow discounts on title insurance for refinancings regardless of which title insurance company you used. You need to both pick up the phone and call around and also use the experience of your loan officer.

Negotiating Closing Costs Through your Loan Officer

Ah, yes, the loan officer. The keeper of the keys—or at least the interest rates. There are a couple of ways to save money as a function of your mortgage.

Increase your interest rate to cover your closing costs.
Negotiate fees from your lender's loan officer.

Adjusting Rates to Cover Fees

In previous examples, you've seen how you can cover closing costs by increasing your interest rate by $1/4$ percent or whatever is needed. The amount needed can be found simply by dividing your closing costs (nonrecurring ones) by your loan amount.

The result is the number of points needed to offset those fees. Refinancing needs to be as close to closing-cost-free as possible. You don't want to add to the acquisition cost, since you'll want to sell your property in the future.

If your closing costs add up to $4,000 on a $200,000 loan, divide $4,000 by $200,000 and the result is 0.02, or 2 points. Increase your rate by $1/2$ percent and compare.

Using a 6.00 percent, 30-year fixed-rate loan and 2 points, you get $1,199 per month and $4,000 in fees. At 6.50 percent, your payment goes to $1,264 per month, or up by $65, but you saved $4,000. You would not "recover" that $4,000 in fees until after the fifth year.

You need also to consider your cash flow when raising your rate to cover costs, but if it made sense to refinance at 6.00 percent, it probably also makes sense to refinance at 6.50 percent, and you're doing it for free.

There's another reason for obtaining a no-closing-cost loan both at the outset and during the course of ownership: Keeping your acquisition costs low lets you follow interest rates and refinance without any costs.

Note here that there's a difference between having no closing costs and rolling your closing costs into your loan amount. And really there's no such thing as a "no-closing-cost" loan, because there is in fact a cost that is associated with your new monthly payment. There are no costs, but there are higher payments.

Putting closing costs into your loan amount means that you have no out-of-pocket expense *and* that you got the lower rate. This increases your cash flow (by $65 per month, as we saw in the previous example), but examining the effect of rolling closing costs into your loan amount versus paying for them out of pocket looks like this:

Rate	Payment	Comment
6.50%	$1,264	No costs
6.00%	$1,199	$4,000 in out-of-pocket costs
6.00%	$1,223	Closing costs are rolled in with your principal

Suddenly the additional monthly cash flow from your investment property has shrunk to $41 from $65 because you rolled your closing costs in with your loan.

Let's also look at the result of financing those closing costs. You've borrowed them for 30 years by putting $4,000 into a 30-year loan. If you hold that loan to full term, that $4,000 really cost you an additional $4,633 in interest.

If neither one extreme nor the other is for you, or if you need as much positive cash flow as possible from a property, yet you still want to keep your costs low, then you can do a combination of a lower rate and reduced fees.

Instead of 6.50 percent and zero closing costs, perhaps 6.25 percent and $2,000 in fees works out better. Perhaps that's a best of both worlds scenario.

Every single lender and mortgage broker can offer a no-closing-cost loan; just remember that there's a big difference between a no-closing-cost loan and one that rolls the fees into your loan amount.

If you get a rate quote from a loan officer who tells you that she has a no-closing-cost loan but tries to sneak your closing costs into your loan, find another loan officer. Either she's not smart enough to know the difference or she's trying to cheat you.

Closing Costs for Flippers

No-closing-cost loan packages are also the choice for flippers, or for those who don't intend to keep the property for any real length of time, say a year or less.

When rates can adjust $1/4$ percent to cover 1 percent toward closing fees, the lower rate with higher costs doesn't work for short-termers. Avoid every possible closing cost when you're investing short term; the advantages of the lower rate will never be realized.

For example:

$200,000 sales price

$4,000 closing costs

$20,000 remodeling/repair cost

6.00 percent rate

Anticipated sales price in 12 months: $ 260,000

The monthly payment in this scenario is $1,199.

$260,000 sales price

Less loan payoff	$ 200,000
Less remodeling	$ 20,000
Less closing costs	$ 4,000
Profit	$ 36,000

Here's the same scenario, but with a rate of 6.50 percent and no closing costs:

$260,000 sales price

Less loan payoff	$ 200,000
Less remodeling	$ 20,000
Profit	**$ 40,000**

Difference in monthly payment for 6.00 percent and 6.50 percent = $65 per month × 12 months = $781

Cost of lower rate with closing costs = $4,000 − $781 = $3,219

You lost $3,232 in profit by selecting a lower rate with costs instead of a higher rate without costs.

Negotiating Through Volume

If you're financing more than one property at a time, either because you're refinancing them or because you're buying them, you're in a bet-

ter position to negotiate closing costs. That's even more true if the units are in one development or perhaps several condos in a condominium complex.

In both cases, you have properties that are in close proximity to one another, translating into an easy appraisal. One title company will pull title reports on the same subdivision, one attorney will handle all closings at the same setting, and so on.

With this scenario, you can expect to get the lowest of all possible closing fees from the various third-party providers. And let everyone know that you're comparing their costs with those of other competitors. This is especially feasible in a refinancing transaction.

With a purchase, often some of the third-party players have been chosen for you; perhaps the title company that is providing the title report is already in the sales contract or the seller has selected a closing company.

But with a refinancing transaction, you get to choose the people you want to work with; hence you get the opportunity to ask for a package deal.

Personally, I have offered discounts to buyers or owners who refinance or purchase multiple properties simultaneously. It saves me plenty of time. Instead of building five separate loan files, I simply compile one loan file, make copies of everything, and change the addresses where needed.

I also have made alliances with other third-party providers, such as title insurance companies and appraisers, to provide lower costs to my borrowers should the borrower select one of the companies I suggest.

Negotiating Fees with your Loan Officer

One final place to negotiate closing fees comes from your loan officer.

You'll notice that our previous example of closing costs listed lender charges such as underwriting or processing fees. In the Good Faith Esti-

mate, these figures will be numbered, and lender fees (the ones you need to most be concerned with) are in the 800 series, with the appraisal listed as line item 803 and the credit report as line item 804.

It is in this section that you'll find lender "junk" fees—fees that you have a good shot at getting waived entirely.

The appraiser wants to get paid, so you won't get the appraiser to be nice enough to waive his charges, and the credit report folks want their money, of course, nice though they are.

Instead, you should be looking purely at the lender charges, those with odd names such as "processing" or "administrative" or "underwriting." Negotiate the best rate you can, then target these fees for waiver first, as the loan officer just might have some discretion over whether or not to charge certain fees.

Lenders charge junk fees, first, because they typically can in any given market, and second, because it helps them to offset the overhead associated with finding, processing, and (hopefully) closing a loan.

In reality, lenders could have long ago waived any fees whatsoever and simply charged higher rates, but they found that they could offer lower rates and offset those rates with loan fees.

A loan processing charge of $400 is the same as $1/4$ point on a $160,000 loan. The lender makes the same amount either way; it's just that with the fee, its rates might appear lower compared to those of other lenders. The problem with this strategy is that all lenders have now adopted this practice and combined rates with their own set of lender fees.

There are usually two types of fees from a lender: required fees and "let's see if we can get them" fees.

For instance, a lender might tell its loan officers that it has two fees: a $300 processing fee, which goes directly to pay the loan processors, and a $400 administrative fee. The $300 is a required fee, while the lender will split the $400 administrative fee with the loan officer if the loan officer collects it.

The difference is that the processing fee is required, but the adminis-

trative fee is not; the lender just hopes to get it to increase the bottom line. However, you won't know whether a particular fee is required or optional. You won't be fortunate enough to be able to say, "Gee, David, you've got two fees here; which one of these can you waive?" and get a direct answer. But you do have to ask.

You can say, "Gee, David, I like your offering, but you're a little high on the closing costs; in particular, I'm not all that fond of your $400 administrative fee. If you waive that today, I'll go with your company."

The loan officer might either stammer a bit or come right out and say, "Okay, we have a deal!"

On the other hand, a required fee doesn't simply get waived; instead, it comes straight out of the loan officer's commission. With a required fee, a loan officer may not be so enthusiastic; in fact, she may decline your gracious offer and risk losing the deal altogether rather than continuing to close the loan but making only a few hundred dollars.

Another interesting twist about closing costs is that some of the costs are set fees, while others are based on a percentage of the loan amount. This is of particular importance when the loan amount of your property is relatively low.

For instance, on a $200,000 loan, 2 points is $4,000 potential credit to your closing fees. But let's say you have a smaller rental or a condo that perhaps has a loan balance of $70,000.

On $70,000, 2 points isn't $4,000 but $1,400. And the closing costs from the lender and the attorney alone add up to that amount. It's much more difficult to get a complete no-closing-cost loan when you're dealing with smaller loan balances.

If your closing costs, including all items from your lender, appraiser, title insurance, escrow—everything—add up to $3,000, when you divide $3,000 by the $70,000 loan amount, the result is 0.0429, or 4.29 points. You would have to increase your rate by more than a full percentage point to cover all the fees.

On the other hand, with a large loan amount, say, $750,000, you

might have closing costs adding up to $5,000, yet that is only 0.0067, or 0.67 point, in "premium" pricing.

Mortgage brokers call this premium pricing the "yield spread premium," and it is the difference in spread from one rate to the next. Mortgage bankers also have premium pricing, but this is called the "service release premium," meaning that the lender will be selling the servicing rights to another lender at some point in the future.

If you have 0.67 point, this typically changes your rate by barely a breath, perhaps 1/8 percent, simply because points as well as origination charges are expressed as a percentage of the loan amount instead of as a flat fee such as that for an appraisal or an attorney charge.

All in all, with a median home price of $210,000 nationally, the rate/point trade-off works in almost every instance and should be considered at every opportunity.

It's important to note here that fixed-rate loans will carry more in premium pricing than adjustable-rate loans, and here's why: Lenders don't really begin making money on a mortgage loan until into the second year. This is because lenders have to pay their loan officers their commission and pay the processor and the office manager and pay for the telephones and computers and insurance and—well, you get the picture. So it's not until about the second year that the monthly interest payments become "net" income.

Red flags are raised when a lender sees an adjustable-rate mortgage loan without points, without lender charges, and without closing costs altogether. This loan has "early payoff" written all over it. If that loan doesn't make it into the second year, the lender will have lost money on it, even though the loan officer made her commission on it.

That's not any concern of yours; you can pay off almost any loan any time you want to. But an ARM coupled with no costs means lost revenue to a lender. A fixed-rate mortgage with no costs doesn't raise red flags, because lenders know that people who take fixed-rate loans typically intend to keep the property longer than those who take ARMs.

To offset the possibility of an early payoff, the lender simply doesn't

offer as much premium on its ARM programs. The most one might find is sometimes only 1 point or so, usually what the loan officer would make on the transaction.

If you're getting rate quotes from lenders and brokers and you can't quite get to a no-closing-cost loan because of the lack of enough premium, this is the reason why. Lenders don't like to make those loans because they're money losers.

If you don't have enough premium to cover your costs, then forgo the ARM and go with a fixed-rate loan. Keep this option open. You'll need to run the numbers, but when it works, it works brilliantly.

First determine the ARM payment plus the costs you'd have to pay, then see what the payments would be with a fixed-rate loan and zero costs. Let's look at a $250,000 loan amount.

For an ARM, a $250,000 30-year amortized loan at a 5 percent rate means payments of $1,342 per month. Because there wasn't enough premium to pay all your closing costs, let's say you would get hit with $2,000 in closing fees.

Next, compare a $250,000 30-year fixed-rate loan at 6.25 percent; that payment is $1,539 a month, but it also means no closing costs because you were able to adjust the rate upward enough to offset all your closing costs.

The fixed-rate program is a better deal.

If you subtract $1,342 from $1,539, you'll be paying $197 a month more with a fixed-rate loan. However, you also had to cough up $2,000 for an ARM. By dividing that $197 into the $2,000 closing costs, you get the number of months it will require before the ARM would have made better sense than the fixed-rate loan because you held onto the property for too long.

In this case, if you go into the eleventh month, you made a mistake. But if you can flip the property more quickly than that, then the fixed-rate loan, even though the payment is higher, is your better deal.

Another word of advice with this strategy is that if you do it too many times with the same broker or lender, you might not find any takers.

You'll need to spread the love around a little bit in order to make this work consistently.

Just don't assume that an ARM is always the best option for the short term.

The Estimated Settlement Statement

Another critical time to review closing costs is when you're getting ready to close on your deal. A few days before your closing, you will receive your Estimated Settlement Statement. This statement is prepared by your closing agent and has a list of all charges and disbursements to both the seller and the buyer.

The Estimated Settlement Statement is so called because it's not the final statement. The final statement will come after your lender, the seller, and you have reviewed it. Sometimes you won't be able to see the estimated statement, only the final one.

Either way, you'll get to see the statement before you go into closing. Or at least you should. Sometimes things get backed up or someone forgets or people just end up being people and don't get that statement into your hands for a review. However, the statement tells you exactly how much you're going to have to bring in and also lets you review it to see if there are any mistakes.

It also lets you compare the final numbers with what your loan officer originally disclosed to you in your Good Faith Estimate of Settlement Charges.

If things are way off base, you need to put the process on hold and get these mistakes corrected.

Notice that I said mistakes. If your loan officer quoted $950 for title insurance and it's $990, that's a good estimate. However, if your loan officer quoted you $950 for title insurance and the final statement shows $1,950, either that's a mistake or the loan officer misled you.

This is also the time to review lender settlement charges as well to

make sure that you weren't charged an extra point at closing time and that your interest rate is what you were told it would be. Getting the statement before you go to closing cannot be emphasized more highly. You need to be able to fix any errors before you go to closing; getting them fixed at the closing table (at least, getting them fixed on time and still making your closing date) may not be possible.

Good loan officers can give you a fairly accurate estimate. A good loan officer knows exactly what an appraisal will cost, how much an attorney's fee is, what an escrow charge is, and so on. This comes with both experience and honesty. Good loan officers stay in business for a long time because of those two qualities.

Credit and Investment Real Estate

Credit is the cornerstone to financing your real estate investments. If you have excellent credit, you're guaranteed the best available interest rates, lowering your monthly payments and maintaining a steady cash flow.

Knowing how credit scores are established, corrected, and affected is critical to financing your investment properties, especially since owning properties will affect your credit score. Making the wrong choices or the wrong assumptions about your scores can affect not only the interest rate you get on a property but, more importantly, whether or not you even get approved for financing.

It used to be that granting credit to an individual was an arduous process. Someone would want to borrow money from a bank to buy some rental properties, and a bunch of folks would meet once a month or so at a loan committee meeting and decide whether or not that person was creditworthy.

Credit was typically issued via relationships with people or businesses that banks knew. If you wanted a loan, you would first get to know

one of the bankers. If you had a loan from somewhere, you could get a loan from somewhere else. If you had never had a loan from anywhere, it would take you some time to get established.

In those days, the rich always got the loans because they had the relationships, established either through previous loans that they had had from the bank or through loans that their parents had had. It was hard to break through.

Fast forward to today. Underwriting decisions are made in moments, not weeks. There is no such thing as establishing a relationship with a banker in order to get credit, unless you're trying to procure an in-house or "portfolio" loan from a commercial bank.

Nowadays, lending decisions are greatly affected by a number, and that number is your credit score. Your credit history is the basis for this score and is the key ingredient in making credit decisions.

Credit scoring has been around for a long, long time. With credit scoring, you get so many "points" for paying on time, so many "points" for utilizing your credit responsibly, and so on, and in the past an underwriter would literally add up all your points and approve, or not approve, your loan.

Credit scoring these days is an ongoing and automated process. It's ongoing because it evolves with your everyday credit use, and it's automated because the algorithms used to calculate your score are preprogrammed into a scoring engine.

But let's back up a bit to see where credit reporting comes from so that you can understand how the score is calculated.

Where Credit Reports Come From

There are three main credit repositories in the United States. A repository is like a library, but instead of being a place where all the books are stored, it's a place where people's credit payment histories are stored.

The three repositories are TransUnion, Experian, and Equifax, and

they are located in different parts of the country. They collect data from businesses and individuals that report those data.

I can see that at some point in the future, there will no longer be a need for three bureaus, but for now, that's what we've got. The reason there are three is that in the past, providing credit data wasn't so automated.

In the olden days, people in California didn't shop at home to buy stuff from Florida. People weren't as transient as they are now; people didn't move so often. We also didn't have national chains with multiple shopping locations throughout the country. Well, maybe we had a Sears store or a JC Penney store where we could order from catalogs, but back then that was about as "continental" as we could get.

When businesses made credit decisions, they would ask you to fill out a credit application. On the credit application, they would ask where else you had credit: the name of the store, its phone number or address, what you owed, and what the monthly payment was.

The owner of the store would then take your application, make some phone calls to the businesses you had bought stuff from on credit, and ask a few simple, albeit blunt, questions.

"Did David buy stuff from you?"

"Did and does he pay you on time?"

"How much does he owe you?"

"What are his monthly payments?"

And the all too popular:

"Would you lend to him again?"

If all the answers came back okay, then you would be able to buy on credit. On the proprietor's terms, of course.

This is a tedious process. If credit decisions were still made like this, we'd still be in the credit stone age. There would be no such thing as

"instant approvals" and such. But it really used to be like this if you wanted to buy a car or a dishwasher. You would have to wait.

Eventually, businesses decided to play nice together and report credit patterns to a central database, the credit repository, where businesses could pull a credit history on someone just the way they would check out a book at a library.

Want to know about Joe Schmoe's credit? Don't call all the businesses Joe has borrowed from; instead, check out Joe Schmoe at the credit repository.

Businesses pay for that. They can't check out your credit for free. In exchange for pulling credit histories, they also contribute credit histories. There's a universal credit give and take.

That was the old way. Welcome to the new way: credit scores.

Along came an automated credit-scoring system that would pull your credit patterns, then assign your credit a number. The higher the number, the less likelihood that you will default. The higher the number, the better your credit; the lower the number, the lower your credit.

Credit scores can range from 300 to 850. I think the highest score I've ever seen was 810 and the lowest was around 440. An 810 score means that you have perfect credit patterns, are never late, make good utilization of credit, and have a long, stellar credit history.

A 440 means that some bad things have happened to you, such as bankruptcies and foreclosures and bad debt judgments.

Automated credit scoring was invented by Fair Isaac Corporation, commonly called FICO, which developed a system that analyzed a person's previous credit patterns and assigned that person a magical number, or score, automatically.

All three credit repositories use the same FICO method. But because not everyone reports to all three repositories, and even if they do, they may not report at the same time, these numbers are almost always different.

So if you get three different scores, which one do the lenders use? The middle one. They throw out the high score and ditch the low score.

They use the middle guy. Because of the geographical and enrollment disparities (not all businesses report to all three repositories, although most do), these numbers will vary.

How Do You Get a Credit Score?

You buy things on credit and pay the money back, and over a period of time your score will begin to appear on your credit reports. Credit scores take into account a variety of credit behaviors, then assign each particular behavior a number, and finally add up all the numbers and voilà!—instant credit score.

Credit scores are most concerned with the most recent two years' history, as that is most likely to be an indicator of what your next two years might be like. The components that make up a credit score are:

Payment history

Balances/available credit

Length of time in credit bureaus

Types of credit accounts

New accounts

Payment History

Your payment history, meaning whether you've ever been late and, if so, by how much, is the most important component of the score. Your payment history represents 35 percent of the total score.

Credit bureaus don't report whether you've been later than your due date; they report only if you've been more than 30 days, 60 days, 90 days, or 120 + days past due.

When you get a credit card statement, it could have a due date of, say, the twentieth of the month. If your payment gets posted on the

twenty-first, while it would be considered late by the credit card outfit—thus possibly increasing your rate and incurring late charges—it wouldn't be considered late by the credit bureau.

There are simply too many due dates to keep track of, and this is the simplest, most convenient method to both report and review payments.

That means that if you were 29 days past the due date but not 31 days past, your credit score wouldn't get hit because you weren't more than 30 days past due. Granted, the cost of your credit will go up because you're past your due date, but for the purposes of calculating a score, it's not an issue.

More than 60 days past your due date? Your score will get hit again, and even more so than if you're 30 days late. The same occurs with a payment that's 90 and 120 + days past due.

If accounts go unpaid and then go into collection, that's still another markdown of your credit score. If the account is charged off, meaning that the creditor has written off your account as uncollectible, that's still another hit, and finally there's an additional hit if the account is sent to the courts for a judgment, meaning that there is now a public record reflecting the bad account.

If too many of these accounts are charged off or go to court, you might file for bankruptcy protection, which would be the final blow to your credit score.

But of course, you'll never get anywhere near that.

Balances/Available Credit

The next most important piece of the credit score pie is your available credit number, which compares how much credit you have available to you with the balances you owe and contributes 30 percent to your overall score.

If you have a total credit line of $10,000 on two credit cards and you owe $4,000, that's a pretty good ratio of balances owed to credit lines, or available credit. Ideally, the secret number is to have a balance of one-

third of your credit lines, Do you have $10,000 available to you? An optimum balance would then be $3,333.

One interesting note about balances: Someone who pays off her debts each month, never allowing a balance to be reported to a credit bureau, can actually have a lower credit score than someone who keeps a balance, as long as that balance is at or below the 33 percent level.

This also means that closing out unused accounts can actually hurt your credit score rather than help it.

But what about mortgages? How do mortgages affect your credit scores if you put very little down? That's a good question, but fortunately for the consumer, mortgages are scored differently from revolving or installment credit lines. If you decide to put 5 percent down on a $100,000 duplex, you're not going to be hurt because the balance versus limit ratio is so much higher.

Credit Myths

These two anomalies in credit scoring run counter to what credit counselors and loan underwriters have suggested for years: Pay off your debt when and if you can, and close unused accounts. In fact, you could probably find articles or publications somewhere today suggesting just that.

While that might be a prudent method of keeping your credit under control, for purposes of scoring, it can be a negative.

Paying off debt and keeping zero balances means that you never reach the 33 percent balance to limit figure. And if you think about it, that sort of makes sense. When lenders extend credit, they want to be paid back, but they also want to make money while doing so. How will a lender really truly know if you can borrow money and pay it back over time if you never keep a balance?

Avoid going over your credit limit; this will also hurt your score and is a critical component of the available credit feature. Not only did you erase your available credit, but you made it go negative by owing more than the amount at which your credit limit is set. If you keep a balance

that is perilously close to its limit, then one finance charge can put you over the top, knocking down your score.

And closing old accounts that have credit lines, an action that used to mean prudent credit behavior, can affect your balance to limit ratio, dropping your score.

For instance, what about that person with a total credit line of $10,000 on two accounts and a $4,000 balance? That's not bad; it's close to the 33 percent level. Now, close the account that didn't have the $4,000 balance. Let's also say that the closed account had a $5,000 limit.

Now you have a $5,000 limit and a $4,000 balance, or 80 percent of your credit line is used up. That will hit your score negatively, simply by doing what some people tell you to do: closing old accounts.

To keep your available credit, don't close old accounts; keep them open.

Notice that these first two score factors make up 65 percent of your credit score. If you concentrate on keeping these two items in line, almost everything else will fall into place. But if you're marginal or you have some credit concerns, you need to pay attention to the final three contributors.

Length of Time in Credit Bureaus

This means "how long have you been using credit?" and it gives you points for being a credit "veteran." It accounts for about 15 percent of your total score.

There's not really a lot you can do to affect this component except wait for time to pass. Your score will automatically adjust upward the older your credit file gets.

This is also another good reason for not closing old accounts. By closing old accounts, you're taking away some history and knocking your length of time component down.

Types of Accounts

Mortgages make up the biggest piece of this pie, followed by credit card accounts and consumer loans. These are called good credit accounts.

Not so good credit accounts are those from consumer finance agencies or other firms that specialize in lending to people with nonexistent or shaky credit, and this score component makes up 10 percent of your score.

New Credit

Opening up new accounts will hurt your score. So will having lots of different businesses pull your credit report for review. This component also makes up 10 percent of your score.

This means that if you don't think you have enough available credit, by opening up a new credit card to increase your credit, you'll also hurt your score at the same time by creating both a new credit inquiry and a new account.

How Real Estate Investments Affect Your Score

A flurry of new account openings could indicate some potential income or credit issues soon down the road.

Pay close attention to your new credit inquiry item. If you're an active buyer of real estate or you anticipate being an active buyer over the next 12 months, you might buy six or eight properties. That means at least six or eight new credit inquiries on your credit report.

Multiple or recent inquiries can hit your score, although not a lot by themselves—say, a couple of points each time you inquire. Credit inquiries over the previous 12 months hurt your score more than the total amount in 24 months.

This also indicates the importance of finding a good lender and sticking with that lender. Having fewer people inquiring into your credit

report will keep your score up. Mind you, it's critical that you shop around for your best financing option, but after you've found a couple of regular "go-to" guys, stay with them.

It's also important to be serious about your real estate purchases. Don't take the plunge unless you're ready to swim the distance. Nonchalant credit inquiries will gradually erode your credit score.

One important thing to remember about inquiries: If there's more than one inquiry for a specific transaction, your score won't get hit as badly.

This means that if you're shopping for a mortgage lender and three lenders want to review your credit, as long as it's within a reasonable period, say 30 days or less, it won't be counted as severely as if you were applying for an automobile loan, a home loan, a new credit card, and a timeshare.

Inquiries for the same type of transaction will affect your score, but barely.

If you are gobbling up properties as fast as you can find them, with inquiries spread out over an extended period of time, pay close attention to the number of inquiries in the previous 12 months and try to spread your purchases or refinancings out over a longer period if possible.

If you have $1,000,000 to invest and you buy one big property with it, you'll have one or two inquiries on your report, depending upon how many lenders you solicit for bids. If you take that same $1,000,000 and buy ten $100,000 properties over 12 months, your score will end up lower than if you made the single $1,000,000 investment.

Inquiries by themselves normally won't hurt your score that much, as they account for only 10 percent of your score, but combining inquiries with any other credit item, such as going over a credit limit, will knock your score down dramatically.

You'll notice that there is no single "fix" in these score categories. Sometimes trying to fix one part of your score can hurt you in another. That's why the score doesn't just look at today, but gives the most weight to the previous two years of history.

CREDIT AND INVESTMENT REAL ESTATE

In fact, about three-quarters of your score reflects your most recent two-year period, whereas little or no account is taken of anything beyond four years. You can have an outstanding collection account that's five years old, but if nothing has happened to it, including paying it off or down, then it's likely that the negative item could remain on the report without affecting the credit score.

Most conventional loan programs underwritten to Fannie Mae or Freddie Mac standards do not have minimum credit score requirements. You heard that right; there is no such thing as a minimum credit score for most conventional loans.

There are certain "boutique" loans with no money down or first-time home buyer programs that do need a minimum score, but in general, you shouldn't get too hung up on your score, unless you need an alternative loan.

Alt loans typically do require a minimum score, usually around 620, but this can be offset by putting more money down or borrowing less or going fully documented instead of stated (documentation levels are explained in Chapter 8). But the score is required nonetheless.

Another type of loan that requires a minimum credit score is loans reserved for the "nonprime" or "subprime" borrower.

Subprime Lending

Subprime loans are designed for people who have had their credit damaged and need an alternative for financing. Subprime loans carry higher rates than conventional or alt loans, but they are there if needed. They should be used only in the short term.

Using subprime lending to acquire investment property needs to be examined closely, but sometimes when properties come up at a time that coincides with a negative credit item on someone's credit report.

How much higher are subprime loans? That depends on your credit score. The lower the score, the higher the rate, but most subprime loans

start out at about 2 percentage points above similar loans reserved for those with good credit, so if a good rate is at 6.00 percent, a subprime loan will be around 8.00 percent. For people with badly damaged credit, rates can be 4 to 5 percent higher. Subprime lenders also categorize their subprime loans with a letter grade, typically from A+ to C−, with A+ being the highest grade of subprime and C− being the lowest.

For marginally subprime loans, those with an A grade, the borrowers have a few features in common:

High loan balances to available credit

Late payments

Paid collection accounts

Credit scores from 600 to 650

Borrowers of B loans have the same features plus:

Outstanding collection accounts

Judgments

Credit scores from 580 to 600

Borrowers of C loans reflect the same features plus:

Recent bankruptcy filing or discharge

Foreclosure

Repossession

Because a grade of C and probably B makes loan acquisition too expensive, these loans are probably less of an option for financing a property and more of a wake-up call that if you're going to get into the real estate investment business, you first need to fix your credit.

Subprime lending fills a need; it is designed not for chronic credit

abusers, but for those who typically have had something bad happen to them, such as losing a job, a divorce, a long-term illness, or, worse, a death in the family.

The typical subprime loan is issued to someone who has had good credit up until a certain point, but then was laid off and couldn't find work, or someone who had an extended illness that wrecked her finances.

Subprime loans are a temporary solution, not a permanent one. This means that while there are lower subprime rates available to you by paying points, the best strategy is to obtain the subprime loan, repair your credit, then refinance later into a conventional loan.

This is why the most prevalent subprime loan is a hybrid with a 2/28 or 3/27 term, meaning that the rate is fixed for two or three years, then turns into a straight ARM for the remainder of the 30-year term.

Subprime margins can be pretty scary—as much as 5, 6, or 7 percent or even more. That's why it's vital that when you take a subprime loan, you do everything you can to get out of it before it adjusts.

You can find subprime loans pretty much anywhere you can find regular loans, but you need to take extra precautions because there are some unscrupulous mortgage brokers who will take advantage of your credit situation and charge you lots of fees and points, making you think that they're the only ones who will approve your loan given your circumstances.

But nothing could be further from the truth. Subprime loans have standard underwriting guidelines just as conventional or government loans do, meaning that you can get the exact same subprime loan from one lender as you can from the next.

That's why I recommend staying away from companies that specialize in subprime lending; instead, work with a mortgage company that you know and ask for its subprime division. Almost every mortgage banker in the business has a unit dedicated to subprime lending.

Bigger lenders and banks typically have a maximum amount of money that can be made on a particular loan, while mortgage brokers may not have any such standard. And since your plan is to refinance out

of the subprime note in a short period of time, say two years, it's essential that you pay no points and, if possible, no closing costs.

Subprime loans also can carry a prepayment penalty, or an additional amount of money that you will owe the lender if you pay off the mortgage early or make extra payments on the mortgage note.

Most prepayment penalties coincide with the initial fixed hybrid term, say two years for a 2/28 loan, but they can last as long as the loan agreement allows.

Repairing Your Credit

So how, then, do you fix your credit if it's been damaged? First, do not use a credit repair service.

Credit repair services don't do anything that you can't do, no matter what they tell you. There is no "secret system" for taking things that don't belong there off your credit report. The credit-reporting system is too dynamic these days to respond to simple "verify or remove" contests, where a borrower would contest a negative item and hope that the response took longer than 30 days, meaning that, according to fair credit laws, the negative item would have to be removed, whether or not it was valid.

If this didn't work the first time, the borrower would start all over, eventually (hopefully) removing the negative item.

Mistakes can be removed, but only if you have documentation for the mistake. I recall a lady who had a Chapter 7 bankruptcy discharge reported on her credit that was a mistake. It wasn't a discharge; it was a dismissal. There's a big difference. She had simply decided that she didn't want to file for bankruptcy after all and dismissed the filing. That was a mistake, and she could document it.

But by taking this process one step further, she got her credit report fixed in one day. Actually, it was less than one day, because I was the one who helped her get the item fixed.

Mortgage companies are customers of credit-reporting agencies. These agencies hire sales representatives and customer service reps who do nothing but make lenders' lives easier. One of the services they offer is correcting a credit report quickly as long as the lender can provide third-party verification of the error.

Consumers can do the very same thing, but it normally takes longer. You have to call here and overnight there and be put on hold, then voicemail, then whatever. It can take forever because you're one of millions of people in the credit system and you're really not the agencies' customer.

But lenders are.

A lender can do what you or a credit repair service can do, only more quickly and for free.

But what happened to my client's credit scores after the bankruptcy had been erroneously reported on her credit report for so many years? After all, her scores were artificially depressed because of that major error.

Let Your Lender Fix it Fast

There is a feature called a "rapid rescore" where a credit-reporting agency will take the corrected information and rerun the score as if the mistake had never been there. It takes about three days and costs around $25 per line item, per bureau.

I rescored my client on just one line item, the bankruptcy, and asked for the rescore from two bureaus and not three, which saved my client another $25. Why did I order only two bureau corrections? Because lenders use only the middle of three credit scores, and by ordering two, I would get my middle score while still throwing out the lowest one.

It worked, and my client's credit scores increased by nearly 80 points.

To repair your credit, remember that you must have third-party documentation, not a heart-rending letter explaining your side of the situation. Credit agencies don't provide the information that's in your credit

report; they only report it. It's someone else who put the data in there in the first place. For a credit-reporting agency to remove something, you have to have verifiable proof.

If you're going to invest in real estate, then good solid credit is a must, and you have to manage it. Keep an eye on your report regularly, and be on the lookout for mistakes that can damage your score without your knowing it.

Lenders can review your score and provide you with worse terms than you thought you would get, all because you weren't actively monitoring your credit.

Documentation of Assets and Rental Income

Earlier in the book, you heard me use the term *degree of documentation*. This simply means how far the lender will go to verify the information you put on your loan application.

This is important because each lower degree of documentation can either require you to put more of your own money into the transaction or increase your interest rate (which could affect your approval), or a combination of both.

Before we go any further, this does *not* mean that you can lie on your application up to a certain point; instead, it means what type of loan you can get approved for based upon the loan requirements being presented.

For instance, a conventional loan could require verification of rental income from other properties in previous years before the rental income on your new property can be counted. But a no income verification loan won't have such a requirement. You have the income from the property

you're going to buy, but because of the particular lending guideline, the lender can't use that income to qualify you for a conventional loan.

So you switch to a loan program where verification of that income is not a requirement.

There are different degrees of verification, and these degrees are:

Fully documented, or full doc

Stated income/verified assets, or SIVA

Stated income/stated assets, or SISA

No income verification, or NIV

No income/no assets, or NINA

No income/no employment/no assets, or NINENA or no doc

Fully Documented Loan (Full Doc)

Plain and simple, this means that everything you put in your application regarding your income, assets, and employment is verified by third parties.

Yes, you completed the application, but the lender won't take your word for it that you make $10,000 per month; instead, it will ask for verification from a disinterested third party, such as the IRS or your employer.

When you verify your income, the lender may ask for tax returns for the previous two years to show how much money you made and also look at your W2 forms for those years.

Most often the income tax requirement is for the self-employed, but it doesn't always have to be, especially when verifying rental income is involved. The lender will also ask for a couple of paycheck stubs covering a 30-day period if you're not self-employed.

Having stubs covering 30 days allows the lender to accurately calculate your debt ratio, or your gross monthly debt divided by your gross

monthly income. A W2 and pay stubs provide the third-party verification that the lender needs in order to document how much money you make.

Fully documented loans also verify your assets, meaning both liquid and nonliquid accounts. Liquid accounts are accounts where you can get the money immediately, whereas nonliquid accounts would include things such as CDs that haven't matured, 401(k) or IRA plans that you can't access without penalties, and other such instruments.

Lenders have to make certain that you have enough money to close the deal, and they do that by reviewing bank and account statements for the previous three months. Lenders demand that the funds needed to close on an investment loan be yours and yours alone. If they review one of your bank accounts that has the $20,000 you need to buy the duplex you have your eye on, the lender will scrutinize the statements, looking for any large deposits that are inconsistent with your income.

This is done to make certain that you're not borrowing from Peter to pay Paul, so to speak. If you need $20,000 to close on a loan, and the lender sees a $20,000 deposit when your job pays you only $7,000 per month, the lender will ask a question: "Where did this come from?"

At first glance, you might say, "What business is it of yours?" but in reality, the lender has a good reason for asking that question. If that $20,000 has suddenly popped up, do you now owe someone else that money? Do you have to pay it back? If you do have to pay it back, then your debt ratio could be skewed.

If you borrowed it, does the person you borrowed it from have an interest in the property that would affect the new lender's loan?

Another aspect of sudden large deposits is that the lender would really like to see a consistent pattern of savings to come up with a real estate investment. This shows some discipline and is usually a reflection of an overall solid profile.

Lenders can also verify via third-party means, using forms called verification forms. Verification forms are sent to your bank or your employer or whomever the lender needs information from and are completed by filling out boxes on the forms that ask, "How much money is in this

account?" "What is the average balance for this account?" and other such questions.

For your employment, the form is typically sent to the owner of the company or the human resources department, asking similar verification questions, such as "Does she work at your company?" "How much does she make?" and "How long has she worked there?"

This form is completed by the bank or the employer, then mailed or faxed back to the lender who is asking all those questions.

Stated Income/Verified Assets

A stated income/verified assets (SIVA) loan means that whatever income you put on your loan application is what the lender will use to qualify you. If you state that you make $8,000 per month, the lender won't send any verification forms to your employer, won't ask for pay stubs or W2 forms, and won't require you to send in tax returns. The lender trusts you.

However, the lender on a SIVA will verify your assets. That means that you need your three months' most recent statements covering your bank, investment, and/or retirement accounts.

SIVA loans are the next highest degree of verification. SIVAs don't mean that you can lie on the application; they simply mean that while you make that money, it doesn't qualify under the lender's fully documented loan guidelines. You still need to make the payments, so whatever you put down on the application still needs to be real.

For instance, if you put down that you make $50,000 per month on a loan application, thinking that you can now qualify for that million-dollar loan, but in reality you make only $5,000 per month, then how in heck can you afford the new mortgage? At 7.00 percent, the payment on a million-dollar loan is nearly $7,000, or $2,000 more than you really make.

Lenders can also look at a SIVA and by reviewing your assets make a roundabout determination as to whether or not your stated income is

realistic. If you report that you make $12,000 per month, and you have zero debt but only $500 in the bank, then there's something really wrong with the application.

With a SIVA loan, lenders may also require that at least six months' worth of PITI, or principal, interest, taxes, and insurance, be verified in a liquid account.

If the property you're buying has a total payment of $2,000, then the lender will want to see account statements verifying that you have $12,000 in the bank above and beyond what is required to acquire the property.

Stated Income/Stated Assets

Stated income/stated assets (SISA) loans are one rung below a SIVA, meaning that neither your income nor your assets are verified. If you put down that you make $10,000 per month and have $50,000 in the bank, then the lender will use those numbers to evaluate your loan request.

Lenders also use some common sense when evaluating a SISA loan. With a SIVA, a lender can look to see if there are liquid assets that could justify a $50,000 per month income, for example.

With a SISA, the stated income and stated assets must be in line with the kind of work you do. If you're a kindergarten teacher making $5,000 per month, hey, that's reasonable in California, but it may not be reasonable in Oklahoma.

If you're a kindergarten teacher and you claim that you make $12,000 per month and you have $100,000 in the bank, then the lender may not approve your loan request because the stated income and stated assets must be in line with your work.

No Income Verification

With this loan type, no income whatsoever is put on the application. Instead of stating an income amount on an application, you leave the income section of the loan papers completely blank.

That also means that no ratios are calculated. Your employment will be verified with a phone call or other type of verification. If you're self-employed, NIVs will require you to have been in business for at least two years.

With an NIV, the lender will ask you to provide a letter from your CPA claiming that you've been in business for more than two years. The letter won't mention anything about income, nor will the CPA be asked to provide tax returns; he will only certify that you've been self-employed for a minimum period.

With an NIV, however, assets are verified and also must be in line with the work.

No Income/No Assets

The next-to-last level of documentation is the no income/no assets (NINA) loan, where both the income and the asset information are left completely blank. No ratios are calculated, and no reserves are required.

The lender will verify that you have a job and may also verify how long you've worked at a particular company or ask for third-party verification that you've been in business for more than two years.

You don't have a CPA, and you've always done your own taxes? Do you have a receipt somewhere for advertising with your company name on it that is more than two years old?

Did you place an advertisement somewhere? Do you have a business license that is dated more than two years ago? You can get creative to meet the requirements for a two-year employment history.

No Doc

The only thing that is verified for this loan is that you are who you say you are; all income, asset, and employment information is left blank.

There's not much more to add here except that this is the absolute

lowest degree of loan verification there is. It also commands the highest rates and requires a larger down payment than any of the previous documentation types. That's the trade-off when you reduce documentation. At first glance, you'd say, "Heck, why doesn't' everybody just fill out a no doc and move on?" The answer is that it gets expensive.

When a lender agrees to relax some lending guidelines, the lender will offset those relaxed guidelines with a higher rate of return—meaning a higher interest rate. Here is a typical trade-off between a fully documented loan and other types, all the way down to a no documentation loan:

Program	Change
Full doc	No change
SIVA	From full doc, increase points by $1/4$ and increase down payment by 5 percent
SISA	From SIVA, increase points by $1/4$
NIV	From SISA, increase points by $1/4$
NINA	From NIV, increase points by $3/4$
No doc	From NINA, increase points by $1/4$ and increase down payment by 5 percent

Let's take a $200,000 sales price with 20 percent down as an example. A full doc loan asks for $40,000 as the down payment.

The SIVA asks for $500 in points plus another $5,000 in down payment.

The SISA asks for yet another $500 on top of the SIVA.

The NIV asks for $500 more than the SISA requires.

The NINA asks for $1,500 more than the NIV needs.

The no doc asks for still another $500 plus another $5,000 in down payment.

The difference between a fully documented loan and a no doc loan is $13,500. This doesn't even take into account credit scores. Lower credit scores can also mean more down payment, more points, or a combination of the two.

Loan documentation levels can also be a matter of convenience. I recall a client who had a hand in several businesses, some limited partnerships and some corporations. His income tax returns were literally nearly eight inches high. And this guy made some pretty good money.

I financed some property for him using a stated income/stated asset loan because it was easier to qualify for and the difference in monthly payment was marginal.

I have had other clients who had a variety of mutual funds, stocks, and retirement accounts with lots of account statements—as many as twenty or more. Instead of trying to verify each and every account, we went stated assets and forgot about trying to verify everything that was there.

Going stated also means that a higher down payment may be required, as well as an increased rate or fees. If you don't want to verify your income or assets in any way whatsoever, then you'd better have a pretty good reason for doing so because it will make it much harder to have good cash flow.

Higher rates as a result of lower documentation levels mean higher mortgage payments and less (if any) net rental income. If you're flipping the property rather than holding it, it might be a good idea to take the higher rate if you don't want to dig through all your tax returns, bank statements, and stock account statements because you won't be renting the property—you'll simply be acquiring it, fixing it up, and selling it within a short period of time. Just remember that this convenience has a price, and it's you who pay it.

Documentation levels have certain clients that they fit and are designed to streamline the loan process.

Documenting Income

Income that is used to calculate debt ratios can come in a variety of flavors. Some people are self-employed, while others work for someone else. Some have interest income, and some get pensions or annuities.

Some play baseball six months out of the year. Some write books. Some are professional gamblers. Some are nurses who work for several different hospitals on a contract basis. Some sell cars. Or yachts.

The fact is that different people get paid in different ways, and for each of these ways there is a method of verifying income. Furthermore, some income can't be counted because it doesn't fall into the qualifying income category.

Let's break down the different types of income and how each is verified and used by lenders to evaluate a loan application

W2 Income

This is the most common form of employment income. You work for a company on a salary or on an hourly basis, get a regular paycheck with all its withholdings, and get a W2 at the end of every year.

Your income is verified by third parties, meaning that your employer sends both you and the IRS a statement showing how much you were paid during the past year. This is the easiest type of income to document. Lenders love W2 income because it streamlines the process and no other verification is required.

W2 income also comes with another benefit: pay stubs from your employer.

When you get a paycheck, your pay stub will show how much you get paid and how often. If you get paid by the hour, it will show an hourly rate and how many hours you worked. If you get a salary, it will also show your gross earnings for that period and what time frame the period represents.

For instance, if you get paid on the first and fifteenth of the month, the pay stub will reflect both the amount paid and for what period, such as, "from 10–01 through 10–15."

A not-uncommon confusion occurs when people get paid every other week, yet still think of two pay periods as their "monthly" income.

If you get paid $3,000 every other Friday, you don't get paid $6,000 per month, although I still see loan applications filled out that way. When this happens, the borrower is short-changing herself.

If you get paid $3,000 every other Friday you make $6,500 per month, not $6,000. When you get paid every other week, your annual income is calculated by multiplying your gross monthly income by 26 (52 weeks divided by every other week) then dividing by 12 (months).

In this example,

$$\$3,000 \times 26 = \$78,000 \div 12 = \$6,500$$

Why is this important? If you want to buy a property that the lender thinks is out of your reach, make sure that the loan officer is calculating your income correctly. Most of all, make sure that you complete the loan application correctly yourself so that there'll be no mistake.

I've seen too many cases where the consumer puts down the wrong income information and the loan officer doesn't double-check the figures. Watch out.

The Self-Employed Borrower

After you've built your real estate portfolio to the point where you want to quit your current job and move into real estate full time, be prepared for a new way of documenting your income and some new rules that will apply to you.

When you're self-employed, the lender first and foremost wants to see that you have been self-employed for at least two years.

This is the part that most frequently trips up real estate investors;

they quit their job, then apply for a new home loan (one that they had been approved for in the past), but now, since they are newly self-employed, they haven't been self-employed for two years and are declined.

How does a lender know that you've been self-employed for two years? Can't you just say so? No, you really can't. That's a stiff guideline, and for a couple of reasons.

First, the lender wants to know if you're successful at being self-employed. Can you make money on your own instead of working for somebody else and getting a regular paycheck? Second, and just as important, can you also run a business as well as being profitable?

Those are two very important questions.

Sure, you need to make money. All too often, businesses look between the sofa cushions for expenses to write off, including mortgage interest and property taxes. But other payments, such as vehicle expense, entertainment, client lunches, and insurance, suddenly become tax deductible for many of the self-employed.

You need to make enough money to cover all your mortgage interest, property taxes, maintenance, and other business expenses and still show a profit. The lender won't use your gross rental income (income before all your deductions) to qualify you; the lender will use your income after all your deductions.

If your deductions eat too much into your gross profit, you could find yourself not being able to qualify because your net income is reduced.

Second, as well as making a profit, the lender wants to see your ability to run a business. Are you making money from one year to the next? Are you showing increased income from one year to the next? Is your business growing or shrinking?

Lenders will examine your tax returns for consecutive years, looking for increased income—and definitely not a loss. That's one of the reasons that lenders require two years' tax returns from self-employed borrowers.

One interjection here: If you've been self-employed for several years

and the past two years weren't as good as the previous years, then feel free to provide three years' tax returns.

Lenders will average your previous two years' income for loan qualification purposes. If you made $80,000 two years ago and $100,000 last year, the lender won't use the $100,000; it will use the average, or $90,000.

Sometimes a business simply has a bad year. If you made $80,000 two years ago and $40,000 last year, the lender not only will drop your income to $60,000 but could also be very wary as to why there was a 50 percent decline in income.

"Is there a problem here?" the lender might ask.

But if you also show that you also made $75,000 three years ago along with the $80,000 and $40,000, you can make a case that the $40,000 was an aberration by providing additional tax returns and an explanation of what happened during that "down" year.

"I bought additional properties that year before I had them rented" or "I had some significant one-time repairs to a property" or some similar answer will suffice.

Being able to not only make money but manage the nuances that a self-employed person has to deal with is part of the package. Some people can make money at a business, yet run it into the ground because of bad management.

What if you make a stated loan application while you're self-employed and the lender wants to see your two-year history of self-employment?

Providing tax returns won't help because a stated income loan doesn't use tax returns.

Lenders will accept a letter from your accountant that says something like, "I'm Sally the CPA, and I have done David Reed's taxes for two years, and he has been self-employed during that time."

This "CPA letter" is common in such instances. The lender just wants to see verification from a third party (your CPA) that you meet the minimum two years' requirement to be self-employed.

You don't use a CPA? Then some other verification will work, such as a business license with your or your company's name and date on it. Heck, I've even used a Yellow Pages ad from a two-year-old phone book.

But here's a trick: Don't quit your day job while you're beginning to invest in real estate if you're planning on becoming a full-time real estate investor. Instead, acquire your property, collect your rent or flip your houses, and do it for a minimum of two years.

Your tax returns will show this self-employment income while you're still working at your current job, and you can have the best of both worlds—getting into real estate investing while qualifying for the lender's two-year minimum self-employed guidelines, all the while still keeping your "normal" job!

Rental Income

Using rental income has a few twists of its own.

For self-employed borrowers, lenders will use tax returns to show rental income, which is reported on Schedule E in the return, then again average it over the previous two years.

For others, a lender will use a lease agreement as verification of rental income, sometimes along with some bank statements showing rent deposits.

If you get $1,500 per month from a rental, a lender will want to look at a lease agreement that states that amount. Knowing that lease agreements can easily be manipulated, it may also look for bank statements showing a $1,500 deposit on or about the first of the month, or whenever rent is due on the property.

If your renter pays you $2,000 per month, be prepared to provide not just the lease agreement but your three most recent bank statements showing a separate $2,000 deposit. If your renter pays you in cash, be sure to deposit that cash in a bank account if you think you'll need that income to help qualify you for future loan applications.

Furthermore, if you're applying for a mortgage and you have dam-

aged credit, a lender can ask for 12 months' bank statements showing that $2,000 deposit. In fact, a lender can ask for just about anything it wants to ask for as long as what it asks for is necessary to approve the loan and it applies that same guideline to everyone, regardless of sex, color, or creed.

There's also a twist as to whether a lender will require tax returns or a lease agreement to verify income. If you acquired the property after you filed your most recent tax returns, the lender will most often use a lease agreement and not the tax return.

If you acquired the property before you filed your most recent tax return, the lender will want to see that tax return to see what you showed as income. You'll also want to keep a copy of your settlement statement that will reconcile the income received from your rental property from the time you bought the property.

If your tax return shows $5,000 in income from last year, but you owned the property for only two months, have your settlement statement handy to show that you bought the property in October and received rental income for November and December. Receiving $5,000 for two months equals $2,500 per month, whereas receiving $5,000 for twelve months equals $417 per month. That's a big difference.

When lenders don't require tax returns for rental income, they'll simply adjust your gross income lower. They'll do this by multiplying your gross rental income by 25 percent and subtracting that figure from your gross income rather than using the full figure. This 25 percent reduction covers maintenance, vacancies, and other deductions commonly associated with rentals.

If you show on your loan application that you receive $1,000 per month in rental income, the lender will automatically deduct 25 percent of that and give you $750 per month for qualifying purposes. This can lead to a loss and a potential problem if you need rental income to qualify you for a new mortgage.

Suppose your mortgage payment is $1,000 and your rental income is $1,000 per month. You're breaking even, right? Wrong. With a deduc-

tion of 25 percent, your income is $750 per month, and you now have a "loss" of $250 per month.

Instead of gaining $1,000 to help you qualify, you are now adding $250 to your liabilities. It's not a wash, it's a bill.

In addition, lenders use your property taxes and insurance along with your mortgage payment to determine net income. Principal, interest, taxes, and insurance, or PITI, is the number used.

Now take a $1,000 mortgage payment plus $150 in property taxes per month and $50 for property insurance, and the PITI figure is $1,200.

You need to collect $1,600 per month to break even. Deducting 25 percent from $1,600 gives $1,200. Then deduct taxes and insurance of $200 per month, and the qualifying rental income is $1,000. Break-even.

Do you need the rental income from the property you're considering buying to help qualify you? Can you afford the new mortgage without rental income?

Unless you have experience being a landlord and collecting rents, managing properties, and everything else that goes along with that, most lenders won't use rental income to help qualify you. No experience, no income.

There's also a problem if you want to use the potential income from a property to help qualify you. For instance, suppose you have been a landlord for more than two years, and you can prove it from your tax returns along with signed lease agreements. However, the property you want to buy is vacant and there is no income stream.

Lenders will not use anticipated income from a rental to help qualify you; there has to be income already there. Just as a lender wouldn't qualify someone based upon using anticipated income as employment income—the person getting a well-paying job—neither will anticipated or expected rents be counted.

Documenting Assets

A fully documented loan that lists assets will need to have those assets verified by third parties; normally that means by your bank or investment

institution. Verification comes from two basic sources: through a verification of deposit, or VOD, or by providing statements from the accounts.

A VOD is a written request from the lender to the bank or investment company asking:

Does this account belong to the borrower?

How much is in the account?

What is the average balance in this account?

The first question is easy to understand, and so is the second. But the third question also reveals another verification secret that lenders like to use: the average balance.

Lenders want to see down payment money come directly from you and your own assets. You can't borrow from someone else to put money down on a property on which you want to borrow still more money.

If your current checking account shows a balance of $75,000, then that's good, right? But lenders also ask for an average balance over the previous 90 days. If the average balance is much less than $75,000, that could indicate that those funds were borrowed from someone else, creating a possible secondary lien on the property you want to invest in.

For example, if your current balance is $75,000, but your average balance over the most recent 90-day period is only $25,000, then there must have been one huge deposit during that 90-day period to bring the current balance up so high. In this case, around $67,000 was deposited at some point during that 90-day time frame to both add to the current balance and adjust the average balance.

Lenders will want an explanation of the origin and terms, if any, of the large deposit.

Another way lenders verify assets is simply by looking at your bank or investment statements. This is easy enough and the least time-consuming way to do this. Upon application, you provide those bank statements to your lender to show that the money is in the bank or invest-

ment account. That way, the lender won't have to fill out a VOD form and send it to your bank.

Remember, though, that if those statements show a $67,000 deposit, you need to be prepared to not only explain but verify the large deposit, just as you would have to with a lender-prepared VOD.

One interesting note here: The better your credit, the fewer statements you may have to provide. If you have excellent credit along with solid debt ratios, a lender might not ask for three months' statements, but only for your most current one. If that's the case, there won't be any sign of a large deposit if the deposit occurred before your most recent statement.

I recall a client who lives in Colorado who bought a condo in Austin, Texas. He provided a statement from one of his accounts that showed a rather large single deposit, of over $500,000.

The underwriter wanted to know where the deposit came from: Was it a loan? My client's credit scores were in the high 700 range, so he needed to provide only one statement, his most recent, and not three.

In fact, it wasn't a loan; it was a retirement disbursement from his previous employer in California, where he had worked for nearly 20 years. The money was perfectly legitimate; it was just that now we had to provide documentation of the source of those funds.

The money had been distributed to him recently, so he needed to get a statement from his previous employer showing how much he was to get and match that amount with what was deposited.

The interesting thing about this verification process was that when he first sent in his statement, he was in between statements and would soon be getting his new one—the statement that did not show the huge deposit, but only the current balance.

Instead of providing yet additional paperwork from various sources tracking down the retirement disbursement, we simply waited for the next statement, which showed only the balance, and provided an explanation letter covering the difference between the two statements.

We did not have to provide third-party verification of the source, as

the client had to provide only the most recent statement. Since there was no large deposit on the most recent statement, we didn't have to explain it. Actually, since the underwriter had already seen the deposit on the previous statement, we did have to explain it, but we didn't have to go through reams of additional paperwork to verify the source of the large deposit.

One last item regarding assets: There are liquid and semiliquid assets that lenders can use to determine whether you have enough money to qualify. Liquid assets are those that you can access at your leisure: bank accounts, stock accounts, and such.

Semiliquid assets are IRAs, 401(k) rollovers, or other retirement accounts. The lender won't make you cash them in but will normally give you credit for 70 percent of the amount noted on your retirement statements.

If you have a 401(k) balance of $100,000, then your lender will credit your application with $70,000 in cash reserves, as this is the approximate amount you would receive after penalties and taxes paid on an early 401(k) withdrawal.

This is important when documenting cash reserves is a requirement of your approval.

Keep Records at the Ready

This brings us to the final part of documentation: Be prepared.

Knowing ahead of time what your lender might ask for means that there'll be less stress during the loan application process. Keep copies of everything, and simply have your very own "mortgage application file" available each time you need it to buy investment property.

At a minimum, keep on hand:

Two years' most recent tax returns, with all schedules

Last two years' W2s and 1099s

A year-to-date profit and loss statement

Three months' most recent statements, all accounts

All lease agreements

All settlement statements from previous sales

Copies of current insurance coverage with premium amounts

Copies of current tax bills showing property taxes

If you keep this information at your fingertips and also current, you'll never be concerned with finding this or locating that—it'll be there when you need it.

All that having been said, do *not* provide all of this documentation at the same time you apply for the mortgage loan; instead, wait until your lender has reviewed your initial loan application.

Mortgage loans used to be underwritten manually, one by one. In the olden days, mortgage loans were documented and verified first, then submitted to the lender for approval.

Now, however, mortgage loans are approved using an automated underwriting system, or AUS.

Loan Approvals in Minutes

With an AUS, either you complete a loan application by yourself online or your loan officer completes it for you, and then the information is electronically submitted to an automated system that automatically "approves" your loan by calculating debt ratios, pulling credit scores, and looking at listed assets.

This process takes only a few moments. Your information is input into the system, and along with your approval, the system gives a list of the things you need to provide—*after* your loan is approved, not before.

The better your loan profile, the less documentation you will have to provide. If you have excellent credit and solid assets, you may have to

supply your bank statements for only one month instead of three. Or the AUS may ask for only one year's tax returns and not two. Or none at all.

The benefit is twofold: The lender reviews only the information required to approve the loan, not every last piece of documentation you've ever had to produce (lenders don't like paperwork either), and you provide only the minimal amount of documentation needed, which also saves you time. But it can also save you more headaches, and there is probably a nice, middle ground.

Each time you apply for an investment loan, you're examined all over again. And if you rate-shop lenders every time and pick the best lender, who might be better in total loan cost by $200, you'll find that you may be providing the same explanations about past income or providing the very same lease agreements or hazard insurance policies.

That's fine as long as you don't start pulling your hair out. From a lender's standpoint, we want loans to go quickly and smoothly as well, but we also want to be within lending guidelines and to make good loans.

As a lender, I want to spend less time dotting i's and crossing t's, and more time getting my clients into properties with the best rates and terms I can, along with the least amount of headaches.

If you have good credit and an initial equity position of 20 percent down, it's smooth sailing for me. And most important, it's smooth sailing for you.

You'll know after your first few investment purchases which level of documentation is best for you, but I can tell you that a stated income, verified assets is perhaps the most convenient in terms of the trade-off between price (minimal, if any), time to close, and paperwork required. This is especially true if you own multiple properties with various income streams.

Creative Financing for Real Estate Investments

There are other sources of financing, ones that don't come from Fannie Mae, Freddie Mac, or alt lenders. In fact, "creative" can simply mean applying existing loan requirements in another, albeit legal, way.

Let's take a moment here first and make it clear that *creative* doesn't mean fraud. Suppose you have a loan officer who says something like, "You know, we might have to get a little creative here to get this thing done."

Run, don't walk.

Falsifying a mortgage application to qualify for a home loan is a felony. Money crosses state lines, making it wire fraud. You sign a loan application that asks you to say, in various formats, that what you're telling is the truth, and so on.

The problem with loan fraud is that the result isn't merely a slap on the wrist or the lender saying, "Oh, that's okay; we really want to make this loan, so we'll overlook the fact that you inflated your income."

Loan fraud has become front and center one of the main focuses of the FBI and state regulatory agencies.

Fraud has become easier to accomplish as a result of the advent of new types of mortgage loans, specifically the stated documentation loans mentioned in the previous chapter. Even if fudging an income amount seems harmless, the consequences can be worse than just losing a property.

For instance, let's say you and your partner decide to buy your first rental property, and you need both incomes to qualify. So both of you apply, and you find out that your debt ratios are too high to qualify for the property you want.

Then you decide, or perhaps your loan officer suggests, that you will instead apply for a stated loan and have your partner put down $10,000 per month income instead of $5,000 per month. Even though this isn't the case, eventually you'll probably make that amount, right? At least, that's what your loan officer is telling you: "Aw, come on. Everybody does it; just put it down; nobody will check it, and you'll own that new property, and besides, you'll make that one day anyway, won't you?"

"It's really not lying if someday you do make that amount. And if you don't buy now, the property will be worth $20,000 more in six months, and by that time you'll have sold it anyway." Says you and the loan officer.

Several things happened during this discourse, but the main ones are that the loan officer told you how much to put on your loan application so that you could qualify, and you agreed and completed the application. So far, both you and the loan officer have committed fraud.

What's interesting about this scenario is that the lender the loan officer works for probably doesn't know about the misstatements. In fact, the lender probably never saw the previous application because the loan was declined and sent to the lender's storage vault in accordance with regulations.

When the new loan application appears, with the brand-new qualifying income, it's simply seen as a new loan application that qualifies for the stated income and asset loan.

You apply, you get approved, and then you move on.

But wait—something happened while you were busy making plans. Your partner lost his job and no longer has an income, not even the one he had before he falsified it. And you can't sell in six months as you intended, because there were suddenly more than a few properties in your price range on the market, so it's going to take some time.

Your partner begins to drain his savings to help pay the mortgage, but soon he tells you that he no longer can. Then you're on your own.

Your tenants move out, and you can't find new ones because the influx of new properties on the market is driving down market rentals. Soon you find you're being squeezed, too. So much so that it could affect your ability to pay your own mortgage.

Your rental house goes into foreclosure, and you lose the property.

Guess what? The foreclosing lender will do a little due diligence to make sure the loan application was on the up-and-up. One way it does that is to compare the income that you and your partner listed on your loan application with the tax returns that you filed with the IRS.

If the IRS shows that your partner made only $5,000 per month and not the $10,000 per month that he swore to, there's a problem here, and a big one. You and your partner can expect a lawsuit.

Loan fraud simply isn't worth it. If you don't have the income to buy a property, then you need to wait; nothing is worth spending time in jail for.

And that's not what creative financing is all about.

Creative financing takes legitimate lending rules and applies them to everyday situations. Creative financing can come from an individual, usually either you or the seller, or from an institution.

Creative Financing From an Individual

The most common type of financing from an individual is seller financing. You find a property you want to buy and have the seller carry the

note. Fair enough. But there are some things that you and the seller need to understand.

From the seller's perspective, she may want to know why you're going for private financing instead of getting financing from your bank or mortgage company. In other words, "I'll finance you, but there must be a problem somewhere, so therefore I'm going to ask for a higher interest rate to offset whatever risk might be involved."

Often the problem may be credit issues, but other times it might simply be that you have income that your lender can't currently use to qualify you, meaning that you don't have a two-year history or meet some other traditional guideline. For instance, you might need rental income to qualify, yet you don't have the necessary two years of landlord experience under your belt.

The Multiple Listing Service, or MLS, will typically show homes that have seller financing as part of the package, so you or your Realtor can use homes with owner financing as part of the search criteria, along with other features such as number of bedrooms and price range.

Why do sellers offer financing and not just cash out of the whole deal? There can be a variety of reasons, but sometimes it's a way to get a good, solid return but still keep hold of an asset.

If someone can get an 8.00 percent return from an investment, that's not bad income, and not only does it come every month, but if the buyer doesn't pay, then the owner can take the house back via a foreclosure.

For instance, suppose a retired couple owns a home free and clear, but the stock market isn't doing all that well and their retirement funds are pulling in maybe 4 percent per year. With seller financing, they can get much more than that 4 percent from a willing buyer.

Note that seller financing will also mean higher than market interest rates. If you can go out and get 6.50 percent on the market, then you might expect to pay 8.00 to 8.50 percent to a seller. The seller knows that you might have a specific reason for wanting seller financing and that

it's likely that you couldn't qualify under conventional terms. In return for that higher level of risk, the seller may ask for a higher rate.

Also be prepared to provide the seller with as much documentation as you might provide to a traditional lender, especially your credit report and your income verification. If your income is hard to verify, show the owner how you're getting paid and how he will get his money.

If there are credit issues, the seller may ask for a larger down payment and increase your interest rate, just as a traditional lender would.

It's up to you. If the property cash flows work out and you can get into the property on terms that you agree to, go ahead and buy the property, and get two years' landlord experience under your belt. If rates are still low, you can refinance the property once you have that experience.

The Seller Carries the Note

Another option for seller financing is to have the seller carry a second mortgage note behind a first mortgage acquired at your mortgage company. This can be a benefit if you want to put less than 20 percent down, yet still avoid private mortgage insurance, or PMI.

For instance, suppose you want to buy a nice fourplex for $300,000 with as little down as possible. You can't find a lender who will loan you 90 percent of the sales price, but you find one who will loan you 80 percent.

With a seller carry, you can put down 10 percent; then the seller carries a second note at 10 percent of the value, and the first lender issues a loan at 80 percent of the sales price.

Sales price	$300,000
First lien note	$240,000
Down payment	$ 30,000
Seller carry	$ 30,000

With this structure, you've put the minimum down and avoided PMI with a seller carry.

Wraparound

A wraparound, or "wrap," is a way for you to buy from the seller where you make the mortgage payment to the seller, and she then turns around and pays her mortgage company.

Your mortgage is "wrapped" around another one. Wraps are negotiated between you and the seller, and any terms you come up with, as long as you both agree to them, are valid.

One note of caution with a wrap: Most conventional loans require that the lender be notified of any change in title, meaning that the property has changed ownership. If this is the case, a wrap may not be your best choice.

Some people say, "Well, who would know?" as long as you make your payments to the seller and the seller continues to make payments to the original mortgage company. And that's a good question; as long as there are no missed payments or other issues with the property, then the original lender might not ever find out.

But it might. And if it does, any agreement you may have had with the seller will be void, and it's likely that you will lose any equity or ownership in the property whatsoever. Since from a title standpoint the property was never transferred to you, if the home goes into foreclosure, you'll lose whatever you put in. From the original lender's viewpoint, the home was never yours, so it is the original owner who is wrapping for you who gets the home taken away from him, and you get nothing.

Assumptions

You can also search for properties that have assumable mortgages, where you not only buy the property but also slide right into whatever mortgage is already on the house. There are two types of assumable mortgages, qualifying and nonqualifying.

Qualifying assumptions mean that, yes, the loan is assumable, but you have to qualify on your own, just as if you were applying for a new mortgage. Nonqualifying means that you don't have to qualify. You can

have terrible credit or no job or some other detrimental credit factor. The house and the note are still yours.

The trouble with nonqualifying assumptions is that there simply aren't that many of them around any longer. FHA and VA loans used to have this nonqualifying feature built into them. The theory was that if a homeowner was having problems paying the mortgage, she could sell the home quickly and have someone else take over the payments, keeping the home out of foreclosure.

The VA stopped including a nonqualifying feature in 1988; the FHA had done so in 1974. Too many people with bad credit assumed these loans and didn't make the payments, starting the foreclosure process all over again.

Assuming that you do find an assumable nonqualifying loan, since the mortgage will be 20 to 30 years old, you'll probably have to come to the closing table with plenty of equity to pay the seller. A seller won't give up that kind of money, and there's no reason for him to do so.

Lease Option

A lease option, or "lease with option to buy," is a method of financing when there are some credit or down payment issues or some other problem that's keeping you from getting conventional financing, yet you still want to acquire the property.

With a lease option, you lease the property for a specific period of time, then buy the property for an agreed-upon price at the end of your lease period.

Say you find a house for $150,000 and you want a lease option. You and the seller agree that you will lease the house for $1,000 per month and will buy the home at $150,000 after one year. Your price is set in stone, and if you did your homework correctly and home prices in that area appreciate 10 percent, then one year from now you will have a $165,000 home that you contracted to buy for $150,000.

Some lease-purchase agreements use a portion of the $1,000 per

month as part of a down payment when you buy the home after one year. While this is certainly legitimate, it is important to note that whatever part of that $1,000 goes toward the purchase must be over and above what market rents are for properties in that area.

If you want $100 to go toward the home and $900 purely for rent, your lender will want to verify that rent for similar properties in that area is in fact $900 per month and not $1,000. If market rent is in fact $1,000, not $900, and you want a $1,200 credit toward your down payment (12 months times $100), the lender won't give it to you.

The $100 per month will be considered part of the rent, and anything the seller credits you with will be considered a gift and the deal can't close with gifts.

To make sure you get properly credited, validate the market rent in your area, either by finding rentals in the newspaper or in listings or by hiring an appraiser to perform a rental survey for you, the best way to determine market rent in such a case.

Lease options are not going to be your best financing vehicle. This technique should be used only if you have no other way of acquiring the property and you have an exit strategy. In fact, the deal really, really has to make sense for you.

First, you'll be subletting the property to others. If you negotiate a purchase price and a rental amount that both is substantially equivalent to the market rent and also adds money above the market rent to go toward a down payment, then what rent will your tenants be paying? You need to have cash flow, right?

If your lease-option payments to the seller are $1,000, then your tenants will have to pay less than that. What seller would do that? Why not just charge the current tenants the market rent?

I mention lease options as a vehicle for real estate investment only because occasionally I see it written or posted somewhere that such a transaction is an easy way to "buy with no money down" or some such. There can be instances where a lease option makes sense, but those occasions are very, very rare.

Creative Financing From an Institution

Portfolio Lending

A portfolio loan is one that the lender keeps in house—in its portfolio. The lender does not intend to sell the loan on the secondary markets anywhere, anytime. Your retail bank offers such loans.

When lenders make loans, they have to conform to lending guidelines. They do so for one main reason, and that's to provide the lender with a level of liquidity, or options. Lenders can make money by selling loans to one another or to Fannie Mae or Freddie Mac, or they can sit back and collect the interest payments each and every month. Or they can do any combination of the two. But this desire for liquidity also means that there can be very few exceptions to the lending guidelines. If a loan requires that you have been self-employed for two years and prove it by providing tax returns, and you've been self-employed for only 18 months, then you probably have to wait. But not with a portfolio loan.

A portfolio loan is designed more for you and less to meet a particular lending guideline. Forget guidelines such as number of properties owned or when you can or cannot use rental income to qualify you.

To apply for a portfolio loan, you don't call up a bank and say, "Hey, I need one of those portfolio loans"; instead, you establish a relationship with your commercial banker. Go to the bank where you have your personal and business checking accounts and schedule an appointment with your banker.

The retail bank will not use an automated underwriting program, but instead will evaluate your overall scenario, just like lenders did in the olden days. Your credit will be reviewed, your income and assets will be verified, and perhaps you will even be asked for a couple of references from business associates.

Portfolio lending can sometimes be a little easier than conventional loans, as once you get your first loan placed, it's easier to get the next one. You've already gone through the approval process, and as long as

nothing has changed, your banker will be more than happy to give you another portfolio loan.

That's what banks do: lend money. Portfolio loans are a bank's strong asset. They are constantly looking for projects to fund.

Portfolio loans also have features that might not fit your financing goals. They are often short term—perhaps a maximum of two to three years. Banks don't like to keep their money tied up for very long. They can't because their profits are interest-sensitive.

If you get a loan from your bank at 6.00 percent and one year later rates are at 8.00 percent, then the bank sees your loan as having a "loss" of 2.00 percent. It's red ink on the bank's balance sheet. That's why portfolio loans can have a very short shelf-life: to give banks some flexibility.

Portfolio loans will also be adjustable-rate mortgages. Your ARM index can change from month to month, and your payments will then change too. A common ARM index for a bank is the prime rate, or the rate banks can charge their best commercial customers. If you're not one of the bank's "top-shelf" customers, you will probably also have a margin of 1, 2, or even 3 percent added to the prime rate.

Portfolio loans also will require a minimum of 20 percent down in most cases. Once you've established yourself as a good bank customer and have all your accounts at that bank, this down payment requirement can be reduced, but it will not be eliminated.

Higher rates, a larger down payment, and shorter maturity—those are the negatives of portfolio loans. The positives are both speed and getting a loan that wouldn't be approved under conventional lending guidelines. It's nice to be able to call up your banker and say, "Hey, David, I need a couple of hundred thousand to buy some duplexes next week."

Equity Transfers

If you're property rich and cash poor, or if you simply don't want to tie up any of your cash to buy investment property, then look around at

CREATIVE FINANCING FOR REAL ESTATE INVESTMENTS   191

some of your current investments to see how much equity might be available to use to buy more property. The easiest and least expensive source of equity is your primary residence. Mortgage rates for owner-occupied properties are usually about 3/8 percent lower than those for investment properties, so examine your primary residence first; it's your cheapest source. And there are two distinct ways of converting that equity into cash: cash-out refinancings and home equity lines of credit, or HELOCs.

A cash-out refinancing entails refinancing your current mortgage while at the same time pulling out additional money that will go directly to you in the form of a check. The maximum cash-out refinancing for almost every loan is an 80 percent loan to value ratio, or 80 percent LTV.

But one note of caution: Pulling out cash up to the maximum will cost you, typically about another $1/4$ point or more. If you cash out to 75 percent of the value instead, there will be no penalty.

Here's an example of a cash-out refinancing on a primary residence.

Value of home	$300,000
Current mortgage balance	$130,000
Closing costs	$ 3,000
75% LTV	$225,000

Now subtract the current mortgage balance and closing costs from the value (as determined by a new appraisal on the property), and the result is $92,000 cash out.

At 80 percent, the refinancing would look like this:

Value of home	$300,000
Current mortgage balance	$130,000
Closing costs	$ 3,000
80% LTV	$240,000

Cash out in this example would be $107,000.

If you borrowed 80 percent of the value instead of 75 percent, you would be hit with another $1/4$ point in fees, or $562, which would be

deducted from your loan proceeds. You paid $562 to get another $15,000. Expensive, but available.

There is no reason to borrow the maximum. If you don't need or want $92,000, but instead want only $50,000, then just borrow that. You're not required to borrow the maximum; you just can't exceed predetermined limits.

But don't do a cash-out refinancing if a refinancing isn't already in your picture. If you have a 7.00 percent rate and interest rates move to 6.00 percent, then it makes sense to refinance, and you can go ahead and pull out cash either for immediate use or to hold for a purchase sometime in the future.

Perhaps you find that you can save money by refinancing, pulling out some equity, and depositing it in an interest-bearing account while you look for the perfect duplex. Don't cash out unless you have another reason to refinance, because there are costs involved in a refinancing just as with any other purchase money mortgage.

A way to tap into your equity without refinancing is simply to get a HELOC. It's quicker and cheaper. A HELOC is a line of credit that is placed in a second, or subordinate, position to your current first mortgage. There are few, if any, closing costs for a HELOC, and normally fees are charged only if you don't use the credit during the course of a 12-month period. Even then the fees are nominal, perhaps a couple of hundred bucks.

There isn't a full-blown appraisal, either; the lender will typically make a value determination using an automated valuation service that looks at recorded sales in your neighborhood and compares them to your property, less any mortgage balance.

A HELOC is sort of like a checkbook. In fact, you'll get a checkbook with a HELOC, and when you need the funds, you simply write a check. Interest will accrue only if you actually use any of the money.

HELOCs are typically limited to 100 percent of the valuation of the property. They can be more or less than that depending upon the type of

loan and other state-imposed restrictions, but for the most part, you can get a HELOC for 100 percent of the value of the property.

Unlike the previous example, you can now borrow more money, and it costs less than a cash-out refinance.

Value of home	$300,000
Current mortgage balance	$130,000
Closing costs	$ -0-
100% LTV	$170,000

The maximum HELOC available is $170,000.

A HELOC can be used over and over again. If you used $50,000 as a down payment on an investment property, then later sold another property, you can repay the $50,000 you borrowed and restore the full amount of your HELOC. It literally is a credit card on your house.

It's also adjustable, which means that the rate you pay on this money can rise and fall with market rates in general.

Another form of second mortgage is an equity second. Instead of there being a revolving line of credit as in a HELOC, the amount of the second mortgage is fixed and you get all the proceeds at the closing table.

An equity second, or a home equity loan, can have a fixed or adjustable rate, and as with all second loans, the rates will usually be a couple of percentage points higher than the rates on first mortgages are.

Equity seconds also have few closing costs. However, you begin paying interest on them immediately because you took money and deposited it in your bank account. Equity lending is available on any property you own; it's just that with your primary residence, it's cheaper. And you can have more than one equity loan if you have the properties to match.

If you have 10 houses and each of them has an equity loan of $10,000, you then have $100,000 available to you to buy still more property. Equity lending is probably the most convenient source to tap when buying real estate.

Securitizing Other Assets

A distant cousin of equity lending is a pledged asset mortgage, or PAM. A PAM securitizes other tradable assets, such as stock portfolios, retirement accounts, or other publicly traded items and is a loan that is guaranteed by those assets.

If you own $100,000 in stocks, you can get a PAM at, say, 50 percent of that amount, or at whatever terms you can agree upon with whoever is holding your stocks and investments for you.

This is a form of equity lending because you're getting a loan based upon the equity (value) you have built up in your portfolio.

Hard Money Lending

One final piece of creative financing is called *hard money.*

Hard money is really a bad moniker. It implies that you're getting your loan from loan sharks who will break your arm if you're one day late or who are interested only in foreclosing on your property.

The fact is, the term *hard money* has simply been around too long to make any changes in terminology, even though hard money lenders themselves try to distance themselves from it.

Hard money is probably best described as being in between borrowing from a bank and taking on a business partner. A partner might be willing to finance your deal, but would want half the profits, and a bank would finance you at prime rate plus maybe a point or two.

First, hard money is for cases where either the property or the person buying it doesn't exactly fit either the conventional or the portfolio mold.

Second, hard money is usually loaned out only for very short terms when compared to 30-year loans. Hard money loans are typically for three months to a year.

Hard money can sometimes be considered as a way to get someone out of a jam. A common instance would be a developer who is almost, but not quite, finished with his project and needs some more funds to finish out development.

The developer would get a hard money loan to finish out the project, then pay back the hard money loan when the project sold.

A hard money lender needs to see a true exit strategy. In other words, how will I (the hard money lender) get my money back?

Hard money deals also require a good solid equity position, usually at least 65 percent LTV but sometimes as low as 50 percent LTV.

These loans depend less on credit and more on the assets involved, and thus they require a solid equity position. You can have damaged credit and still qualify for a hard money loan; you can even have hard-to-prove income as well because the hard money lender is banking on the sale of the project.

It's this sale of your project that you have to make clear.

Hard money loans also close quickly, sometimes in a matter of days rather than weeks, but while they're quick, they're also a little pricey when it comes to interest rate—often 5 to 10 percent above the prime rate.

But that's okay because the loan is for such a short term. It's cheaper than other alternatives or no alternative at all.

Hard money lenders typically get their business by advertising or by making calls to local banks telling the bank that they'll take referrals of deals that the bank can't do. If there's enough equity in a property, there's really no situation where a deal can't be done.

Blanket Mortgage

A blanket mortgage, as the name implies, is one big loan that covers several properties. This type of mortgage is available at your retail or commercial bank.

Blanket mortgages will most often require 20 percent down and can carry either a fixed or a variable rate. They're cheaper because there's only one closing for, say, 10 properties, but you won't get the absolute lowest rates for these loans.

Blanket mortgages are designed to purchase several similar proper-

ties in a neighborhood or several units in a condominium project simultaneously at one fell swoop. Blanket loans help you acquire a multitude of properties with one note in a quick fashion.

With a blanket mortgage, it's important that you have a reconveyance clause, which allows you to sell one property at a time and still keep the original note. Some blanket mortgages won't allow for a partial conveyance, meaning that if you want to sell one unit, you'll have to either sell them all or find new financing. The benefit with a blanket is that it's simple and is usually used when you find a terrific opportunity and want to close quickly.

If you found 10 houses you wanted to buy, you'd traditionally have to have 10 separate closings, which could quite possibly drive you through the roof. With a blanket, you'd have one loan for 10 properties.

Blankets are considered to be commercial loans; therefore you can get a blanket loan at your retail or commercial bank.

1031 Exchange

You've no doubt heard the term "1031 exchange" with regard to investment real estate. It is called that because the "1031" is the section of the IRS tax code that deals with tax deferment.

A 1031 exchange isn't really a method to finance real estate but a way to transfer equity from one property to buy another, deferring income taxes on the sale of the property being sold.

Say you have a duplex that's worth $200,000 that you paid $100,000 for and you want to buy another duplex for $200,000. Instead of selling the duplex for $200,000 and getting taxed on the $100,000 gain, you instead find a like property to "swap" by exchanging your property from the one you wish to buy.

You can use a 1031 as your down payment should the equity in your current property not be enough to completely purchase the new one. Your $200,000 duplex for another $200,000 duplex would be a straightforward exchange. But if you wanted to buy a $300,000 duplex and

needed to finance the remainder, you'd have to come up with the balance just like with any other real estate loan.

1031s entail several rules you need to follow, and you'll need counsel to help make sure you're complying with all the IRS guidelines regarding property exchanges. For instance, a 1031 swap must be for like properties. You can't swap a bed-and-breakfast for your duplex, for instance.

If you have the opportunity to take advantage of a 1031 exchange, make sure you explore this method of transferring gains to invest in still more investment real estate while deferring income taxes on those gains.

Appraisable Assets

You can sell anything that has a value in order to get funds for buying real estate and getting financing. And I'm not kidding.

Do you own gold coins? Do you have artwork? Do you have the finest baseball card collection this side of the Mississippi? If assets can be appraised by an independent third party, you can convert those assets to cash.

Lenders want to verify the source of the funds you use to close. If you need $15,000 to close, then the lender wants to make sure that your $15,000 belongs to you and not to someone else. You didn't borrow those funds from someone else who just might have a legal interest in or hidden lien on the property you're about to purchase.

This is why sudden deposits need to be verified, and if you sell assets for cash, those assets must be something that can have an unbiased value. But you must have the asset appraised before you sell it.

I recall a client in Austin, Texas, who wanted to buy a bed and breakfast and needed to come up with some additional cash for a down payment and cash reserves. He was a book editor, and he also collected rare books on the side.

He sold two of his books, but he first had them appraised by a bookseller, who graded the books; he had a bill of sale, a copy of the check

from the buyer, and a copy of the deposit slip and bank statement showing the deposit.

The underwriter who reviewed the application was not, of course, that big a book collector and had no idea of the value of the books my client had sold. Heck, who would unless you were in the business, right?

The underwriter not only reviewed the appraisal stating the approximate value of the books my client sold, but also reviewed some listings I had provided that I had printed off from eBay auctions showing the very same book, its grade, and what it sold for.

You can't just show up at closing with a box of Liberty silver dollars or a stamp collection. But if you have anything that's appraisable by a third party that can be bought and sold in the open market, then you have an asset that you can use to buy a property.

Builder-Owned Mortgage Companies

While this is not exactly creative financing, there is definitely a twist, and there are some things you need to be on guard for when you are dealing with a builder-owned mortgage company. Of builders who build houses in new subdivisions, nearly every one has its own mortgage firm, or at least an affiliation with such a firm.

When you sign a contract, there will be a stipulation that you must apply to the builder's mortgage company. You don't necessarily have to use the builder's lender, but at a minimum you have to make an application with it.

So far so good, right? You can't have too many people bidding for your business, right?

There will be incentives for you to work with the builder's company, and those incentives are sometimes easy to identify and sometimes not so easy. For instance, suppose your builder will pay 2 points toward your closing fees if you use its lender. That's not bad. But you need to do your own homework before you sign on the dotted line.

A builder-owned mortgage company doesn't have a corner on the

mortgage market. It gets its mortgage rates from the very same wholesale lenders that other brokers do, and the loan officers at that company get paid the very same way that others do.

If a builder offers you 2 points, that sounds like a good thing, but if you compare the quote from the builder's mortgage company with a quote from an outside lender, you'll often find it's a shell game.

I recently closed a loan for a client who bought a newly built rental from a developer who would pay her 2 points to go toward closing costs. The problem was that while the builder's mortgage company "credited" her with 2 points, it also charged 2 points for the same exact rate I could get her. When I pointed this out to the client, it was one of those "aha!" moments. She then confided in me that she had fallen for this the last time she had bought a house from the very same builder.

Don't assume that you're getting a better deal from the builder just because he's paying points or origination fees. You might find that the lender will charge you 2 points, then credit those same points, making the whole thing a wash.

Another thing to watch out for with a builder's mortgage company is the sales contract. Read it carefully, because some contracts have a clause that says something like, "If the builder's mortgage company finds you a mortgage loan and you don't take it, you'll forfeit your deposit."

Still another client of mine lived in Texas but was buying in the Washington, D.C., area. His contract had that language, and it turned out to be very harmful.

The buyer had to sell one of his properties to buy the new one, but his old property wasn't selling and he was approaching his closing date. In fact, his debt ratios with the old and new mortgages, plus his current primary mortgage, were so high that he couldn't qualify for conventional financing.

His ratios were nearly 100 percent, meaning that the total house payments added up to almost everything he made each month—before taxes and withholdings!

The buyer was going to pull out, but the builder reminded him of

the clause in his contract. The builder's mortgage company did indeed have a loan approved for him; it was a no document loan, with no income, employment, or assets being used to approve him. He had excellent credit, but he still hadn't sold his other property.

And he was in trouble. Not only did the builder's mortgage company have him approved, but because his was a no doc loan, his interest rate was significantly higher than what he had originally wanted. He tried to decline the loan, but the builder said, "Fine, but according to the contract you signed, you'll lose your $10,000 deposit."

The buyer was between a rock and a very hard place. If he took the loan he couldn't afford and his property still hadn't sold, he could be foreclosed upon. If he didn't take the loan, he'd lose his $10,000.

I couldn't help him out because I wasn't licensed in the D.C. area, but I did call both the builder's mortgage company and the builder; they basically could have cared less.

The buyer eventually agreed to buy another property if he could find a buyer for the one he had originally agreed to purchase (another shell game), which gave him more time to sell his other rental. He reduced the price enough to sell it quickly and bought the new property from the builder, although he held his nose the whole time when he was signing the closing papers.

The final thing to look at is offers of free upgrades if you use the builder's mortgage company: "Use my mortgage company and I'll throw in an upgrade package that normally costs $20,000."

Again, sounds good. But why would a builder "give" you $20,000 to make only $2,000 on a mortgage loan? It doesn't make good business sense. When you're offered such an incentive, try to compare the true retail price of that incentive (you can always go down to Home Depot or Lowe's and get quotes on the very same thing) with what the builder is offering you.

It's simply hard to judge with upgrade packages. Just make certain you've compared other lenders and mortgage brokers before you take the plunge. I'm not saying all builders' mortgage companies are bad; they're

not. It's just that comparing mortgage loans can be confusing enough without trying to account for upgrades.

You may never have a need for creative financing. But sometimes you may find that you've stumbled across a property that you want to invest in, yet your finances are not quite ready for conventional lending. The creative alternatives in this chapter are all legal and have all been used in the open market. If someone or some business entity approaches you with any type of financing strategy that is not listed in this book as legitimate, then beware.

Epilogue

Making bad financing decisions can wipe out your profits and turn a good deal into a bad one. So can paying too much for closing costs or getting ripped off by a bad loan officer.

When you buy real estate as an investment, remember that you're the person who makes everything go—or not go. Realtors and loan officers get paid commissions when you close a deal. Attorneys make money from you, and so do appraisers and title insurance companies. Suddenly everyone is after your business, and this can be overwhelming. That's okay; they're trying to make money just like anyone else.

But remember that once your deal closes, all those people go back to doing every single day what you may do occasionally. Loan officers close loans every day, and Realtors sell houses every day. It's easy for them to overlook the fact that you're a person and not a transaction. Keep a cool head and remind yourself, while you're in the middle of being a real estate investor, that nobody gets paid unless you close your deal, on terms that make financial sense for you. Nobody. So make sure the financing works for you.

Glossary

Abstract of title. A document used in certain parts of the country when determining whether there are any previous claims on the property in question. The abstract is a written record of the historical ownership of the property that helps to determine whether the property can in fact be transferred from one party to another without any previous claims.

Acceleration. Paying off a loan early, usually at the request or demand of the lender. This is usually specified by an acceleration clause within a loan document that states what must happen for a loan to have to be paid immediately, but it most usually applies when payments are late or missed or there has been a transfer of the property without the lender's permission.

Adjustable-rate mortgage. A loan program where the interest rate may change over the life of the loan. The rate is adjusted in accordance with terms that have been agreed upon by the lender and the borrower, but typically it will change only once or twice a year.

Amortization. The process by which a loan is fully paid off over a predetermined period of time through equal payments made at regular intervals; such a loan is sometimes called a "fully amortized loan." Amortization terms vary, but generally accepted terms run in 5-year increments from 10 to 40 years.

Appraisal. A report that helps to determine the market value of a property. This report can be prepared in various ways as required by a lender, from simply

driving by the property in a car to a full-blown inspection complete with full-color photographs of the real estate. Appraisals compare similar homes in the area to substantiate the value of the property in question.

APR. Annual percentage rate. The cost of money borrowed, expressed as an annual rate. It is a useful consumer tool for comparing different lenders, but unfortunately, it often is not used correctly. The APR is useful only when the same exact loan type is being compared from one lender to another. It doesn't work as well when comparing different types of mortgage programs with different down payments, terms, and so on.

Assumable mortgage. A mortgage that lets buyers take over the terms of the loan along with the house being sold. Assumable loans may be fully qualifying or nonqualifying. With nonqualifying assumable loans, buyers can take over the loan without having to be qualified or otherwise evaluated by the original lender. With qualifying assumable loans, while buyers may assume the terms of the existing note, they must qualify all over again as if they were applying for a brand-new loan.

Balloon mortgage. A type of mortgage where the remaining balance must be paid in full at the end of a preset term. A 5-year balloon mortgage might be amortized over a 30-year period but have the remaining balance be due, in full, at the end of 5 years.

Banker. A lender that uses its own funds to lend money. Historically, these funds would have come from savings accounts from other customers of the same bank. But with the evolution of mortgage banking, that's the old way of doing business. Even though bankers use their own money, it may come from other sources, such as lines of credit, or from selling loans to other institutions.

Basis point. One one-hundredth of a percent. Thus, 25 basis points is $^1/_4$ of a discount point, and 100 basis points is 1 discount point.

Bridge loan. A short-term loan that is used primarily to pull equity out of one property for a down payment on another. This loan is paid off when the original property is sold. Since these are short-term loans, sometimes for just a few weeks, only retail banks generally offer them. Usually the borrower doesn't

make any monthly payments and pays off the loan only when the property is sold.

Brokers. Mortgage companies that arrange a home loan between a banker and a borrower, similar to the way an independent insurance agent operates. Brokers don't have money to lend directly, but they have experience in finding various loan programs that can suit the borrower. Brokers don't work for the borrower, but instead provide mortgage loan choices from other mortgage lenders.

Bundling. The act of putting together several real estate or mortgage services in one package. Instead of paying for an appraisal here and an inspection there, some or all of the buyer's services are packaged together. Usually this allows the service provider to offer discounts on all services, although when the services are bundled, it's hard to look at all of them to see whether you're getting a good deal or not.

Buydown. Paying more money to get a lower interest rate. This is called a permanent buydown, and it is used in conjunction with discount points—the more points, the lower the rate. A temporary buydown is a fixed-rate mortgage that starts at a reduced rate for the first period, and then gradually increases to its final note rate. A temporary buydown for two years is called a 2–1 buydown. A buydown for three years is called a 3–2–1 buydown.

Cash out. Taking equity out of a home in the form of cash during a refinancing. Instead of just reducing your interest rate during a refinancing and financing your closing costs, you finance even more, putting the money in your pocket.

Certificate of Eligibility. The VA form that tells you and your VA lender both if you have VA entitlement available to use to buy or refinance using a VA loan, and if so, how much. It is required on every VA mortgage.

Closing costs. The various fees involved when buying a home or obtaining a mortgage. The fees can come directly from the lender or from others in the transactions whose participation is required if a good loan is to be issued.

Collateral. Property owned by the borrower that is pledged to the lender in case the loan goes bad. A lender makes a mortgage with the house as collateral.

Comparable sales. The part of an appraisal report that lists recent transfers of similar properties in the immediate area of the house being bought. Also called "comps."

Conforming loan. A Fannie Mae or Freddie Mac loan that is equal to or less than the maximum allowable loan limits established by Fannie Mae and Freddie Mac. These limits are changed annually.

Conventional loan. A mortgage using guidelines established by Fannie Mae or Freddie Mac and issued and guaranteed by a lender.

Credit report. A report showing a consumer's payment history along with the consumer's property addresses and any public records.

DD-214. The number of the VA form number that shows your discharge information from the armed services.

Debt consolidation. Paying off all or part of one's consumer debt with equity from a home. This can be part of a refinanced mortgage or a separate equity loan.

Debt ratio. Gross monthly payments divided by gross monthly income, expressed as a percentage. There are typically two debt ratios to be considered: The housing ratio (sometimes called the front ratio) uses the total monthly house payment plus any monthly tax, insurance, PMI, or Homeowners' Association dues divided by gross monthly income, and the total debt ratio (also called the back ratio) uses is the total housing payment plus other monthly consumer installment or revolving debt. Loan debt ratio guidelines are usually denoted as 32/38, with 32 being the front ratio and 38 being the back ratio. Ratio guidelines can vary from loan to loan and from lender to lender.

Deed. A written document evidencing each transfer of ownership in a property.

Deed of trust. A written document giving an interest in the home being bought to a third party, usually the lender, as security.

Delinquent. Being behind on a mortgage payment. Delinquencies are typically recognized as 30 + days delinquent, 60 + days delinquent, and 90 + days delinquent.

Discount points. Percentages of a loan amount; 1 discount point equals 1 percent of a loan balance. Borrowers pay discount points to reduce the interest rate on a mortgage, typically lowering the interest rate by $1/4$ percent for each discount point paid. This is a form of prepaid interest to a lender. Also called "points."

Document stamp. Evidence—usually with a literal ink stamp—of how much tax was paid upon transfer of ownership of property. Called a "doc stamp" in certain states. Doc stamp tax rates can vary based upon locale. Some states don't have doc stamps; others do.

Down payment. The amount of money initially given by the borrower to close a mortgage; it equals the sales price less financing. It's the very first bit of equity you'll have in the home.

Easement. A right of way previously established by a third party. Easement types can vary, but they typically involve the right of a public utility to cross your land—for example, to access an electrical line.

Equity. The difference between the appraised value of a home and any outstanding loans recorded against the property.

Escrow. A term with two meanings, depending upon where you live. On the West Coast, there are escrow agents whose job it is to oversee the closing of a home loan. In other parts of the country, an escrow is a financial account set up by a lender to collect monthly installments for annual tax bills and/or hazard insurance policy renewals.

Escrow agent. On the West Coast, the person or company that handles the home closing, ensuring that documents are signed correctly and that the property transfer has taken place legitimately.

Fannie Mae. Federal National Mortgage Association. Originally established in 1938 by the U.S. government to buy FHA mortgages and provide liquidity in the mortgage marketplace. Its charter was changed in 1968, and it now purchases conventional mortgages as well as government ones.

Fed. The Federal Reserve Board. Among other things, the Fed sets overnight lending rates for banking institutions. It doesn't set mortgage rates.

Fee income. Closing costs received by a lender or broker other than interest or discount points. Fee income can be in the form of loan processing charges, underwriting fees, or other such assessments.

FHA. Federal Housing Agency. Formed in 1934 and now a division of the Department of Housing and Urban Development (HUD), it provides loan guarantees to lenders who make loans following FHA guidelines.

Final inspection. The last inspection of a property, showing that a new home that is being built is 100 percent complete or that a home improvement is 100 percent complete. This lets the lender know that its collateral and its loan are exactly where they should be.

Fixed-rate mortgage. A mortgage whose interest rate does not change throughout the term of the loan.

Float. An active decision not to "lock" or guarantee an interest rate while a loan is being processed. This is usually done because the borrower believes that rates will go down.

Float down. A mortgage loan rate that can drop as mortgage rates drop. There are usually two types of float, one being used during the construction of a home and the other during the period of an interest-rate lock.

Foreclosure. The bad thing that happens when the mortgage isn't repaid. Lenders begin the process of forcefully recovering their collateral when borrowers fail to make loan payments. The lender takes your house away.

Freddie Mac. Federal Home Loan Mortgage Corporation (FHLMC). A corporation established by the U.S. government in 1968 to buy mortgages made under Freddie Mac guidelines from lenders. Similar in structure to Fannie Mae.

Fully indexed rate. The number reached when a loan's index and its margin are added together. This is how the rate on an adjustable-rate note is determined.

Funding. The actual transfer of money from a lender to a borrower.

Gift. When buying a home, a situation in which the down payment and closing costs come from someone other than the borrower instead of coming from the borrower's own accounts. Usually such gifts can come only from family members or from foundations established to help new homeowners.

Ginnie Mae. Government National Mortgage Association (GNMA). A government corporation formed by the U.S. government to purchase government loans like VA and FHA loans from banks and mortgage lenders. Think of it as Fannie Mae or Freddie Mac, only it buys government loans.

Good Faith Estimate. A list of estimated closing costs on a particular mortgage transaction. This estimate must be provided to the loan applicant within 72 hours after the receipt of a mortgage application by the lender or broker.

Hazard insurance. A specific type of insurance that covers homeowners against certain destructive elements, such as fire, wind, and hail. It is usually an addition to homeowner's insurance, but every home loan has a hazard rider.

HELOC. Home equity line of credit. A credit line using a home as collateral. The customer writes a check on the line whenever he needs it and pays only on balances withdrawn. It's much like a credit card, but secured by the property.

Homeowner's insurance. An insurance policy covering not just hazard items but also other things such as liability and personal property.

Impound accounts. Accounts set up by a lender to receive the monthly portion of annual property taxes or hazard insurance. As taxes or insurance comes up for renewal, the lender pays the bill using these funds. Also called "escrow accounts."

Index. The basis for establishing an interest rate, usually with a margin added. Almost anything can be used as an index, but that most common are U.S. Treasuries or similar instruments. See *fully indexed rate.*

Inspection. A structural review of the house that looks for defects in workmanship, damage to the property, or required maintenance. An inspection does not determine the value of the property. A pest inspection looks for infestation by insects such as termites or wood ants.

Intangible tax. A state tax levied on personal property. An intangible asset is an asset not in itself but because of what it represents. A publicly traded stock is an intangible asset. It's not the stock itself that has the value, but what the stock represents in terms of ownership.

Interest rate. The amount charged to borrow money over a specified period of time.

Jumbo loan. A mortgage that exceeds current conforming loan limits.

Junior lien. A second mortgage or one that is subordinate to another loan. This term is not as common as it used to be. You're likely to hear simply "second mortgage" or "piggyback."

Land contract. An arrangement in which the buyer makes monthly payments to the seller, but the ownership of the property does not change hands until the loan is paid in full. This is similar to the way an automobile loan works: When you pay off the loan, you get title to the car.

Land to value. An appraisal term that calculates the value of the land as a percentage of the total value of the home. If the value of the land exceeds the value of the home, it's more difficult to find financing without good comparable sales. Also called lot to value.

Lender policy. Title insurance that protects a mortgagee from defects or previous claims of ownership.

Liability. An obligation of the borrower. Liabilities can be things that show up on a credit report, such as student loans or car payments, but they can also be anything else that one is obligated to pay. It's the ones on the credit report that are used to determine debt ratios.

Loan. Money granted to one party with the expectation of its being repaid.

Loan officer. The person typically responsible for helping mortgage applicants get qualified; she assists in loan selection and loan application. Loan officers can work at banks, credit unions, or mortgage brokerage houses or for bankers.

Loan processor. The person who gathers the documentation required for submission of a loan application. Along with your loan officer, you'll work with this person quite a bit during your mortgage process.

Lock. The act of guaranteeing an interest rate for a predetermined period of time. Loan locks are not loan approvals; they're simply the rate your lender has agreed to give you at the loan closing.

Margin. A number, expressed as a percentage, that is added to a mortgage's index to determine the rate the borrower pays on the note. For example, suppose the index is a six-month CD at 4.00 percent and the margin is 2.00 percent. The interest rate that the borrower pays is 4 + 2, or 6.00 percent. A fully indexed rate is the index plus the margin.

Market value. In an open market, the value of a property that is both the most that the buyer was willing to pay and the least that the seller was willing to

accept at the time of contract. Property appraisals help justify market value by comparing similar home sales in the subject property's neighborhood.

Mortgage. A loan on property where the property is pledged as collateral. The mortgage is retired when the loan is paid in full.

Mortgage-backed securities. Investment securities issued by Wall Street firms that are guaranteed, or collateralized, by home mortgages taken out by consumers. These securities can then be bought and sold on Wall Street.

Mortgage insurance (MI). An insurance policy, paid by the borrower with benefits paid to the lender, that covers the difference between the borrower's down payment and 20 percent of the sales price. If the borrower defaults on the mortgage, this difference is paid to the lender. MI, also called "private mortgage insurance" (PMI), is typically required on all mortgage loans with less than 20 percent down.

Mortgagee. The person or business making the loan.

Mortgagor. The person(s) getting the loan; the borrower.

Multiple Listing Service (MLS). A central repository where real estate brokers and agents show homes and search for homes that are for sale.

Negative amortization (neg-am). An adjustable-rate mortgage that can have two interest rates, the contract rate or the fully indexed rate. The contract rate is the minimum agreed-upon rate that the consumer may pay; it is usually lower than the fully indexed rate. The borrower has a choice of which rate to pay, but if the contract rate is lower than the fully indexed rate, the difference between the two payments is added to the loan. If your contract payment is only $500 but the payment at the fully indexed rate is $700 and you pay only the contract rate, $200 is added to your original loan amount. This is not for the faint of heart or for those with little money down.

Nonconforming. A mortgage loan in an amount above the current Fannie Mae or Freddie Mac limits. Also called "jumbo mortgages."

Note. A promise to repay. There may or may not be property involved, and a note may or may not be a mortgage.

NOV. Notice of value. The VA name for your appraisal.

Origination fee. A fee charged to cover costs associated with finding, documenting, and preparing a mortgage application, usually expressed as a percentage of the loan amount.

Owner's policy. Title insurance for the benefit of the homeowner.

PITI. Principal, interest, taxes, and insurance. These figures are used to help determine front debt ratios.

PMI. Private mortgage insurance. See *mortgage insurance (MI)*.

Prepaid interest. Daily interest from the day of the loan closing to the first of the following month. Also can be in the form of a discount point.

Prepayment penalty. A monetary penalty paid to the lender if the loan is paid off before its maturity or if extra payments are made on the loan. Prepayment penalties are sometimes categorized as "hard" or "soft." A hard penalty is an automatic penalty if the loan is paid off early or if extra payments are made at any time or for any amount whatsoever. A soft penalty lasts for only a couple of years and may allow extra payments on the loan as long as they do not exceed a certain amount.

Principal. The outstanding amount owed on a loan, not including any interest due.

Points. See *discount points*.

Realtor. A member of the National Association of Realtors. This is a registered trademark; not all real estate agents are Realtors.

Refinancing. Obtaining a new mortgage to replace an existing one.

Sales contract. A written agreement, signed by both the seller and the buyer, to buy or sell a home.

Second mortgage. A mortgage that assumes a subordinate position behind a first mortgage. If the home goes into foreclosure, the first mortgage must be settled before the second can lay claim. Sometimes called a "piggyback" mortgage.

Secondary market. A financial arena where mortgages are bought and sold, either individually or grouped together into securities backed by those mortgages. Fannie Mae and Freddie Mac are the backbone of the conventional secondary market. Other secondary markets exist for nonconforming loans, subprime loans, and other types of loans.

Seller. The person transferring ownership of and all rights in your home in exchange for cash or other assets.

Settlement statement. A document that shows all financial entries during the home sale, including sales price, closing costs, loan amounts, and property taxes. Your initial Good Faith Estimate will be your first glimpse of your settlement statement. This statement is one of the final documents put together before you go to closing and is prepared by your attorney or settlement agent. Also called "Final HUD-1."

Survey. A map that shows the physical dimensions of any structures and where they sit on the property. It also indicates any easements that run across or through the property.

Title. Ownership in a property.

Title exam/title search. The process in which public records are reviewed to uncover any previous liens on the property.

Title insurance. An insurance policy that protects the lender, the seller, and/or the borrower against any defects in title for or previous claims to the property being transferred or sold.

Underwriter. The person who physically approves the loan, making sure that the loan meets lending guidelines, and signs off on the documentation submitted.

Verification of deposit (VOD). A written form sent by the lender to a financial institution to verify the amount of funds in an account. This form also shows how long the account has been open, everyone who has a claim to the account, and any deposits and withdrawals from or to the account.

Verification of employment (VOE). A written form sent by the lender to an employer to verify an applicant's employment. This form also shows how long

the applicant has worked at her job, how much the applicant makes, and any recent raises or bonuses.

Yield spread premium (YSP). The difference in basis points from one rate to another offered by a wholesale lender in return for a higher rate. The opposite of discount points, which are paid to get a lower rate, YSPs are paid by the lender to get a higher rate. They are often used to offset borrowers' closing costs and to provide a no-points, no-fee mortgage loan.

Payment Tables

Payments per Thousand Dollars Financed

Find the interest rate, move across to the Term column, and multiply that number by the number of thousand dollars financed.

Example: 6.50 percent, 30-year term on $150,000

$6.32 × 150 (thousands) = $948.00 principal and interest payment

Rate	40 years	30 years	25 years
2.500	$3.30	$3.95	$4.49
2.625	$3.37	$4.02	$4.55
2.750	$3.44	$4.08	$4.61
2.875	$3.51	$4.15	$4.68
3.000	$3.58	$4.22	$4.74

3.125	$3.65	$4.28	$4.81
3.250	$3.73	$4.35	$4.87
3.375	$3.80	$4.42	$4.94
3.500	$3.87	$4.49	$5.01
3.625	$3.95	$4.56	$5.07
3.750	$4.03	$4.63	$5.14
3.875	$4.10	$4.70	$5.21
4.000	$4.18	$4.77	$5.28
4.125	$4.26	$4.85	$5.35
4.250	$4.34	$4.92	$5.42
4.375	$4.42	$4.99	$5.49
4.500	$4.50	$5.07	$5.56
4.625	$4.58	$5.14	$5.63
4.750	$4.66	$5.22	$5.70
4.875	$4.74	$5.29	$5.77
5.000	$4.82	$5.37	$5.85
5.125	$4.91	$5.44	$5.92
5.250	$4.99	$5.52	$5.99
5.375	$5.07	$5.60	$6.07
5.500	$5.16	$5.68	$6.14
5.625	$5.24	$5.76	$6.22
5.750	$5.33	$5.84	$6.29
5875	$5.42	$5.92	$6.37
6.000	$5.50	$6.00	$6.44
6.125	$5.59	$6.08	$6.52
6.250	$5.68	$6.16	$6.60
6.375	$5.77	$6.24	$6.67
6.500	$5.85	$6.32	$6.75
6.625	$5.94	$6.40	$6.83
6.750	$6.03	$6.49	$6.91
6.875	$6.12	$6.57	$6.99
7.000	$6.21	$6.65	$7.07
7.125	$6.31	$6.74	$7.15

7.250	$6.40	$6.82	$7.23
7.375	$6.49	$6.91	$7.31
7.500	$6.58	$6.99	$7.39
7.625	$6.67	$7.08	$7.47
7.750	$6.77	$7.16	$7.55
7.875	$6.86	$7.25	$7.64
8.000	$6.95	$7.34	$7.72
8.125	$7.05	$7.42	$7.80
8.250	$7.14	$7.51	$7.88
8.375	$7.24	$7.60	$7.97
8.500	$7.33	$7.69	$8.05
8.625	$7.43	$7.78	$8.14
8.750	$7.52	$7.87	$8.22
8.875	$7.62	$7.96	$8.31
9.000	$7.71	$8.05	$8.39
9.125	$7.81	$8.14	$8.48
9.250	$7.91	$8.23	$8.56
9.375	$8.00	$8.32	$8.65
9.500	$8.10	$8.41	$8.74
9.625	$8.20	$8.50	$8.82
9.750	$8.30	$8.59	$8.91
9.875	$8.39	$8.68	$9.00
10.000	$8.49	$8.78	$9.09
10.125	$8.59	$8.87	$9.18
10.250	$8.69	$8.96	$9.26
10.375	$8.79	$9.05	$9.35
10.500	$8.89	$9.15	$9.44
10.625	$8.98	$9.24	$9.53
10.750	$9.08	$9.33	$9.62
10.875	$9.18	$9.43	$9.71
11.000	$9.28	$9.52	$9.80
11.125	$9.38	$9.62	$9.89
11.250	$9.48	$9.71	$9.98

11.375	$9.58	$9.81	$10.07
11.500	$9.68	$9.90	$10.16
11.625	$9.78	$10.00	$10.26
11.750	$9.88	$10.09	$10.35
11.875	$9.98	$10.19	$10.44
12.000	$10.08	$10.29	$10.53
12.125	$10.19	$10.38	$10.62
12.250	$10.29	$10.48	$10.72
12.375	$10.39	$10.58	$10.81
12.500	$10.49	$10.67	$10.90
12.625	$10.59	$10.77	$11.00
12.750	$10.69	$10.87	$11.09
12.875	$10.79	$10.96	$11.18
13.000	$10.90	$11.06	$11.28
13.125	$11.00	$11.16	$11.37
13.250	$11.10	$11.26	$11.47
13.375	$11.20	$11.36	$11.56
13.500	$11.30	$11.45	$11.66
13.625	$11.40	$11.55	$11.75
13.750	$11.51	$11.65	$11.85
13.875	$11.61	$11.75	$11.94
14.000	$11.71	$11.85	$12.04
14.125	$11.81	$11.95	$12.13
14.250	$11.92	$12.05	$12.23
14.375	$12.02	$12.15	$12.33
14.500	$12.12	$12.25	$12.42
14.625	$12.22	$12.35	$12.52
14.750	$12.33	$12.44	$12.61
14.875	$12.43	$12.54	$12.71
15.000	$12.53	$12.64	$12.81
15.125	$12.64	$12.74	$12.91
15.250	$12.74	$12.84	$13.00
15.375	$12.84	$12.94	$13.10

15.500	$12.94	$13.05	$13.20
15.625	$13.05	$13.15	$13.30
15.750	$13.15	$13.25	$13.39
15.875	$13.25	$13.35	$13.49
16.000	$13.36	$13.45	$13.59
16.125	$13.46	$13.55	$13.69
16.250	$13.56	$13.65	$13.79
16.375	$13.67	$13.75	$13.88
16.500	$13.77	$13.85	$13.98
16.625	$13.87	$13.95	$14.08
16.750	$13.98	$14.05	$14.18
16.875	$14.08	$14.16	$14.28
17.000	$14.18	$14.26	$14.38
17.125	$14.29	$14.36	$14.48
17.250	$14.39	$14.46	$14.58
17.375	$14.49	$14.56	$14.68
17.500	$14.60	$14.66	$14.78
17.625	$14.70	$14.77	$14.87
17.750	$14.80	$14.87	$14.97
17.875	$14.91	$14.97	$15.07
18.000	$15.01	$15.07	$15.17

Rate	20 years	15 years	10 years
2.500	$5.30	$6.67	$9.43
2.62	5$5.36	$6.73	$9.48
2.750	$5.42	$6.79	$9.54
2.875	$5.48	$6.85	$9.60
3.000	$5.55	$6.91	$9.66
3.125	$5.61	$6.97	$9.71
3.250	$5.67	$7.03	$9.77
3.375	$5.74	$7.09	$9.83

3.500	$5.80	$7.15	$9.89
3.625	$5.86	$7.21	$9.95
3.750	$5.93	$7.27	$10.01
3.875	$5.99	$7.33	$10.07
4.000	$6.06	$7.40	$10.12
4.125	$6.13	$7.46	$10.18
4.250	$6.19	$7.52	$10.24
4.375	$6.26	$7.59	$10.30
4.500	$6.33	$7.65	$10.36
4.625	$6.39	$7.71	$10.42
4.750	$6.46	$7.78	$10.48
4.875	$6.53	$7.84	$10.55
5.000	$6.60	$7.91	$10.61
5.125	$6.67	$7.97	$10.67
5.250	$6.74	$8.04	$10.73
5.375	$6.81	$8.10	$10.79
5.500	$6.88	$8.17	$10.85
5.625	$6.95	$8.24	$10.91
5.750	$7.02	$8.30	$10.98
5.875	$7.09	$8.37	$11.04
6.000	$7.16	$8.44	$11.10
6.125	$7.24	$8.51	$11.16
6.250	$7.31	$8.57	$11.23
6.375	$7.38	$8.64	$11.29
6.500	$7.46	$8.71	$11.35
6.625	$7.53	$8.78	$11.42
6.750	$7.60	$8.85	$11.48
6.875	$7.68	$8.92	$11.55
7.000	$7.75	$8.99	$11.61
7.125	$7.83	$9.06	$11.68
7.250	$7.90	$9.13	$11.74
7.375	$7.98	$9.20	$11.81
7.500	$8.06	$9.27	$11.87

7.625	$8.13	$9.34	$11.94
7.750	$8.21	$9.41	$12.00
7.875	$8.29	$9.48	$12.07
8.000	$8.36	$9.56	$12.13
8.125	$8.44	$9.63	$12.20
8.250	$8.52	$9.70	$12.27
8.375	$8.60	$9.77	$12.33
8.500	$8.68	$9.85	$12.40
8.625	$8.76	$9.92	$12.47
8.750	$8.84	$9.99	$12.53
8.875	$8.92	$10.07	$12.60
9.000	$9.00	$10.14	$12.67
9.125	$9.08	$10.22	$12.74
9.250	$9.16	$10.29	$12.80
9.375	$9.24	$10.37	$12.87
9.500	$9.32	$10.44	$12.94
9.625	$9.40	$10.52	$13.01
9.750	$9.49	$10.59	$13.08
9.875	$9.57	$10.67	$13.15
10.000	$9.65	$10.75	$13.22
10.125	$9.73	$10.82	$13.28
10.250	$9.82	$10.90	$13.35
10.375	$9.90	$10.98	$13.42
10.500	$9.98	$11.05	$13.49
10.625	$10.07	$11.13	$13.56
10.750	$10.15	$11.21	$13.63
10.875	$10.24	$11.29	$13.70
11.000	$10.32	$11.37	$13.78
11.125	$10.41	$11.44	$13.85
11.250	$10.49	$11.52	$13.92
11.375	$10.58	$11.60	$13.99
11.500	$10.66	$11.68	$14.06
11.625	$10.75	$11.76	$14.13

11.750	$10.84	$11.84	$14.20
11.875	$10.92	$11.92	$14.27
12.000	$11.01	$12.00	$14.35
12.125	$11.10	$12.08	$14.42
12.250	$11.19	$12.16	$14.49
12.375	$11.27	$12.24	$14.56
12.500	$11.36	$12.33	$14.64
12.625	$11.45	$12.41	$14.71
12.750	$11.54	$12.49	$14.78
12.875	$11.63	$12.57	$14.86
13.000	$11.72	$12.65	$14.93
13.125	$11.80	$12.73	$15.00
13.250	$11.89	$12.82	$15.08
13.375	$11.98	$12.90	$15.15
13.500	$12.07	$12.98	$15.23
13.625	$12.16	$13.07	$15.30
13.750	$12.25	$13.15	$15.38
13.875	$12.34	$13.23	$15.45
14.000	$12.44	$13.32	$15.53
14.125	$12.53	$13.40	$15.60
14.250	$12.62	$13.49	$15.68
14.375	$12.71	$13.57	$15.75
14.500	$12.80	$13.66	$15.83
14.625	$12.89	$13.74	$15.90
14.750	$12.98	$13.83	$15.98
14.875	$13.08	$13.91	$16.06
15.000	$13.17	$14.00	$16.13
15.125	$13.26	$14.08	$16.21
15.250	$13.35	$14.17	$16.29
15.375	$13.45	$14.25	$16.36
15.500	$13.54	$14.34	$16.44
15.625	$13.63	$14.43	$16.52
15.750	$13.73	$14.51	$16.60

15.875	$13.82	$14.60	$16.67
16.000	$13.91	$14.69	$16.75
16.125	$14.01	$14.77	$16.83
16.250	$14.10	$14.86	$16.91
16.375	$14.19	$14.95	$16.99
16.500	$14.29	$15.04	$17.06
16.625	$14.38	$15.13	$17.14
16.750	$14.48	$15.21	$17.22
16.875	$14.57	$15.30	$17.30
17.000	$14.67	$15.39	$17.38
17.125	$14.76	$15.48	$17.46
17.250	$14.86	$15.57	$17.54
17.375	$14.95	$15.66	$17.62
17.500	$15.05	$15.75	$17.70
17.625	$15.15	$15.84	$17.78
17.750	$15.24	$15.92	$17.86
17.875	$15.34	$16.01	$17.94
18.000	$15.43	$16.10	$18.02

Index

www.tandf.co.uk/journals/RSHI

From Routledge Journals

Social History

Editor: Janet Blackman,
University of Hull, UK

Founding Editor: Keith Nield

**Listed in the Thomson Reuters Arts & Humanities
Citation Index®**

For more than thirty years, *Social History* has published scholarly
work of consistently high quality, without restrictions of period or
geography. *Social History* is now minded to develop further the
scope of the journal in content and to seek further experiment in
terms of format. The editorial object remains unchanged - to enable
discussion, to provoke argument, and to create space for criticism
and scholarship.

In recent years the content of *Social History* has expanded to
include a good deal more European and American work as well as,
increasingly, work from and about Africa, South Asia and Latin
America. In the main, the bulk of this work has taken traditional
form - that is, the shape of the scholarly article has determined the
form of presentation, its narrative styles and its footnote apparatus.
In some circumstances this format can constrain originality, at the
worst, or, maybe less bad, it serves to limit conceptual or
theoretical risk. We do not wish to argue here that the tradition is
without merit. Far from it. Yet we do not judge it appropriate for all
purposes. On the contrary, *Social History* will also welcome work
which, rather than reproducing past practices, seeks innovation in
focus and presentation.

Visit www.tandf.co.uk/journals/RSHI for:
- Online sample copy
- Call for papers
- Instructions for Authors
- Back issues
- Content alerts
- Pricing and Ordering